Nancy

Mary & Ann
Thanks for the hospitality

Dick

Military Beginnings

EARLY DEVELOPMENT OF AMERICAN AND MARYLAND FORCES

Richard J. Martiny

John Ogilby's map <u>Nouae Terrae - Mariae Tabula 1635</u> courtesy of the Maryland Historical Society; Edward Bennett Matthews' <u>Map showing the counties of Maryland during the period 1637 - 1650</u> and Thomas Kitchin's <u>A Map of Maryland with Delaware Counties etc.</u>, collection of the Maryland State Archives, used with permission; map <u>Forts Built in Maryland and Pennsylvania</u> by William Ansel, Jr., used with permission; print <u>Fort Mount Pleasant - Cumberland</u>, used with permission; maps <u>Forbes Route to Fort Duquesne</u> and <u>Braddock's March</u>, by Dr. Allen Powell, used with permission; map <u>New England and Atlantic States, 1766 - 1783</u>, by Martin Lubikowski, used with permission; map <u>Battle of Brooklyn and New York</u>, by Colin Determan, used with permission.

ISBN: 1482649497
ISBN 13: 9781482649499

Library of Congress Control Number: 2013904070
CreateSpace Independent Publishing Platform
North Charleston, South Carolina

Military Beginnings

EARLY DEVELOPMENT OF
AMERICAN AND MARYLAND FORCES

Richard J. Martiny

John Ogilby's map <u>Nouae Terrae - Mariae Tabula 1635</u> courtesy of the Maryland Historical Society; Edward Bennett Matthews' <u>Map showing the counties of Maryland during the period</u> <u>1637 - 1650</u> and Thomas Kitchin's <u>A Map of Maryland with Delaware Counties etc.</u>, collection of the Maryland State Archives, used with permission; map <u>Forts Built in Maryland and Pennsylvania</u> by William Ansel, Jr., used with permission; print <u>Fort Mount Pleasant - Cumberland</u>, used with permission; maps <u>Forbes Route to Fort Duquesne</u> and <u>Braddock's March</u>, by Dr. Allen Powell, used with permission; map <u>New England and Atlantic States, 1766 - 1783</u>, by Martin Lubikowski, used with permission; map <u>Battle of Brooklyn and New York</u>, by Colin Determan, used with permission.

ISBN: 1482649497
ISBN 13: 9781482649499

Library of Congress Control Number: 2013904070
CreateSpace Independent Publishing Platform
North Charleston, South Carolina

Military Beginnings

EARLY DEVELOPMENT OF AMERICAN AND MARYLAND FORCES

Richard J. Martiny

John Ogilby's map Nouae Terrae - Mariae Tabula 1635 courtesy of the Maryland Historical Society; Edward Bennett Matthews' Map showing the counties of Maryland during the period 1637 - 1650 and Thomas Kitchin's A Map of Maryland with Delaware Counties etc., collection of the Maryland State Archives, used with permission; map Forts Built in Maryland and Pennsylvania by William Ansel, Jr., used with permission; print Fort Mount Pleasant - Cumberland, used with permission; maps Forbes Route to Fort Duquesne and Braddock's March, by Dr. Allen Powell, used with permission; map New England and Atlantic States, 1766 - 1783, by Martin Lubikowski, used with permission; map Battle of Brooklyn and New York, by Colin Determan, used with permission.

ISBN: 1482649497
ISBN 13: 9781482649499

Library of Congress Control Number: 2013904070
CreateSpace Independent Publishing Platform
North Charleston, South Carolina

Contents

Maps/Illustrations

Introduction

In the spring of 1776, after forcing the British troops to withdraw from Boston, General George Washington brought his army to New York, the assumed location of the next British landing and the next major battleground. Being short of troops, he urgently requested the Continental Congress to provide him with as many soldiers as they could, with the further stipulation that the new troops have longer enlistment periods than their predecessors. His belief that short term men did not make effective soldiers, first formed in the 1750s and 1760s, was more than reinforced around Boston. Congress obliged, requesting additional troops from the colonies in early June.

For all of their experience with warfare, Americans remained innocent of battle - general engagements - until August, 1776. If, during the colonial period, they had seen, or taken part in, intense fighting, they had never yet experienced fighting of the scale and duration of general action, of anything comparable to the Battle of Long Island. Encounters between colonists and Indians were comparatively small, sharp and brief; it was far easier to break the power of Indians by destroying their crops, supplies and villages than by bringing them to action. Imperial conflicts of the eighteenth century required much larger forces and extended service. But the colonists had served mainly as auxiliaries to British troops and most campaigns had ended with sieges or with engagements in which the regulars did much of the fighting.

New Englanders, sustained by the British fleet, had captured Louisburg by siege in 1745; regulars and provincials captured it again in 1758 and Ft. Ticonderoga in 1759. In the climactic battle of the Seven Years/French and Indian (SY/FI) War in America, colonists skirmished along the flanks of the British army that captured Quebec. However, even during the opening years of the Revolutionary War, Americans fought only detachments of regulars at Lexington and Concord, Bunker/ Breed's Hill, Quebec and Charleston. Casualties were high, but forces were small and fighting was brief.[1]

The first Maryland troops to march in response to Congress' call were the regiment commanded by Colonel William Smallwood. Arriving in New York, the regiment was assigned to a brigade ultimately commanded by General Stirling on the extreme right flank of the American forces on Long Island.

The American Army they joined was decidedly inferior to the British forces assembling at New York. The Americans did have the moral advantage of fighting in defense of their homes, families and institutions; they were buoyed by a general enthusiasm for a revolution that was then in its zenith; they knew, as yet, comparatively little of the defeat and suffering that could and would come with war; and they had in Washington a Commander-in-Chief who knew how to make the most out of popular feelings. But apart from their enthusiasms and innocence, there was little that favored the Americans. It was not just that the British generals were more talented and more experienced in combat than the American commanders; or that the British had better weapons or more abundant supplies. It was primarily that the British Army was better prepared than the Americans to endure the shattering experience of battle, of a general action fought at close quarters with muskets, bayonets and cannon. British regiments were stronger and more resilient than even the best of the Americans. They were filled with soldiers who were, on average, five to ten years older and who had served together nine or ten years longer than the rank and file of Continental lines. There were in some regiments, like the Royal Welsh Fusiliers and the 37th Foot, men who had fought at Miden, Quebec and Vellinghausen, men whose presence alone could steady their younger comrades. In short, British regiments had had time to build the deep sense of community and the automatic response to command that were essential in eighteenth century combat; that sustained a regiment under fire and that, in turn, made its fire truly effective. [2]

British forces, including Hessians, arrived in New York and established camp on Staten Island. They included units which had withdrawn from Boston to the eastern coast of Canada, units that had originally been stationed in Nova Scotia and Newfoundland, and units from England and Europe. They crossed to Long Island to engage the Americans in August, 1776. The British planned to outflank the Americans through a pass on the American's left flank, all the while attacking them vigorously on their right flank to keep them engaged and prevent their withdrawal. The British deception succeeded. After getting through the pass they moved against the American left flank, rolling it up, while occupying them with strong attacks on their right.

Stirling eventually realized that he had to withdraw his troops or they would be crushed between the attacks coming from his front, left and left rear. However, he needed time to do it. The withdrawal route was precarious, through a swamp previously deemed impassable and over an 80 foot wide tidal creek with the tide in full flow. He ordered the Marylanders to cover the withdrawal and led them in doing so.

The Marylanders, under their fourth ranking officer, that day third in command, took on the English soldiers, marines and Hessians, numbering more than ten times their number. They attacked five times, forcing their opponents to withdraw. Their sixth attack was unsuccessful. About to be overrun from their left and front, they withdrew. They had more than 250 soldiers killed or captured, over 60% of the force they started the day with. Many additional troops were wounded. However, they had stymied the British attacks and allowed the other American units to successfully withdraw and find shelter in previously prepared fortifications.

The battlefield, modern or ancient, is a noisy, smelly, confusing, frightening and extremely dangerous place. It takes a long time to train a person to perform individual tasks and then to utilize them effectively in functioning as part of a cohesive unit in such an environment. This is what armies do. More specifically, in the eighteenth century, this is what the regular, standing European armies did and what part-time citizen soldier militias tried to do, the latter with extremely limited success.

Smallwood's Regiment became a Continental Army unit and, hence, was deemed a "regular" one. However, the regiment had been authorized just seven months before and had spent the spring of 1776 forming, organizing, equipping and training. The first time it had acted together as a cohesive unit with all of the companies present had been about seven weeks before the battle when they gathered together at Head of Elk to march north. They had no apparent military background as a unit and, in fact, were in their first fight together. Their commander and his deputy were not present on the day of the battle. They were commanded by the third ranking officer currently with them, but, actually, the fourth in command; a man with no experience in battle either individually or in command of any group of soldiers of any size. That they were able to perform in the manner that they did, against professional soldiers, is nothing short of phenomenal.

Who were they? Where did they come from? How was their unit formed? Was there any long standing military tradition that they had grown up with that allowed them to easily and successfully adapt to combat in such a short period of time? What military forces did Maryland have available in the mid-1770s that enabled them to field such a unit? How had Maryland protected itself in the 140+ years since the first landing on St. Clements Island? What military force structure did the first Marylanders use as a guide and where did it come from?

This is the beginning in answering those questions.

1. Amateur to Professional, The Old Country

NEAR EAST AND EUROPE

Many centuries prior to the Christian era organized armies under formal discipline and employing definite systems of battlefield tactics appeared in the empires of the Near East, rivaling in numbers and in the scope of their conflicts anything that was to appear in the west before the nineteenth century. In the fourth century B.C. Alexander the Great of Macedonia brought all of these empires and dominions under his control in a series of rapid military conquests. In doing so, he carried to the highest point of development the art of war as it was practiced in the Greek city-states. The Romans built on the achievements of Alexander, and brought the art of war to its zenith in the ancient world. They perfected the legion, a tactical military unit of great maneuverability, comparable in some respects to the modern division; performed remarkable feats of military engineering; and developed elaborate systems of fortification and siege craft.

Rome's military institutions, along with its political organization and economy, underwent progressive decay after the second century A.D The Roman empire in the west was succeeded first by barbarian kingdoms and then by feudalism, a highly decentralized political system. A multitude of warring nobles exercised authority over local areas of varying size. Warfare in Europe became, for the most part, a monopoly of the ruling classes, for only men of substance could afford horse and armor. Each knight owed a certain number of days of military service to his lord each year in a hierarchical or pyramid arrangement, from the mass of knights to the king. However, lords who were strong enough defied their superiors, including the king.[3]

The organized, structured armies of the Near East, Greece and Rome had come from somewhere. They didn't just appear as so many sown dragons' teeth. They developed from the concept of the tribal warrior band which, in turn, evolved into what today we would call the militia. The militia principle lays the duty of performing military service upon all a community's free male citizens. Failure or refusal to fulfill the duty usually entailed severe penalties, up to and including loss of citizenship. [4]

The basic concept of the militia – that every man has the right and duty to bear arms in defense of national freedom, law and order - is nearly universal. Among primitive peoples, the tribal fighting force, of necessity, included all able bodied males. From this developed the concept of linked political and military responsibility and privilege. In the city-states of Greece, among the Germanic and Celtic tribes, and in early Rome, youths were admitted to manhood by qualifying as fighting men. The whole population of free men voted on the question of peace and war. If they chose war, they formed themselves into the army that fought it.

Such a force, however capable for home defense, always proved unsatisfactory during long wars, especially those involving operations against distant enemies. Such campaigns kept the citizen-soldier absent from his farm or his trade for ruinously long periods. They also demanded a higher level of competence and specialization than the citizen-soldier could offer. As a result, on a limited basis, both in Greece and in Rome, the long-service professional gradually replaced the citizen-soldier. As this happened, the average citizen generally lost interest in military matters unless his home locale was being attacked. This was a theme that kept repeating itself down over time.[5]

The provision and training of manpower affects the outcome of battles, campaigns and wars. Manpower systems have displayed great consistency through the past 2,500 years of Western warfare. The Greeks used a militia which, engaging in some practice together, had a measure of tactical proficiency. Based in small cities, it also had some cohesion and unit spirit. The Roman militia, inexpensive compared to a standing army, had the benefits of large numbers and potential reserves. This stood them in good stead in resisting Hannibal's invasion of Italy. However, again, the militia could not fight long wars especially those far from home, which explains why the Greeks and the Romans ultimately adopted professionals. The militia did, however, excel in transitory operations. A large number of raiders, such as Arabs or Magyars, many of whom came from civil life, did not really constitute a professional force. Militia had even greater advantages in the defense against raids. Acting on the defensive, often with the aid of fortifications, placed fewer demands on the militia's limited tactical skill.[6]

The concept of a militia is associated with the phalanxes of the Greek farmer citizens. The Greek city-states required military service of all able bodied free male citizens. Such service was usually of short duration, and the Greek citizen-soldiers fought locally to defend their own land and city-state. They fought each other in the small states' quarrels. However, they might combine against a common danger, such as offered by the Persian Empire in the sixth and fifth centuries, B.C. Rome, in pre-Republican years, imported its tactics from the Greeks. The word "militia" comes from the Latin term "miles", meaning soldier. The Roman Army, from which that of the Caesars ultimately descended, had its origins in phalanx warfare. Rome's farmer soldiers would progressively yield to paid professionals. The Greeks, however, did not make a complete transition, preserving the individual city-state militias. This, in turn, ensured that the stronger, semi-barbarian Macedonians would overrun all of them. Nevertheless, the militia idea would survive. With the rediscovery of classical learning in Renaissance Europe, it came to seem as good as that of the rule of law or civic pride. [7]

The military forces of the Middle Ages only superficially conformed to the militia or professional models. Although an urban militia had a basic similarity to the Greek pattern and, like it, depended tactically on dense masses of pike men, the rural militia hardly deserved the name. Without drill, and often with agricultural implements instead of weapons, it lacked even the cohesion of an urban force because of its dispersal in many tiny villages. Some rural military, however, had better characteristics. The Swiss, for example, with their more compact valley communities, possessed an armed and trained force, one hardly distinguishable from regular soldiers. [8]

In the fifteenth century Italy city-states, instead of relying on mercenaries for defense, made it a condition of citizenship that all free men of property should purchase arms, train for war and do duty in time of danger. This describes the militia system. The term includes the fyrd of Anglo-Saxon England and its equivalent in Continental Europe. They were based on the principle that free men must bear arms. It had been brought from Germany by the barbarian invaders, was carried on by the kingdoms that succeeded Roman rule, and remained in force until, in the military crises of the ninth and tenth centuries, it was overtaken in importance by the summons to the horse keeping vassals, ultimately the knights. [9]

The "upper level" of Germanic militia was the enrolled militia or select fyrd. They were farmers, merchants, serfs, tinsmiths, blacksmiths and craftsmen of all sorts. The only thing they had in common was their enlistment with the militia. Generally, they were used only within a hundred miles of their homes. They were permitted to return home, save in times of grave danger and immediate peril, to plant their crops and harvest them. Their training was minimal, but adequate, given their use. The house-carls (the king's household guards) were given the job of training the militia. It was designed to employ the select fyrd individually in units made up on the spot. They were not enrolled to enter battle as a trained and cohesive unit. In general, they were deployed as simple infantry. On occasion they were used as a defensive mass, normally in non-critical positions.

Most men of the times had simple weapons skills, being able to use a pike, a sword or an axe. Many could use a bow. While receiving some elementary training on these weapons, it was felt that there was no great need for developing the militia's military skills. A skilled militia might one day prove to be an even greater threat to the house-carls in the event of a popular uprising against the king. Each man was required by law to provide his own weapons. However, laws also limited his ownership of weapons. The poorer men would be provided weapons. Horses were reserved for use by officers, nobles and the mounted house-carls.

Below the enrolled militia/select fyrd was the great fyrd. It consisted of all able bodied men from the ages of fifteen or sixteen to sixty. It was the last ditch effort of an invaded people. It was never used offensively. Defensively, it was only used in the immediate area where an invader was operating. It was generally unorganized, undisciplined and untrained. [10]

Eventually, a major defect in the militia system became apparent. It laid duty on the property owning alone. Hence, it limited the number of men a state could put in the field to a number lower than that of all of its able-bodied male residents. [11]

The Persians employed a professional army of soldiers who had greater proficiency resulting from continuous service. They were essentially full time, with service year after year. Constant warfare ultimately forced the Greeks to partially transition from a militia to a system of professional soldiers. The Romans, starting like the Greeks with a militia, likewise began utilizing a long-service career army, an exemplary in its organization and discipline. In contrast to the militia, career soldiers had greater individual skill, and additional tactical preponderance provided by their ample experience in working together in units. This also gave the men mutual confidence and enhanced each unit's sense of community.

Medieval professionals differed markedly from the Roman and Greek models. Medieval armies decentralized their regulars into small garrisons and even individuals scattered over the countryside rather than having a permanently embodied and partially concentrated force. This system produced soldiers with adequate, often greater, skill, but rarely furnished units accustomed to discipline and subordination, experienced in working together, or possessed of much sense of community. The more frequent employment of individual professionals for a year's campaign, either directly or through military contractors, did little to mitigate the deficiencies of the medieval system of mercenaries, even though groups of men would remain together over the winter in anticipation of a contract for the coming year. Not until the latter part of the seventeenth century did European professional armies take the far more effective Roman form of regulars who lived and trained together year after year with the support of an organized and adequately funded commissariat. As a result, the militia lost most of their significance. [12]

Beginning in the medieval era and remaining essentially unchanged through the seventeenth century, the "standing army" of the king or overlord stood at the top of the military organization. It was well ordered with the best weapons systems the king could afford. It was a professional army, the soldiers therein having no other profession. On occasion these troops would be hired out to the king or state. In the original medieval conception, these men were called house-carls, the troops quartered by the king in his own castle. Many, if not all, would have been mounted troops. They would be uniformed or, at least, in clothing or a clothing armor combination that would differentiate them from commoners. They would be employed in battle as the king saw fit. At times such men were recognized as mercenaries; that is, they were available for hire for pay, or for booty payable directly to them, as opposed to hirelings rented out by the king. [13]

During the Renaissance leaders of city – and nation – states found themselves in a dilemma. To keep their economies expanding, their people had to work, not make war. On the other hand, survival and growth demanded a trained army. The solution was to use some of their major product – money – to hire armies of mercenaries. One result of this was that anyone could now be a soldier; the elitism of knighthood was gone forever, and armies slowly began to increase in size. It also meant that the overlord, or leader, was no longer dependent upon his vassals. Thus, power slowly shifted from the many to the few.

A Roman, Flavius Vegetius Renatus, author of <u>De Re Militari</u>, was rediscovered during this period. He became, next to Caesar and his <u>Commentaries</u>, the most influential military writer into the nineteenth century. His primary message was discipline. He wrote that "[v]ictory in war does not depend entirely upon numbers or mere courage, [but] only skill and discipline will ensure it." To Vegitius, martial discipline and training distinguished a soldier from a civilian. Without discipline "there is no longer any difference between the soldier and the peasant."

In important ways, the rediscovery of discipline as a means of exacting control over an army was emblematic of modern war in its infancy. Borrowing directly from Vegitius and others, Maurice of Nassau (Orange) rediscovered drill in the late sixteenth century as the best means of instilling discipline and esprit de corps. From his example, foreigners in the Dutch service quickly spread his ideas throughout Europe. The Netherlands, for at least a short time, was "the school of war whither the most martial spirits of Europe resort to lay downe the apprenticeship of their service in armes" noted John Bingham in the introduction to his translation of <u>The Tactics of Action Or an art of Embattling an army after ye Grecian manner</u> in 1616. The successes of Sweden's Gustavius

Adolphus in the Thirty Years' War confirmed Maurice's concepts and were, perhaps, even more influential in spreading the gospel of discipline. Discipline meant control, and drill was the means of achieving martial discipline. What had been unwieldy, unorganized masses were gradually shaped by constant drilling into sophisticated, disciplined organisms ready to change shapes on command and increasingly capable of refined battlefield movement. With a clearly defined chain of command that ran from the lowest ranking non-commissioned officer back to an absolutist monarch, over time armies became powerful, efficient, and obedient weapons, especially fearsome to external enemies and internal dissidents. By the eighteenth century the armies were more stable and more responsive to manipulation than anything known since classical times. The rediscovery of discipline, this seemly subtle, even minor change, proved to have an enormous impact on warfare throughout the eighteenth century.

The development of disciplined, well-drilled armies paralleled an increasingly multifarious society. To build such an army required the investment of a great deal of time effort, and treasure. It was often the most expensive and pressing activity of sixteenth and seventeenth century nations. States could no longer be dependent on patriotic, but ill-trained, ill-disciplined, short term militia. Therefore, the gradual movement toward permanent paid standing armies became universal throughout Europe, finalizing the divorce of king and armies (rulers) from the populace (ruled). Its implementation, systems and regularity of training, and forms of enforcing discipline, however, varied greatly with each nation's armed forces at differing times. [14]

From the mid-sixteenth century onward European campaigning was dominated by the foot soldier. Increasingly he was the permanently employed servant of one royal master – a "regular" soldier armed and clothed in a uniform manner. The first such soldiers had appeared in the employ of the Spanish kings at the end of the fifteenth century. France and the Hapsburg lands were the next monarchies to establish large regular armies. By the end of the seventeenth century they were the distinctive mark of all kingdoms which aspired to great nation status. The populations of the regions too small, too remote or too poor to maintain armies of their own – Switzerland, Scotland, and the Balkan borderlands – contributed to the new military labor market by furnishing mercenary regiments which were hired and maintained by the rich states on a regular basis.

The model on which the bodies of regular infantry were based was still that of the old mercenary company of the late Middle-Ages. The tactical unit remained the company, commanded by a captain, with a lieutenant and sergeant-major as his principal assistants. Under the new configuration, however, the rule, or 'regiment' of a colonel, appointed by the king, was imposed on groups of companies for administrative purposes. These regiments, about a thousand men strong, became the principal instrument through which the European states settled their religious, dynastic and political differences from the seventeenth to the nineteenth century. [15]

The term *Colonel* derives from the Latin "small column." As a rank, the term arose in late sixteenth century Italy where it referred to the officer in charge of a column (Italian colonna) or field force. The term is first attested to as *Colonnello*, but is perhaps a truncation of something like *Capitano Colonello*, Captain of the column. This was the Captain designated to command the column. In this context *Colonna* seems to refer to a force marching in column rather than to a battle formation – a battle, or battalion of pike.

As the office of Colonel became established practice, the Colonel became the senior Captain in a group of companies which were all sworn to observe his personal authority – to be ruled, or regimented, by him. This regiment, or governance, was to some extent embodied in a contract or a set of written rules, also referred to as the Colonel's regiment or standing regulation(s). By extension, the group of companies subject to a Colonels' *regiment* came to be referred to as his regiment.

With the shift from primarily mercenary to primarily national armies in the seventeenth century, a Colonel, normally an aristocrat, became a holder and proprietor of a military contract – the right to hold the regiment – from the previous holder of that right; or directly from the sovereign when a new regiment was formed or the incumbent died. Originally, the Colonel of the regiment was as much a business entrepreneur as a tactical commander, and considerably more so when he left the field command to a "lieutenant colonel" or professional director, while he confined himself to managing the business side of the enterprise. He was provided the king's warrant to beat the highways and byways for recruits; he was paid by the head for each one brought in; he thereafter had the concession for feeding, clothing and equipping them, from which he was free to enrich himself to the extent his conscience might allow. Regiments, like modern armament plants or electronic factories, were frequently as much a speculative enterprise as a response to calls of patriotism. Venous and callous as this system may seem, it arose from the fact that, in the absence of effective governmental administrative techniques, private enterprise was the only available recourse. It was considerably modified as the eighteenth century advanced and as more and more competent government bureaucracies began to take over more centralized control of military operations from the free-play of individual initiative. [16]

French cavalry units were called regiments as early as 1588. Again, the word was derived from the Latin *regimen,* a rule or system of order, and describes the regiment's functions of raising, equipping and raining troops. As a regiment acquired individuality, colors, a coat of arms, distinctive uniform and insignia and achievements in battle, it also became a central object of loyalty, pride and the espirit de corps of its soldiers. [17]

The French term regimen entered military usage in Europe at the end of the sixteenth century, when armies were evolving, as discussed above, from collections of retainers which followed knights, to formally organized, permanent military forces. At that time regiments were usually named for the commanding Colonels, and disbanded at the end of the campaign or war. The Colonel and his regiment might recruit from and serve several masters (countries). Later it was customary to name the regiment by its precedence in the line of battle and to recruit from specific places, e.g. the cantons in Switzerland. In 1479 the French formed their 1st Infantry Regiment from the ancient "Bandes de Picardies." The still existing Swedish Life Guards were formed in 1521.

Each regiment was responsible for recruiting, training and administration. The regiment came to be permanently maintained. Each developed a unique espirit de corps because of its unitary history, traditions, recruitment and function. Usually the regiment was responsible for recruiting and administering a soldier's entire career. [18]

When groups of companies were combined to form a regiment and regiments to form armies, the officers of the company, evolved from those in medieval mercenary companies, were replicated as "general" to the larger body; hence, Captain General, Lieutenant General and Sergeant Major General, with their subsequent modern grades. At the same time, functional appointments came into existence within armies, notably those of the quartermaster, who was concerned with housing the troops, and the adjutant, who was the commander's assistant. Rank came, in time, to be applied to such appointments so that they might be Major Generals too. The consolidation of this system and the standardization of rank were slow to happen. Cromwell's Chief of Staff in the mid/late seventeenth century, for example, held the rank of Sergeant Major General. From the sixteenth century onward, however, the principle upon which modern command organization works could be clearly discerned. Administrative duties had been allocated to officers who were subordinate to the commander. Necessary though they were to the management of the army, their performance had been recognized as different from that of directing the army in battle, for which the senior general had to be freed from routine. [19]

In additional to the fundamental technological advances, such as the development of gunpowder and weapons to use it, and the consequent revolution of fortification design, accompanied by the introduction of heavily armed oceangoing vessels, the other great changes to conduct of war were economic and political. They gave rise to the standing or permanent army, organized and led by professional soldiers in service to the state. [20]

In the sixteenth and seventeenth centuries the relationship between military developments and the rise of the European state was fundamental. As Sir George Clark wrote: "A state tightened its organization to be strong against its rivals; and the strength which it acquired in the contest for power strengthened its government at home." The declining military value of the feudal horsemen mirrored somewhat the restriction of his political influence. The threat posed by over-mighty subjects waned. The new armies were not only subject to direct royal control. They were recruited, in growing measure, from the inhabitants of the state they defended and were uniformly clad and trained. Their officers and NCO's took station in a more formalized hierarchy. They were more reliable than the mercenaries who had played such a large part in European history for centuries past.

The growth of armies increased opportunity as well as widening risk. The social distinction between horseman and foot soldier diminished until neither birth nor wealth dictated a soldier's choice of arms. Although the nobility strove to retain its grip on command, it was not universally successful. War brought many a humble youth military rank, social status and, on occasion, hereditary nobility. It also gave employment to young men from the unfertile or disputed peripheries of Europe: Scots and Irish adventurers left an enduring mark on the continent's armies.

The structural changes to European militaries which began in the sixteenth and seventeenth centuries were to end the career of one profiteer, the recruiting captain. A survivor of the "free lance" of the Middle-Ages, his service was a matter of contractual arrangement. In most European armies regiments were still owned by the proprietor colonels who regarded them, at least in part, as a financial enterprise. However, by 1660 they were no longer the quasi-independent contractors of yesteryear. They held commissions from the king; wore his uniform, not their own; and were subjected to the penetrating stares of a new generation of military bureaucrats. Paymasters and muster clerks, intendants and commissaries all materialized to further centralize control of armies and to ensure, within the limitations of the day, that soldiers were properly fed, clad and armed. The military bureaucracy offered its own prospects for advancement to men who found administration more congenial than combat, and it too might confer nobility. [21]

During the seventeenth century the firearm replaced the pike as the basic infantry weapon. The original firearm, the matchlock musket, suffered from several serious defects as a military weapon: it was cumbersome; reloading was long and complicated; the chance of a misfire was extremely high, particularly in damp weather; and the lit match required to ignite the gunpowder charge betrayed positions in the dark. These defects, particularly at close quarters, required a portion of each unit to carry pikes for defense against enemy cavalry or pikemen.

A technological breakthrough occurred in the second half of the century with the introduction of a new firing mechanism. It relied on the spark produced by a piece of flint striking a steel plate to set off the propellant charge. The flintlock musket was lighter and more easily handled than its predecessor, had a higher rate of fire and was easier to maintain. Late in the century development of the socket bayonet complimented the flintlock musket. It slipped around the muzzle of the musket without blocking it, turning it into a pole weapon, eliminating the need for pikemen.

Whether produced at government arsenals or by private contractors, all eighteenth century muskets were inaccurate. Weighing over ten pounds and with a barrel over a yard long, they were difficult to aim. Flints tended to wear out after only twenty rounds. Even under ideal conditions the effective range of these smoothbore weapons, which fired one ounce balls (1/2" to 3/4" in diameter), was only about one hundred yards. An average soldier under the stress of combat could fire three rounds per minute for short periods, but he required considerable training to accomplish this feat. Since care in reloading was a major factor in influencing accuracy, only the first round loaded before combat was completely reliable. [22]

The Thirty Years War (1618-1648) initially began between Catholics and Protestants in Germany. Eventually it involved much of the rest of Europe, especially Gustavius Adolphus of Sweden. It marked a major turning point in methods of warfare and military organization. While it would have occurred without him, Gustavius not only sparked tactical changes, he also transformed organization. His was the first true European professional army. His infantry squadron, consisting of approximately 500 men, was called a battalion by the French, and this designation has persisted to the 21st century for the basic combat command. The battalion usually consisted of four companies. Three battalions were combined into brigades (equivalent of modern regiments or brigades) for combat. This was not an entirely new concept. What was new was Gustavius' decision to make the brigade a permanent unit within a permanent command hierarchy, the origin of the modern regimental officer system. The regiment, or brigade, was commanded by a Colonel, the battalion by a Lieutenant Colonel and the companies – whose origins were the free companies of earlier centuries – by Captains.

The establishment of permanent units hastened the almost universal adoption of a proprietary system, which had already begun to replace the vestiges of feudalism and of free companies, as we have seen. The permanent Colonel was the proprietor of his regiment, accepted by the king as a permanent officer, and authorized personally, and through him his Captains, to raise men. Initially, with armies being raised only for a campaign and disbanded afterward, the troops raised by the proprietary system were volunteers, carefully selected from the available and willing manpower. However, as the armies became permanent, the standing units were not disbanded and were kept up to strength by regular influxes of recruits, usually provided by the Crown. This, combined with financial considerations in maintaining year-round units, gave the Crown increasing right of supervision over the administration and training of the regiments. This, in turn, somewhat restricted the proprietary rights previously exercised by the Colonels and Captains.

The proprietary system could be profitable. A commander was paid for the number of men mustered, as well as for their weapons, equipment and subsistence. In addition to the profits to be derived from the economical exercise of his proprietorship (to say nothing of the possibilities offered by parsimony and fraud), an officer could sell his proprietary interest when he retired. Thus, officers' commissions were valuable and could be purchased, a system which continued in the British Army, for one, into the nineteenth century.

In the latter part of the seventeenth century the French extended the concept of a permanent combat military hierarchy upward from the regiment to army commander. Hitherto the king or prince of the realm was usually the titular "general" of an army. The second in command – often the field commander – was the Lieutenant General, almost invariably a nobleman, who usually exercised direct command over the aristocratic cavalry. The infantry was normally commanded by a senior professional soldier, who was usually called the Sergeant Major General or Major General. He was charged with the responsibilities for forming up the army for battle and with the care of the various administrative duties of the campaign. When the army was disbanded at the end of a campaign, as was usually the case until the very end of the century, the Lieutenant and Major Generals lost both command and rank. Usually they reverted to their proprietary positions as Colonels of permanent regiments.

By the end of the century the French revived the old title of Marshal, which became a permanent rank for a commander of a field army in the absence of the king. With several armies normally in the field simultaneously, they established a permanent list of officers with sufficient experience and distinction to warrant them serving as a Major or Lieutenant General, or a Marshal, of an army. In time the relative position of officers on the list established precedence for command. Thus, for the first time since the fall of Rome, the permanent classification by rank and not by the temporary position one happened to be occupying appeared. Over time the national ranking lists and, hence, seniority, were extended to the ranks of Colonel and below. This eventually undermined the proprietary system of independent regiments, which mostly disappeared in the eighteenth century. [23]

New tactical formations and doctrine between 1688 and 1745 took advantage of the technological advances in firearms. The emergence of the infantry as a major factor on the battlefield gained momentum from the growth of the importance of firepower. Beginning with the War of Spanish Succession (1702-1714), Generals sought literally to blast the enemy off of the field with concentrated fire delivered at close range. They moved away from the massed formations which had characterized the era of the pike and adopted a deployment in long lines (linear tactics). By mid-century infantrymen in nearly every army stood three deep to bring a maximum number of muskets into play. The critical firefight took place at ranges of between fifty and one hundred yards.

These weapons and tactics required adjustments in organization. As we have seen, since the sixteenth century the regiment had formed the basic component of an army, providing administrative and tactical control over a group of companies. The need for better fire control in battle led to many complicated experiments. Ultimately, each army turned to a more manageable sub-element, the platoon, whose fire could be controlled by a handful of officers and noncommissioned officers. Coordinating the actions of a number of these basic elements of fire (normally eight) produced the battalion, the basic element of maneuver. Most regiments were composed of two or more battalions; except in the British Army, where the regiment and battalion were normally synonymous. The relationship between the company, the administrative entity, and the platoon varied. However, by the end of the century, most armies were making them interchangeable. Filled with rank and file trained to fire in unison at areas rather than individual targets, these units constituted the latest advances in organization during the period of the SY/FI War (1754-1763).

A second major development during the eighteenth century was improved handling of armies on the battlefields. At the beginning of the century, armies marched overland in mass formation and took hours to deploy into line of battle. A commander who felt at a disadvantage refused battle and either marched away or took refuge in fortifications. Engagements normally occurred when both Generals wanted to fight. Several reforms were introduced to force battle on an unwilling opponent. The cadence of march step and standardized drill maneuvers sought to reduce the time needed to display, and the confusion associated with forming, a line of battle. These changes allowed a commander to adjust his formations to the changing flow of battle without risking total disruption of his ranks. Brigades and Divisions controlled the movements of several battalions and increasingly became semi-permanent. [24]

There are several different historical interpretations to describe the changes which took place in military organization, tactics and weaponry during the latter stages of the Renaissance. According to one, the important developments were between 1560 and 1660. Armies grew much bigger and came increasingly under state control, which were both a cause and a consequence of their increased size and efficiency. There was a resultant loss of individuality, with the need for better organization, good training – especially in drill – and strict discipline. Another sees the "revolution" taking place over a longer time span, 1550 – 1720, with another constraint being removed in that period, that of finance. Fiscal thresholds, which in the past had limited the capacity of rulers to make war, were crossed with the development of more sophisticated credit machinery in most European states. Much more could be spent on the sport of kings – war. Still others have expressed different views; specifically, that the changes in warfare did indeed take place, but at varying rates in different places, with the fluctuations in the size and organization of armies depending upon need and breakouts of peace. All of these theories have merit, but the last appears to offer the best overall explanation. [25]

The military revolution occurring during the sixteenth and seventeenth centuries in Europe was also the direct result of continuous ongoing conflicts and the desire to win. New tactics were developed in the Netherlands, Sweden and France involving greater maneuverability and linear formations on the one hand and less mobile siege warfare on the other. Campaigns became more complex and protracted. The emphasis on drill and coordinated movement required well trained and properly disciplined troops. In consequence, more and more states acquired standing armies. The essence of the military revolution was the increase in the size of national armies and in the number of troops deployed on the field of battle. In the space of some two hundred years these increased tenfold. By the last quarter of the seventeenth century the Spanish Army consisted of 70,000 troops; the Dutch 110,000; the French 120,000; the Swedish 63,000 and the Russian Army 130,000. [26]

The relationship between economic demands and the size and composition of armies was dramatic. Broadly speaking, a monarch had to balance the competing claims of productivity and military efficiency. With great tracts of Europe not even yet under cultivation, let alone producing a surplus, a growing population was thought to be the *sine qua non* for economic growth. But in the Seven Years' War, the Prussian Army lost three times its own strength in men, suffering 180,000 deaths.

Prussia, like most other European countries, employed mercenaries in order to lessen the impact of unproductive labor on her economy. About a fifth of the Austrian Army and up to a third of the French Army came from abroad. As one French General said, each foreign soldier was worth three men, one more for France, one less for the enemy, and one Frenchman left to pay taxes. In peacetime, therefore, the military ethos was predominantly that of the mercenary. At the same time the officer corps became more aristocratic. The purpose was to link and subordinate the nobility to the crown and, increasingly, to the idea of the state. The aristocracy's relative loss of independence is well illustrated by the ending of the Colonel's proprietary rights in his regiment; although as late as 1789 in France there were still vestiges of it. The more noble the officer, the fewer ties he had with the mercenary.

The status of the private soldier declined. Desertion became rampant. The monarch had a choice. If he had a well motivated army, home production would be neglected. The alternative was to place greater weight on home production and so accept the inevitability of an army whose social characteristics would place distinct limitations on its performance. The latter was more appealing because, by using mercenaries and nobles, military officers were removed from the ken of the emergent bourgeois classes. If either they or their employees were taken from their more productive roles, then the national harmony would suffer; so too would their ability to pay the taxes which kept the army in the field. A protracted and costly war was, therefore, additionally undesirable because it could force the monarch, in raising money to pay for it, to have to secure the approval of the representative institutions for his proposed taxation. [27]

As mentioned above, the armies were composed predominantly of infantry, with cavalry and artillery as supporting units. During the seventeenth century an infantry formation normally included a number of pikemen, who protected the musketeers when they reloaded. By the end of the century, however, the pike sections were disappearing. As the relatively new gunpowder weapons were improved, commanders came to rely more on the volume of firepower that an army could deliver and less on the effect of shock weapons like the pike. Moreover, a way was found to give the musket the power of shock – by fitting a small pike, the bayonet, on the end of the barrel without plugging it. The standard weapons of the infantry in the seventeenth century were, first, the matchlock, and then the wheel lock. By the eighteenth century they had been supplanted by the flintlock, which was easier to load and fire, surer in discharge, and superior in range and accuracy. It remained in use in armies until the 1840s. [28]

By 1700, with the invention of the socket bayonet that could be fitted on the end of the flintlock musket without plugging the barrel (the first ones had), as noted above, the pike disappeared entirely, along with the helmet and body armor that had primarily been designed for protection against pikes. Commanders relearned to maneuver large bodies of troops on the battlefield and to employ infantry and cavalry and artillery in combination. As we have seen, national armies composed of professional soldiers came once again to resemble the imperial forces that had served Alexander the Great and the Roman emperors.

In the late seventeenth and eighteenth century warfare the nobles, again, served as officers, their positions in their kings' armies replacing the military distinction they had earned leading their own knights. Princes, counts, earls, marquises and barons, who had held position by hereditary right, royal favor or purchase, filled the higher commands, while gentlemen of lesser rank usually served as Captains and Lieutenants. Advancement to higher rank depended as much on wealth and influence at court as on demonstrated merit on the battlefield. The officers were hardly professional in the modern sense of the word. They might well first enter the service as mere boys through inheritance or purchase of a commission. Except for technical specialists in artillery and engineering, they were not required to attend a military school to train for their duties. [29]

Eighteenth century Europe's social structure and weapons technology dictated the basic organization and tactics of the armies. Society still bore an aristocratic imprint. Despite the growth of the royal bureaucratic state and the development of commerce, the nobility preserved and even expanded its privileges and power. Armies reflected noble preeminence. In France great aristocrats with court connections dominated the highest military posts. Lesser noblemen filled the lower commissioned ranks. Commoners did manage to enter the officer corps and comprised about a third of the total. Bourgeois officers could attain high positions in the artillery and engineer corps. In these service arms proficiency outweighed concern with status; however, high rank in the cavalry and infantry remained an aristocratic preserve. Noble influence was so strong that the government often created new posts for such men even though the French Army was overloaded with officers. In 1740 there was one officer for every eleven men. In 1758 there were 364 generals and 389 brigadiers for fewer than 300,000 men. A similar situation prevailed in other eighteenth century armies. In Sweden in the 1760s, two-thirds of the officers were of noble extraction and 89 percent of the generals were aristocrats. In Prussia, by the latter part of the century, there were 379 field grade infantry officers; only 2 percent were commoners. Frederick II preferred to employ foreign nobles rather than to allow native commoners to enter the officer corps. In Russia about 90 percent of the officers were aristocrats.

Aristocratic officers were not professionals. They did not regard themselves as military men. Rather, they looked upon their commissions as an adjunct to their hereditary status. Aristocratic military men were reliable in battle and personally courageous; but few of them studied war on a systematic basis. Some individuals did become proficient commanders. Some even contemplated the fundamental of strategy and tactics. However, states had no effective means at their disposal to provide a minimum level of training for the officer corps as a whole. Officers frequently left troop training duties to their non-commissioned officers and took extended leaves. When in the field, they lived in relative luxury, especially the commanders. Governments, in an effort to improve their army's efficiency, tried to limit the number of horses, coaches and servants that one officer could take along on a campaign. Success, however, was marginal since aristocratic officers tended to regard war as part of their special life-style rather than as a distinct profession.

For a man lacking influence or money, promotion was excruciatingly slow. In 1760, for example, a poor officer became Lieutenant Colonel, but only after he had serves thirty two years on active duty. Governments did try to force prospective purchasers of commissions to demonstrate a minimum level of ability and sought to provide for advancement based on demonstrated talent; but, purchase and influence remained the dominant road to higher rank.

The enlisted men in the eighteenth century provided Continental armies with their professional component. They served from six to twenty five years. In practice, most private soldiers stayed in the ranks until released by death, wounds, desertion or old age. The economic structure dictated in large measure governmental recruiting policies. Europe was basically agrarian, with primarily subsistence farming and small middle classes. Governments encouraged businesses to provide themselves with increased taxes and strategic goods. States searched among economically marginal groups for recruits, those producing the least taxes. Consequently, the unemployed, poorly paid workers, vagabonds and criminals filled the enlisted ranks. Many, if not most, governments hired foreigners. If volunteers and mercenaries were insufficient, rulers might conscript peasants or serfs, but they always preferred to fill their armies with the economically disadvantaged. [30] More than a sprinkling of paupers, ne'er-do-wells, convicts and drifters were in the ranks. Since recruiting extended across international boundaries, mercenaries continued to form part of every European army. Discipline, not patriotic motivation, was the main reliance in making these men fight. Penalties for even minor offenses ran as high as a thousand lashes. Executions by hanging or firing squad were frequent. The habit of obedience inculcated in the drill ground carried over into battle. Many claimed that the men advanced because they preferred the uncertainties of combat to the certainty of death if orders were disobeyed. [31]

Standing armies were expensive, and governments spent a remarkably high percentage of their resources on the military. Every Continental power used over half of its annual budget on the armed forces. Despite large expenditures, armies remained fairly small. Governments simply did not have the money to create larger standing forces. Europe lacked the taxable wealth and credit institutions to produce more money for the military. Democratic resistance to royal efforts at fiscal reform further restricted governmental fiscal options. Further, given the prevailing social structure, monarchs could not realistically plan to create a reserve system or a citizen army. Desertion, a problem common to all armies, made it impossible to establish a ready reserve; and no monarch would willingly arm the lower classes. Governments, therefore, had to maintain standing forces at levels approaching full strength. They had little choice but to trust their armed security to small standing armies led be aristocrats and staffed by long service enlisted men from society's lower orders. Hence, European professional armies of the seventeenth and eighteenth centuries. [32]

England

The collapse of the Roman Empire led to the revival of the European militias. Beginning in the Germanic area of Europe, by 605 the concept of the obligation of every able-bodied man to defend his society had reached England through the Angles and the Saxons. The fyrd, a levy of able-bodied freemen, locally organized and controlled, was established. It incorporated two concepts. Each male was obligated to military service and citizen-soldiers had to provide their own weapons and equipment. Lacking any formal system of training, the real value of the fyrd was its ability to mass a great number of armed men at critical points on short notice. It became embodied in what was called the "Great Fyrd", consisting of the entire free male population of military age. It bound males for defense only and traditionally only for service close to home. By 894 an increasing population made it possible to leave half of the fyrd to work the farms while the other half campaigned.

At first the legitimate sovereign could call out the Great Fyrd if men might return to their homes by nightfall. Five calls occurred during the Danish invasion of 1016. There is no evidence of attempts to train the whole universal body, but individuals were expected to turn out when called with whatever weapons they could acquire. There was probably some sort of periodic manpower muster held to determine liability/availability for service.

The pre-Norman governments of Britain, in need of a less unwieldy reserve, employed what was called the "Select Fyrd" based on land ownership. While the obligation of the ordinary people for service in war could not compare with that of their social betters, especially in the future under the feudal system, it did exist. The Anglo-Saxon fyrd was based on a personal obligation to defend the country as well as an obligation based on landed wealth. The possessor of five hides of land (varying in size by county, from 40 to 120 acres) was required, when called by his suzerain, to provide and equip one soldier. Further, he was required to pay four shillings for each hide of land. The sum of twenty shillings was expected to see the soldier through two months of service, the customary limit of his duty. The assumption was that the same person would, if possible, turn out for any particular five hide area at each call. He would thus become a relatively practiced warrior. There is some evidence, also, that when not on active service he was required to train in arms with comrades and so gain practice in cohesive action. Failure to perform fyrd service was considered a serious offense, punishable by a fine. The fyrd did not long survive William I's Conquest in 1066. On one occasion it was called out by William Rufus (II), only for his officials to take from the men the money they had been given for their subsistence. This was so more effective mercenary troops could be hired. [33]

While the mass of peasants were serfs bound to a noble's estate, freemen did exist in towns and the countryside. They continued to bear arms on occasion as infantry, often as despised adjuncts to the armies composed of heavy cavalry. This yeoman class was always stronger in England than on the Continent. Even after the Norman Conquests had brought feudal institutions to England, the tradition of the fyrd, if not its formations, remained alive. The English kings came to recognize the value of a general levy as a counterweight to turbulent nobility. In 1181 Henry II declared, in his Assizes of Arms, that every freeman should keep and "bear arms in [the King's] service according to his order and in allegiance to the Lord King and his realm."

Facing a civil war, Henry had turned to the militia for additional support. In the Assize he formally levied the military obligation of every adult male in defense of the realm. Citizen-soldiers were required to arm and equip themselves based on their social status and economic standing. They were obliged to train periodically under the local militia officer and to be ready for the King's call to service. Henry's Assize formally codified into English law the role of the militia and represented a turning point in the history of governments laying military obligations upon citizen-soldiers. The nature of the weapons the freemen kept was dependent on what they could afford. Further, as stipulated, they could use them only in the service of the king. Over the next century the practices mandated by the Assizes were not regularly enforced. Edward I felt obliged to reaffirm them in the Statute of Winchester in 1285. It dictated that all free men must provide themselves with arms and armor "to keep the peace." Edward confirmed two roles for what was becoming the militia: to be a key stone in the defense of the island and to maintain law and order within it.

During the fourteenth century competition between the monarch and Parliament resulted in constraints on the militia's employment. In 1327 Edward III stipulated that the king might not order the militia to serve outside the county of origin unless England itself was invaded, the "sudden coming of strange enemies into the realm." The militia's "range" could be extended only if the soldiers agreed and if they were paid to do so. Concerned about the Crown's power to impress all Englishmen into military service, Parliament passed other laws specifying that no citizen could be compelled to perform military service without the legislature's consent. Further, militiamen could serve outside their native county only in the instance of "great necessity." With legal restrictions on the militia's employment overseas, the English monarchs turned increasingly to mercenaries for foreign ventures and the militia deteriorated significantly. Despite these restrictions, however, in times of danger English monarchs, relying on royal prerogative, overrode the stipulated geographical limitation. Edward III invaded Scotland with militiamen, but the results of overstretching the system did not justify the cost. Later, Elizabeth I moved militiamen beyond bounds without their consent. However, her Council was so sensitive about the constitutionality of her action that they felt it necessary to arrest and detain those persons who challenged the process. In general, it was considered better to develop some sort of contractual methods to procure men for overseas excursions. [34]

The institution of the militia emerged from the traditions of the fyrd as augmented by Henry II's Assizes and Edward's Statute. It was organized on a county basis, but owed allegiance to the central government. The militia was based on the principle that a freeman had an obligation to fight for his country in war and to prepare to fight in time of peace. It was a part-time citizen army, to be called out in an emergency – to repel an invasion – and then return to the citizen mass from whence it had come. It was established when Englishmen had feared a professional army as an instrument of tyranny in the hands of an ambitious king and before Britain had embarked on foreign ventures that demanded professional forces. By the seventeenth century, when the colonies were being settled, it was declining in vigor. [35]

In the early sixteenth century the county militia was not intended to produce an expeditionary force. Only volunteers, willing or otherwise, could be sent abroad. Often the militia was reluctant to quit its own county; nor was it an obedient military instrument. Continental monarchs might find their mercenaries awkward or even mutinous over money and conditions. The English militia could be awkward in different ways. It was a cross-section of county and town society, from the lords and gentry who mustered and led it to the peasants and yeomen who left their fields and cottages with long bow and bill. Its enthusiasm could be enlisted for national purposes, but not necessarily for policies interesting the monarch alone.

From a purely military point of view, the increasing sophistication and professionalism of war lowered the value of the shire levies. The occasional enjoyable day at the muster or butts was no substitute for thorough tactical skills or experience won in arduous marches and bloody battles. The advent of fire arms had widened the gulf between the professionals and the militiamen. The handling of harquebus's and volley firing involved uniform movements not required by archery. Moreover, the militia could not be kept in the field for a long campaign because farms, estates and shops urgently called them home. [36]

True professional forces, the instruments of kings, had been taking form in England since the middle of the fifteenth century. However, the economy of Tudor England could not support so expensive an establishment. By this time, also, the feudal military system had virtually disappeared. In the reign of Queen Mary, domestic turmoil, religious fanaticism, and an increasing military threat from Spain resulted in a militia revival. In 1557, the last year of her reign, she attempted to make some sort of army out of the mass of potential citizen soldiers. An act of Parliament, "An Acte for the Having of Horse, Armour and Weapon," specifically repealed the Statute of Winchester (1285) and established new regulations. They altered the traditional military responsibilities of the sheriff and redefined military obligations. All men between sixteen and sixty were required to serve. For the provisions of horses and equipment, the nation was divided into ten classes based on yearly income. The wealthier a man was, the more equipment he was required to provide. Wealthy men were also required to provide the resources for those too poor to arm and equip themselves.

The regulations strove to make the county the basis of military organization. The office of County Lord Lieutenant was created to supervise and command the militia, building on Henry VIII's system of appointing certain nobles to be Crown Lieutenants for specific regions in emergencies. The positions were filled by important members of the local gentry. They were to be responsible for mustering the local militia, inspecting arms and equipment, and conducting periodic training. However, lest the Lord Lieutenant develop into another kind of independent aristocratic authority dangerous to the crown, the office was not permanent. It was only filled in emergencies. Under the Lord Lieutenant was a hierarchy of deputies who worked without pay. Among them were sheriffs, who from the time of the fyrd had dealt with citizens as soldiers while serving as the highest ranking royal official in the area. They also included constables of the hundreds, justices of the peace and commissioners of musters. A second act, "An Acte for the Taking of Musters," aimed at eradicating some of the major functional shortcomings and abuses of the militia. [37]

The attempt to build an army of citizen-soldiers rested on the muster, a mandatory gathering of able-bodied males, aged sixteen to sixty, in order to examine the individuals, their weapons and horses, and such armament as it was the responsibility of the towns and counties to maintain. Although the practice was ancient and steeped in tradition, the musters had become sporadic and unsystematic at best. Training as a regular adjunct of peacetime musters had become virtually unknown until Elizabeth I's Muster Law of 1572. It required her subjects to form and train in units against the danger of a Spanish invasion. Musters were required to be held four times a year and payment was a authorized for attendees

The commissioners of musters were employed by the Crown. Except for them, the gatherings were carried out by local officials, most of who were serving without pay. The musters were held at traditional gathering places and were social as much as military events. People looked forward to them and took part as a break from the monotony of their lives. They ate heavily and engaged in fights, some of them mock battles which gave pleasure to all. Despite the festive atmosphere, Elizabethan musters were the first time in English history that there were systematic attempts to train citizens as soldiers. Militiamen gathered to train in units. Men who failed to appear at musters or training days, or who turned out without the equipment required by law, were subject to fines. In times of stress the officials collected the fees; at other times they grew careless. Because of a general disinclination to military exercise, tension existed between the government and the people over training, especially during peacetime. As a solution, a select corps was created that was well trained and well supplied. The resulting units were referred to as "trained bands." [38]

As part of the Elizabethan recasting of the militia, the structure and organization of the English County levies were radically changed to transform them into the backbone of a national army. Modernization was forced on Elizabeth's Privy Council by external and internal threats. On the one hand, there was the worrying possibility of a confrontation with Spain in the near future; on the other, there was the more urgent problem of subversion by English Catholics whom the Pope had absolved from their oath of allegiance in 1570. The reforms created a core of twelve thousand part-time soldiers, selected from the County levies, who were given training, armor and weapons. They were placed under officers drawn from the local gentry who were chosen on account of their devotion to the Crown and the Church of England. The trained bands, or train bands, were supported by a reserve of sixty three thousand infantrymen, who were supplied with equipment, but not instruction, as well as three thousand cavalrymen. Overall command was in the hands of the Lords Lieutenant of individual shires, who were selected for their local standing and loyalty. Equipment was stored locally. The system was designed for domestic security and, where possible, the trained bands were not deployed abroad. By 1573, London train bands included 3,000 militiamen who trained three times a week. Ten years later, in 1593, 12,000 men out of 150,000 carried on the muster rolls were members of train bands. Elizabeth called them out in the summer of 1588 as the Spanish Armada approached the British Isles. Traditional obligatory service never was attractive, not least because it disrupted men's lives and reduced their income. Evasion had always been commonplace and was connived at by venal officials who profited from various rackets. However, desertion was cheaper and, therefore, a more popular alternative to purchasing one's way out of a military obligation. [39]

As stated earlier, Elizabeth's Privy Council, building on Mary Tudor's regulations, delegated to the Lords Lieutenant the power to carry out their orders for home defense. They created the structure of trained bands primarily for economic reasons, to save money. The new Lords Lieutenant and their deputies took charge of the mustering and the arming of the trained bands, together with all other measures necessary for military defense. These included the maintenance of beacons (for signaling approaching danger, like Spanish fleets along the English coast), the raising of the military rate, the funding of recruits for overseas expeditions and the like. At their best, when the national mood, in time of invasion threat, was cooperative, units of the militia were regularly trained, sometimes by professional officers. They could be introduced to new weapons, e.g. the pike and the musket, with some hope, in due course, of their being mastered. A typical county in the front line of war from the 1580s, such as Kent or Essex, might muster 4,000 trained men. In the north, a poorer region, such as Lancaster, whose defense and contribution to forces sent to Ireland was no less vital, could produce 500 trained and armed men. A further 4,000 in so called freehold bands, a second line of defense, were available. However efficient the system was, it still depended on the willing. [40]

Leadership in war came most easily for those who exercised in it civil society. Official instructions issued in 1586 for the training of levies specified that they should be commanded by "ensigns and captains well affected to her Majesty and the state, the eldest son of the chief gentlemen or of others of like station." A man accustomed to showing deference to the squire would find no difficulty in taking orders from him or his son. What mattered most was that the officer possessed a natural authority, rather than any experience or technical skills. Others more skillful in martial arts might be appointed as lieutenants or other officers. [41]

It was not until after 1588 that the position of Lord Lieutenant became a permanent appointment. His responsibilities covered the complete range of military activities, from mustering and training to leading men in action if there was fighting in England. He also had the task of levying men for service overseas. He was responsible for morale and public order. He could arrest and punish people who spread rumors or caused alarms or commotions. The Lord Lieutenant often had other functions within the general Tudor system of unpaid local government, such as that of ecclesiastical or grain commissioner, or commissioner for public loans. To help in these duties, the Lord Lieutenant called on the Justices of the Peace and others of his fellow gentlemen to act as his deputies (up to five or six, often with one to a large town) or as Commissioner of Musters.

At the summer musters to which all men between sixteen and sixty were summoned, the county levies were assembled, counted and divided into companies of 100 men under a captain, a gentleman of the county. Two paid officers appointed by the Lord Lieutenant, the Muster Master and the Provost Marshal, carried out the detailed work of the musters. Men fit for service or manual labor were picked and given some sort of training. Every county had its muster book in which was entered a record of the men, equipment and state of training in every hundred. The Privy Council periodically scrutinized these books which, in effect, constituted the "order of battle" of the militia. These summer musters, with progressively more complex training as the art of war progressed, were extremely unpopular. No penalties could prevent a large amount of shirking. Training was intermittent, a few days at a time during the year. The men selected for training were known, not very accurately, as "trained bands."

As a military instrument, the Elizabethan militia was useless except against similar levies such as rebels or Scots. The mistaken faith in the system was never put to the test because of English geography. The result was that long after most Continental nations had abandoned levies or militia as a first line national army, the English remained faithful to it. A tradition of amateurism became more and more deeply engrained. In the emerging professional armies of the Continent, while the nobility and the gentry provided the bulk of the officers because of the feudal traditions and privileges of their class, they were, in general, qualified to command troops because of their professional status and experience. Under the English system, as discussed previously, the nobility and gentry commanded simply because of their social position; the hierarchy of the county became the hierarchy of command. The Elizabethan militia constituted not merely the home army; it formed the pool from which expeditionary forces were levied and assembled. The armies had to match their skill, equipment and organization against the current standard of European warfare. They were the nearest thing that the Tudor military system produced to the increasingly permanent armies of the Continent. [42].

Over 100,000 men were raised for overseas service in the last two decade of Elizabeth's reign. This was fifteen percent of all able-bodied males in a population of less than 5 million. Some had to be drawn from trained bands. Large numbers were impressed by the Lords Lieutenant, each region contributing to the nearest war zone: the southern counties to the Low Countries, the northwest to Ireland, the four northern counties to the defense of the Scottish border.

Over time the decline of the Elizabethan war machine in times of peace and governmental parsimony which followed was compounded by social and political changes. The Lord Lieutenancy and the trained bands shared in this general decay and neglect. The failure to pass a Militia Act which would update and clarify the military obligations of subjects throughout the early Stewart period was symptomatic of wider malaise. Musters became less frequent, the interest in military matters declined, and the essential positions, the backbone of the militia, were either avoided by the working gentry or suffered from being the prey of local political rivalries. The Lieutenancies became hereditary in certain aristocratic families. [43]

From Anglo-Saxon times, before the Conquest in 1066, free men were obliged to undertake military service for sixty days in a national emergency. Local communities paid the overall bill for the transport and wages of the draftees. In Scotland, the Crown paid. Successive acts had been passed by the English and Irish Parliaments that specified when and how county levies were to be raised, the nature of the men's equipment and who was to bear the costs. This legislation was widely ignored. No minor lord or tenant farmer would waste money on weapons, or armor just to provide ill-paid, obligatory and irksome military service. In 1599, faced with widespread indifference, the Scottish government abandoned wide spread levies and chose, instead, to depend on men directly raised by the nobility from among their own circle of clients and tenants. [44]

By the seventeenth century the Anglo-Saxon fyrd had been transmuted into the militia. It was still concerned with military defense on the local scene like the fyrd, but was otherwise quite different. Hardly more than a tenth of the men of the county belonged to the militia. It had become a social as much as a military organization composed mainly of the county's substantial men. Only the fairly well off could afford the musket, ball and shot, the pike, sword and other military paraphernalia with which each member had to equip himself. Cast, as well as the Crown's eagerness to keep often restless lower classes unarmed, prevented most men from joining. The militia mustered once or twice a year. Citizens from all parts of the county gathered to watch the troops perform their drills and perhaps engage in a sham battle. The rest of the day was given over to drinking and other pleasures. The militia now played no part in the conduct of war. England's isolation gave little cause to fear invasion. By Cromwell's time in the 1640s the militia had become mainly a police force to put down riots and other internal disturbances. [45]

By the middle of the eighteenth century the average British male had lost his intimate knowledge of weapons and fighting. Charles Lee, a former British officer turned American General, pointed out that "the lower and middle people of England ... [are] almost as ignorant in the use of the musket, as they are of the ancient catapulta." The militia tradition in England had lost much of the vigor of earlier times, although, technically, men between the ages of eighteen and forty five were eligible for five year stints which they could commute by hiring a substitute or paying a fine. As the militia was funded by a land tax, it was controlled by the landed gentry. The military lists of the period are simply a catalogue of the leading county families. In many cases a regiment of militia became a very exclusive country club. [46]

In 1757 the militia was ordered to be raised by ballot. During the eighteenth century, especially the first half, the militia increasingly became a reserve for a regular professional army, not an alternative. Compulsory service in the militia did not, therefore, indicate a progression towards a true citizen army, particularly as the obligation was hedged around by exemptions and could be avoided by the procurement of a substitute. [47]

Britain's standing army and foreign troops for hire were supplemented by the militia, not replaced by it. Before the Militia Act of 1757 it had become a largely ineffective force which was rarely mustered in large units or employed. Therefore it lacked military experience and expertise. The Jacobite Rebellion of 1745-46 and the threat of French invasion during the Seven Years (SY)/French and Indian (FI) War led to the militia's reorganization and, eventually, to the regular embodiment of a national militia. After 1762 the county militia was required to drill for twenty eight days a year. Militiamen became subject to military law while on active service. By 1764 nearly 28,000 militiamen were under arms.

While their military proficiency improved during the second half of the eighteenth century, the militia was not tested in battle against regular troops. Confined by law to its native land, it was primarily a bulwark against foreign invasion, albeit a somewhat flimsy one. As such, it was the least important component of Britain's military effort. However, it did serve to familiarize many more Englishmen with the use of arms and the character of military life. While they by no means became military strategists, most learned how to drill and the rudiments necessary to defend the nation. [48]

Great Britain enjoyed a unique status among the great powers of Europe because, ultimately, its strong navy gave it security from attack by its neighbors. One consequence was that the British Army lagged behind the other European armies in adopting the reforms of the sixteenth, seventeenth and eighteenth centuries. Another consequence was that the militia lingered on. By the seventeenth century, for all intents and purposes, and with the possible exception of the city of London's train band, its military role was nil. However, the tradition or, more correctly, the myth of the tradition, strengthened with the institution's demise. Ironically, the myth of the militia became more influential than the actual militia ever had been. This concept was especially true among two groups: those who perceived a large, professional standing army based in England as a real threat to civil liberties; and those who migrated overseas. The dearly held custom transplanted to America represented a tradition in the classical mold of a free people dropping their scythes and shouldering weapons to fight off the invaders; and then, the battle won, of going home to resume cutting hay. As in republican Rome, no need existed for a professional army as long as a virtuous, well armed, free citizenry stood guard, or so the tradition went.

By mid-eighteenth century, while enjoying and profiting from its geographic security and naval supremacy, Britain had adopted the major European military reforms. In fact, it had led the way in introducing many techniques of infantry fire control. Its slow and ad hoc growth as an institution, however, had produced an inefficient and extremely complex administrative and logistical superstructure. Authority and responsibility were divided between two major army commands (the British and the Irish establishment), between the Army proper and the Ordnance Department (controlling artillery, engineer and munitions), and between the civilian Secretary at War and the military Commander-in-Chief, when that office was filled. Strategic direction was shared by two or three civilian Secretaries of State. At times the various individuals responsible for these chains of command cooperated and the system functioned well. However, when break down occurred, the British Army appeared leaderless and inept.

Unless engaged in extensive hostilities, the British maintained a small standing army by European standards. After 1763, the end of SY/FI War, the Army numbered about 39,000 men. In wartime, they could count on a Hanoverian force of 34,000. Since George I, the English kings had been, and George III continued to be, hereditary rulers of Hanover. They could also call on an Irish garrison of 12,000. Mercenaries were available as well, primarily from the smaller Germanic states who "rented" their units out en-mass. Wealth, geography and naval dominance had allowed Great Britain to act as a major power without the financial burden of a large standing army. [49]

The beginnings of the English standing army can be traced to the pre-Norman period amongst the guardsmen whose duty was to defend the Saxon kings. Canute the Dane, who ruled from 1016 to 1035, enlarged the force. These House Guards became professionals by reason of continual

48

service and may be considered the forbearers of later regular armies. It was with a mixed force of House Guards and Select Fyrd that King Harold unsuccessfully tried to expel William from England in 1066. [50]

Paid troops were important in English armies as early as the eleventh and twelfth centuries. The employment of mercenaries, hardened professionals mostly drawn from the Low Countries, was a notable feature of the period. Such men formed a high proportion of the paid elements in English armies. The skill of the mercenaries is well attested to in the Chronicles. In some circumstances, most notably those of civil war, they might prove more loyal than English troops, provided they received their rewards. These men, however, were extremely unpopular. And it was not only foreigners who might be paid for their service. The troops of the royal household were usually paid, as were those temporarily hired to bolster the household's numbers. [51]

In the fourteenth and fifteenth centuries England was one of the most effective states in Europe, with a much feared army and the military capability to command a sizable empire on the Continent. However, from the mid-fifteenth century, when the artillery of Charles VII won the decisive victory of Castellan and drove the English out of almost all of France, to the year 1558, when Elizabeth lost her Continental foothold at Calais, British military might underwent a marked decline. Between the end of the Hundred Years War (1453) and the outbreak of hostilities with Louis XIV in 1689, England ceased to be a major military power in Europe. With the exception of Henry VIII's delusions of grandeur at the beginning and end of his reign, English military activity for a period of more than two hundred years consisted of naval warfare, civil war and the occasional, all too often unsuccessful, expedition to aid a friendly Continental power. In a period of ferocious and continuous warfare, England was remarkable for its lack of participation in international conflict and for its many years of peace. England was not a major participant in the so-called "Military Revolution" of sixteenth and seventeenth century Europe.

The Tudor monarchs opposed a standing army because it was likely to enhance aristocratic power. In the seventeenth century successive Parliaments opposed a standing army because it was likely to enhance the power of the executive. In either case, such opposition could be effective only as long as the state as not under direct military threat. Provided no foreign foe was able to invade the kingdom and that no domestic power challenged the state's monopoly of legitimate violence, England could remain the least militarized of European powers. Her military commitment could be confined to the navy, domestic militia fit only for defensive warfare and to the occasional body of professionals paid to fight abroad.

This pattern of military development, which contrasted with the emergence of standing armies among the major Continental powers, is often attributed to England's peculiar strategic position; it's an island. England's insularity, together with her prowess as a naval power, provided adequate protection against foreign invasion. Another significant factor was the change in the character of warfare. The increased size of armies meant that a full scale cross-Channel invasion of England was both a complicated and costly operation. England was sheltered not just by her insular position, but also by the scale of war in early modern Europe. [52]

Drafts of county levies were never a substitute for professional soldiers, no matter how well equipped and dressed.

These formed the bulk of the contract armies that served in France and elsewhere during the fourteenth and fifteenth centuries. Men were frequently raised on the estates of the commanders. Those chosen would wear the commander's livery and, wherever possible, were mounted. From among the ranks of such men emerged the first English career officers, men of often lowly birth who showed outstanding abilities which earned them commands. [53]

When Henry VIII came to the throne in 1509 England had not fought a campaign in Europe since the conclusion of the Hundred Years War in 1453, as mentioned above. English military ideas had failed to progress beyond those of Agincourt. On the other hand, medieval English military institutions had been deliberately demolished by Henry VII in his determination to impose the authority of the Crown on the great nobles. He forbade private armies or retainers, except under special royal license in the case of a trusted magnate. No new royal military organization had replaced the abolished medieval source of troops. Unlike other European monarchs, he had not needed a royal army to suppress his over-mighty subjects by force and reunite his kingdom. Further, there had been no need for a large foreign expeditionary force. Thus, by 1509 the English late medieval system had disappeared without replacement, except for the royal bodyguard of two hundred men. Henry VII had created it in the first year of his reign, the Yeomen of the Guard, who survive into the twenty-first century. [54]

The first permanent English military department and military administrative officer of state, established during the reign of Henry VIII, were, respectively, the Ordinance Department and the Master of Ordinance. They were created to deal with artillery, a new and growing technology.

The Master was a person of distinction, usually a peer. His department produced guns designed for both the army and navy; only the mountings were different. When Henry VIII died in 1547, both the military troops and their administration were still backward compared with the professionalized and increasingly long standing armies of the Continent. The permanent guards and garrisons in new forts and towns of strategic importance were the only standing force in peacetime, apart from a handful of Yeomen of the Guard and gentlemen pensioners. Some garrisons were large, up to 500 men. However, the English land forces in 1547 did not begin to compare to those of the Continental monarchies. [55]

English military men were aware of ongoing changes in tactics and organization throughout Europe. They could read about them in any number of military manuals which were circulated throughout Europe and translated into several languages. The new tactics were even put into practice by Cromwell's armies. However, in the most important change in European warfare, the increased scale, England lagged behind. In the last quarter of the seventeenth century the British army had only 15,000 men. It was smaller than it had been in 1475. The numbers exceeded 30,000 during the Commonwealth and the Protectorate (when civil conflict and an exchequer filled with revenues from sequestered royalist lands made a large army politically necessary and fiscally possible) and during the last years of James II's reign. As we have seen, for much of the period between the late fifteenth and late seventeenth centuries England virtually lacked a standing army. While other European nations acquired such forces, the English state relied increasingly for domestic defense on the militia and its trained bands. Only foreign expeditions were manned with professional soldiers drawn from the bodies of paid retainers or foreign mercenaries, the militia not being required to serve overseas. [56]

In the course of the seventeenth century the English popular militia fell into eclipse. Its ineptitude helped cause the Civil War. At its outset there was no standing army and few professional soldiers. The opening campaigns of the war reflected this generally amateurish approach. However, over time and through experience, trained soldiers and able commanders began to emerge. In his quest to restore stability in the country, Cromwell increasingly relied on what had become professional standing regiments of soldiers. Charles II had good reason to depend on professional soldiers almost exclusively, and the history of the English regular army is usually dated from his reign. The English militia fell into virtual oblivion and the professional army became the almost exclusive land force of the state. [57]

Immediately after the restoration of Charles II in 1660, while Commonwealth men were still restless and rumors of plots and insurrections were rife, the militia again fulfilled the only function it had ever carried out effectively, that of amateur political police and riot force. Yet, even for this it was soon felt to be inadequate in the face of the apparently serious new danger to the state. This apparent danger produced another, and major, step forward in the history of English military institutions: the retention of regimented bodies on men in peacetime.

Apart from some small non-regimental units that had always garrisoned coastal forts and fortified towns, it had been intended at the restoration to retain only the King's bodyguard which had accompanied him into exile to guard his palace and person. Upon his return, Charles had found four existing armies made up of those of previous opponents, the

New Model Army, and his own group of exiled Irish and royalists. Determined to avoid the example of his Cromwellian predecessors whenever possible, he reduced the army to its lowest possible extent, leaving a small residue to protect the royal palace and the first overseas colonies. Some of the units were disbanded, some became mercenary units, and still others were sent to fight overseas. Since Charles had insufficient funds, a large army was out of the question; but a military royal household of "guards and garrisons" to protect the royal person and the key points of the kingdom was both feasible and realistic. On November 23, 1660, the 1st Footguards, later known as the Grenadier Guards, was formed consisting of twelve companies of 100 men each. It was started as two regiments drawn from Charles' overseas guards that were quickly merged into one.

In January, 1661, a fanatical Fifth Monarchist, Samuel Venner, led an armed uprising in London which seemed to the newly restored King and his supporters more dangerous than mere plots. The ongoing disbandenment of the remaining New Model Army units under General Monck, former Commander-in-Chief, was halted. Only two regiments were left. On February 14, 1661, both regiments disbanded and were immediately reconstituted in the royal service. The infantry became the Lord General's, or 2nd, Regiment of Footguards, later the Coldstream Guards. The cavalry was reformed as the Lord General's Troop of Guards. Subsequently merged with cavalry troops from Charles' overseas guards into the Earl of Oxford's Regiment of Horse, it exists today as the Royal House Guards (Blues), amalgamated with the Royal Dragoons in the Life Guards.

Also as a result of Venner's revolt, the government called the Scottish troops in French service back to Britain. The

French regiment had been raised in 1633 and later absorbed Scottish units which had fought under Gustavius Adolphus of Sweden. Although the regiment returned to the French in 1662 and served until 1678, with one two year break, they date their seniority in the British service from 1661 as the First Royal or Scots Foot, now the Royal Scots. Charles' Queen, Catherine of Broganza, brought Tangier to the English Crown as part of her dowry. The Tangier Regiment of Foot was formed as a defense against the Moors. The regiment was brought to England in 1684 as the Queen's Regiment of Foot, today the Queen's Royal Regiment. In Scotland the Commonwealth regiments were not disbanded on the Restoration, but in 1662 were taken into Portuguese service. The Restoration meant that England and Scotland became separate kingdoms again with separate military establishments. This lasted until the final union of the two kingdoms in 1707. Its royal regiments are now represented by the Royal Scots Greys, the Scots Guard, and the Royal Highland Fusiliers.

Hence, the oldest regiments in British history trace their lineage back to 1660-1661 and to the odd combination of a Fifth Monarchy Plot and a Roman Catholic dowry. However, despite opinions to the contrary, this was not a great watershed in British military developments. In fact, no definitive date for the creation of the army can be fixed. By 1661 the British aversion to standing armies was already strong. Those politicians/statesmen who decided to retain the last two regiments of Monck's Commonwealth Army and the pre-1660 royal regiments had no intention of creating a standing army. They were merely temporarily reinforcing the guards of "his Majesty's person" in order to maintain public order. There had been "guards and garrisons" in peacetime for centuries.

Fifty years later the Mutiny Acts were still proclaiming that a standing army in peacetime without Parliament's consent was illegal. Troops in Britain were still described as "guards and garrisons." Although those regiments became permanent, Monck, Charles, and his minister Clarendon had not planned to make them so.

Charles maintained this relatively small standing force of about 6,000 men built from the remnants of his royal guard and the Cromwellian New Model Army. The regiments and a smattering of garrison companies cost the King ten per cent of his annual income from Parliament. In fact, it didn't even cost him that. Charles supported this essentially unconstitutional establishment with little aid and no approval from Parliament. He was able to do so because of a secret subsidy which his uncle, Louis XIV, paid him. When his brother James succeeded him in 1685, he openly defied the public mood more than Charles had ever been willing to do by enlarging the standing army to 53,000. It steadily grew even larger, rising to 93,635 in 1694 to deal with war in Ireland, Scotland and the Low Countries. After the Peace of Rijswijk in 1697, Parliament reduced the army down to a cadre of 7,000 men although it did not remain at that level for long. [58]

After the stalemating of James II in the Glorious Revolution, Parliament, to guarantee its jurisdiction in the military sphere as elsewhere, produced the Bill of Rights, stating that "the raising and keeping of a standing army within the kingdom in time of peace unless it be with the consent of parliament, is against the law." The resolution of the constitutional position of Parliament vis-a-vis the Army was demonstrated by the Mutiny Act. It was an annual law, first enacted in 1689, which legalized the Army's existence, regulated its discipline, and was a principal means of assuring

Parliamentary supremacy over the military. It authorized the trial of soldiers by courts martial for one year only. Without yearly renewal the Crown would have no legal foundation upon which to discipline the Army. This measure, together with the practice of granting Army appropriations, which normally accompanied it, only for one year, prevented the Sovereign's ruling for an indefinite period without calling a Parliament, in the manner of Charles I. Originally brief, the successive Mutiny Acts grew lengthy and complex. Without it the Army would cease to exist. [59]

After 1688 the scope of British military involvement changed radically. Britain was at war more frequently and for longer periods of time (60 of the next 95 years), deploying armies and navies of unprecedented size. Wars were now conducted on a greater scale than earlier military operations. The state's military role made it the most important single factor in the domestic economy; the largest borrower and spender, as well as the largest single employer. Britain acquired a standing army and navy. She became, like her main rivals, a fiscal-military state, one dominated by the task of waging war.

Though it expanded enormously, Britain's military activity retained much of the pattern it had assumed prior to 1688. The sizeable peacetime standing army was new, but weak. The practice of hiring foreign troops to fight in Europe persisted. The sums spent on foreign regiments and armies were far greater than ever before. Both of these tactics helped circumscribe the scope of the standing army. Between 1703 and 1713 the army averaged nearly 93,000 men, with 144,650 in final year of the war under British arms. After subsequent reductions it rose again to 70,000 men in 67 battalions. The SY/FI War saw a significant increase, to in excess of 90,000 in 120 battalions.

Britain's peacetime forces were much smaller than those of wartime. The peacetime army numbered about 35,000 in the first half of the eighteenth century and 45,000 after the SY/FI War. The reduced peacetime regiments were stationed in Britain, in outposts of the empire such as Gibraltar, and, eventually, North America, which needed constant protection, and, above all, Ireland. This latter location had the advantage, from the point of view of the ministers at Westminster, that a large portion of the peacetime force was kept on the Irish establishment, funded by the Irish taxpayer and kept out of view of the English Parliament. However, they could be transferred quickly to England if the need arose. After 1688 England had a standing army, a body of professional "effectives" which was in a constant state of readiness and which provided the core around which a wartime army was built. They were a more effective base than their larger European counterparts because they were required to serve year round. They were not dismissed at harvest time or granted long peacetime leaves of absence, like the Prussians. [60]

In the eighteenth century Britain was fighting its wars with professional armies and navies, like its European counterparts. Its growing quest for imperial power and subsequent need to fight in foreign lands forced it to turn to professionals, albeit much later than its allies and opponents. In all countries the raising of an army was an onerous and expensive task. The officers came from the nobility and gentry and were easily enlisted. But the rank and file had to be recruited from the lowest classes, from men who had no other place to go and were amenable to offers of bounty and threats of force. Once raised, a professional army was a resource to be husbanded. It was difficult, if not impossible to replace.

Hence, commanders did not risk battle until they were reasonably certain of victory, or had no choice but to fight. [61]

Although younger sons of the aristocracy and gentry dominated the British Army's officer ranks, it was much freer from aristocratic influence than many of its European counterparts. About two-thirds of its officers purchased their commissions according to tariffs established in 1720 and subsequently updated. Many of the remaining third had been "volunteers" who served in the ranks in the hope of attracting favorable notice, or NCOs who were commissioned in large numbers in wartime. The officer of this period was far from being the red coated booby of popular mythology. There was certainly a sprinkling of incompetents, but, as one author said, "the British Army was ... led by an officer corps of the most considerable experience, made up of men who, by and large, entered the service for life and got by on steady, competent service."

During the eighteenth century the status of private soldiers declined. The British Army supplemented voluntary enlistments by drafting "all such able-bodied, idle and disorderly persons who cannot upon examination prove themselves to exercise some lawful trade or employment." Soldiers' lives were dominated by the demands of the drill-ground and they were subjected to discipline which brought with it the constant risk of corporal punishment, whether from the casual blow of the sergeant's stick or the more deliberate attentions of the cat o'nine tails. However, once a man had finished his recruit training he might, at least in peacetime, expect to spend much of his time off duty, helping with the harvest or even taking up a civilian trade. For much of the period soldiers were billeted on private households or lodged at inns in garrison towns. Billeting was a source of friction between

monarchs and their subjects, the more so because it was sometimes used as a means of punishing refractory citizens. By the
end of the eighteenth century troops were often housed in
purpose built barracks, the long, austere blocks which are
features of many fortresses.

The seventeenth century had seen the birth of national
armies in which mercenaries played a declining part. Sweeping
native males into their ranks denuded the work force and
reduced income from taxation. Thus, armies found themselves increasingly dependent again on foreign recruitment.
In 1709, 81,000 of the 150,000 British soldiers in the field
were actually foreign: either exiles, often French Huguenots,
serving for pay, or regiments from German states hired out
by their rulers. This high proportion of mercenaries was one
of the causes of the Army's most prevalent disease, desertion.
It also led to ironic confrontations: at Fortenay in 1745 the
Irish Brigade (the "Wild Geese") in the French service played
a prominent part in defeating the British; at Trenton in 1776
King George's cause was defended by Colonel John Rall's
Hessian Brigade. [62]

During the seventeenth and eighteenth centuries, in both
British and American forces, the terms battalions and regiments were virtually synonymous and used interchangeable.
British regiments deployed to America, or formed there, normally consisted of two battalions; one deployed and one serving as an administrative unit at the regiment's territorial base.
This territorial base unit was responsible for recruiting new
soldiers from the surrounding area and training them. Upon
completion of their training they would then be reassigned
to the serving battalion. On rare occasions there would be a
three battalion regiment, two deployed and one recruiting
and training in the "home" area.

The typical infantry regiment consisted of ten companies, eight "battalion" and two 'flank." The flank companies, one of grenadiers and one of light infantry, were so called because when the regiment was drawn up into battle lines, they were positioned on each flank or wing. The grenadiers would be on the right, the position of honor, and the "light bobs" on the left. The grenadiers were generally the largest men in the regiment and the light troops were the smallest. Within units, regiments/battalions and companies, the troops were put into formation by size, largest to smallest from right to left. It looked better and helped with uniformity. This desire for 'smartness" led to the size disparity. The sizes of the grenadiers and the light infantry troops also were a factor in their deployment. The smaller "lights" were presumably more agile and better able to deploy as skirmishers, using cover, concealment and movement to safely move around the battlefield and harass the incoming enemy troops. The grenadiers were more imposing looking and were supposed to disconcert the enemy by their very size and apparent ferocity (hence the large bearskin headwear eventually used), scaring them into flight. It often worked.

On paper, though rarely in reality, each company had 56 privates. In actuality, there were fifty three because three were fictitious "contingency" men whose pay was collected by the company commander to defray the cost of the weapons' repair and other company expenses. In addition, each company would have a captain, a lieutenant, and ensign, three sergeants, three corporals, a drummer and a fifer. A colonel, a lieutenant colonel and a major formed the regimental headquarters leadership. A chaplain, a surgeon, a surgeon's mate, and a quartermaster completed the establishment. A British battalion, complete with its flank companies, had 642 officers and men and could muster 560 muskets (privates and corporals). However, the difference between paper strength and battle strength was usually significant due to losses through illness, casualties, desertions and shortfalls in recruitment. [63]

In seventeenth and eighteenth century England, according to radical Whig opposition ideology, property-holding citizens organized as militia would naturally stand up to those who would resort to military force as a means of despoiling liberties. An extremely significant personage in the struggle between power and liberty, then, was the citizen-soldier who came forth as the Minuteman in Lexington and Concord in Massachusetts in 1775. From the mid-seventeenth century on, Whig opposition writers had extolled the citizen-soldier. In particular, they were reacting to Oliver Cromwell's New Model Army. It became, in their view, an instrument of repression, with little concern for popular rights after it had swept the royalist supporters of Charles I before it in the 1640s. The reason seemed to be that Cromwell's soldiers hardened into regulars whose loyalty in time of flux devolved onto a tyrannical Puritan leader, all at the expense of liberty.

Commentary in condemnation of standing armies and in praise of the citizen-soldier in the modern era may be traced to early sixteenth century Florence and the writings of Nicolo Machiavelli: in The Prince (1513) he said "that no state is safe unless it has its own arms ... . Your own arms are composed of your subjects or citizens or dependents, all others are either mercenaries or auxiliaries." John Harrington in Commonwealth of Oceana (1656), in turn, carefully defined the independent citizen as the individual who held property, such as a free hold estate. Such persons, by virtue of property holding, had clear economic stakes in the preservation of society. Likewise, it was a fundamental duty of the citizen to keep and bear arms in the defense of public liberty and personal property.

To Harrington, and other seventeenth century opposition writers, the ideas of propertied independence and the militia were inextricably tied together. Since independent proprietors, those with a demonstrable stake in society, should naturally provide for the public defense, they would never become a "threat to the public liberty or public purse." If they did, they would be attacking the very polity in which their property gave them a clear stake, which would have been contradictory behavior. The presence of a standing army in any country denoted to Whig ideologues that luxury, corruption, power and tyranny were to various degrees threatening property, liberty and life itself. An active militia, by comparison, denoted that citizens were taking their obligations seriously and were behaving virtuously.

While this philosophy ultimately took root in America, the radical Whig pamphleteers had little influence on government activities in England. Parliament maintained and supported a peacetime standing army, despite persistent opposition Whig cries. It could do so because of the language contained in the Bill of Rights from the late seventeenth century which mandated that any regular military establishment must be clearly subordinate to civil authority. Likewise, all citizens were to have the right to bear arms in defense of the state.

Militia units did exist, yet Parliament relied most heavily on a well trained standing army. It exercised civil control through yearly appropriations and the annual Mutiny Act, legitimizing the military establishment and prescribing a code of discipline. Propertied citizens generally did not worry about the implications of a standing army in their midst. The establishment remained the backbone of imperial defense, although with sharply reduced manpower when not at war. [64]

There is a theme running through the development of the science and structure of military forces that keeps reoccurring over time, from culture to culture, society to society, nation to nation. As a society becomes more complex and specialized, the military forces increase in complexity and formal structure. The result is a completely professional army. As the nation moves toward a lessening of power and, ultimately, disintegration, as all eventually have, its military forces follow a similar path.

Among man's earliest, most primitive ancestors males were the hunters, the protectors of territory and the acquirers of new territory. They were warriors. Every male was expected to fill that role. He had individual responsibility to be part of the collaborative effort to defend the group. This structure and attitude continue to exist in unsophisticated peoples. Witness the "uncontacted" tribes in the Brazilian Amazon River Basin who appear to be acting in that manner without regard for the more sophisticated developments of surrounding societies.

Over time, in various societies and cultures, life became more complex. Agriculture developed, and then light industries and trade. Nation states evolved from the various tribal groups. Military defense was still essential for the state's, the society's survival. However, the cost of maintaining a group of people who only fought was beyond the reach of the state, even if anyone thought of it The solution was still the concept that every man was a warrior with an obligation to defend his society/culture/nation. Hence, the formal development of militias or militia-like forces.

Development within society continued apace. While there was a consensus that defense was essential, more and more of the members didn't have time to devote to military training, much less to leaving their homes for extended periods of time on military campaigns. The losses in productivity, agricultural production and tax revenue for the state were too great. Further, if there were extended periods of no military danger, people lost interest. Their attention was not on defense but on their day to day lives. The solution was the development of professional soldiers as part of regular standing military units. Most nations started with mercenaries; men who, for whatever reason, were willing to fight for pay for whoever would pay them. As more funds became available and the perceived need grew, countries organized their own citizens as full time soldiers.

There were countless variations on this theme over time, each society's development dependent on multiple, changing factors. But the central theme of military development remained the same. Developments in technology required adaptations in tactics and strategy. Failure to do so had disastrous consequences (e.g. the slaughter in World War I), but basic soldiering remained the same. The military leaders in the sixteenth through the eighteenth centuries had to learn how to utilize the emerging weapons technologies while moving larger and larger groups of men around the battlefield. They were relearning the lessons of the Egyptians, the Assyrians, the Persians, the Greeks, and the Romans, among others, in organizing, maintaining and moving large military units around the battlefield while incorporating new technologies into their tactics and strategy.

Although similar in many respects to those in other countries, military developments in England were also significantly different. Through a combination of geography, political development, societal development and happenstance, a formal, structured, professional standing military force developed much later in England than on the Continent. Even once initiated, it developed slowly due to monetary considerations as well as lack of necessity. Also unique to England, the strong philosophical and political opposition to a standing army, interwoven with opposition to the Crown and dominant political party in the seventeenth and eighteenth centuries, slowed down a fully developed army on the Prussian or French models. Ultimately, this opposition lost its impact on the decision makers, especially as England's desire to participate in overseas expansion and international politics grew, along with the resultant military requirements.

This philosophical aversion to and fear of long term standing armies made its way to America where it was espoused by the leading thinkers and political leaders. These men, and their successors, continued to believe in the benefits of citizen-soldiers and the nobility of seventeenth and eighteenth century successors of Cincinnatus long after their English counterparts had moved on. Many of them were instrumental in fomenting opposition to Britain, declaring independence, waging a war, writing the U.S. Constitution, and, then, organizing and running the first government under it. The belief and mythology surrounding the citizen-soldier continues in this country to the present day.

And the strength of nations and their militaries continues to ebb and flow. The ancient process is ongoing.

2. New World Militia

ORIGINAL SETTLEMENTS

On April 10, 1606 James I granted a charter authorizing two groups, one centered in London and the other in Plymouth, to establish plantations in Virginia. At that time Virginia was the name given to all of that part of North America claimed by Great Britain. Self defense was an integral part of the charter. Members of the first colony (Jamestown) "shall and may inhabit and remain there, and shall and may also build and fortify with any the same, for their better Safeguard and Defence, according to their best Discretion, and the Discretion of the Council of that Colony." The colonists were required to take with them "sufficient Shipping and Furniture of Armour Weapons, Ordinance, Powder ... necessary for the said Plantations and for their use and Defence there." They were granted the right to "transport the Goods, Chattels, Armour, Munition and Furniture ... to be used for them, for their ... Apparel, Food, Defense, or otherwise." [65]

The English promoters of the first English colonies knew something of the hazards of America. From the beginning, all of the colonial charters authorized defensive armaments. In 1607 the Virginia promoters instructed the settlers to form themselves into three groups immediately upon landing: one to erect fortifications for defense, one to serve as a guard and to plant a crop, and the third to explore. The first ships were stocked with weapons. Pikes and swords were supplemented by firearms, primarily matchlocks. The matchlocks, in turn, were eventually replaced with flintlock muskets. All of these weapons, especially the firearms, required extensive training. Laws required that every able-bodied man, with a few exceptions, be given training in firearms, swords and pikes. The citizen-soldier was required to drill in formation; possess, maintain and provision his weapon; and maintain his equipment ready for immediate use. Although faltering in military capability and effectiveness, the Elizabethan militia is what they knew. Shortly after her death, they brought that with them too. [66]

The first English settlers in America came prepared for warfare. Military considerations, especially defense, were important in their lives. Virginians knew that the Spanish objected to their presence. They expected to be confronted by hostile Indians, as did the early settlers of Plymouth and Massachusetts Bay. They were not mistaken. Harassed by hostile Indians, in addition to Spanish, French and Dutch colonial rivals also often hostile to their survival, in a wilderness three thousand miles and many months from Britain, the colonists were ever mindful of the need to protect themselves. The British Crown offered little more than company charters and proprietor grants. It originally expected the colonists to defend themselves.

Thoughts of war weighed heavily on the minds of these early English settlers. At any moment a belligerent fleet might appear on the horizon or the stillness of a dawn could be shattered by war hoops. These threats to the settlers' very existence were genuine and prudence dictated that they take measures to defend themselves. The first colonists were products of a tumultuous, violent epoch in European history. Although the England they sailed from was relatively peaceful, to the aspiring colonists weapons of war were essential tools. They would no more have crossed the ocean without hoes or Bibles than have left their blunderbusses, crossbows and pikes at home. Their understanding of war derived from fundamental and ancient sources. It was influenced greatly by the seemingly endless ferocity of sixteenth century Old World religious and secular life.

The charter of Massachusetts Bay stated that the inhabitants were "to incounter, repulse, repell and resist by force of armes, as well as by seas as by lands" any attempt to invade or destroy their community. The Maryland charter referred directly to the remoteness of the proprietary "placed among so many barbarous nations" and to the "incursions as well of the barbarians themselves, as of other enemies pirates and ravagers."

Maryland's first military law, contained in the Royal Charter, stated "that in so remote a region, placed among so many barbarian nations, the incursions as well of the barbarians will be feared, therefore we have given, and – for us, our heirs and successors do give by these presents as full and unrestrained power as any captain-general of an army hath had, into the aforesaid now Baron of Baltimore, and to his heirs and assigns, by themselves, or by their captains or other officers, to summon their standards and array all men of whatsoever condition or wheresoever born, for the time being in the said province of Maryland, to wage war, and to pursue, even beyond the limits of their province, the enemies and ravagers of aforesaid, infesting those parts by land and sea, and … to vanquish, and captivate them, and the captives to be put to death, or, according to their discretion, to save and do all other and singular things which appertain, or have been accustomed to appertain, unto the authority and office of a captain-general of an army." Simplistically, Baltimore was the general of an army wresting control of what was to become Maryland from whoever had it and protecting it from all comers. [67]

Cecil Calvert, Lord Baltimore and Lord Proprietor of Maryland, was very aware of the potential dangers his new settlers faced. In his instructions to them he directed the colonists to be ready for any emergency: against Indian massacre, Spanish attacks, eruptions from Virginia to the south, or aggressions from New Netherlands in the north. To this end, a fort was to be immediately constructed and universal military training put into effect.

In describing the site of St. Mary's City in May 1634, Leonard Calvert, the first Governor, wrote his brother Cecil "we have seated ourselves within one-half mile of the river, within a palisade of one hundred twenty yards square, with four flanks. We have mounted one piece of ordinance and placed six murders [small cannon] in parts most convenient, a fortification (we think) sufficient to defend against any real enemies as we have reason to expect here." As further defense "people were enforced not only to labor by day, but to watch in their turns by night." [68]

Leonard and his brother George also described to Cecil the initial landings and their encounters with the Indians. The town they call "St. Marie's; … we bought … for hatchets, axes, hoes and clothes, a quantity of the same 30 miles of land … And that which made them more willing to sell it, was the wars they had with the Susquehanock, a mighty bordering nation, who came often into their country to waste and destroy ... Yet, seeing we came so well prepared with arms, their fear was much less, and they would be content to dwell by us." However, the colonists were cautious. The first thing the settlers did on landing was to build a guard-house for their defense. [69]

The new Maryland colonists were immigrants facing the prospect of life in a hostile environment. Short term survival depended on preparation. Aware of this fact, in 1635 associates of Cecil Calvert, at his direction, prepared a pamphlet entitled A Relation to Maryland. It contained instructions on what the gentlemen adventurers on Calvert's upcoming expedition to America should bring. It listed essential provisions and their price, presumably for helping potential colonists estimate the cost of going to America. The list included food, clothing, bedding, tools and "Armes. For one man: one musket, 10 pounds of powder; 40 pounds of Lead, Bullets, Pistoll and Goose Shot, of each sort some; one sword; one belt; one bandelere and flaske: In(ch) match" at a total cost of 2 pounds, 5 shillings, 6 pence. [70]

The colonizers in England sent armaments with the settlers. In the first two settlements, Jamestown and Plymouth, however, these proved inadequate in both kind and number. Pikes and steel armor were not useful against the Indians. In contrast, Massachusetts Bay, with past examples to learn from and with more adequate funding, spent 22,000 pounds – one ninth of its original capital – on twenty cannon and enough infantry gear for one hundred men. Individuals brought their own store of arms too. After food, arms and armaments accounted for the greatest expenditures. Thus, individually and collectively, the Puritans arrived in New England ready to defend themselves. Once afoot in the New World, defense would always be a primary concern.

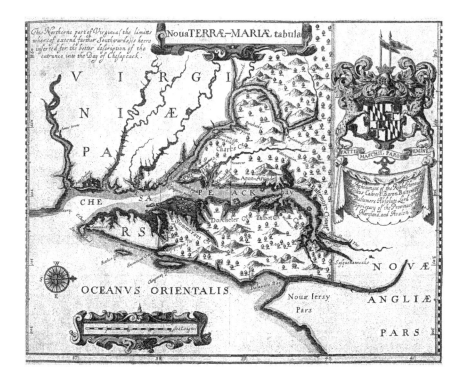

However different the agencies that founded the various colonies in North America may have been, all of them, as well as the colonists themselves, believed that a military obligation rested on every free white male settler. Accordingly, the charters issued by the various English kings to the colonizing agencies gave their representatives the right "to assemble (in) Marshal Array and put in warlike posture the inhabitants of said colony." This clause referred specifically to able-bodied men aged 16 to 60. These, led by constituted authority, were authorized to "expulse repell and resist by force of Arms ... and also to kill slay destroy by all fitting ways ... all and every Person or Persons as shall attempt the destruction invasion detriment or annoyance of the ... inhabitants." These words, taken from Charles II's charter to the colony of Connecticut, are not found verbatim in other charters, but the same ideas and powers are present. The charter granted to the last of the original colonies, Georgia, speaks specifically of the militia as the "backbone of colonial defense." [71]

Elizabeth I's government sent professional soldiers into the counties of England to assist in making citizens into soldiers. With similar intent, the organizers of every colony sent one or two professional soldiers with the first group of settlers. Their main task was to instruct the male colonists in the use of arms and military formations and, in some cases, to lead their trainees. The overall English concept of a small group of professional soldiers and a large group of citizen-soldiers, with various levels of training, was applied by the Crown. The boatloads of colonists included professional military men, such as Virginia's Captain John Smith, Plymouth's Captain Miles Standish, John Endicott of Salem (Massachusetts Bay), and John Mason of New Haven. It was not by accident that such military men accompanied the first settlers. While the lure of adventure may have prompted these men to volunteer for a perilous and hazardous mission, it was by design that some professional soldiers were included in the passenger lists. [72]

The Pilgrims of Plymouth hired Captain Miles Standish in 1620 to organize a "train band" from among their number as a protection against Indian raids, organized under the blanket of the Mayflower Compact. The Puritans of Massachusetts Bay included a number of men with professional military experience along with the military supplies brought by the colonists. In addition to John Smith, several of Virginia's early governors were military men. During the "beach head" stage of the earliest colonizations, the hired captains had authority to enforce discipline and training by the most draconian means necessary.

However, they often found that much of their European experience meant little in the wilderness of America. [73]

In some cases, all of the military preparation prior to landing proved immediately beneficial. The Jamestown trading post organized itself into a virtual regimental garrison, complete with companies and squads. Within the first month of the initial landing the settlement was attacked by Indians. The attack was only repulsed with the help of cannon fire from the still anchored ships. By the end of the first month a fort was completed, mounting cannon at each of its triangular corners. In 1608, seventeen months after the initial landing, John Smith became the undisputed leader. A mercenary by trade and veteran of many campaigns on the European continent, Smith imposed military discipline and training in order to guarantee the settlement's survival and to provide the means for offensive action against the Indians. After further improving Jamestown's defense and organizing the settlers for work details and guard duty, Smith began a training regime designed to prepare the citizen-soldiers to compete in open battle against Powhattan's braves.

For the next few years the settlement was virtually collocated around the fort and its protective artillery. In 1612 Governor Dale, a former soldier, arrived when the colony was close to extinction from starvation. Dale imposed military discipline on every colonist based on the laws governing the army in the Low Countries. His policy was successful in impressing the Indians and allowing the colonists to farm and hunt peacefully. This, combined with Dale's restoration of the economy, permitted a gradual relaxation of universal military discipline. [74]

On November 11, 1620 one hundred Pilgrims landed and established Plymouth Colony. They had hired Captain Miles Standish, a veteran of the wars in the Low Countries (the Netherlands), to serve as military advisor. The warning of an Indian raid on February 16, 1621 prompted action. The following day the Pilgrims formally elected Standish as their Captain and military commander. They further gave him complete authority in military matters.

Standish moved quickly to impose order and discipline. He organized the Plymouth militia into four squadrons, or companies, and instituted a thorough plan for watches, guards and alarms. The colonists realized that their survival was at stake and gave Standish broad powers to instill discipline and levy punishments. When one recalcitrant colonist refused to stand watch and called his commander a "beggarly rascal," Standish clapped him in irons. Frequent musters and training sessions became common. Over time militia activities became an integral part of the colony's social structure.

The Massachusetts Bay Colony, with its later settlement date, profited from the experiences of the earlier settlements. In 1629 its first expedition left England for Salem with a militia company already organized and equipped with the latest weapons. John Endicott served as Massachusetts Bay's first militia leader. He established a trading post at Salem. The following year he helped complete the organization of Salem's first, arriving, militia company.[75]

According to tradition, among the Adventurers who disembarked at what was to become St. Mary's City, Maryland in March 1634 were two militia Captains. Although, as in other early colonies, all able-bodied Marylanders were obligated to help defend the province, the Captains called for volunteers to establish a professional armed force or "trained band." A night watch guard was set up immediately. The Maryland militia was born.

Who the militia Captains were and what their backgrounds and military experiences were are not clear. For that matter, how many "Adventurers" arrived with the <u>Ark</u> and the <u>Dove</u> and who they were is also unclear and unknown with any exactitude. Based upon available evidence, the new Marylanders to be arrived with military capability, including weapons. The disembarkation in the vicinity of what was to be St. Mary's City included an honor guard and full military panoply, to impress the Indians with their power if for no other reason. One of the first orders of business was the construction of a stockade/fort that mounted several small cannon for protection. While this was going on, someone organized and led patrols and night watches to ensure the settlers' safety. All of these activities indicate that the original group of settlers included several individuals with more than rudimentary levels of military expertise and experience and with enough leadership skills and/or visible support from the Province's political leadership to ensure compliance with their directives. It is just difficult to determine who they were. It is even more difficult, if not impossible, to determine if they were soldiers of fortune, ala John Smith or Miles Standish, or just leaders whose military experience was limited to militia activities in England.

In the opinion of Harry Wright Newman, in <u>The Flowering of The Maryland Palatinate</u>, a complete and accurate list of "Adventurers" (his term) in the <u>Ark</u> and the <u>Dove</u> remains, and will remain, unknown. The same is true for the exact number of those Adventurers. It was officially reported to the government that the Oath of Allegiance had been administered to about 128 people while the ships were in the Thames River at Tilbury, downstream from London. Some authors contend that as the oath was repugnant to Catholics, since it required the individual to, among other things, swear allegiance to the King as the Head of the Church, they boarded the ships elsewhere, after the oath had been administered, to avoid taking it. If true, since there were a number of identified Catholics, the Adventurers would have exceeded 128 people. Others, Newman among them, contend that at least some, if not all, of the Catholics must have taken the oath, hoping for subsequent absolution. As a minimum, the Calvert brothers, Leonard and George, and the Commissioners, Thomas Cornwallys and Jerome Hawley, Catholics all, must have been on board from the moment the ships sailed from London and, hence, must have taken the oath. The total number of Adventurers, then, could drop back closer to the 128 reported oath takers.

In a letter to the Earl of Stratford Cecilius, Lord Baltimore, stated that "[t]here are two of my brothers gone with very near twenty other gentlemen of very good fashion and three hundred laboring men." In 1634 Father Andrew White, one of the original Marylanders, wrote A Relation of the successful beginnings of Lord Baltimore's plantation in Maryland in which he recounts the voyage of the Ark and the Dove, the initial meetings with the Indians and the settlement at St. Mary's. In 1635, at the direction of Lord Baltimore, A Relation of Maryland was prepared and distributed to help generate interest in immigrating to Maryland and to outline what it entailed. It began with an abridgement of White's earlier Relation. They both include only the names of seventeen gentlemen and no other figure for the number of passengers is given. In the House of Lords shortly after the ships sailed Lord Baltimore put the number of passengers at about two hundred. A subsequent legal case, published in 1653, stated that Baltimore sent "about 200 people to begin and seat a Plantation." In 1757, in a message to the Lower House of the General Assembly,

Governor Sharpe, after reviewing then existing records and documents no longer available, stated that the "first settlement (St. Marie's Citie) had between two and three hundred other persons," in addition to the Calvert brothers.

The best approximation is between 150 and 200 people arrived in Maryland on the Ark and the Dove in early 1634. David Bell in Passenger List of the Ark and the Dove, a compilation of many other passenger lists which will be discussed below, lists 162 names of individuals identified by at least one source, if not more, as having been on the ships, including crew members. Again, exactitude is difficult to achieve in the absence of passenger manifests. It is further complicated by the death of some of the people enroute and the disembarkation of some passengers and embarkation of others at the ships' ports of call enroute in the Caribbean and in Virginia.

During the intervening centuries there have been numerous attempts to construct passenger lists for the Ark and the Dove. Starting with the gentlemen mentioned in White's Relation, the lists were developed by historians and genealogists using correspondence, government records, probate and estate documents and other sources. In 2003 David Bell published Passenger List of the Ark and the Dove mentioned above. It is a compilation of a number of passenger lists of several different authors/ researchers/ organizations including: Robert E. T. Pogue, Harry Wright Newman, Rhoda Fine, a listing of Gentlemen/Gentlewomen of the Voyage, John T. Marck, and The Ark and the Dove Society. The latter, in turn, was drawn from work by Gus Skordas and Carson Gibb. George Mackenzie and the Russells, George Ely and Donna Valley, also did research in the field which Bell did not include. Dr. Lois Carr did extensive research on early St. Mary's and Maryland residents, developing an extensive set of index cards with biographical data. Collectively this resulted in a listing of the passengers, or, at least, a partial one, that can be used to identify the early Maryland military officers and leaders.

Before exploring that further, however, two other issues have to be addressed. First, in a practice that continued through the early Revolutionary War era and beyond, but was especially prevalent during the colonial/pre-Revolutionary War period, men assumed the title of the military rank they acquired and used it as a form of address and as a part of their name, an honorific title. They continued to use it until another, higher rank was acquired or until their death. Further, in correspondence and publications discussing or dealing with past event(s), the individual's currently held/used military title was used, not the one he may have had during the time period being discussed. Second, in addition to the obvious social differences between the gentle folk and those of the laboring class among the passengers, there was a distinction between those who emigrated and those who were transported, between those who paid for their passage and those whose passage was paid for. While somewhat different than its predecessors in aims and tolerance, the voyage of the Ark and the Dove was at core a commercial venture. There were investors, some of whom were passengers and others who didn't make the voyage. One method of investment was to pay for the cost of transporting what were referred to as servants. The return on the investment would not only be the potential labor of the person being transported, but also, just as importantly, and maybe more so, a grant of land from the Proprietor for each individual whose passage was paid for. Land was the perceived greatest source of wealth at that time. The term servant had a different meaning during that period and in that context than it does in modern times. Many of the "servants" among the Ark and the Dove passengers were actually members of the gentry, gentlemen and gentle-women. Many were younger sons seeking their fortune who took advantage of someone's willingness to pay their way in return for some work, potentially, and giving up a claim for some land. Subsequently, many of them became successful and well to do, some wealthy planters, and participated fully in the governing of the Province.

Who then, among the first settlers, were the military leaders, the "militia Captains?" In Father Andrew White's <u>Relation of Maryland</u> the voyage of the ships is recounted, along with the initial meeting with the Indians and the creation of the settlement at St. Mary's. However, there is no mention of any militia Captains. The same is true in the subsequent <u>Relation</u>. Leonard Calvert, along with being appointed Governor by his brother Lord Baltimore, was also given several military titles, including Admiral and Lieutenant General. The latter appears to have been the most regularly used and was meant to indicate that he was the on the ground representative and executor for the Proprietor/General. Regiments of that time and later were developed along the same line, with the Colonel/Proprietor/Owner of the Regiment overseeing its organization, arranging its employment, and reaping the monetary rewards while his Lieutenant Colonel led the unit in the field. While the Lieutenant General could have been one of the "militia Captains," and may have personally directed military activities such as the organization of protective patrols and night watches, as well as the design, construction and arming of the first stockade, it is probable that he delegated these responsibilities to other men.

In identifying who the "militia Captains" were, there would appear to be two basic criteria: they had to be among the first settlers; and, they would, presumably, be identified with a military rank during that initial period. Future military activity, especially in leadership positions, might be another indicator, but not a conclusive one. There are several candidates who meet some of these criteria. Richard Gerard, Esquire, arrived on the Ark and the Dove, transporting five men whose land rights he assigned to the Jesuits, along with a manor granted him by Lord Baltimore. In 1634/1635 he was present at a skirmish in which four men were killed. He returned to England prior to the January 1637 Assembly. Subsequently, he had an extensive military career in Europe, primarily in support of the Stuarts. He achieved the rank of Lieutenant Colonel. However, beyond his presence at the above mentioned skirmish, there is no indication that he was a military leader in Maryland.

John Price was transported by the Wintour brothers, Edward and Frederick, Esquire, sons of Lady Wintour. He arrived with the original settlers. He may have left Maryland and returned by 1636, this time with servants (transportees) of his own. On February 18, 1638 he was elected to the General Assembly while living in St. Michael's Hundred. In 1647 he was Captain of the Fort at St. Ingo's. In January 1659, as Colonel John Price, he was appointed a member of the Upper House of the Assembly, the Governor's Council, by Lord Baltimore. However, he was also a participant in the opening session of the first General Assembly on January 25, 1637. He is listed as being present, but with no military rank. Some of the other participants were listed with military ranks. In December 1642 he was listed among a large group of men being assessed taxes, expressed in pounds of tobacco. Again, he was listed without military rank while the ranks of others were given. It appears that his military rank/title was acquired after 1634.

The Russells in <u>The Ark and The Dove Adventurers</u> listed Major Thomas Baldridge, but also indicated that there is no indication of how or when he, and his brother James, arrived. Both are included in the passenger lists of the Ark and the Dove Society, Harry Wright Newman and Gentlemen/Gentlewomen of the Voyage. Robert E. T. Pogue also lists James, but not Thomas. However, none of them list Thomas' rank of Major. James was a member of the first General Assembly in 1637 and Thomas appears attending the second Assembly session of that year. Thomas was appointed Sheriff and Coroner of St. Mary's Hundred on March 20, 1638 for a term of one year. This gave him the rank of Sergeant, which may not have been considered a purely military rank at that time. Subsequently, at least, the Sergeant of the Hundred was responsible for organizing the militia members for the Captain. In an order dated August 28, 1642, Thomas was referred to as a Lieutenant in charge of the southern part of St. Mary's Hundred. The order outlined procedures in case of Indian attacks and was the first mention of an officer's rank for Thomas. Lois Carr's biographical files indicate that Thomas was a Captain in 1649.He was also referred to as "Capt. And Commander of those Rebels" during Ingle's Rebellion. He moved to Virginia in 1651, probably right after Ingle's Rebellion.

The participants in the first General Assembly session in January 1637 included several men with military rank. Among them were Captain Robert Evelin and Captain Henry Fleete. Fleete was primarily a fur trader from Virginia who had set up shop on an island in the Potomac River. He was a fierce competitor of, and an opponent of, William Claiborne of Kent Island, who also worked the Susquehannah River region. While he became a prominent member of the St. Mary's community and supported the Calverts against Claiborne, there is no record of his involvement in military action. Evelin was the Commander of Kent Island, a prominent military and political position given the fighting between the forces, albeit small in size, of the Calverts and Claiborne. However, Evelin is not shown as having been among the original Adventurers by any source.

There were seven of the original settlers that the various compilations show with military rank and one other additional candidate. They were: Captain Thomas Cornwallys, Esquire, Commissioner, who emigrated; Major John Hallowes (Hollis, Hollows), Gentleman, who emigrated; Captain John Hill, Gentleman, who emigrated; Lieutenant William Lewis, Gentleman, who was transported; Captain Robert Vaughan, Esquire, who was transported; Captain Robert Wintour, Esquire, who emigrated; Captain Henry Fleete; and Jerome Hawley, Esquire, Commissioner. As discussed above, Fleete was primarily a transplanted Virginia Indian trader. Jerome Hawley was a prominent settler, one of the two Commissioners on the voyage, the other was Cornwallys, who became the initial members of the Governor's Council. However, there is no indication that he was involved in any military activities.

Nothing is known of Captain John Hill other than that his name included in White's <u>Relation of Maryland</u>. All indications are that Major John Hallowes military rank was acquired well after the initial landings. William Lewis was an early steward or Chamberlain to the Jesuits, among the initial settlers, and in charge of their redemptioners, i.e. those they transported, or whose transportation they paid for in return for service. However, he was not included in the listing of Father White's servants. He was among the listed participants in the January 25, 1637 General Assembly session. However, while he presented proxies for five other planters from St. Mary's, indicating some level of prominence, he was listed without military rank. Carr listed him as a Sergeant in the militia in 1638 and as having been the High Constable of St. George's Hundred in 1637/38, the same time period that Robert Vaughan is listed in the office. He was a Lieutenant in 1642 and a Captain in 1647, the same year that he was appointed Commander of Kent County. Wright maintains that although he was not styled as a Lieutenant until 1640, he obviously was one of the early militia officers of the Province.

Captain Robert Vaughan is not directly listed as being on the <u>Ark</u> or the <u>Dove</u>, but all evidence points to him having been there and he is included in every compilation except Pogue's. Although he was transported, indicating a somewhat lower social status, he witnessed the last will and testament of George Calvert on July 10, 1634 less than five months after the initial landings. Further, there is no record of another ship arriving in the intervening time. Although an Anglican, he was held in great confidence by Governor Leonard Calvert, possibly indicating long association and friendship before the beginning of the Maryland settlement. On January 5, 1637, three weeks prior to the opening General Assembly session, Cecilius Calvert appointed Vaughan, identified as "our trusty Robert Vaughan of St. George's hundred Sergeant of the trained band," High Constable of the St. George's Hundred, on the west bank of the St., George's River. This implies several things. In the intervening years the military organization within the Province had grown outside the immediate vicinity of St. Mary's City; and that Vaughan occupied a position of military authority prior to the appointment. In 1638 he assisted Governor Calvert in gaining control of Kent Island. As Sergeant Vaughan he led the force subduing Palmer Island,

Claiborne's trading post in the mouth of the Susquehannah River. In late June Vaughan provided the Council an inventory of the goods seized on Palmer Island, and possibly on Kent Island as well. In 1640 he was referred to as "Lieutenant Vaughan" in an order of the Council. In 1642 Lord Baltimore made him Commander of Kent. Also during that period he was addressed as "Lieutenant of our Ile and County of Kent." During the Assembly of January 1648 he was addressed as Captain. So, although his officer rank was acquired several years after the initial landings, Vaughan was an active military leader during that period. Wright maintains that Robert Vaughan was one of the two principal military officers of the Province during the early, formative years. The other was Thomas Cornwallys.

Thomas Cornwallys (Cornwallis) was one of two Commissioners accompanying the Calverts on the Ark and the Dove, the other being Jerome Hawley. Upon their arrival in America Cornwallys became one of the three members of Governor Calvert's Council, in effect the Upper House of the Assembly, who served as close advisors to the Governor. He was a major investor in the Calvert project and one who participated in his investment. In Maryland he was a significant entrepreneur. He emigrated (i.e. paid for his own passage) and transported (i.e. paid for the transportation of) servants, not only on the initial voyages, but for a number of years thereafter. Between 1634 and 1651 he transported at least 71 servants to Maryland. As just mentioned, he had transported a number of people on the first voyage, including taking over the responsibility for five or more from a fellow Adventurer who died. Many of his transportees subsequently became plantation owners and acquired the title of Gentleman. Between his arrival in 1634 and his final departure for

England in 1659 Cornwallys acquired extensive land holdings, much of it as a result of the large number of people he had transported and the land grants associated therewith. He held several political offices and, in the opinion of several authors including Harry Wright Newman and Lois Carr, was Maryland's chief military officer.

In every contemporary reference, no matter how early, Cornwallys is referred to by his military title of Captain, implying that he probably acquired it before he set sail from England. On the first day of the opening session of the General Assembly on January 25, 1637, Cornwallys is among those listed with his military rank. The others were Leonard Calvert as Lieutenant General, Captains Wintour, Fleete and Evelin, and Sergeants Vaughan and Baldridge. As pointed out above, Wintour was a ship commander, Fleete a fur trader, and Evelin not among the first group of Adventurers. Vaughan and Baldridge, especially the latter, appear to have that rank, at least in part, as a result of being constable of a hundred.

On February 12, 1637 the Governor and Council ordered a military expedition, to be led by Governor Calvert, to subdue Kent Island. Cornwallys was a member of the Council. The order directed, among other things, that "for his [Calvert's] better assistance … it was thought fit and so ordered that Captain Thomas Cornwallys, Esq. … should go along with the Governor, and be aiding and assisting him to the uttermost of his power for command of the forces according to such directions as he shall receive from the Governor, during his expedition." The order was signed by Calvert, Jerome Hawley and John Lewger, the other two members of the Council, but not by Cornwallys. On May 27, 1638 Governor Calvert appointed "my good friend" Thomas Cornwallys to act as Lieutenant

General of the Province in his, Calvert's absence. This was the highest military appointment in the Province, giving him command of all military forces (essentially the militia), and making him, in effect, Deputy (acting) Governor. Calvert made the appointment again on May 8, 1641, when he was going to be out of the Province in Virginia.

On January 23, 1642 Cecilius Calvert appointed and authorized Cornwallys to "have and use all necessary and sufficient power for the levying and mustering of soldiers within the Province and for making with them an expedition upon the declared enemies of the Province ..." He did so "relying upon your [Cornwallys'] prudence and experience in martiall affaires." On August 18, 1642 Cornwallys was given a commission to "leavie men and Command them ..." preparatory to leading a subsequent military expedition. Finally, on April 17, 1643, Calvert used the same words, describing Cornwallis' "known prudence and experience in military affaires" in appointing him "Captaine General" of a military expedition against the Susquehannocks. He was selected, among other reasons, because of his ability to recruit men, make them at least partial soldiers and get them to follow him. He was deemed a good commander.

So, then, who were the two initial militia commanders? Cornwallys and Vaughan seem likely candidates. There could have been other individuals with previous combat military experience in one or more of the ongoing European or Middle Eastern conflicts who filled the role of military expert(s) for the newly landed Marylanders, ala John Smith or Miles Standish. However, if there were, their identities are not readily apparent. Cornwallys' and Vaughan's subsequent involvement in the highest levels of the Province's government, Cornwallys' involvement with the Calvert expedition early on at the highest level and his significant monetary investment, and the subsequent financial success both had in Maryland seem to militate against their being involved at that basic level militarily. However, the size of the force involved wasn't great, fewer than 200 men. Self protection, if no other reason, would dictate that everyone be involved. John Smith, twenty years earlier, had been secretly selected as one of the Council members and leaders of the Virginia colony before the expedition set sail, to the shock of his fellow colonists. Subsequently he came to be in charge of the entire operation. So, Cornwallys' and Vaughan's later activities do not militate against their having been the early military leaders. However, this is merely supposition and not provable with any certitude. What is known is that these new Marylanders were conscious of the potential dangers, organized and prepared themselves to meet them, and someone, probably Thomas Cornwallys and Robert Vaughan, led them. [76]

The British government and early colonial promoters/organizers were aware, at least to some extent, of the potential dangers of establishing settlements in the American wilderness, populated, even if somewhat sparsely, with potentially hostile Indians. At least one group of organizers, the Calvert's of Maryland, had direct first-hand experience with wilderness America before sending out their first party of settlers. They all attempted to protect the settlers, or, rather, directed and enabled the settlers to protect themselves. They provided instructions for mounting defenses, for constructing protective fortifications and for organizing and maintaining defensive forces. They sent military supplies to arm the forces and experienced professional military men to train the colonists in the arts of war.

The thing they did not send were any regular soldiers to defend the settlements. They didn't send them for a very simple reason, there were none to send. There were a few professional regulars on duty in the country. However, they were the King's guards or the garrisons of some of the coastal fortifications and fortified towns. There were none available for overseas deployment to Europe, much less to the New World.

The first settlers were influenced by what they knew and where they came from before they landed in America. Over time they acquired new information, learned about new trends in Europe and new methods of doing things. But they were still people of their time and experience. English military developments moved slowly. There were no large regular English military units until the latter part of the seventeenth century; fifty to sixty years after the first settlements were started. Further, the initial number of troops under arms was relatively small. Many leaders may not have been all that aware that they existed. Even if they were aware of the developments and wanted a comparable organization for their community, they ran into a major impediment, how to pay for it.

The leaders of the colonies used what they knew and developed it to their needs. They took a military system that was waning in influence and importance at home, adjusted it as required, and successfully employed it to keep themselves safe from external threats for over 150 years.

Development of Militias

In the beginning, the unknowns of a new and strange land nurtured the colonists' fear of enemies and attack. The tragic fate of the Roanoke Colony in 1587 and the more recent Indian massacre of the Jamestown settlement in 1622 remained fresh in memory. In New England settlers were acutely aware of their vulnerable situation. On every side the topographic features of wilderness and coastline far from England combined with recurring alarms and Indian fights to instill a defensive psychology. Their situation reinforced the defensive mentality that seventeenth century Puritans brought with them to the New World, thereby generating a social and cultural environment in which the institution of a militia would grow and flourish. Universal armed defense thus became an unquestioned policy. [77]

The military organizations the colonists created reflected the military tradition of the English colonists. They predominated over the French, German, Dutch, Irish, Scots and Scotch-Irish settlers. It was also an outgrowth of the way in which the colonies were established. The colonies, and the settlements within them, were founded and developed over a span of more than a century, in a piecemeal fashion. As settlement further encroached in Indian lands, they struck at the closest targets. The initial response to the Indian threat was at the local level. The first military organization to appear was local in makeup. But almost immediately, it became part of a larger organization, the colonial militia.

The early colonists' understanding of war derived from fundamental and ancient sources. It was influenced greatly by the seemingly endless ferocity of sixteenth century Old World religious and secular strife. In the New World their ideas about war and the military were altered and adapted to the exigencies of survival, circumstance, time and space, and their opponents. The transformation occurred so naturally and so smoothly that the colonists scarcely perceived that they were modifying their Old Country ways. The development of what became the American way of war was a continually evolving process. Old World models were trans-figured and shaped to fit practical colonial needs; needs dictated in large part by New World experiences. European advances in the art of war were eagerly studied, but not dog-matically followed in America, for that would have been impractical. So, each colony developed something of its own character, the basic military establishment. The militias mir-rored the colonies' evolving needs, hopes, fears and growing complexities. With time, the children and grandchildren of the early settlers became less like their European cousins. No longer Englishmen, neither were they part of an overarching American culture. Rather, they became provincial or colonial hybrids, with differing institutions, traditions, concepts, iden-tities and ways of war.

The colonists utilized the militia format in their military organization because it was the form they knew the most about and because they retained a fear of a standing army. Even if they had been receptive to the idea of professional army, they lacked the resources to support one. Moreover, for the kind of warfare they had to wage, a professional army was not practical. Campaigns by and against Indians were generally of short duration, and a professional force would have been a needless expense. [78]

Most of the early settlers came to America aware that war in some form might play a role in their everyday lives. An early visitor to Plymouth, a settlement relatively untroubled by hostile natives, saw men march to Sunday meeting carry-ing muskets that they kept beside them through the service. The musket to the early seventeenth century American was as central to his daily life as the hoe.

In a letter to England Edward Winslow recorded Plymouth's first Thanksgiving Day. In addition to describing the feast and the Indian invitees, he also emphasized that "amongst other recreations we exercised our arms, many of the Indians coming among us." This exemplified a legitimate physical recreation even as it offered a brave exhibition of the colonists' armed strength and martial spirit. Captain Standish commanded the small band of Puritan militia, calling out orders forming the martial figures, directing the handling of the guns and their firing. Clad in but a few pieces of armor, the small band marched in files while bearing pikes and cumbersome matchlocks. The Indian guests witnessed a strange spectacle of English militiamen massed in an open field marching and wheeling on command; or, even stranger, experienced at close range the smoke and noise of discharging firearms. For the Pilgrims, however, the martial show upheld tradition since it invoked a heritage of training days in their old English home. There the sight of family and neighbors drilling had long been emblematic of the strength of will of every Englishman to defend his land from the invasion. The exercise of arms by Plymouth's handful of citizen-soldiers signaled a determination to be at the ready and to use force, broadcasting the will to fight to establish and hold their New England in the wilderness. [79]

The colonies were much too poor to permit a class of able-bodied men to devote themselves solely to war and preparation for war. Every colonist had to contribute all of his energy to the economic survival of his colony and no colony could afford to maintain professional soldiers. Yet, through most of the seventeenth century every part of the colonies remained subject to military danger, potentially from Spain, France, and the Dutch and Swedish settlements, and actually from the Indians. The potential dangers were very real. Spanish settlers, working from Florida, had established enclaves at least as far north as the coast of present day South Carolina. Spanish Catholic missionaries were massacred by Indians on the York River in Virginia, between the site of Jamestown on the James River and present day Yorktown. The Dutch in the Hudson River Valley, and the Dutch and Swedes in the Delaware River Valley, expressed initial willingness to defend their claims and expand them with force of arms. The French threatened from the north and, eventually, from the west, primarily through their surrogates, the Indians. The actual danger, early on, however, was from the indigenous Indians. Therefore, every colony needed military protection, and every colony, save the pacifist Quaker settlements, sought to obtain it by invoking the historic principle of a universal obligation to military service to create a military force of armed civilians. [80]

The early colonists lived in small, widely scattered homesteads, or small settlements. The leading European powers were generally unwilling, or, in England's case, unable, to send anything more than token regular forces to protect their distant colonies in America. By and large, the colonies had to provide their own defense. They relied on their militias raised from the able-bodied men of military age, although these were civilians in arms and not trained soldiers. Most would fight to protect their own farms or those of their neighbors. However, they were unwilling to travel far or to campaign against the Indians for long, especially when they had to return home to bring in the harvest. They were almost identical in attitude to their predecessors in the Anglo-Saxon fyrd and the English militia, just with a different enemy and in a different country. Colonial governments were also often reluctant to go to the aid of another neighboring country, i.e. colony. [81]

The need to defend the relatively poor and sparsely settled colonies against both Indian tribes and European powers led to different military arrangements in America than had been used in England, such as raising temporary armies of paid soldiers (mercenaries) for overseas expeditions and small trained bands of militia for local defense drawn from the theoretical general militia of all able-bodied men. Defense played a major role in colonial life. Although the Royal Navy, supported by a few fortifications equipped with cannon, defended the coastline, the colonies themselves bore the burden of their own defense. No colony could afford to maintain enough troops to meet all of the contingencies, so all relied on the concept of a citizen-soldier to defend the community. Within two years of its founding in 1607 Jamestown had organized itself into a virtual regimental garrison, complete with companies and squads. Plymouth, on the advice of Mile Standish, formed four companies (squadrons) of militia. The Massachusetts Bay Colony, profiting from the experiences of the earlier settlements, established a militia company in Salem, their initial settlement, in 1629. By 1636 three permanent regiments had been formed throughout the colony. [82]

In circumstances similar to Virginia, the later colonies established similar systems of universal military obligation. Plymouth did so early, and a Massachusetts Bay law of 1631 decreed that all males between sixteen and sixty must provide themselves with weapons and form units for training. In Maryland and New York the governors, working under instructions from their proprietors, had militia organizations well established before the legislatures got around to passing military laws. However, generally, the obligation to military service came to rest on legislative enactment.

Pennsylvania, the Quaker colony, was an exception to the rule of compulsory obligation. William Penn made it his practice (with one exception) to appoint a non-Quaker as his Lieutenant Governor so that in case of war someone could take command of the province untroubled by scruples concerning the use of force. The conversion of Penn's family after his death assured the continuance of this policy. However, Quakers long remained in control of the assembly, manipulating the distribution of seats to maintain their ascendancy long after their share of the population ceased to warrant it. As long as they did so, they obstructed measures of self defense. [83]

If the rules of warfare were different in America, particularly away from the cleared ground of the Eastern seaboard, so too was the composition of military forces. Whereas in Europe the military obligation eventually fell on a small, professional class of soldiers, in America it fell on nearly all; or warfare at some time or another took place everywhere. No person was immune from the military obligation in times of crisis. Even in the older settlements, where fear of armed invasion receded with the passing years, weapons continued to be prerequisite for obtaining food and protecting property. [84]

English settlers brought from their homeland two social attitudes that had a profound influence on America's continued development. Steeped in ancient tradition and codified into English law, the militia tradition called for the compulsory service of all free males between the ages of sixteen and sixty. In the early North American settlements colonial leaders readily adopted the philosophy and the specifics of militia service first learned in England. Additionally, the colonists brought to the New World a deep and abiding fear of standing armies as repressive agents of ambitious monarchs.

In the seventeenth and eighteenth centuries the American militia performed a number of vital military functions. First and foremost, citizen-soldiers organized and armed themselves during prolonged struggles with the Indians. In the absence of military assistance from Great Britain, the militia system alone guaranteed the success of early the English colonies. As the Indian threat receded, militiamen found themselves more and more engaged against other colonial powers. Battles against the Spanish and the French, as well as service alongside British regulars, often revealed the militia's best and worst aspects. By the late 1700's, the militia was bulwark against unwelcome British intrusion into colonial affairs. [85]

One of the most fundamental notions incorporated by the colonists from English traditions was the belief that an individual who benefited from membership in a society had an obligation to use his talents and resources for the good of the society at large. In the military realm this meant that every free, able-bodied male was required to own weapons and, when necessary, offer his services under local leaders to defend the community. Thus, everyone participated in the defense of a society in proportion to the benefits received from it. [86]

In early America nearly all of the males between the ages of sixteen and sixty, whether freemen or servants, were required to be listed (enlisted) into their local militia company and to attend company musters and regimental training days. Such occasions in Colonial America during the seventeenth and eighteenth centuries were considered serious events.

There were some exemptions from enlistment in the militia: for magistrates, public notaries, deputies to a legislature, ministers of the church, schools masters, students, physicians, masters of ships, fishermen, herdsmen and invalids.

There were few Jewish families in the early colonies and prejudice against non-Christians was such that they were not welcome in the militia. The enlistment of African Americans, either slave or free, was generally forbidden by law. However, despite these exemptions and restrictions, formal or informal, in times of severe emergency, every white male was expected to serve. [87]

Regular armies are standing armies. Since before Cromwell, Englishmen had preserved a fear of standing armies as instruments of oppression. Even the Puritan founders of Massachusetts Bay, Cromwell's co-religionists, had subscribed to that theory. When they set up their citizen militia, the military structure was created primarily as a response to the threat from England. [88] Throughout most of the seventeenth century the Crown refused to give substantial military aid to any colony. That would have cost money, which it refused to spend. The London Company assumed most of the burden in Virginia, as did the Dutch West Indies Company in New Netherlands (New York). However, in both instances the expense proved prohibitive. A better solution to a unique problem had to be found quickly if the colonies were to survive. The settlers found it, or thought they had, in their experience at home, the militia. [89]

The colonists' military system, following English precedents, rested primarily on the concept of universal service for able-bodied males of military ages who received military training. Those men kept their own weapons. In New England they at first elected, and later nominated, their own officers in each town. In the Chesapeake, the local officers were appointed by the governor, usually from members of the local court. But in all of the colonies local men officered and led the militia. The notion that a citizen-militia provided the cornerstone of a free government and a protection against tyranny and absolutism was as strong in America as in England. Standing professional armies, besides being expensive, were perceived as threatening civil liberties. In addition to foot soldiers, troops of cavalry and batteries of artillery also appeared in most colonies with the growth of a colonial upper class that often preferred service in these semi-exclusive units to ordinary militia duty. Colonies also built up public supplies of arms and powder. In times of emergency or war, governments could impress (press) militiamen into armies serving under martial law. However, in many colonies the charters or enabling legislation for the militia specified that it could not be made to serve beyond the colonies' borders. [90]

The institution of the militia was built into the fabric of the earliest colonies. The necessity not only to protect the colonists' settlements, but also, where expedient, to expand their holdings, meant that every able-bodied man from the ages of sixteen to sixty was required to show up, armed, for regular training. If necessary, they were also required to make themselves available for longer periods of service.

In the beginning it had been a decidedly convenient arrangement for Britain to set up what were essentially trading satellites. They were charged with the responsibility of defending themselves with little financial drag on the mother country. It was only after the conclusion of the SY/FI War in 1763, and the subsequent inability of the colonist's to protect themselves against European powers as well as the perceived need to separate the colonists and the Indians, that the cost/profit ratio of Britain's empire shifted in an uncomfortable direction, significantly increasing Britain's national debt. [91]

Laws regulating the militia were among the earliest enacted by colonial assemblies. Typical of the importance attached to a proper organization was the statement of the Massachusetts General Court: "The well ordering of the militia is a matter of great concernment to the safety and welfare of this Commonwealth." Although the laws varied in detail, they agreed in principle-all able-bodied males between certain ages owed military service to a colony and had to enroll in their local militia. Every colony enacted such a compulsory training law except Quaker influenced Pennsylvania, which permitted a volunteer militia. The laws usually stipulated that males between sixteen and sixty were liable for service. Certain occupational deferments were allowed: sheriffs, justices, ministers, teachers and other public servants, as mentioned above. Most colonies excluded blacks, others only slaves. However in times of crisis, such as an Indian raid, they were likely to be impressed into service. [92]

With the exception of Massachusetts Bay, which designated an elected sergeant major-general, colonial legislatures entrusted command of the militias to the governors, while still retaining surveillance and ultimate control. They voted the necessary funds, oversaw their expenditure, and investigated the conduct of operations. Thus the assemblies, their educated members mindful of classical examples of Caesar and the Praetorian Guards, and with the spectacle of Cromwell's military dictatorship before them, established in American the principle of civilian control of the military and guarded it. [93]

Representative government was introduced in Virginia through the Assembly of 1619. Civil law continued the executive decisions of previous governors of a general military obligation. After the colony had barely managed to put down the Indian uprising in 1622, the Assembly, on March 25, 1623, imposed a statutory requirement that all inhabitants of the colony "go under arms." In accordance with instructions from the Crown, which had newly assumed direct control of the colony from the Virginia Company, in 1626 Governor Yeardley defined the military obligations as extending to all males between seventeen and sixty. In 1627 one Richard Bickley was punished on a rack and with a fine for failing to take up arms when so ordered. In 1639 the Assembly reinforced the Governor's instructions by providing that every male of legal age, except Negro slaves, should be compelled to finish his military service whenever the occasion for it arose. [94]

In July 1623 the Plymouth Colony directed "that all and every person within the colony be subject to such military order for training and exercise of arms as shall be thought meet, agreed on and prescribed by the Gov'r and Assistants." On April 12, 1631, the Court of Assistants in Boston issued an order for the Massachusetts Bay Colony, setting forth that "a watch of 4" be kept nightly at Dorchester and Waterton and that "eftey [every] man that finds a musket shall, before the 18th day of this month, (and soe always after) have 1 3/6lbs of powder, 20 bullets and 2 fothsome [fathoms] of match, under penalty of 10s for eftey fault." The same order then provided "that eftey captaine should traine his company on Saturday everie week."

In 1645 the General Court of Massachusetts dictated that the governor "with the advice and consent of the Council," could raise and transport "such part of the militia ... as they find needful, or oblige them to march into any ... of the provinces or colonies ... without their free and voluntary consent." On May 14th of the same year it decreed that "all youth within this jurisdiction from ten years ould to ye age of sixteen years, shall be instructed ... upon the usual training days, in ye exercises of armes, as small guns, half pikes, bowes and arrows ... pvided yet no child shall be taken to ye exercise against yir parents minds." On August 16th the Court ordered "chief commanders in ye hundred, who shall be ready, at half an hour's warning upon any service they shall be put upon by their military officers." [95]

On September 1, 1636, the General Court of Watertown, Connecticut decreed that the able-bodied men in "every plantation shall traine once in every month" under the supervision of "their military officer," and imposed fines on those absent without cause or who neglected to provide themselves with arms. In the following year the General Court decreed the "all persons that are above the age of sixteen years except magistrates and church officers, shall bear arms, unless they have, upon just occasion, exemption granted by the courts; and every male person within this jurisdiction, shall have in continual readiness, a good musket or other gunn, fit for service, and allowed by the clerk of the band, with a sword, rest and bandoleers, or other serviceable provision in the roots thereof ... " [96] The original military law for the Carolinas, drafted by John Locke in 1669, read "[a]ll inhabitants and freemen of Carolina, above 17 years of age and under 60, shall be bound to bear arms and serve as soldiers whenever the grand council shall find it necessary." [97]

In Pennsylvania, with Quakers in charge of the Assembly, assemblymen would not authorize a provincial militia, and pacifism was only one of the reasons. They were willing enough to support volunteer soldiers who were not principled against military service. However, they feared the power that a militia would put in the hands of the Governor appointed by the Proprietor (William Penn and his descendants): perhaps a power to impress men into service against their will; certainly a new engine of patronage that the selective appointment of officers would provide; possibly use of the militia to win elections by forceful means. [98]

It wasn't until the middle of the eighteenth century that such attitudes in the Pennsylvania Assembly began to change; and then only through a significant shift in public opinion. In July, 1741, during King George's War, French and Spanish privateers sailed up Delaware Bay, plundering and raiding. Benjamin Franklin published a pamphlet calling on the sixty thousand non-Quaker residents of Pennsylvania of military age to organize their own defense. He followed up by organizing a mass meeting which, in turn, resulted in a volunteer association that soon grew to ten thousand men. They furnished themselves with arms, formed companies and regiments, and met to drill. Franklin also organized a lottery to finance a fort and artillery. Later, when Indians were raiding the frontier during the SY/FI War, the Quakers were finally pressed into yielding control of the Assembly, which they had controlled through gerrymandering long after they had become a shrinking minority within the colony. The Assembly then created a military force, though still without compulsory service. Pennsylvania was finally beginning to establish a local military force comparable to that of its sister colonies along the Eastern seaboard. [99]

Maryland had also created a military force, but over one hundred years earlier. The Proprietor, Lord Baltimore, had made the Governor, his brother, his "Lieutenant General, Admiral, Chief Captain, and Commander as well by sea as by land." He gave the Governor power to appoint and instruct all military officers under him and instructed him to cause all men able to bear arms to be trained weekly or, at least, monthly.

But unless the Proprietor himself supported a standing force within the province, which he was financially unable to do, it would take an effective act from the Assembly to provide for a strongly organized, well equipped and well disciplined militia.

Within a few years of the establishment of Maryland's first settlements, relations between the Indians and the colonists began to deteriorate. In 1637 a militia bill was one of the first legislative acts sent over by the Proprietor. In the next session of the Assembly this detailed bill outlining required military actions failed to become law. In its stead, in 1638, the Council passed an "Act for Military Discipline" establishing a militia. It also provided that "the captain of the military band," at the direction of the lieutenant general/governor, should "use all power necessary, or conducing, in his discretion to the safety or defence of the province. And the Commander of Kent to do the like in that Island."

The Act required that "every person within his, her or their house able to bear" arms had to arm "one Serviceable fixed gunne of bastard musket boare, one pair of bladeers or shott bag, one pound of good powder, foure pounds of pistol or musket shott and sufficient quantity of match for locks and of flints for firelocks and before Christmas next shall also fund a sword and Belt for every such person." No inhabitant was to give an Indian a gun, shot or powder. When an alarm was sounded, each inhabitant was to answer fully armed. The militia was first organized in St. Mary's County, and then expanded beyond that original county. The households of St. George's Hundred proposed the organization of the militia under the Act of 1638. They chose George Pye, Burgess, as their commander early in 1639. He was charged with the enumeration of all freemen who might bear arms in defense of the colony.

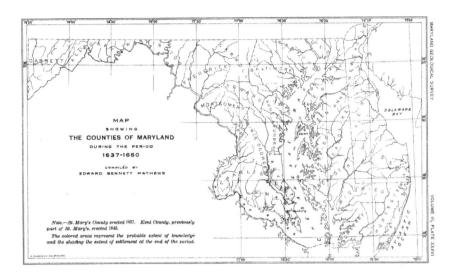

A commission was issued to Giles Brent, Esq., a member of the Council, bearing the date May 29, 1639, "appointing him to be captain of the military band next under our lieutenant general, requiring him to train and instruct all the inhabitants of our said colony able to bear armes (those of our Council excepted), in the art and discipline of war on holidays or any other time there should be need, and by himself or his sergeant or other officer, once a month if he should find it needful, to view [in] every dwelling house within the said colony the provision of necessary arms and ammunition and where found any defect to amerse the party failing at his discretion, so that it exceed not 30 pounds tobacco for one default, and further to punish any delinquent in any kind offending against the discipline military." At the discretion of the lieutenant general/governor, he and subsequent Captains were authorized to use and command all of the power which they deemed necessary for the defense of the province. [100]

The inspection that Brent was to conduct periodically was based on an act of the Assembly in March 1639, engrossed for a third reading, but laid over, which dictated required armaments. It required every householder to have at all times in his or her house, for every person "able to beare armes, One Serviceable fixed gunn of … musket boare one pair of bandoleers or shot bag one pound of powder foure pound of pistol or musket shott and Sufficient quantity of match locks and of flints five locks." [101] In 1641 Governor Calvert, by proclamation, directed that "noe man able to bear arms shall go to church or chapel or any considerable distance from home without a fixed gunn and 1 charge at least of powder and shott." [102]

The local government developed in Maryland was based on a basic geographic subdivi- sion, the county. The number increased from three in 1650 to fifteen in 1773. In 1650 Anne Arundel County was established embracing "all that part of the province, on the west side of the Chesapeake Bay, over against the Isle of Kent, called Providence by the people thereof." Land grants show that the people of Providence extended from Herring Creek on the south to the Patapsco River on the north, with the Severn River as a central meeting place. Charles County was also created in 1650 out of territory on the north side of the Patuxent River. It was a county grant, i.e. virtually giving it to Robert Brooke, a close friend of Lord Baltimore's. When Brooke later became a leader in the independence movement of Virginia settlers, he was deprived of his command by the simple expedient of changing the name of the county to Calvert. Disputes over the exact boundaries in relation to Anne Arundel continued into the nineteenth century.

With a steady influx of people into the current Charles County area, the Lord Proprietor and Governor were soon receiving complaints that the distance to St. Mary's Court

House was too great for the efficient transaction of business. On April 13, 1658 the Governor's Council ordered the creation of a new county to take care of the more distant settlements. On May 10, 1658 Governor Fendall issued a proclamation reviving the name Charles in honor of the Proprietor's son and heir. The wording of the proclamation actually gave the new county an elastic northern boundary, "as far as the settlements extended." It was not until the establishment of Prince George's County in 1695 that the county lines were clearly defined.

The establishing proclamation for Charles County appeared to intend to include all of the land west of the Patuxent River. It is likely, however, as the area which later became Prince George's was settled, that the official business of settlers living in the watershed of the Patuxent was transacted in Calvert because of the convenience of water transportation. Early Charles County actually was focused on the watershed of the Potomac River.

In 1695 Prince George's County was formed, again, out of Charles' northern territory, extending as far south as Mattawoman Creek, although not all the way to its mouth on the Potomac. Rather, the boundary cut north to a point almost directly across from the current site on Mt. Vernon in Virginia. Extending from the Patuxent to the Potomac, Prince George's had received its definitive western limit in 1748 by the creation of Frederick County. Their boundary was a straight line running from the lower side of the mouth of Rock Creek north (through the current District of Columbia) to the Patuxent River, west of present day Laurel. Frederick, then bordered on Prince George's, Anne Arundel and Baltimore Counties. Its lower portion became Montgomery County in 1776.

Baltimore was formed partially out of the northern portion of Anne Arundel in 1659. The head of the Patapsco River was its western limit, as well as that of Anne Arundel. The establishment of Frederick in 1748 moved the boundary eastward. Its northern limit was Pennsylvania. Western Maryland, from 1658 to 1776, was successively included in the geographical limits of Charles, Prince George's and Frederick Counties. In 1776 the Provincial Convention divided Frederick into its upper (Washington), middle (Frederick) and lower (Montgomery) districts.

Counties were divided into hundreds as the population increased, subdividing again if necessary. The concept of the hundred came from feudal England, where it was used as a geographic subdivision based on one hundred hides. A hide was a unit of land measure varying in size from 1 or 5 to 20 or 30 acres depending on location. The hundred was a unit of representation in the general Assembly. It was also the principle organ for military service, taxation, the administration of justice, and police regulation. Each hundred had its military unit which was trained by the sergeant. Arms and ammunition were allocated and inventoried by the hundred. For service in garrison or in any expedition against the Indians or obstreperous neighbors, each hundred was required to contribute its quota of men and to submit taxation for their maintenance. [103]

As this structure for a military force was being developed, the people of Maryland, represented in the Assembly, wanted to ensure that military power was kept within their control. In 1649 the Assembly passed an act providing for a meeting of the freemen of each hundred at some place within their hundred on the last three days of the month from April to September. At those meetings such ordinances were passed as those present deemed necessary for the defense of their hundred during the following month. The commander of the hundred was tasked to see that the ordinances were put in place. [104]

On October 20, 1654 Maryland revised its militia act. The legislature mandated the annual inspection of arms of each family since the law required that each man between the ages of sixteen and sixty own a firearm suitable for militia use. Each head of household was made responsible for arming himself, his sons and servants of military age. Military exercises, while mandated by law, were left to the discretion of the officers. One June 3, 1658, The Council of Maryland again ordered the County Lieutenants to draw up, and continue to maintain, a list of men eligible for militia service. The parameters remained ages sixteen to sixty, and included indentured white males. Officers were responsible for forwarding the full list of eligibles to the Colonial Secretary. No mention was made of blacks, slaves or free, or of Indians.

In 1661 the General Assembly, now under Puritan control, passed another militia act. However, unlike previous legislative acts, this one was detailed, updating the bills passed in the past three decades. Its preamble stated that for want of necessary law, training had been neglected, even in times of danger. It authorized a colonel, lieutenant colonel, major and captain to enlist such persons between sixteen and sixty as they saw fit, provided that a uniform proportion was kept between those enlisted and the entire population of any district. The officers were to train the troops fourteen times a year and more frequently if ordered by the Governor and Council. Everyone was required to bring their own weapon, powder and shot to training. Compliance was secured by the imposition of fines and imprisonment in some cases. [105]

In 1671 the Assembly ordered that the militia, as a *posse comitatis*, "to doe your utmost for the preventing and suppressing all and all manner of Riots and seditions and Rebellions, Rioters, seditious and Rebellious assemblies and meetings within our said Province." The Assembly thought that, in times of unrest, the militia alone could be trusted to "secure the publick peace." In 1675 it authorized the creation of mounted militia. "None should appear at the appointed place of rendez-vous there to be mustered, but such as are armed as followeth, viz. each Horseman a good, Sufficientable Sword, one well-fixed Gun or Carbine, and one good well-fixed pistol." Militia of foot were to be provided with "a Sword and musquet or other Gun to be well-fixed and fitted up."

In 1678 the Proprietor requested the Assembly to provide an act of recognition of his powers, so that soldiers might be better regulated. The Lower House (Delegates) demanded a copy of the charter and insisted that the Upper House (Council) sign it as a true copy. They refused. The Lower House, finding that an act for militia was all that was desired, subsequently consented to it. The bill being discussed, and ultimately passed, had very little change from the previous act of 1676. It empowered the Governor to enlist as many men, ages sixteen to sixty, as he thought appropriate. The Governor, with the consent of the Council, was given the authority to appoint the superior, or senior, militia officers. He would call out such portion of the militia as he thought necessary to quell insurrections, defend against invaders and repel Indian attacks. Each man was to appear with a good gun and "six shoots of powder." The fine for failure to appear at muster was 100 pounds of tobacco, with the proceeds to be used to purchase trumpets, drums and flags. Men fined for failing to provide arms could have their penalties voided if they purchased a gun within 18 months. The act continued the policy of providing public support for the families of men killed or injured while serving with the militia.

A horse troop was authorized for each county. Priests, delegates, magistrates and constables were exempted from serving. Booty was to be equally divided among the soldiers. Provisions were made against extraction by press masters, and the expenses of any war were to be levied by equal assessments upon those eligible to be taxed by the Assembly. To limit the expense of too frequent meetings of the Assembly, the Governor and Council were empowered to make levies on the people for payment of small charges, the total amount not to exceed fifty thousand pounds of tobacco yearly. The law remained initially unchanged through the resumption of control by the royal government.

Assemblies in Maryland, generally speaking, exercised considerable jurisdiction over military strategy and policy, allocating monies to raise only the number of soldiers that they had approved for the purposes they had agreed to. Assemblies did not hesitate to refuse requests from the Crown, the Proprietor, or the Governor. In the late seventeenth and early eighteenth centuries the Governor and Council repeatedly requested that changes be made to provide the province with a more serviceable militia. They recommended that the militia officers be given greater power, that a master adjutant be appointed to train the militia sixteen times a year, that every six taxable citizens be required to furnish one well equipped infantryman, and that every nine provide one well equipped trooper.

The Lower House essentially ignored their requests, letting them languish in committee. While minor, inconsequential changes were made, no meaningful changes were approved. Attempts got caught in the ongoing disputes and contests for control between the Lower House and the Governor and Council. In 1701-1702 the Lower House declined to obey a royal order to send money and men to the defense of New York. Even during the SY/FI War of the 1750's and 1760's Governor Sharpe ran into continuous resistance when he attempted to organize, or, more importantly, pay for troops to defend Maryland and defeat the enemy. The Lower House ignored his requests, authorized troops but failed to provide adequate funding, or placed restrictions on the deployment of the troops and/or the utilization of the funds or the taxation needed to generate the funds, severely limiting Maryland's participation in its own defense both within and without the colony's boundaries. [106]

On May 27, 1697, the Assembly, feeling that the existing militia laws placed too heavy a burden on the people, resolved that "the militia of this Province be modeled anew, it being deemed impossible that the present act in force about the same should be complied with by means of the poverty of the people." The new act required full armament and muster only of "every fourth or fifth taxable [male]." The remainder of the "taxables" would constitute an untrained reserve, to be used only in the case of an emergency. Those who were to serve would be chosen by their neighbors whom the law "obliged to find a Trooper, Dragoon or Footman, according as it shall be agreed upon with necessary arms." [107]

In 1733 the legislature moved to repair some perceived deficiencies in the basic militia law, noting that "several sums of Money laid out in the Purchases of Arms and Ammunition for those Purposes have not had the desired effects in a proper Regulation of the Militia of the Province by Reason of some Defects in the Laws already made." Pilferage of arms seems to have become a major problem, with many commanders being unable to account for arms issued to them. The updated law reaffirmed the power of the Governor to call out and command the militia, to enter into contracts for the purchase of arms, and to distribute them among the various county militias through the officers, and to make the officers responsible for the security of the arms. Militia units could be held liable to replace missing firearms, if necessary by assessing the whole company. Each Company Commander was required to make "a List of [public] Arms which [the] Colonel can find in his County, together with an Account of the Condition such arms are in." The law directed that "all Public Arms shall be marked with such Marks, and in such a Manner, as the Governor, or Commander in Chief, shall think proper, to denote such Arms to belong to the Publick." Buyers and sellers of public arms were liable for fines of 40 shillings each.

The law also reaffirmed the power of the superior officers of the counties to call out, drill, exercise, train and discipline the militia units "to the End that every Person inlisted or inrolled … may improve and render themselves fit for Duty and Service." It gave the commanders greater authority to discipline, levy fines, or order corporal punishment against the militiamen who failed to maintain order and proper decorum at musters. No servants were to be enrolled in the militia "unless upon such an Emergency as may be judged necessary and proper by the Field Officers of the respective county." [108]

Without support from the colonial legislatures the governors' military authority was virtually nonexistent. The colonial executives needed money to establish and maintain even a meager military force. Since governors had few monetary resources at their immediate disposal, they looked to the assemblies. As the years passed, new governors soon discovered that the maturing American legislatures appropriated money only upon their own terms, stipulating the size of the force, the pay of the men, and the length of their service. Further legislative measures eroded the governors' authority by stating where men would serve, by naming commissions to oversee militia expenditures, and by demanding a voice in the selection of officers. Still another check upon the executives in several colonies was an annual piece of legislation, somewhat like the British Mutiny Act, giving the militia legal existence as well as an organizational structure.

In their struggles with the governors, the colonial assemblies pursued a course set by the English House of Commons. Army affairs were one of the principal subjects of controversy between the Crown and Parliament in the seventeenth century. However, the assemblies went well beyond the Commons in using the purse to limit executive dominance. For colonial Americans, it was not enough to believe that military power should rest with the civil authority. Ultimately, they placed military power in American hands. Civil control came to mean legislative control. [109]

Defense of the colonists and their settlements rested overwhelmingly with themselves and their militia, especially in the earliest days. The King had traditionally conferred all military power in the royal colonies upon the governors. A Royal Governor was an impressive figure. The local militia, from the vicinity of the capital/principal town, normally the best dressed and best drilled in the colony, had an integral part in the welcoming ceremony for the new chief executive.

The governor's commission, received directly from the King, proclaimed him "Captain-General" or "Commander-in-Chief." He was empowered to appoint all officers to the colony's military establishment and they were subject to his authority alone. He could arm and employ all residents of the colony in repelling invasions, carrying out the King's commands, and suppressing internal rebellion. [110]

As the settlement in Virginia continued to grow, the Governor began to exercise his functions as commander of the military forces by appointing subordinate commanders over militia districts. The district commanders then chose their own juniors, though all commissions came from the Governor. In addition to military officers, the district militia commanders took on civic duties as well, such as compelling church attendance. They became sufficiently busy that lieutenant commanders eventually were commissioned to give assistance. [111]

The county commander combined civil and military leadership in one person. As head of the county commission, he was commander in fact as well as name. Use of the title continued through the 1640's. Subordinate officers of the militia served by his appointment, with the Governor's approval. Through his authority in civil affairs, problems of overlapping or conflicting jurisdiction were effectively eliminated. The title of "commander " disappeared after the middle of the century when separate military commissions were issued for each county to a board of officers whose head usually carried the rank of Colonel. However, the basic administrative principle of the earlier system remained in effect. The county militia commissions were distinct, but there was a marked overlap in personnel and responsibility. The chief magistrate and the Colonel were, more often than not, the same man.

Everywhere a majority of the commissioners of militia held a place in the County Court.

In the seventeenth century the county sheriff, whose office tended to be occupied in turn by the justices of the peace, exercised not only police functions, but also collected taxes, some royal or proprietary revenues, supervised elections and made election returns, and generally administered the county courts. By law the county militia was controlled by a separate officer. In fact, the ordinary militia officers, often themselves justices of the peace or members of the Assembly, tended to run affairs; an indication of the way in which a county elite - often the same men held positions as justices of the peace, militia officers, representatives to the Assembly and church vestrymen - now tended to appear.

In mid-seventeenth century Virginia the county remained a convenient unit of apportionment in all militia levies. Upon its official family fell the obligation to apportion the levy among its men of military age; to provide required supplies by a further levy upon all inhabitants; or, if the call to arms came in harvest season, to make an assessment of labor for care of the soldier's crops. Whatever authority the commissioners of the militia may have lacked, the county commissioners had. To seek a clear line of demarcation between the two jurisdictions would be to bother about questions that rarely bothered the commissioners. In times of serious and common emergency the joint task was carried out under the general rules and assignments emanating from Jamestown. On other occasions there appears to have been some inclination to regard local trouble with the Indians as a distinctly local problem, and to leave a county to work out of its own difficulties at its own cost. [112]

In Massachusetts, a Sergeant Major initially commanded the militia regiments, assisted by a Muster Master. As the militia system expanded, the highest ranking officer became the Sergeant Major General, later shortened to Major General, of the colony. In some cases it was an elective post, selected by a vote of those who were to serve under his command. He provided for the general provisions for the militiamen, procured communal arms and ammunition stores, mustered the militia, saw to their training, commanded the forces in the field, and even, on occasion, provided the provisions himself. While the post certainly gave him great opportunity for personal advancement, he was, in general, a citizen-soldier whose real interests lay in his own profession separate from the military. Many such men parlayed the Major Generalship into political office.

Military advisors were assigned to both colonial governors and colonial legislatures. While the soldier might choose their officers, in some cases, the total management of the militia system was entrusted to professionals and political advisers. Civilian control over the militia was firmly established. The legislature controlled the budgets of the militia in all cases, including expenditures for training. Committees of the legislatures ordinarily investigated all actions involving the militias. The colonial charters spelled out the actual conditions of legislative control. English law limited the sovereign's (and, hence, the governor's) control of the militia units as a defense against their misuse in support of tyranny. [113]

When the government of Maryland was first organized, it appears that the Proprietor only appointed a governor (his brother Leonard Calvert), two or three commissioners to advise and assist him, and a surveyor. In reorganization in 1636, the commissioners designated a Governor and a three man Council, Thomas Cornwallis (Cornwallys), Jerome Hawley and John Lewger. Lewger was secretary, register of the land office and receiver general. Hawley was appointed treasurer. The Governor and Council then began the creation of local governments, the first step being the creation of hundreds and counties. Over the hundred, as well as the county, they appointed a military commander; over the hundred a constable; over the county a sheriff and an increasing number of justices of the peace. These justices of the peace, with a clerk, soon came to constitute the county court. In 1648 the first Muster Master General was appointed. He was paid by fees and held office at the Proprietor's and Governor's pleasure. He appears to have been a kind of Commander-in-chief, subordinate to the Governor. He saw to it that the military regulations of the government were carried out and that drills were duly held. He probably exercised martial law when needed and carried out the penalties for disobedience. [114]

The first use of the title "Commander "in Maryland was on Kent Island in 1637. There was a need for someone to both "command and govern" the people. A majority of the people of Kent coming from Virginia, where the position existed and was commonly used, it was only natural that the precedent provided should have been followed. In December, 1637, George Evelyn received a commission as Commander of the Isle of Kent. He had power to choose six or more capable men for his consultation and assistance, to hold courts for minor civil and criminal cases, and to appoint peace keepers with allowance for fees identical with those "usually belonging to some or like officers in Virginia." By 1644, if not before, St. Mary's had a court with a Commander and two other Commissioners. By the end of the decade, the institution had acquired a position in the government of Maryland comparable in all particulars to that of the County Court in Virginia. However, the position and title, which had emphasized an early combination of military, political and judicial leadership in the county, was not long lasting. It disappeared after 1658. Thereafter the presiding justice in the County Commission was commonly known as the judge, a title that served to mark a new distinction between civil and military commands. [115]

The early colonial militia units were organized in imitation of the English "trained bands," with comparable proportions of musketeers and pike men. They were commonly called "train bands" as late as the early eighteenth century, especially in New England. A "train band" would usually be a company sized unit of about 50 men drawn from a village or town ward, which would form a part of a county regiment. Troops of mounted militiamen began to appear in the 1640's. While remaining rare, their members could be either volunteers or enrolled (i.e. involuntarily enlisted). Horses were expensive and mounted men had to provide their own animals. However, it became a general practice to allow one troop to each territorial regiment of infantry. Artillery units were even rarer. Early artillery gunners were individual specialists who might be grouped together. The first such unit was raised in Boston in 1638. Common practice was to mass such cannon as were available with individuals selected from the general draft for field service. [116]

The keystone of the militia system was the company. Formed within a township, a county, or, perhaps, a city, the company had a geographical rather than a numerical basis. Numbers depended upon the male population within any given geographical base. The vitality of the company depended on the quality of the officers.

The town militia, usually the first unit to appear, consisted of a company or "train band," in New England, of fifty to sixty men. Over time, the standard authorized size of a company increased in direct proportion to the increasing population of the supporting geographical subdivision. When a maximum strength of two hundred men was reached, a new company was formed. These early companies were infantry, two-thirds of the men being musketeers and the remainder pike men. Earlier than in Europe, as early as 1675 in Massachusetts, pikes were recognized as outdated and were replaced with firearms.

At first, except for the governor and council, the companies were the sole level of militia organization. As their populations increased the several colonies began to establish regiments. Massachusetts was first in 1636, Virginia in 1652, Maryland in 1658 and South Carolina in 1685, among others. The county was the common base. However, where the population grew dense, the area could be more restricted. In a county the companies could be widely dispersed and regimental control would necessarily be loose. Both companies and regiments, no matter how loose their organizations, provided rosters of officers and men that became essential starting documents in any sort of mobilization of manpower for military purposes. Here, at least on paper, was a roster of names and a chain of command.

Each colony provided, at least formally, for a regimental organization based on the companies of a county. In some colonies the regiments assembled once a year, but in others the rule was once every four years. Many of the colonies allowed cavalry companies/troops, which operated as scouts

with the infantry. A few colonies authorized artillery compa-
nies/batteries, which could perform the latest European evolutions with field and siege artillery. [117]

In New England small units of men, trained bands or
"train bands," met and drilled under arms in every village
and distant hamlet, carrying on their martial activities with
great autonomy. Their only supervision came from their officers, for the most part elected by popular vote. Every trained
band constituted a local military unit, made up of relatives
and members of the same church, neighbors and townsmen.
They were comparable to today's Reserve and National Guard
units located in small and/or rural communities. There was
no system of paid substitution for militia drill; nor was the
obligation to bear arms and possess arms limited to freeholders, for lesser men and servants also bore an obligation.

The larger towns normally had more than one unit.
Massachusetts Bay "train bands," now "companies," had
strengths numbering from sixty five to two hundred men. As
previously noted, initially two-thirds would be musketeers and
one-third pike men. When a town had more than two hundred able-bodied men of military age it formed additional
companies. Towns with fewer than sixty five banded together
to establish a company. As early as 1636 the Massachusetts
General Court had amalgamated the companies into three
regiments, territorial groupings, the North, East and Boston
Regiments. Eventually each county came to have a regiment,
so that regimental strengths varied.

The Court also appointed the Governor and three assistants "to consulte, direct and give command for ye managing
and ordering of any war that may befall us." This military
committee was specifically granted power to "presse" men,
horses and carts into service as needed. Provision was also

made for pensioning any individuals "maimed and hurt" in military operations. In 1652 Virginia amalgamated the militia companies of Charles City and Henrico Counties into a territorial regiment. The other colonies, in turn, took similar action.

Growth in each colony led to innovations in their militia system and structure. In Massachusetts Bay an excess of non-commissioned officers over European norms allowed for the forming of separate elements, or "demi-companies," which received a field test in a 1635 punitive expedition against Indians on Block Island. When the colony then grouped its fifteen companies into three territorial regiments in December 1636, it became the first English-speaking government to adopt permanent regiments. In England they weren't formed until later in the seventeenth century. Other colonies followed: as we have seen, the militia companies of Henrico and Charles City counties in Virginia in 1652, Maryland and Plymouth in 1658, the rest of Virginia in 1666, and Connecticut in 1672. [118]

In the early days of Maryland the hundred was the basis of division of the province, a reversion to the old English feudal custom. The hundred was the unit of representation in the General Assembly. It was also the principal organization for taxation, the administration of justice and police regulation, as well as military service. The militia was organized on the basis of the hundred, with each having a train band. All men of the hundred between sixteen and sixty years of age and able to bear arms met, chose a commander and arranged whatever they thought necessary for the common defense. They were trained by the hundred by their sergeant. The inventory of arms and ammunition was taken by the hundred. In 1649 the Assembly directed that once a month, for five months, the freemen of each hundred would assemble "at some appointed place and there pass such orders and ordinances as they judge necessary for their defense."

The Puritans in the mid-seventeenth century enacted legislation requiring each county to have a Captain and other officers to see that the inhabitants were properly supplied with arms. Subsequently, the Proprietary government appointed Colonels for each county. The Colonels were usually members of the Council. The Governor, by virtue of his commission, was Commander-in-Chief and led the troops in person. The troops of the hundred were still a train band and had a sergeant to train them. His fees were sometimes regulated by the Assembly. Systems of alarm upon signs of danger were carefully arranged and were rigorously enforced. [119]

In 1638 the Maryland Assembly gave the Governor, as advised by his Council, authority to organize the militia as he saw fit. He just wasn't given much support to do so. Early on he appointed Captains for St. Mary's and Kent Island. He, or the Captain, appointed a Sergeant for each hundred. By 1648 he placed the mustering and training of the militia of the whole province under the general supervision of a Muster Master General. In 1671 this position was supported by a tax of four pounds of tobacco per poll. The office was phased out in 1689.

On June 12, 1658 militia companies were gathered into two regiments, North and South. Fines on defaulters among the militia troops were used to pay for the purchase of drums and flags for the units. There was also a "Governor's Own Company" which was not part of either regiment. By 1661 each county was placed in the charge of a Colonel. Under the Colonels were Majors, Captains, Lieutenants and Sergeants. On some occasions, when war was threatening, a Major

General, the rank derived from the older Sergeant Major General, was appointed for each shore.

In the early years of the province the Captain, with the aid of the Sergeants, was authorized by the governor to muster and train the militia as often as he saw fit. He was also authorized to view arms and ammunition at every dwelling house and to fine anyone found inadequately equipped. Finally, he was authorized to execute martial law for the suppression of mutiny and to make war against the Indians in case of a sudden invasion of the province. [120]

Over the course of the next century, Maryland's militia structure developed in complexity. The muster rolls from 1732 to 1748-49 show a diversity of types of troops. The listing is not complete because some of the counties are missing and others only have brief lists of names. However, it serves to give at least a representative sample, if not a complete order of battle. Listed are: St. Mary's, commanded by Colonel George Plater – 4 Troops of Horse under LTC Jordan and 5 Companies of Foot under LTC Clark; Charles – 3 Troops of Horse and 7 of Foot – 985 men total; Calvert – 3 Companies of Foot; Prince George's – 4 of Foot and 1 of Horse; Somerset, commanded by Colonel Robert King – 7 of Foot and 2 of Horse; Dorchester – 8 of Foot and 11 of Horse [These seem questionable because they are so large relative to the other counties.]; Talbot – 4 of Foot; Cecil – 7 of Foot; Queen Anne's – 4 of Foot and 1 of Horse; Worcester – 5 of Foot. While the companies of some of the counties may have operated independently, several of the counties showed a basic regimental structure. [121]

The militia leaders were hardly more effective than their troops. The senior officers were primarily politicians with little or no knowledge of war or the equipping and raising of armies. Their junior officers were from the same mold. They had to be popular with the men to be chosen for commissioned rank and to continue to hold it once it was theirs. All officers of the formations serving during the colonial wars of the seventeenth and eighteenth centuries had, to a greater or lesser extent, to be responsive to the wishes of the men. Those who commanded regiments or battalions were leaders in civilian life: the squire, the tavern keeper or the merchant. Indeed, if teachers and parsons were included, they were normally the only persons who could read and write, translated by the emergency of war into military commanders. [122]

High ranking militia officers were almost invariably planters, merchants or lawyers whose appointments were made directly by the governor and/or legislature. On the other hand, the preponderance of militia officers, the captains and subalterns (lieutenants), came from the large free holding class and were chosen locally, either by election or appointment. As the Connecticut Assembly phrased it, "[w]e consider that our officers generally are chose out of the best yeomen of the colony who live on their own lands in peace and plenty ..." These officers had various military and administrative obligations besides bearing arms. The senior officers, generally the community's wealthiest men, were usually obligated by law to furnish the drums and colors if levied fines did not cover the cost. [123]

Company officers were designated in ways that varied from colony to colony. In New England, a full company would usually elect its officers. Elsewhere the choice was sometimes made by election, and sometimes by appointment from high ranking officials of the government. Whatever method of choice was used, the positions carried with them enhanced social prestige.

Highlighted by appropriate sermons and prayers, the election of officers marked a special day for a militia company in New England. Apart from an interlude when Massachusetts Bay officers were appointed, the general rule prevailed that officers of a company were elected. This held true until the Bay became a royal colony and acquired the New Charter in 1691. Massachusetts Bay's example set the precedent for the New England militia in the seventeenth century. Rhode Island held elections until 1718, while Connecticut continued to do so throughout the eighteenth century.

While elected militia officers usually had the approval of the local establishment, they always had to garner support from their potential troops. Standing "treat" to the company at the close of a day's drill offered an opportunity to gain popularity, with the obligation usually rotating among the officers. Treating and martial conviviality indicate that New England's militia leadership reflected general popularity first and military expertise or command skills second. It was not martial skill alone, but rather broad standing in the community, combined with the personal regard of the soldiers, that garnered the popular vote to command. The requirement to win votes, to share conviviality and be a good fellow, kept the officers in close contact with their men. Military discipline, as traditionally conceived, would be nonexistent amid such relationships between officers and men. However, New England was isolated from traditional relationships and symbols of even royal authority. Most often the personal popularity of the local captain claimed the loyalties of the men over some distant King or Queen. Hence, the person of the company commander symbolized a neighborhood and became a rallying point for the soldiers' loyalty. Election to rank also meant that the officer's loyalty was primarily to the men who elected him, his company. Local associations made military leadership, not the King's commission alone.

When regiments were established, the governors and legislatures all had a hand in the selection of their officers. In royal and proprietary colonies, e.g. Maryland, the governor and council selected the Colonels and their subordinates, in some cases with the consent of the legislature. In other colonies, the Assemblies nominated officers and the Governor commissioned them. Whatever the type of colony, it was rare for the Governor to appoint an officer whose duty was to take care of the logistics in peacetime. Commissaries and quartermasters appeared only when troops actually took to the field.

Even though there were different militia systems throughout the colonies, certain generalizations applied to all of their officers, especially the senior ones: a substantial citizen could not decline a commission except for drastic reasons; and a commissioned officer could not resign at his pleasure, but had to be released by the Governor. In early New England they had to be members of that self limiting minority, the congregation. In the South, officers had to own specific quantities of land. In South Carolina, for example, a Captain had to be the owner of at least forty acres. In all of the colonies the officers occupied fairly high stations in a deferential society. [124]

By the latter half of the eighteenth century the number of exemptions from militia service in some colonies had grown extensively. In North Carolina, "no member of his Majesty's Council, no members of the Assembly, no Minister in the Church of England, no Protestant Dissenting Minister ..., no Justice of the Superior Courts, Secretary, Practicing Attorney, no man who has borne a Military Commission as high as that of a Captain or Commissioned Officer who has served in the army, no Justice of the Peace, ... no Clerk of the Court ..., Practicing Physician, Surgeon, Schoolmaster having the Tuition of ten Scholars, Ferryman, Overseer having the care of six taxable slaves, Inspectors, Public Millers, Coroners, Constables, Overseers and Commissioners of Public roads, Searchers and Brach Pilots ... shall be obliged to enlist themselves at such musters." [125]

Early America was primarily an agrarian society. The overwhelming majority of the troops, the private soldiers, if not farmers themselves, relied on farming to feed themselves and their families. Men who were very often at the demands of the farming cycle could not make commitments that took them away from their farms for long periods. Men involved in the trades who had families to support did not have the luxury of dedicating themselves to campaigns for long periods of time, no matter how impelling the reason for the campaign might be. The history of colonial warfare is punctuated by what may seem the most egregious betrayals by the militia who, on the expiration of their term of service, simply picked up and headed home. [126]

All militiamen were obligated by law to possess arms. Many obligations were specified in the colonial militia laws and the men could be fined if they did not meet the requirements. The monies collected were, as previously mentioned, used to purchase the unit's drums and colors, or equipment for common use, helping to relieve the burden of the wealthier senior officers. Early train bands in New England included pike men, but very few remained by the middle of the seventeenth century. The armament of the early musketeers generally consisted of heavy match lock muskets with rests. However, the lighter flintlock muskets became plentiful by the 1630's and predominant by the next decade.

Due to differences in terrain, tactics and strategy from England, military equipment in America changed. Most of the accoutrements common in the seventeenth century British military – long pikes, heavy matchlocks with rests, carriage cannon, brightly colored uniforms, ponderous supply trains and female camp followers – vanished. A lighter, shorter musket, easier to carry through the forest, with its barrel coated brown to reduce reflection, came into use. The men wore moccasins and carried backpacks thirty pounds lighter than those of British soldiers. The packs had blankets, field provisions, and, perhaps, extra moccasins. Body armor was favored by the early settlers and remained in use for many years, along with the heavily padded coats and jackets which came to replace it. By the 1640's both had gone out of use with the foot troops as too cumbersome. However, some officers, who could afford it and who used it as much as a status symbol as for protection, continued to use the armor well into the latter half of the seventeenth century. Officers' gorgets, the symbolic representation of their knightly armor, were rarely seen. As exceptions, cavalrymen in Massachusetts wore buff coats, helmets and breast and back plates until the end of the seventeenth century.

The men began wearing clothing that blended into the forest background, either buckskins, or shirts and breeches dyed dark green. Those coming from the current frontier region probably wore their everyday clothes which blended in. Initially, the required swords and edged weapons were varied as they were largely individually owned. Cutlasses, normally thought of in more nautical settings, were especially popular. By the end of the seventeenth century many militiamen had given up carrying the expensive and cumbersome swords and sabers. Militia laws eventually omitted them from the lists of required arms. They were replaced with axes, hatchets, tomahawks and scalping knives. Pikes, including halberds for the sergeants and half pikes for the officers, became reserved primarily for publics drills and ceremonial parades in the large towns. They were rare in the rural communities. Bayonets, meant as a replacement for the pike, slowly became more popular once they could be attached to the musket without blocking its muzzle bore. However they continued to be scarce unless furnished by the colonial government. Uniforms themselves for the non-elite militia infantry units remained rare until the eve of the SY/FI War. [127]

In the early days of the Virginia militia, the freemen were required to supply themselves with proper arms and equipment. These usually consisted of a smooth bore musket, ammunition, clothing and food for a short expedition. Most of the colonies followed suit, directing that every household should provide its own arms. However, if a household lacked the means to do this, various methods came into use to supply them. These ranged from mandatorily working for someone for a set period who would then provide the worker's arms, to special taxes to provide arms for the poor. In addition, most local authorities maintained reserve supplies of muskets to arm those too poor to buy them. They also collected stores of ammunition and sometimes small cannon that could be dragged along through the wilderness. For very long campaigns, the colonial government had to take charge. The Assembly would appropriate the money for supplies and designate the supply officers to contractors to handle purchasing and distribution.

Grants to colonial Proprietors originally included a monopoly on the sale of arms within their territory, but these were soon rescinded. In Maryland a 1639 law curbed sales of arms in which the profit exceeded 100 per cent. All colonies kept public arms, but only in New England were the stocks anywhere near adequate. However, the use of public arms always created problems. Weapons loaned to the poor for drill were often not returned; weapons in private hands were not always kept in good repair. The town system in New England was more effective in enforcing the maintenance of these stocks than were the counties and other large jurisdictions.

Writing in 1676 about Massachusetts, Edmond Randolph said that "their trained bands are twelve troops of horse and six thousand foot; each troop consisting of 60 horses besides officers, all are well mounted and completely armed with back, breast, head piece, buffe coat, sword, carbine and pistols each troop distinguished by their coats [presumably different colored lapels and facings]. The foot also are very well furnished with swords, muskets and bandoliers."

Cannon required heavy investment. It was usually made by governments, but sometimes by individual artillery companies. In return, these companies received special privileges, such as freedom from any draft. The established churches usually stood behind and supported military strength. In Massachusetts, Cotton Mather used church funds to purchase cannon. The men who served in the artillery units were volunteers.

Horsemen initially acted as scouts for the foot units. As their numbers increased they formed themselves into troops. Citizens who could equip themselves with horses and appropriate accoutrements volunteered for service in these troops, often in return for exemption from the draft and for certain tax advantages. Even though the early horse soldiers rode their work animals, the mounted service was expensive. In addition, Massachusetts, for example, required a cavalryman to possess about 100 pounds worth of property. [128]

From the beginning of the province, the directives of Maryland's governor that everyone able to bear arms should provide himself with arms and ammunition were not well complied with. The meager supply of arms and the nature of the controversy that arose around the issue not only directly increased the executive's weakness, but also contributed significantly to the growing hostility between the Lord Proprietor and his governors on the one hand, and the citizens and their delegates in the Assembly on the other. In 1664 and 1666 the lower house initiated action to increase the available supply of arms and ammunition; in the later case directing that each county have a magazine stocked with weapons and ammunition. Also in 1666, the province purchased 140 snaphance muskets (predecessors to the lighter, more accurate flintlock), 140 cutlasses and belts, 50 carbines for "Horsemen" and ammunition as part of the reserves counties were required to maintain.

In 1671, when responsibility for supplying arms and ammunition shifted from the people to the Proprietor, the issue became embroiled in the ongoing dispute between the Proprietor and the delegates on the revenues flowing to the Proprietor and what the monies were used for. The Assembly repeatedly attempted to either have the Proprietor pay directly for certain activities or provide monies from taxes, to include those on certain activities or revenues that had traditionally gone to the Proprietors. He, in turn viewed this as a reduction of his revenues and either refused to fund the activity or refused to approve the bill taxing him. This conflict continued well into the eighteenth century, up through and including the period of the SY/FI War in the 1750's/1760's. As direct results of this ongoing, long term dispute there was a consistently limited supply of arms and ammunition, as well as a limited number of trained soldiers from the militia to use them. [129]

During the early settlement periods the colonial militia soldiers wore no formal uniforms. They drilled and fought in their everyday clothes like their contemporaries in English militia units. Over time, just like in England, more and more units began to wear uniform clothing. The design and color scheme varied from colony to colony and, often from unit to unit within the colony. In 1695 a troop of Maryland Dragoons was shipped arms and equipment purchased in England. The dragoons were armed with carbines having "round locks and varnished stocks," with "carbine belts and swivels" and "caro-tuch boxes and belts" as well as "horse pistols [with] round locks varnished stocks and brass caps" which went into the holsters of their dragoon saddles. The troop had "6 dragoon drums" and "6 brass trumpets" for its musicians, and carried a small "union flag" as its standard. No clothing is mentioned in the description and no uniform is known. However, members of the troop would have been men of some means, and they were probably asked to parade wearing a red coat – the color worn by English dragoons - which all probably had in their wardrobe, with hat, breeches and boots suitable for riding.

Colonel Abraham Barnes of St. Mary's County was a wealthy shipper in Annapolis, a member of the Assembly, and a Major in the militia in 1746, promoted to Colonel in 1755. Based on his portrait in uniform, it appears that Maryland militia officers in the mid-eighteenth century opted for all scarlet dress, which included the coat, waistcoat and breeches. Colonel Barnes had gold buttons, gorget and sword hilt, and a crimson sash over his shoulder.

From 1756 Maryland provincial soldiers were furnished with "1 Coat, 1 Pair Breeches, 1 Pair Stockings, 2 Shirts, 1

Hat and 1 Pair of Shoes." However, there is no indication that this was a specific uniform, but rather a basic clothing issue of some sort. By 1757 this had changed. Descriptions of two deserters from Beall's Company reveal uniform clothing consisting of red coats with metal buttons and sleeves "tur'd up black," red breeches, white shirts and black hats with white trim. This color scheme was in contrast to the uniforms of most of the other colonial militias which had gone to blue coats uniform with facings (lapels and cuffs) of varying colors. In 1758 Marylanders serving with General Forbes appear to have been neglected, at least for cold weather clothing, victims of the ongoing disputes between the Assembly and the Governor. Forbes complained in October that they had "no manner of clothing but one blanket each" and "no shoes, stocking or breeches" or anything else against the "Inclemency of the weather" so that "Flannel jackets and blankets were added to the supplies provided them." [130]

British regulars were issued much less clothing than their French counter-parts, and the American militia even less. In most instances, as mentioned above, the militiaman was expected to bring his own gun, receiving a small bonus to defray its cost. By the mid-eighteenth century he was issued a blanket, a coat and a "soldier's hat." They rarely had uniforms, at least not the enlisted men, turning out for drill in everyday clothes and certainly not their best. If the militiaman was issued a musket because he had brought no firearm of his own, it was usually one discarded by the British Army after it had been worn out by war in Europe.

Over time, however, the amount of equipment provided to militia troops by the government had increased significantly, comparable to what had happened with the Head Count soldiers of the Roman Army during the late Republic

(The Head Count were from the lowest Roman social order with no money to purchase weapons and armor when they joined the Army. They weren't allowed in until the days of Gaius Marius.). In North Carolina, just prior to the Revolution, militiamen, by law, were to be provided "a well fixed Gun ... a Cartouch Box, Sword, Cutlass or Hanger." In addition, at musters they were required to have "at least Nine charges of powder made into cartridges and sizeable Bullets or Swann Shot and three Spare flints, a worm and a picker ... ." [131]

Sick or wounded soldiers could not expect much from the medical service of the seventeenth or eighteenth centuries. Normally each battalion or regiment had its surgeon and, perhaps, an assistant surgeon. Dysentery, the "bloody flux," was the most common disease among armies of the day. Failure to provide sanitation in the latrines was the most likely cause. Small pox was another widespread disease.

The basic food was salt pork packed in barrels of brine that would preserve it for months; that is until waggoners began to drill holes in the barrels so that the brine would leak out and the meat spoil, both lightening their load and increasing their profits through additional sales. When beer and rum ran out among the colonists they resorted to making spruce beer, which was quite tasty and may have been an effective remedy against scurvy. No would think of touching water except for washing clothes and their bodies, albeit infrequently. The danger of illness from drinking the water of the day, probably highly polluted, was too high. This too is a carry-over from their homes in England and elsewhere in Europe. [132]

In none of the colonies did the officer corps include a permanent staff, planning or "housekeeping" officers. During peacetime there weren't any commissary or quartermaster organizations to look after supplies. A permanent staff was not needed. Most campaigns against the Indians lasted only a few days and the militia reported with their own weapons and provisions. If an expedition was to be of any duration, the colonial government took over the logistical operations, providing what supplies were needed and appointing temporary staff officers to distribute them. Procurement was a simple process compared to what it would become in later and more complex wars. Food could usually be procured locally. Although most arms had to be imported, there were some resources of production. Probably one-third of the muskets used by the colonists in the seventeenth century were made in small domestic plants. Gunpowder was manufactured in a number of mills. There were even a few foundries that cast cannon. [133]

In early colonial times the survival of the community and the lives of its members could well depend on the proficiency of the militia. At fixed times every male within the age limits, equipped with his own musket, ammunition, clothing and provisions reported to his town or township or hundred or county seat or designated muster site for drill. At these meetings the men would engage in marching and other parade ground formations; in musketry practice; and, more often, as conditions became more settled, in social, festive, and/or political activities. On occasion the men of a local company trained with men from other units.

The frequency of training fluctuated with the degree of danger. In the early seventeenth century, in the early days of the colonies, company drill often took place weekly. This was true in Virginia and Massachusetts. The General Court of Plymouth initially stipulated that drills be held six times a year. A Massachusetts law of 1631 called for weekly drills to be every Saturday because of the perceived insecure conditions. Over time, in periods of perceived lesser danger, the frequency of drills dropped. By 1637, in Massachusetts, it seemed safe enough to drill less often and training days were set at eight a year. In some of the other colonies, they were reduced to six days yearly and in still others to four. When danger reappeared, such as during King Phillip's War in 1675-1676, Massachusetts reinitiated intense training, meeting as frequently as twice a week.

As regiments were formed, legislatures also established their training/assembly requirements. The regimental assemblies were normally scheduled once a year and were usually well attended. Some locations decreased the frequency to once every three years, but this was an exception to the annual rule. Volunteer units, like artillery batteries, especially those in towns, would normally meet more frequently than the current laws required. Some of their meeting time went to fraternal activities, but some of it was always reserved for military matters. [134]

Militia musters were brought into the English colonies without much modification from the Elizabethan practice. The carnival mood and escape from monotony became as much a part of the American muster as it had been of the English. So too did the flamboyant uniforms and martial swagger bordering on burlesque. What did not migrate across the ocean was the practice of paying militiamen for appearing at musters, or the office of the Commissioner of Musters. The prestige associated with being a militia officer was substantial. Such service was considered an honor. The men who became officers were called by their military rank for the rest of their lives as a mark of respect. The laws requiring periodic training also stipulated fines to help encourage attendance at the musters. However, these laws did not overcome the reluctance to train when there was no current conspicuous danger in the area and there had not been any for some period of time. [135]

Besides fear of attack and laws requiring drill, positive inducements encouraged men to undertake militia training earnestly and willingly; or, at least, without complaint. Incentives adhered in the very nature of training day itself. Time set aside for martial activities meant a brief respite from the repetitive everyday labor of a provincial farmer, mechanic, artisan or tradesman. It required a coming together of men in a serious communal effort; yet an effort that permitted sociability and good fellowship. The stated military days with their paraphernalia of guns, bullets and powder, the marching, shooting and sham fight composed one of the few sanctioned and legitimate recreations in seventeenth and early eighteenth century colonial life. This was especially true in Puritan dominated New England. Military training meant allowable exercise, a useful diversion and, as such, offered a permitted break in the routine of work. The marching, maneuvering, volleys and mock fights of training day not only advanced the team effort of sport, but also permitted individuals to excel on their own.

Joint training days and musters promoted wider competition. Individual soldiers from every part of the county vied with each other in shooting, while the train bands (companies) competed in the execution of drills and the contest of sham battles. Competition stimulated local pride in the town's company. An element of play and the competition of team spirit always undergirded the mandated militia operation.

In every community the militia had its own designated space for drill. Martial activities often took place in the town center, on the common or green nearest the meeting house, or in a designated field nearby. In New England towns, commons had a pastoral purpose as communal grazing grounds. However, from the beginning specific portions of town commons, including the Boston Commons, were set aside as training grounds. [136]

On training days the community's militia company generally assembled on public grounds, held roll call and said a prayer, then practiced the manual of arms and close order drill. There might also be target practice and sham battles. This would be followed by a pass in review and inspection by the militia officers and other local officials who were present. The morning's military activities were followed in the afternoon, when times weren't too perilous, by refreshments, footraces and other sporting events, games and socializing. They ended, at least for one Virginia muster, with hog heads of punch being rolled out which "entertained all the peoples and made them drink and fighting all evening, but without mischief." The fines collected for failing to attend drill helped finance the whole system. The officers planned and conducted the training, but also had other responsibilities. They were expected to lead the troops in battle, to supervise the construction of any local defenses and to keep custody of the public supply of powder, ammunition and armaments. [137]

The conduct of war in the late seventeenth century through the eighteenth century in Europe centered on the deployment of infantry, with cavalry and artillery generally serving as support arms. Battles were conducted according to formal rules, with strict maintenance of order; almost as though the commanders were playing a mammoth chess game using individual units of troops as their chessmen. The men stood packed in ranks in full view of the enemy. Camouflage and concealment played no role. In the eighteenth century, opposing armies simply exchanged musket volleys until one side faltered sufficiently for the other to overwhelm it with a bayonet charge.

The formal tactics were dictated, in part, by the nature of the weapon used: the single shot, muzzle loading, smooth bore musket. An experienced soldier could load and fire his musket three or four times a minute. The complexity of the loading process virtually dictated that a soldier had to be standing to complete it. A musket could hit a man-sized target at ranges only up to 100 yards. For maximum effect, commanders found that the volley fire produced a shock effect that hit an enemy force harder than shots fired individually. The key to success, then, was massed fires. The key to maintaining massed fires and, hence, effective infantry units, was maintaining close order formations. [138]

Such units, with rigid, formalized formations and tactics, were not completely appropriate for the conditions the colonists found themselves in, both in terms of the terrain they were fighting over and the initial opponents they were fighting against. Further, no one could expect farmers and tradesmen who received military training in their spare time to be instantly ready to take the field against armies of well trained military professionals. Programs for training citizen-soldiers were not based on that expectation, but rather on the assumption that some military training and organization was better than none. The citizens' military training was designed to offer a useful foundation on which to build something more in a military emergency. The American colonial militia organizations had little expectation of having to fight large armies of professional soldiers. Their function was mainly to fight Indians, or, occasionally, white troops of their own character, such as French Canadian militia during the SY/FI War. It wasn't until the Revolution that militia units were required to engage large professional formations. Nevertheless, the colonies wanted to extract as much military values as possible from the limited period of training, despite the inherent problems in designing and executing such a program. [139]

In the eighteenth century Swiss and German craftsmen on the Pennsylvania frontier developed the Pennsylvania rifle (commonly referred to as the Kentucky rifle). It was a far more accurate firearm than any musket. It was a lighter and less cumbersome weapon than the rifles the Englishmen had known in their homeland. Though even the best rifle of the eighteenth century posed troublesome difficulties in loading and firing, they did much to cancel out the Indians' previous advantages in weaponry (bows and arrows vs. match-lock and flintlock muskets; speed and accuracy initially over-came greater firepower).

It has been claimed that the average colonial militiaman could fire his musket five times a minute, well above the standard for professional soldiers. However, this is highly doubt-ful because each time he fired he would stop and take cover. In advancing he could not fire so rapidly; if prone, to offer the enemy the smallest target, he dared not betray himself, squirming around to make the many motions necessary to reload or raising his head repeatedly to make sure of his target. At best, a good militia soldier could fire his flintlock only twice a minute. Even this frequency could not be attained if there was a bayonet plugged into the muzzle of his musket.

As long as a colonial community remained a frontier community, the part-time soldiers of its militia company were likely to be fairly competent Indian fighters, no matter what occurred on training days. As the frontier receded, the inhabitants of the older communities gradually lost their skills in shooting, forest lore and Indian fighting, simultaneously diminishing the military prowess of their militia. More and more of the militia of the long settled communities had to rely not on frontier experience, but on European military manuals to guide them in their training. These manuals taught the increasingly formalized type of warfare being developed by European professional soldiers, with tactical systems designed for the open plains favored by Europeans as battlefields, as opposed to the woods favored by the Indians. Out of necessity, the colonists came to rely more and more on friendly Indians for success against their Indian foes. George Washington, a Colonel in Virginia's militia, studied Humphrey Bland's <u>Treatise on Military Discipline</u>, first published in 1727 and the leading English tactical manual of the day. He recommended it to other militia officers that they might better mold their part-time soldiers into approximations of the men-at-arms of Europe. It was widely read throughout the colonies. [140]

The Maryland Governor and the Assembly were among those concerned about the disciplines and training of both officers and men in the militia. In 1723 the Assembly attempted to help rectify the deficiencies by purchasing copies of a military training manual. It purchased "4 ½ dozen" books on military discipline from a London printer which it issued to militia officers throughout the Province. The legislature also considered hiring an experienced military officer to train both the troops and the officers. However, there is no record that they did so. [141]

The militia in America, while modeled on that of England, was also very different. It drew its members from the community, town in New England and county elsewhere. Officers, whether elected or appointed, usually came from the gentry. Members were required to equip themselves. Muster days continued to resemble a carnival. However, the American version was no longer comprised overwhelmingly of the upper classes. Most able-bodied men from sixteen to sixty were required to serve. Behind the new assumption that men had a duty to protect their community lay another, that men, all men, had the right to bear arms. Initially, fear of Indians outweighed fear of internal revolt. They built from there. [142]

Generally, colonists enjoyed the trappings of military service, the formalities of muster days, the parades, the pomp and the enhanced sense of oneness, of community. Colonial New England, as well as elsewhere in English America, accorded militia leaders special marks of distinction. Though distinctive uniforms and other insignia were generally nonexistent during the early years, the scrupulous designations of militia rank carried over into social life, as we have seen. Officer rank was eagerly vied for since it was a fairly easy means of achieving status. Once elected or selected, a man used his rank as a title for life, or until the next wartime promotion. For the most part, being a militiaman was as much a social function as membership in the Congregational or Anglican churches. [143]

The colonial militia system, with extensive responsibilities even in prolonged periods of peace, was profoundly important in shaping American politics. Except for slaves, just about every adult male served in the militia at some point in his life, making it the single most persuasive political institution affecting the daily lives of Americans. Even individuals technically denied the franchise in local elections participated in the process by which junior officers were elected or selected for units. Many political leaders gained their first responsible position in government as company commanders in their local militia. When war threatened, Provincial service provided other opportunities. The wide spread use of grants of land as recruiting bounties provided propertiless laborers and younger sons the chance to gain a homestead and, therefore, to rise in the social structure.

Military skill also opened the door for individual officers to raise their economic standing and join the social elite. A clear understanding that the militia and Provincial units had an important function in protecting society did make Americans of all political views read contemporary political philosophers in a special way. These citizen-soldiers passionately believed that defense of life and liberty was an integral part of the citizen's duties, not something that could be left to a professional force responsible to a distant government. [144]

Mock war and military exercises, as part of membership in the militia, remained some of the main occupations and recreations of the men of Maryland through the middle of the eighteenth century, just like in other colonies. They served as attractive "recruiting" tools to make the service of the citizen-soldiers more amenable. While continued service was mandatory, "enjoyable" activities made it less contentious. The militia strengths in Charles County in 1748 illustrate the point. They were as follows:

Cavalry		Infantry(Foot)	
CPT Arthur Lee	73	CPT William Theo-bald	108
CPT Allen Davis	73	CPT Richard Harrison	182
CPT William Hanson	78	CPT John Thomas	82
		CPT Barton Warren	102
		CPT Samuel Chinn	90
		CPT Francis Ward	136
		CPT John Stoddert (previously in Prince George's County by late Act Of Assembly)	61
Total	**224**	**Total**	**761**

Note the disparities in the size of the Infantry companies. As in most, if not all, of the other colonies at this time, Maryland's and Charles County's militia units are organized geographically. The available manpower is not spread across the units. [145]

As the colonial settlements grew in size and complexity, so too did their military capability and their military arm, their militia. The size of the units, the sophistication of the weapons systems, the logistical systems and the administrative systems all grew and improved. The next thing to determine is could they field a fighting force and how effective was it? Could it fight?

3. Militia Employment

COMPOSITION AND USES

American methods of warfare were a composite of the Old World and the New. The setting and the adversary gave preponderance to one or the other. The most salient European inheritance in fighting the Indian was the white man's superior social organization, which enabled the colonials to act collectively. This was virtually impossible for the Indian war party, usually little more than a body of individual warriors attracted by the prestige of the chief. [146]

The early settlers quickly learned to fight the Indian by his own rules. They soon saw that the close order drill practiced on muster days was a useless tactic against Indian warriors. "It is one thing to drill a company in a plain campaign and another to drive an enemy through desert woods" said a contemporary. Instead, they marched through the forest "at a wide distance from one another ... [as] this was an Indian custom to march then scatter." It was customary to put out scouts on the flanks to anticipate a surprise attack. Unnecessary talk was discouraged and smoking was forbidden. At the first sign of attack the leader shouted "tree all" and all dove for cover. The colonists adopted the Indian strategy of total war. However, English brutality was not simply a reaction to Indian barbarism. The seventeenth century

Europeans brought with them long standing traditions of brutality towards opponents.

The colonials' use of Indian tactics – ambush, hit and run, mobile detachments, and personal marksmanship as opposed to mass fire – continued until well into the eighteenth century. On April 29, 1756 the <u>Maryland Gazette</u> reported that "Thomas and Daniel Cresap (sons of Col. Cresap) went out about three weeks since with sixty People, dressed and painted like Indians, to kill the women And children in the Indian Towns, and scalp them, while their warriors are committing the like Destruction on our Frontiers." [147]

The independent spirit of the militia was rooted in something fundamental in colonial society; the idea of a contract between those who served and the political body that demanded they serve. The establishment of each colony had been based on a contract implicit in the colonial charters. The obligations of each colony to Britain were to be balanced, in theory, by the responsibilities and obligations of the mother country. Militiamen were keenly aware of the contractual relationship, made between free men, not coerced, and often invoked it to the discomfiture of the military and political hierarchy.

Within each colony, however, not all were equally bound by the militia contract. Some, in the lower reaches of colonial society – slaves, Indians, white indentured servants and apprentices, and itinerant laborers – were exempt; not from some humanitarian impulse on the part of the white oligarchy, but because it was considered too dangerous to arm groups that might, at some future time, turn the military experience the wrong way. In any event, these people were property, someone else's property, and the rules and rights of property were at the heart of colonial society. It would only be under the severest pressures of war that these often unwritten rules would be bent or broken. At the other end of the social scale, the more powerful could escape the inconveniences of militia service by paying a fine or hiring a substitute, an avoidance long established in colonial tradition.

In 1716 Governor Spotswood of Virginia wrote to the Board of Trade "[n]o Man of Estate is under any obligation to Muster, and even the Servants of Overseers of the Rich are likewise exempted; the whole Burthen lyes upon the poorest sort of people." A comparison of the original 1669 militia ordinance and the 1774 Militia Act for North Carolina shows how wide a gap had opened between the generally inclusive demands of the original ("all inhabitants and free men ... above 17 years of age and under 60") and the much more lenient expectations of the latter, which excluded many categories of freeholders, including clergymen, lawyers, judges, millers, overseers, and constables. In other colonies the exempted included, as well: magistrates, clerks of the court, sheriffs, physicians and surgeons, ministers and deacons, schoolmasters and students, mariners, miners and iron furnace workers, and, as already mentioned , black and indentured servants. The hierarchy of Virginia was acutely aware of the political fallout if too many militia obligations were placed on its core constituency. The General Assembly regularly restricted militia service to those who were "not freeholders or house-keepers qualified to vote at the election of Burgesses." Eventually, in all of the colonies, those who served on active duty were overwhelmingly young, free and white. [148]

Beyond mental attitudes and postures, continual wars and border clashes, especially in New England, tangibly affected everyday life in towns and villages. There were very real socio-economic effects. The area repeatedly and willingly bore the substantial costs and negative economic effects of Indian wars, border clashes, and military expeditions. Added to these were the social costs of burned villages and farms on the frontier, as well as the frequent disruptions to family life on the border when family members were sent to the coast for safety, or even captured by Indians. Although the militia was never activated to fight long term in all of the various struggles, it was from the militia's ranks that young men were recruited to soldier on the frontier or go off on a military expedition. If enough local young men did not volunteer, then the town's quota of required recruits had to be met by a draft from the local militia company's roster. Sometimes the forays offered something of an adventure for young men, and such part-time soldiering was considered a justified and honorable endeavor. Given the small population in towns and villages, the effect on succeeding generations of young men's participation must have been considerable. In tandem with the militia training days, individual participation in military expeditions shaped a tradition of an aggressive and armed stance in defense of hearth and home. [149]

The effectiveness of the militia was tied to the imminence of danger. Early Virginia ordered every Sunday to be a training day, with all males being required to bring a musket to church and drill after service. A decade later muster days were reduced to once a month. After an Indian onslaught in 1622 that nearly demolished the colony, yet left enough settlers alive to reply with a murderous offensive, a complacency set in that led them to neglect "to stand up on their guard or keep their arms fit or ready around them." The colony survived another attack in 1644 and, in the relaxed atmosphere that followed, musters were reduced to three times a year. As the

Indian menace waned, the militia became mainly a social obligation. A third of the Massachusetts legislature tacked military titles on to their names to indicate their status. In Virginia's House of Burgesses the proportion ran higher. [150]

As the frontier pushed westward and local military threats declined, the demand for full mobilization decreased. Along the ever moving and changing frontier, the continuing need for military skills or, at least, a warlike mentality was obvious. In most settled areas, by contrast, basic military skills among militiamen atrophied at about the same rate that the illusions of their military prowess increased. But even when the coastline and the frontier were literally one, typical militiamen bore little resemblance to the mythological, sharp shooting Indian fighters like Cooper's Hawkeye. The militia system was not designed to produce military units for combat. Rather, its mission was to ensure that men were armed and had a modicum of training.

Shortly after its creation, the colonial militia split. One branch was the general, universal service militia that became, by the mid-seventeenth century, a home guard whose role was more social and political than military. Men could indulge themselves in their taste for military life without the harshness and boredom of campaigning. It provided little that passed as military training, even by seventeenth or eighteenth century standards; nor did it always act as something of a contemporary depot for units in the field. For actual campaigning, colonial magistrates and legislatures found it less disruptive to a colony's economy, militarily advantageous, less distasteful and cheaper to field units of volunteers, some of whom, admittedly, were drafted. [151]

The militia was for defense and could be used only close to the area it was supposed to defend. The militia units, similar to their predecessors in England, were not designed for use in sustained combat. They were designed for use in emergencies and for short run defense against invaders and hostiles. The decentralized nature of the militia militated against its use as a combat weapon and a source of tyranny. Although formed into companies and regiments, the militia units were not designed to be combat units except in emergencies. They came to be the source of trained manpower for armies when armies where needed. They were, in most instances, to provide skilled citizen soldiers for an army, but they were not themselves an army. In the opinion of some authors they served the same purpose as the twentieth century's selective service system.

The colonists normally stopped their troops at their own boundaries. While the South Carolina charter gave the proprietors the right to use their citizen-soldiers outside the colony, in 1690 the Assembly forbad it. Subsequently, the legislature of North Carolina gave express permission to use its militia in South Carolina and Georgia. Another limitation was length of service. Since most of the militia soldiers were farmers, they relied on their own labor for sustenance. Thus colonial custom provided that the standard period of active service was three months. The time limitation, coupled with that on space, made the militia a defensive instrument only. For continuous or distant operations a different method of procuring manpower was needed. [152]

"Divers Gentlemen and others being joined in military company desire to be made into a corporation, but the Council considering from the example of the Pretorians and among the Romans and the Templers in Europe how dangerous it might be to erect a standing authority of military men which might easily in time overthrow the civil power, thought it fit to stop it betimes; yet they were allowed to be a company, but subordinate to all authority." Thus John Winthrop, Governor of the Massachusetts Bay Colony, in 1638, noted in his Journal the creation, on February 13ᵗʰ of that year, the first unit of organized volunteer militia in North America. While Winthrop was penning his remarks a system of compulsory military service was already at least eighteen years old and growing in the North American colonies. [153]

New Englanders had developed both a warlike outlook and a legal military organization in the earliest period of settlement. The danger of attack by Indians made them warlike. The military organization had followed them from England, modeled after the Elizabethan Muster Law of 1572. By 1643, when the United Colonies of New England were formed for mutual defense, the colonists were actually arming and training themselves to take the field at short notice. In 1645 the Massachusetts Council passed a regulation ordering militia commanders "to appoint out and to make choice of thirty soldiers in ye hundred, who shall be ready at half an hour's warning upon any service they shall be put by their chief military officers." [154]

In the seventeenth and eighteenth centuries wars in New England raged so frequently that every generation saw men summoned to the colors. Procedures had become fixed by custom as well as by law. Generally, the wars were fought by volunteers. The militia was rarely called up, though selective impressments from militia ranks would sometimes occur. Men would volunteer only for service under officers whom they respected and trusted. Officers and men understood that a covenant existed between them and the officers knew they would lose community standing if they violated that covenant. They also might lose all of their troops through desertions. [155]

Eventually supplemental military institutions emerged for frontier defense. Hired military volunteers began to range the wilderness throughout colonial America, patrolling outposts and giving warning of Indian attacks. Other volunteers combined with friendly Indians for offensive operations deep in the wilderness where European tactics were ineffective. The volunteer concept matured during the colonial wars. Regiments completely separate from the militia were raised for specific campaigns. These units called Provincials, or, in Maryland, State Troops, were patterned after regiments in the British Army and were recruited from the militia, often during regular drill assemblies.

In 1645, to cope with a major Indian confrontation, the Virginia General Assembly directed that each group of fifteen titheable persons produce and maintain a soldier for an extended tour of duty. Behind this lay the power of the authorities to press (impress) men into service and, if necessary, to employ the militia draft. The military force that took form consisted of indentured servants, unemployed men, vagabonds and prisoners released for this service, a cross section of the bottom level of Virginia society. A quasi-standing army, it remained on duty for two years and eight months. In 1698 Governor Webb used indentured servants, mostly Irish Catholics, to create a similar army. Other examples can be found in almost all of the colonies.

The volunteer branch of the militia was generally made up of young men with neither land nor families of their own. Communities as a whole, or the colonial legislatures, shared in maintaining these volunteer units, offering land bounties, for example, in exchange for service in a campaign, payable upon completion of the service. This contractual form was scrupulously adhered to by both parties, including what the volunteers judged as fair treatment, or they went home. From this branch of the militia, not the general militia, came the contingents of colonials who served alongside the British in the colonial wars.

These volunteer forces, unlike the general or regular militia, were built from the top down. The governor would select the commander who, in turn, would recruit and enlist his men. The choice of a commander was made with regard for his popularity in the colony since this directly related to his ability to persuade officers and men to serve under him. The militia was the main base of recruitment and the officers were almost invariably men whose previous experience was in the militia. However, as noted above, indentured servants, drifters and others without military obligation were also enlisted. The enlistment period was only for the duration of a campaign, at best a year or so. Colonial assemblies had to vote money for pay and supplies. They were usually parsimonious as well as unwilling to see volunteer forces assume any of the status of a standing army. With short enlistments, inexperienced officers, and poor discipline by European standards, even the best of the colonial volunteer units were, like the militia, often held in contempt by British officers.

An informal and unacknowledged alternative to the militia system had come into use. The alternative troops were not raised through the militia organization, but through special officers who were given orders to recruit volunteers and, if necessary, to impress men who were not protected from such arbitrary action. To expedite enlistment, the seasoned colonies offered various inducements to volunteers, including additional pay, freedom from impressments for a period of time, a share of the plunder, and land grants, among others. In spite of this alternative system for raising men, the militia system remained the mechanism for large scale mobilization in case of an attack serious enough to threaten the life of the colonies. The system remained useful for defense, but not for aggressive military action. [156]

In the late 1650's, as we have seen, the Maryland Assembly made some important changes to the Militia Act. By 1655 the government had begun to make a distinction between the common, or general, militia and that which had been specifically equipped and trained. Initially, provision for the better arms was the responsibility of the men themselves. This proved to be too expensive for many. In 1657 the Assembly passed a law formalizing the distinction between the popular militia and the select militia. Each county was to maintain a list of all eligibles, that is, all able-bodied men between sixteen and sixty. The authorities "out of that list [would] select such persons to be of theyr constant Trayned Bands they shall judge fittest both for their ability to Body, Estate & Courage." The select group was to receive colonial equipment of the best order and additional training. The colony was to "muster, Exercise and train up in the art of warre and disciplinary military and in all things to do as any Captaine of a Company of foote or of right ought to do." The colony would provide for the major maintenance of public arms, although the citizens were responsible for normal care. The law provided for substantial penalties for failures to muster and train as ordered. Payment of fines was to be made in pounds of tobacco. In 1658 the militia was organized into two districts, divided by the Patuxent River. [157]

Despite the disheveled state of most provincial militia units, Americans took great pride in their system of armed defense built on the concept of the virtuous citizen-soldier. From its beginnings in Virginia, through the next 130 years, the militia system kept adapting to the problems of the moment. The early militia, especially in New England, had been essential in defense against the Indians, while militia units during the 1730's and 1740's in the South played a large part in guarding the white population against individual slave depredations and group uprisings. Over time the militia became the exclusive province of the free, white, adult, propertied males, usually between the ages of sixteen and sixty. Thus Indians, slaves, free blacks, indentured servants, apprentices and indigents came to be excluded from militia service. In actuality, a primary function of the militia turned out to be protecting the propertied and the privileged in colonial society from the unpropertied and underprivileged. [158]

Although Americans celebrated their militia and sought to rely on it for defense, the militia almost never was, according to some historians, an effective fighting force. After the first few decades of English settlement, the militia was not properly armed or trained. The colonists came to rely on volunteers, as we have seen, as well as friendly Indians and the few British regulars available to provide security to keep the hostile Indians, as well as other Europeans, at bay. When the English colonists had serious fighting to do they eventually came to depend on the British Army.

Americans were satisfied with their poorly armed and trained militia because the colonies were, in the main, peaceful and remarkably secure, again in the view of some historians. Whites did treat slaves, Indians and other minorities brutally. But whites rarely assaulted other whites, almost never killed one another, and offered little armed resistance to their governments. While some writers contend that the British colonies were at war more than one-third of the time between the founding of Jamestown and the SY/FI

War, others say that "in the vast expanse of time from 1607 to 1775 peace was the norm." The colonists were sometimes drawn into wars by Europeans. However, even then, battles in America tended to be less costly than those in Europe. [159]

In colonies with universal military service there grew up a distinction between the common militia and the volunteer militia. Few occasions arose requiring the whole able-bodied manpower of a colony or district, the compulsory service companies and regiments, in their entirety. Even when some military expedition might have made complete mobilization desirable from the military viewpoint alone, other considerations, such as home defense and the need to tend crops, generally forbade it. Therefore, the compulsory service companies and regiments rarely took the field in all their strength. Rather they served as training commands and replacement pools from which troops were drawn in emergencies to form the units that actually conducted operations. When troops were needed for a campaign the legislatures assigned quotas to the local military districts. The local officials then called for volunteers. They could draft (press/impress) men when sufficient numbers did not come forward. Usually compulsory service was limited to expeditions within the colony. However, militia laws often empowered the governor to employ troops outside the colony's boundaries for stipulated periods in special circumstances. [160]

The call for service from the governor or regimental commander became a mechanism for compelling the compulsory service men with an obligation to assemble, normally by companies, at the muster site. Once assembled the Captain would explain to the company the required quota and ask for volunteers. If the number of volunteers did not fill the quota, he would, as has been noted, resort to a draft. However, he normally could not impose it at the muster because drafting required legal action. In Massachusetts constables were given warrants which they had to serve individually on each draftee. Even then the impressed man could avoid service by paying a fine or finding a substitute. When the duty extended beyond the legal term of service, officials had the power to impress replacements for the men who had the right to return home. The legislatures also sometimes permitted a draft of men to serve outside the colony.

The volunteer forces were normally built from the top down. The commanding officers were first chosen by the governor and/or the assembly. The men were enlisted by them from among the volunteers generated in response to their district's quotas. The choice of a commander was made with due regard for his popularity in the colony since this was directly related to his ability to persuade officers and men to serve under him. The militia was the main base for recruitment and the officers were invariably men whose previous experience was in the militia. However, previous restrictions began to be lifted and indentured servants and drifters without military experience were also enlisted. [161]

A major expeditionary force was mounted in 1740 against Cartagena, a keystone of the Spanish empire in America, located in present day Columbia. Under the command of Admiral Edward Vernon 5,500 soldiers and sailors sailed from the British Isles. The colonies recruited and sent to the rendezvous in Jamaica 3,500 men who had either responded to the lure of plunder or had been impressed. Once the colonial force reached Jamaica the cost of its maintenance shifted to England, but the cost in lives continued to rest on the colonies. Disease took such a toll that no more than 600 of the colonials lived to return home.

In 1745 more than 4,000 Massachusetts men gathered for an expedition against Louisburg in Canada. These men, and others like them, were a new type of soldier in the colonies. They may have been on the militia rolls, but they had not been called up from them. They were predominantly young, single, landless and poor; in need of the money being offered for military service. Most of them volunteered, but some had been impressed. Like the enlisted soldiers of Europe, they generally came from the lowest social stratum. However, unlike the Europeans, they were free to enter or stay out of service, and they were rarely in it for a large portion of their lives. [162]

Although a viable tradition of one colony sending its men to defend the settlements of another did not exist, some of the northern colonies had joined in offensive operations against the French in Canada. Since it was hardly feasible to call out the whole militia, technically almost the entire white population, leaders generally gathered a body of the younger, better trained and better equipped militiamen, along with other volunteers, of the sort described above. Frequent use was made of the bounty, most often a monetary grant the citizen received upon enlisting for a set period or campaign. [163]

As discussed above, in the event of emergencies, generally, individuals were drafted, either voluntarily or by press, from the territorial units into provisional regiments. The size of the provisional units was determined by the colonial government's assessment of the adequate strength needed for the job at hand. When the emergency ended, those temporary formations were disbanded and the citizen soldiers returned to their original home units. The officers of these territorial groupings were usually elected by the popular vote of the men of each unit, especially in New England; military ability rarely determined their choice.

The emergency units followed in general the normal English regular tables of infantry organization. They were usually one battalion regiments of ten companies each, two of which, termed grenadier and light respectively, were classed as flank companies, elite units in the colonial formations. Over the years it became common practice to assign the growing spate of volunteer companies (called up from their respective territorial regiments) into the flank positions of the emergency formations. The men called up for temporary field service were enlisted for short terms only: from one to three months, or, in some cases, for the duration of some specific campaign or specific objective. When their obligations were concluded they quickly disbanded and went home. [164]

As the colonies began to rely more on volunteers, as opposed to common or standard militia, there naturally grew more or less permanent formations of those persons willing to volunteer for active duty. The common or standard militia was territorial and based on the principle of compulsory service. The volunteer militia was the formation whose recruits choose membership in it, generally with the understanding that they would respond to the first calls for active service. As early as 1645 Massachusetts Bay provided that 30 soldiers in each militia company were to be ready for service at a half-hour's warning. Volunteers were sought for this role, out of which grew the minute men of 1775. The militia's cavalry and artillery formations tended to be elite volunteer units, with the volunteer militia sometimes choosing their recruits on the basis of exclusivity. [165]

From the late seventeenth century the colonies raised a variety of troops to serve for limited periods of time against the Indians and, later, against the French. The colonial legislatures would vote laws enabling these units to be raised, usually consisting of infantry regiments together with a few companies of rangers (Men lightly dressed and equipped to serve as quick reaction forces as well as scouts and intelligence gatherers.). They were recruited from volunteers lured by bounties and wages. The length of service was usually reckoned to be for the time required for the expedition.

The coming of age of American provincial units as quasi-regular troops came during the SY/FI War. They were normally authorized in May of each year and were in pay for service until November, when the men would be discharged. In some colonies a few companies were maintained during the winter to guard the frontiers. The great majority of these units had uniforms. Officers were appointed by the provincial governor and they received provincial commissions. Many officers were appointed in successive years. Thus, by 1760 units had a good proportion of officers and soldiers who were veterans of several campaigns. Recruiting, however, was consistently below the establishments authorized by the colonial legislatures. In 1760, for example, they enlisted 15,942 of the 21,180 authorized. Nevertheless, the units did contribute to the British war effort. [166]

By the summer of 1756 it had become quite apparent that little reliance could be placed on the militia to assist in Virginia's defense. Its answer was to develop a professional force, the Virginia Regiment. The regiment had its origins prior to General Braddock's arrival in North America. After his defeat the Virginia House of Burgesses expanded the regiment and put its establishment on a more regular footing. However, recruiting efforts flagged, producing only 500 men, half the required number, in the first three months. This was a crisis for the officers because they needed a specific number of recruits before the governor would confirm their commissions. It resulted in some of the officer creating phantom companies.

With such a shortage of troops, in the spring of 1756 the Burgesses extended the provisions for drafting single white men from the militia, with fines for officials who did not comply. This resulted in widespread local protests which, in turn, resulted in local authorities often drafting vagrants or undesirables who had no link to the county. This, coupled with provisions allowing draftees to either hire replacements or pay a ten pound fine for noncompliance, resulted in draftees who were poor and/or had few community ties. [167]

The European threat of the eighteenth century called forth responses that went far beyond the original conception of the militia. War against France and Spain required larger forces, serving for longer periods of time and traveling greater distances. The answer was the volunteer force, paid and supplied, often armed and clothed by the government. The power of the governor to raise and command the militia, accordingly, came to mean less and less, while the military role of the legislature grew larger. The shift in power from royal governor to colonial assembly had many causes, but the change in the character of warfare was not the least of them.

While some of the volunteers for military expeditions in the eighteenth century were militiamen, they were by no means all of them, as we have seen. There were several classes of men, whose total number was growing after 1700, who fell outside of the militia structure. They included: friendly and domesticated Indians, free Negroes and mulattos, white servants and apprentices, and free white men on the move. These were precisely the men who, if given a chance, were most willing to go to war. As the militia companies tended to become more social than military organizations, they became hallmarks of respectability or, at least, of full citizenship in the community. A growing number of those who did the actual fighting were not the men who bore a military obligation as part of their freedom. [168]

Although militiamen developed a record of sorts in tracking down recalcitrant slaves, wiping out discrete Indian bands, and entertaining an admiring populace with drill routine on muster day, citizen-soldiers did not earn much of a record in full scale wartime combat. During the imperial years of 1689 – 1763 there were few encounters that brought the militia glory. Indeed, most propertied colonists seemed to forget that extraordinary efforts were required to get provincial citizens to fight the French and the Spanish.

Virginia, in supporting regular army units during the SY/FI War, chose to move its militia out of the province. The Assembly, composed primarily of the planter-elite, passed legislation that placed the burden of service on "such able-bodied men, as do not follow or exercise any lawful calling or employment, or have not, some other lawful and sufficient maintenance." Local candidates for front-line combat, as opposed to home-defense, were to be those who came from the poor and indigent classes, who had, as a class, been excluded from militia service. The rigors of actual open field combat had been set aside as appropriate calling for the poorer sort, with upper class leadership, while the middle class filled the militia. [169]

Military Engagements

Utilizing the resources available to them, the colonists in America created military forces to protect themselves from hostile inhabitants and European opponents, their citizen militias. Rudimentary at first, they grew in size and complexity as their respective colonies grew and became more complex societies. The quality of the force, the involvement of the local population, the logistical and administrative support provided and the training conducted were all directly impacted by the settlers' perception of the degree of imminent danger they were in as well as the resources they had available. As the frontier, with its constant danger of Indian attacks and, later, European incursions, moved further and further west, the longest settled areas lost immediate interest. The governments found that the compulsory service units weren't very effective, even if they could muster the necessary strength to be involved in a fight. More and more they came to rely on ad hoc volunteer units that, in turn, achieved a high degree of permanency. Having developed and prepared these military forces, the next issues to address are where the colonists used them and when. First, a brief overview of events and units primarily outside Maryland.

The relationship between the English and other Europeans in the colonies had been intermittently a military one since the beginnings of English and Europeans in the Americas. The outcome of the sixteenth century raids against the Spanish on the South Atlantic and the Caribbean had been a practical relinquishment of Iberian claims to sovereignty of North America's Atlantic coast above Florida and the West Indies. English contests with the Dutch had broken the hold of the United Provinces in the Atlantic trades, although not their supremacy in the East Indies. In their turn, the wars of the late seventeenth and eighteenth centuries would mark an English response to French competition, a contest for supremacy in the West Indies, for access to

Spain's American colonies, for the bounty of Canada and the interior of North America.

With these aims the American settlers largely agreed. Their own commercial ambitions and cultural and religious prejudices, as well as their fears of French and Spanish hostility led them increasingly into the great struggle for empire. Yet Americans did develop their own views of tactics and strategy. They showed a willingness to act to defend their own particular colonies, but less readiness to contribute to the aid of other colonies or to support imperial military schemes with no direct relevance to themselves. Many Massachusetts settlers believed that the Crown, and not their colony, ought to be responsible for the defense and safety of northern New England, and often refused men or supplies to defend it. Maryland and Virginia sent few men and little money for the protection of New York when it was requested. [170]

Ft. Christiana, on the site of present-day Wilmington, Delaware, was well situated for defense. It was partially surrounded by swamps, limiting overland access and avenues of attack. It also provided easy access to the Delaware River, allowing easy loading and unloading of ship cargos. The two corners that faced the river, along the northeast corner, were mounted with cannons from the Kolmar Nyckel, the ship that brought over the first Swedish colonists. The fort's initial garrison consisted of 25 men. Two log houses were built within the fort. However, it was primarily a trading post, not a military bastion. By 1640 the walls had collapsed due to neglect. They were repaired, but by 1644 the fort needed a complete overhaul. By 1654 it had to be rebuilt again. The work wasn't completed when the Dutch captured it in 1655. In 1644 34 people, only three of them soldiers, resided at the fort. By 1655 the population had only increased to about

100, very few of whom were soldiers. The Dutch, led by Peter Stuyvesant, captured it with 300 soldiers and seven ships. [171]

Militia service in New England was initially against Indian raids, of which the Pequot War of 1636 – 37 in the Connecticut River Valley had given a fore taste. The subsequent King Phillip's War in 1675 – 76 in Connecticut, Rhode Island and Massachusetts sent a shock wave through the northern colonies. Terrifying though they were on the warpath, the Indians never threatened the extinction of the colonies by their own efforts. It was their alliance with the French which made them formidable and it was, therefore, directly against the French that the colonists' military efforts were made: by William Phips in 1680 – 90, by Francis Nicholson in 1711, by William Pepperell in 1745, by George Washington in the South in 1754, and by John Johnston and William Shirley in 1755.

From the 1690's onward the militias of the northern frontiers, in particular, began to acquire real competence in forest warfare, along with a readiness to turn out rapidly for duty in all seasons. While this woods savvy actually applied only to a minority of the provincial troops, as a group, they were more at home in the woods than the King's regulars, who eventually became more engaged in the American conflicts. The professionals had little stomach for woodland operations. As the conflicts with the French intensified during the eighteenth century, portions of the militias of the increasingly prosperous New England and Atlantic colonies were developing into semi-regular forces, expensively equipped and capable of mounting some autonomous operations against the enemy as they did at Louisburg in 1745. [172]

When war came to the middle colonies in 1755, it came to a region that had witnessed little previous contact. Since

Bacon's Rebellion in 1676 and the Iroquois victory over the Susquehannocks the following year, there had been little warfare in the region. The colonies had avoided the conflict that had so dominated the early settlements of other colonies. Because of these long periods of peace, unlike the New England colonies, which had witnessed repeated conflicts with both their French and Indian neighbors and, consequently, had something of a martial tradition, they were unequipped to wage war. The Virginia militia, which had been honed into the colony's principal defense force in the seventeenth century, had become more of a social institution than a military force. Pennsylvania did not even establish a militia until the 1750's in response to the SY/FI War. [173]

Virginia precipitated the SY/FI War when Governor Dinwiddie aggressively sent militia detachments into the Ohio country to assert the expansionist claims of the Ohio Company investors (of whom the Governor was one, along with other prominent, influential Virginians) against the rival, and similarly expansionist, French claims. In his attempts to expel the French from the Ohio country in 1754 (west of Virginia, just across the Ohio River which became Virginia's western/northwestern boundary), Dinwiddie knew that the House of Burgesses would not agree to draft the militia. On February 24, 1754, he wrote Governor Sharpe of Maryland: "I prorogued our Assembly this Day. They had given 10,000 [pounds] this money for the Support of His Majesty's right to Lands on the Ohio in Consequence thereof I design to immediately raise five or six Companies of men to march to Will's Creek [later Ft. Cumberland; present-day Cumberland; Maryland territory] with all prudent Expedition ... ."

Because of the Burgesses' reluctance to utilize the militia, Dinwiddie, as he indicated to Sharpe, attempted to induce men to volunteer. Since the promise of spoils was negligible, even Lord Thomas Fairfax, a very powerful landlord (George Washington's neighbor and, more importantly, mentor), could not oblige his tenants to enlist. In six weeks only 300 men had volunteered. Of them, 100 were Indian traders who had a special interest to protect. The other 200 were from the lower reaches of society. This was George Washington's command, given to him after the incapacitation of his original commander, among other reasons, because of his position as a substantial planter with rising prospects and impeccable connections.

Support to oust the French from the western frontier was less popular elsewhere than it was in Virginia. Even there, except among the gentry and high government officials who were Ohio Company investors, it was tepid at best. Getting a concrete expression of support from their respective Assemblies was not an easy task for the governors. The attempts at action also got caught up in the ongoing and growing rivalry between the lower (popular) houses of the legislatures and the proprietors and royal officials that existed in virtually all of the colonies to a greater or lesser extent.

Pennsylvania began to act, starting to reverse its previous pacifistic stance and eventually allowing a voluntary militia. North Carolina's Assembly voted 12,000 pounds in support of the campaign. A detachment of North Carolinians started towards the rendezvous at Wills Creek, but mutinied and was forced to turn back. Maryland found an additional reason for dragging its feet in support of the coming war. Its western and southwestern boundaries were in dispute, with Virginia claiming, and eventually getting control of, land that had been clearly granted to Maryland in its royal charter. This all combined to make it easier to lay a heavy burden on the colony that had the most to gain, Virginia. The Maryland Assembly rebuffed Governor Sharpe when he appealed to it for resources to support Virginia and the other colonies. The delegates asserted that they could not see the need for such expense because the colony was not actually being invaded. They refused to fund troops for the campaign. This attitude was to persist as the hostilities increased. [174]

On September 1, 1754, less than two months after Washington's defeat at Great Meadows, Colonel James Innes was appointed the commander at Wills Creek by Governor Dinwiddie. A short time after assuming command, and on his own initiative, Innes began construction of a fort near the mouth of Wills Creek on the Maryland side of the Potomac. A small stockade was completed in about a month and named Ft. Mount Pleasant. Governor Sharpe, having been commissioned "Lieutenant of the Forces to be sent against the Forces who have invaded his Majesty's Dominions ...," went to western Maryland to inspect what was being constructed.

In a letter to Dinwiddie, Sharpe reported "... I found the Independents preparing for themselves barracks, having already completed the small Stoccado Fort about which you were advised they had been employed; but as the Fort they have finished is exceedingly small its Exterior Side not exceeding 120 feet I conceive it requisite or rather absolutely necessary to have another much larger raised on an adjacent or much more elevated piece of ground & I hope they will be able to finish it this winter." Ft. Mount Pleasant was subsequently renamed by General Braddock for the Duke of Cumberland when he, Braddock, was using it as a staging area for his expedition against Ft. Duquesne. Dinwiddie referred to it as a "King's Fort" which just happened to be in Maryland. Until the fort was formally turned over to Maryland, it was not under the jurisdiction of its governor. This is why Dinwiddie of Virginia tried to play such a large role in its construction, staffing and utilization in this mid-eighteenth century period. It was also the reason that the composition of the forces there were so diverse. There were provincial troops from Maryland and Virginia, as well as Independent Companies of British regulars from New York, North and South Carolina. At various times there were also contingents from regular British regiments. Initially the provincial troops were all under Colonel Innes' command. [175]

The SY/FI War did not alter the militia system of the colonies. The system had supplied manpower, but so had the alternative method of producing short term standing forces, manned in part by volunteers and in part by pressed men. More often than not the provincial commander came from a roster of militia officers. Trained companies, still known as train(ed) bands in some areas, did not provide quick manpower during the war. They seldom turned out as companies, but, rather, were the source of detachments of men that joined with similar detachments from other companies to make new ad hoc units. In New England, where the trained bands were generally more efficient than elsewhere, detachments were constantly engaged in defending new settlements before those settlements could defend themselves. Mobilization would have been faster and more efficient if the trained bands had been inducted intact. [176]

The departure of the French from America after their defeat during the SY/FI War, and the consequent lessening of the Indian danger, had the effect of loosening the bonds between Britain and her colonies. The colonists, at least subconsciously, did not feel as great a need for the Crown's protection. At the same time that they were asserting their self sufficiency, they were also relaxing their military strength. This brought about an abrupt decline in the militia's fitness to fight and overall quality after 1763. Drills were neglected and not taken seriously. Musters were poorly attended with few, if any, consequences. Training in many places became a farce. Energetic men were no longer putting themselves forward to be officers. Those already holding commissions often tended to lapse into lethargy. Many of them were conservative stay-at-homes to whom the value of their rank was the standing their association with the British government brought them. In fact, some colonies no longer attempted to enforce the laws requiring drill and came to rely on volunteer militia units for their defense, the forerunners of the later National Guard. [177]

On the eve of the American Revolution Timothy Pickering suggested that if the colonies reformed their militias they would never need standing forces. To achieve this desirable and low cost position it was necessary to involve the elites once more in the militia. Because it was so simple to avoid service by paying a fine, the upper levels of society had stepped aside and allowed the militia to be operated by less competent men. Pickering's solution was to simply require participation and close what he called the avenues of erosion. Over 230 years later Pickering's analysis provides a quick synopsis of the problems of a modern day military draft as well as possible solutions. [178]

As policies of the British government grew more ominous, in the view of the colonists, they lacked the local means to oppose the representatives of the Crown and its armed forces in America. Their protests were mere words. The dissenting colonists required a force of their own. In a local military revolution in 1774 they set about building one.

In September the voters in Worcester County, Massachusetts, a center of military activism since King Phillip's War, chose to require the senior officers of the militia to resign their commissions. The purpose was to force out the pro-British officers, especially the senior ones, and to replace them with others of sterner stuff, i.e. pro-American sentiments. Each county town was to select a third of its men between sixteen and thirty years of age "to be ready to act at about a minutes warning." Each was also to appoint a committee "to supply and support those troops that shall move in any emergency." The Worcester resolutions were to provide a model for military reorganization throughout the colonies. [179]

Maryland's military activity from its founding through the mid-eighteenth century was relatively limited, especially compared to the New England colonies. Further, unlike most, if not all, of the other colonies, Lord Baltimore's royal grant precisely defined Maryland's boundaries, or so it was thought. When the charter was issued on June 20, 1632, no one could have told Lord Baltimore even the approximate size of the grant. The boundaries, apparently so clearly stated in Article III, traced the outline of Maryland from the ocean along the fortieth parallel "unto the true meridian of the first fountain of the river of the Pattowmack," thence along the south bank of the river to a point "where it disembogues" into the Chesapeake, and then eastward along the parallel that runs through Watkin's Point to the Atlantic Ocean. Its limits were: on the north, the fortieth parallel of north latitude: on the west and southwest, a line running south from this parallel to the farthest source of the Potomac and, thence, by the farther, or, western, bank of that river to the Chesapeake Bay; on the south, by a line running across the Bay and the peninsula to the Atlantic; and on the east, by the ocean and the

Delaware Bay and River. Its western boundary should have been the head of the South Branch of the Potomac which, in fact, is further west than that of the North Branch which was ultimately used. It included, therefore, a portion of present day Virginia on the Eastern Shore, all of the present day state of Delaware, a large tract of land in Pennsylvania (to include the sites of part of present day Philadelphia, all of York and Gettysburg) and much of present day Northeastern West Virginia.

On the surface limiting conflicts with its neighbors over disputed territory, in fact these fixed boundaries were the causes of numerous disputes between Maryland and the surrounding colonies, to include military action. The vagueness of the boundaries with what became Pennsylvania and already existing Virginia, along with Swedish and Dutch claims which not only competed with and overlapped between themselves, but also with British claims, led to repeated confusion. Colonists were victimized by the issuance of conflicting land grants emanating from the several authorities. Legal deployment of militia normally was limited to only to service within a colony's own territory. When militia units were chasing marauding bands of Indians and crossed into disputed territory there were occasional diplomatic crises. By the late seventeenth century there had been armed clashes for some years, although on a minor scale. [180]

After the arrival of the Ark and the Dove on the Chesapeake in 1634, there was no major clash of arms in Maryland for several years, unlike what had happened in Virginia, almost thirty years earlier. The Indians were at first friendly. In fact, the local inhabitants willingly sold Calvert and his associates their land and some of their dwellings. They had been in the process of moving on due to increased harassment from more aggressive tribes to the north, so they viewed the new arrivals as fortuitous. The only military action of note in the first years was the construction of the fort at St. Mary's, although in 1635 CPT Henry Fleete led a party to the Patuxent River to protect trade conditions. [181]

During the seventeenth century military activity in Maryland was a mixture of internal conflicts, disputes with neighboring settlements and colonies, and attacking and being attacked by Indians. The Province grew and prospered with relatively few troubles or altercations with the local Indians. In fact, local Indians used the colonists for protection against incursions by hostile Indians, such as the Susquehannocks, the Iroquois from the north, and the Nanticokes on the Eastern Shore. Likewise, the colonists began to use the local Indians as a buffer against sporadic raids by those same hostiles. For several years, until the settlements spread farther afield, the arrangement worked well both for the colonists and local tribes. However, by the 1640's this situation began to change when freemen of the colony demanded a greater voice in colonial affairs and the Susquehannocks and other Iroquoian tribes began raiding the livestock of outlying settlements. By 1638 St. Mary's settlement had its trained band of 128 men. In the early 1640's captains were appointed for "every hundred" men. In April 1650 the Assembly allowed a full time garrison of six men under a captain in the fort at St. Inigo harbor, just south of St. Mary's

As Maryland expanded and grew in population the militia that was maintained not only guarded against Indian raids, but also provided armed support to governmental authority during periods of civil strife. The most sustained period of conflict took place between supporters of Charles I and those of Parliament when civil war erupted in England in 1642. For almost twenty years the civil war raged intermittently in the province. In March 1654 the primarily Catholic supporters of the royalist Calverts and the primarily Puritan supporters of Parliament fought each other. The Maryland loyalists were defeated with some 40 men killed at a battle on the Severn River. The militia was later ordered to disarm any inhabitant suspected of disaffection towards the Province's government, which meant Catholics, Quakers and Baptists. They were henceforth denied the rights of citizens for more than hundred years, until the Revolution.

By the 1660's the struggle had subsided and the primary duty of the militia was to protect the settlers from Indian raids. In the early days of Maryland the authorities fostered fair treatment of the Indians. Unlike colonies to their north and south, they refused to use military power to intimidate or exterminate entire villages for the wrongdoing of a few braves. However, as settlers pushed the frontier further westward in the late seventeenth century confrontations with the Indians became more commonplace. [182]

William Claiborne, a member of the Virginia Council and Treasurer of Virginia, as well as a royally licensed trader with New England, Nova Scotia and the Dutch in Manhattan, had established a trading post on Kent Island prior to the establishment of Maryland. Kent Island, renamed from John Smith's original designation of Winston's Island, had been within Virginia's original patent. However, it was subsequently included in the land granted by Maryland's charter. When notified that his land now fell within Maryland's jurisdiction, Claiborne was incensed. With the support of dissident elements in Virginia, he resisted what he felt was an incursion.

The contest between Calvert and Claiborne was far from an academic argument over a phrase, *hictamis inculita* (hitherto uncultivated), in Baltimore's charter. All such land within the boundaries described in his charter was given to the Proprietor by royal patent. Claiborne contended that his Kent Island establishment was, in fact, a cultivated and inhabited place, and that he had, indeed, at his own expense, settled and cultivated the island before the charter had been issued. Accordingly, he claimed full ownership of the soil and exemption from Baltimore's jurisdiction and overlordship.

William Claiborne illustrates a type that surfaced in the outer reaches of Britain's overseas possessions, giving a turbulent cast to the early years of colonial history. Claiborne had fought unrelentingly against Lord Baltimore being issued a charter. As Secretary of the Virginia Council, he had acted in his official capacity to prevent the King from granting land from within the boundaries claimed by Virginia. In addition, he also had personal motives. Several years earlier, as noted above, Claiborne had established something like a colony of his own half way up the northern arm of the Chesapeake Bay, on the Eastern Shore. He had selected his ground with an eye to both carry on trade and establish a plantation (farm) on Kent Island. It was the largest offshore body of land in the Bay, flat, well drained, and cut off from the shore by a narrows navigable only an armed sloop or wherry, designed for defense of the island. Here he had erected a fortified trading post staffed with retainers, approximately 100 in 1634 when the <u>Ark</u> and the <u>Dove</u> arrived, who cleared the forest to lay out fields, orchards and pastures.

These properties clearly lay within the Maryland patent, but Claiborne stubbornly refused to acknowledge Baltimore's jurisdiction. On the other hand Governor Leonard Calvert, equally stubbornly, determined to assert the Lord Proprietor's (his brother's) rights to the soil and government of the island. The impasse had complications touching Claiborne's financial backers in England, the mercantile firm of William Claberry and Company, and his rival in the Chesapeake fur trade, Captain Henry Fleete, who sided with Baltimore.

In 1635, less than a year after the first landings in St. Mary's, a pinnace belonging to Kent Island was captured by Marylanders for trading in Maryland waters without a license. Claiborne armed a shallop, the Cockatrice, with 30 armed men under Lt. Ratcliffe Warren, whom he commissioned to seize any vessels belonging to the government at St. Mary's. Calvert sent out two armed pinnaces, the St. Helen and the St. Margaret, under the command of Thomas Cornwallys (Cornwallis). They met on April 23, 1635 in the Pocomoke River, the first naval engagement in the inland waters of North America. Warren's party fired first, inflicting casualties. Cornwallys returned fire, killing Warren and two others, forcing the surrender of the Cockatrice. On May 10th there was another engagement in the harbor of Great Wighcomoco (or Pocomoke) in which Thomas Smith commanded a vessel of Claiborne's and, apparently, inflicted casualties. Round 2 went to Claiborne. [183]

While Claiborne's involvement waned after the events of 1635, the attempts of his successor commercial interests and their attorney, George Evelin, to dominate the area urged Maryland authorities to send a force and reduce it formally. On February 12, 1637, as a result of Kent Island's long standing resistance to Proprietary authority, the Governor and Council directed that "the governor should sail, in person, to said isle of Kent, and take along with him a sufficient number of freemen, well armed, and there, by martial law ... reduce

the inhabitants ... to their due obedience to the lord proprietor, and by death (if need be) ... and so order that Captain
Thomas Cornwallys, esquire, and one of the council of this
province, should go along with the governor ... for the command of the forces, according to such directions as he shall
receive during the expedition." [184]

The outcome of this expedition is not recorded, leaving
the results open to several different interpretations. James H.
Fitzgerald Browne stated that the expedition must not have
been too successful because Claiborne's forces remained
entrenched on the Island. Perhaps, because only free men
could serve in the militia and because the majority of the
indentured people of Kent in Claiborne's service were not
aware of such legal niceties, it is reasonable to presume a
repulse of the attackers. J. Thomas Scharff maintains that
since any violent confrontation would have been subsequently
mentioned/discussed in the legislature, it is presumed that
the threat of force was sufficient to settle the disputes peacefully. William K. Browne supports Scharff in his contention
that limited, if any, resistance was offered. At any rate, a few
days after Calvert's initiation of military action he returned,
bringing with him Thomas Smith, leader of the affray at
Great Wighcomoco. Smith was subsequently charged with
piracy and murder, tried, convicted and executed. [185]

In May 1638 the Council, conceiving that "in so remote
an Iland as the Ile of Kent and situate among divers Savage
nations, the incursions as well of the Salvages as of other enemies, pyrate and robbers may probably be in feare," appointed
John Bateler "Captaine of the military band of that Ile of
Kent in all martiall matters" with "full power to leavie muster
and traine all sorts of men able to beare arms and in case any
sodiane invasion of Salvages or Pyrates to make warre and

to use all necessary meanes to the resistance and vanquishing of the enemy." However, from the desultory character of
military references after the Council's actions, it would seem
that the militia provisions became obsolete. Despite the periodic problems caused by the Susquehannocks, expeditions
against marauding Indians did not, by records, normally
exceed twelve men. [186]

While the whites were busy fighting among themselves,
some of the local Indians had also been active. Numerous
minor forays upon Kent Island settlers and others by hostile
Indians of the Eastern Shore were coupled with attacks by the
Susquehannocks, which were chiefly directed at the friendly
Patuxents and Piscataways. However, Maryland's resources,
just five years after the first arrivals, were not extensive, limiting the size and the scope of their military expeditions. This
was best illustrated by the general orders signed by Governor
Calvert and his Council on May 18, 1639: "… it is found necessary … to make an expedition upon the Indians on the
eastern shore upon the public charge of the province, …
That a shallop be sent to Virginia [to purchase supplies of
arms, ammunition and food] …; and likewise that a pinnace
be sent [against] the Susquehannocks sufficiently victual and
manned, and 30 or more shots with necessary officers be
allowed after the rate of 100 lb. of tobacco per month … and
2 sergeants double the said roll … ." The 30 marksmen plus
command group were loaded into two pinnaces and a skiff.
Some of the soldiers were volunteers, but some were there as
part of their compulsory service. [187]

The results of the expedition are unknown. However,
it must have had some success because in 1640 it was
only thought necessary to declare war against one of the
tribes instead of several. On January 3, 1640 Governor

Calvert, because "Certaine Indians of the Nation called the Maquantequats have committed Sundry Insolences and rapines upon the English inhabiting this Province" and refused the satisfaction that was demanded "and therefore compelled us to enforce them thereunto by the Justice of Warr," commissioned Nicholas Harvey [Hervey?] to go "with any company of English as Shall be willing to goe along – so they exceed the number of twelve men sufficiently provided of arms to invade the said Mancantequats and against them and their lands and goods to execute and Inflict what may be inflicted by the Law of War and the pillage and booty therein gotten to part and divide among the Company that Shall performe the Service." Similar declarations of war, or commissions for military service against the "Susquihanowes" and other Indians were issued year after year, sometimes as frequently as two or three times a year. [188]

About this time news reached the Maryland settlers that the Susquehannocks and other Indians were being supplied with firearms and taught how to use them by Dutch and Swedish traders from the Delaware River and Hudson River Valleys. Governor Calvert wrote to Governor Berkley of Virginia referring to a previous "joint expedition by both colonies" and requesting that they mount one against the traders. Calvert's efforts came to naught and then became submerged into difficulties with the Assembly concerning the manner of raising troops and supplies. A central part of this dispute was the Governor's attempts to exempt employees of the executive estates. Calvert was opposed by CPT Thomas Cromwell, but the Assembly eventually agreed with him. In 1643, while Calvert was in England, Cromwell raised a company of volunteers to engage the Susquehannocks and was successful. A second expedition the same year directed "against the Susquehannoes or any [of] their orders," also led by Cromwell, was not as successful. It appears that it met with disaster, possibly an ambush. [189]

By 1640 it was evident that the Indians in Maryland were growing dangerously restless. However, the records of the province offer only indistinct impressions of sporadic attacks upon outlying farms, scanty references in the proceedings of the Assembly, with a confused impression as to what was done by way of reprisal, counterattack or negotiation. Between 1640 and 1643 Governor Calvert was active in outlawing certain tribes and urging war with them. However, in 1643 some members of the Council blocked action. Previously, in 1642, the freemen of the Assembly appear to have been the pacifists in the case. Father White, one of the original group of settlers, wrote in 1642 that he was compelled to abandon the Piscataway mission (located almost directly across the Potomac from the later site of Mt. Vernon) because of its "proximity to the Susquehannocks," adding that "an attack having been recently been made on a place of ours, they slew three men whom we had there and carried away the goods, to our great loss and unless they be restrained by force of arms, which we little expect from the counsels of the English, who disagree among themselves, we will not be safe."

The opposition to the Governor's proposed "march against the Indians" in the Assembly involved important principles and precedents concerning the real or alleged rights of the freeman versus the declared prerogatives of the Proprietary, or, in this case at least, of his brother and representative, Leonard Calvert. By late 1642 a "great opposition" arose to the urgent plea from the Governor to proceed against the Indians. This opposition must have begun in the form of a debate as to the advisability of such a march.

Governor Calvert, however, informed the House that he "did not intend to advise with them Whether there should be a march or not, for that judgment belonged to himself, as appeared by the clause patent touching the power of war and peace; and a motion was made by the Secretary that a bill might be drawn up for the levying of twenty pounds of tobacco per head toward the charge of it." Whereupon it appears that the Delegates "desired to have the patent to peruse and respite until the next morning to advise of their answer." The main problem appears to have been that the people evidently feared that future abuses would arise out of the proposed methods of calling out freemen, especially in regard to commissioning the officers of the militia. [190]

The Susquehannocks to the north and the Nanticokes to the east attacked the more docile tribes still in Maryland, and even some of the outlying English plantations, the commonly used term for a homestead or farm. In 1642 they murdered several settlers, burned their houses and seemed to be plotting more serious activities. Governor Calvert began to take measures for defense. Signals were agreed upon by which news of an attack could be passed swiftly from plantation to plantation; officers were appointed to command the militia. The most defensible house in each hundred was designated as the location to which women and children were to be conveyed. On June 23, 1642 Calvert appointed Robert Evelyn, former military commander of the Isle of Kent to "command all English in or near Piscataway and train them in discipline of war and to punish delinquencies. He was not successful. Calvert's attempt to interest Virginia in a joint expedition against the Indians and their European weapons suppliers, as we have seen, was also unsuccessful. [191]

In direct response to the perceived dangers from ongoing Indian raids and skirmishes a makeshift organized military structure began to emerge. A fort had been erected at or near the Patuxent River in the neighborhood of several scattered settlements. As a further precaution, Mr. Henry Bishop was authorized to take command of the fort, which was to form a rendezvous for the inhabitants in case of dangers. On August 28, 1642 a proclamation was issued "[f]or the purpose of reducing the inhabitants having dispersed in several plantations to some places of better strength, in case of any sudden inroad of Indian robbers and pillagers." It created an alarm system, along with forts or fortified houses for settlers to gather in. It appointed commanders for various gathering points and established guard and defensive procedures. It also commanded that " all several persons of the said several hundreds, able to bear arms, be obedient and assistant unto the said several persons respectively appointed to take charge and command as aforesaid, or they will answer to the contrary at their peril." [192]

Maryland declared war on the Susquehannocks on September 13, 1642. A best as can be determined, the declaration was motivated by a desire to halt the incursions of the Susquehannocks into territory occupied by Maryland's "client" tribes – including the Piscataways, the Patuxents and Yoamacoes. Whatever the cause, militiamen did not mobilize until sometime between July 1643 and June 1644. The Susquehannocks continued to be aggressive on Maryland's northern and western frontiers, destroying a mission station, while the Nanticokes on the Eastern Shore threatened the colonists across the Bay. As mentioned above, having assisted the Governor of Virginia previously in punishing the Indians of the Eastern Shore for an attack upon settlements of that colony, Governor Calvert proposed a joint expedition against the Indians and their arms suppliers with two hundred men drawn equally from the two colonies. The current attacks were happening too far from Jamestown to concern the Virginia Council and they evidenced little interest in participating. Calvert, however, considered the danger real and took vigorous action within Maryland. As previously noted, he directed all of the frontier settlers to be withdrawn into forts and blockhouses, proclaimed martial law and authorized the local commanders to call out every third man capable of bearing arms. These actions, coupled with proclamations limiting the Indians' access to the settled areas on pain of death, proved to be successful and the threat subsided. Hence, the delay between the 1642 declaration and the mobilization.

Governor Calvert departed for a visit to England in April 1643, appointing Giles Brent Governor in his stead. An April 17th Brent issued a commission to Captain Thomas Cornwallys (Cornwallis), Esquire, appointing him Captain General of a force to be lead against the Susquehannocks. Cornwallis, having a "propensenes to goe a march upon the Susquihanowes," was authorized "for vindication of the honour of God … and the English race upon those barbarians and inhumane pagans … to levie volunteers and do all other things requisite for the training of the souldiers punishing of insolences vanquishing the enemies and disposing of the spoils." He was authorized to take, if necessary, every third man to make up the number required and to lead forth the expedition at such time and in such manner as he deemed fit. Cornwallis was chosen, among other reasons, because he possessed the full confidence of the militia. Instead of using a draft for troops, however, at his recommendation he was authorized to raise and organize a body of volunteers.

Cornwallis was not expected to, nor did he, immediately begin preparations to depart. The day after his commission was issued the Council determined to raise a company of ten good marksmen and post them as a garrison, fully armed and equipped, upon Palmer's Island, in the mouth of the Susquehanna River as it entered the Chesapeake Bay. They were able to monitor the movement of the Susquehannocks, whose fort was a few miles above the falls on the eastern bank. They were also able to prevent Indian war parties from coming down the Bay to assault the colony.

The Susquehannocks continued to become more formidable. As previously noted, they were being furnished with firearms and instructed in their use by the Swedes of Delaware and the Dutch of New Amsterdam. They carried on a wholesale traffic in arms and ammunition with the Indians bordering on the English and French colonies. Their motives were both mercenary, for they were primarily merchants, and strategic, to generate the maximum amount of difficulties for their competitors. The Dutch were claiming the Delaware River region and were attempting, ultimately with some success, to overwhelm and control the Swede's territory. In the lower Delaware River Valley they both were occupying land granted to and claimed by Maryland.

Captain Cornwallis subsequently was granted authority to attack the marauding Susquehannocks and this time he used it. There are no surviving official records of the results. However, it appears that the Indians fled from the militia's guns. Plantagenet in his 1648 work New Albion, as quoted in Streeter's Papers, stated that the Swedes settled on the Delaware had sold arms and ammunition to the Indians, "[T] hey had hired out their soldiers to the Susquehannocks, who, training the tribe to the use of arms and to European tactics, had led them into Maryland and Virginia, and assisted them to take the chief of the Potomacks prisoner, and to subdue the eight Indian Tribes in Maryland that had been civilized and subjected to the English Crown." He then goes on to say that the Susquehannocks and their allies numbering 250 were defeated by Cornwallis and his force of 53, with minimal losses to the latter.

Cornwallis received still another commission for a subsequent expedition which, if ever made, is not on record. However, it, or a subsequent one (the record is unclear as to which) must have ended disastrously. Fifteen Marylanders were taken prisoner, with two being tortured to death. The troops had fled in such haste that they abandoned their arms, including two field pieces, precious artillery very rare in the colonies. In 1644 Captain Henry Fleete was commissioned to negotiate with the Susquehannocks at Ft. Piscataway on the Potomac. Among other things, he was directed to obtain the restitution of "as much as he could get of the arms and other goods lost or left in the last march upon them, at least the two field pieces." [193]

While the expeditions against the Susquehannocks were ongoing, internal strife also resumed. Captain Richard Ingle, an associate of William Claiborne of Kent Island, was discovered hovering around the settlements with an armed ship, attempting to stir up trouble with disaffected colonists. Ingle claimed that the acting Governor, Giles Brent, had persecuted him because he, Ingle, was opposed to the royal prerogative. Ingle was captured, but quickly escaped and rejoined Claiborne. When Governor Leonard Calvert returned in September, 1644, after almost a year and a half's absence, he found the government in great difficulty. Some inhabitants, for example, were refusing to pay for or serve in expeditions

against the Susquehannocks who had attacked the outlying settlement at Mattapoint, at the mouth of the Patuxent
River, about five miles north of St. Mary's fort. Calvert also
found Claiborne in possession of Kent Island. He dispatched
a reconnoitering party across the Bay to watch the insur-
gents and make preparations to dislodge them. However, the
efforts were unsuccessful.

In February 1645 Claiborne, Ingle and supporters invaded
the Western Shore as a direct result of ongoing difficulties
in England. After plundering and robbing throughout the
colony, Ingle landed an armed force and took possession of
St. Mary's City. In his opinion Maryland was ripe for a revolution against the Crown and royal authority. Claiborne had
actively revived his claim to Kent Island. Ingle presumably
made prisoners of those members of the Assembly and such
others as offered resistance or objection. Many of the colonists refused to take an oath of submission to Parliament.
Ingle's distinctly anti-Catholic bias caused Calvert and others
to flee to Virginia, whose power structure was staunchly royalist. While there Calvert was busy defending the rights of Lord
Baltimore and trying to gather support to retake control of
Maryland.

The "revolt" flamed out quickly. Within a few months,
because of political developments in England and with a well
armed, but unspecified, military force that he had raised in
Virginia, Calvert returned to St. Mary's and resumed control
over the Western Shore. He was able to pick up the reins
of government with little or no objection. He reconquered
Kent Island and regained control of the Eastern Shore by
April 1745. He then died, on June 9, 1645, and was succeeded
by Thomas Greene, a member of the Council. Greene's new
government was immediately preoccupied with the problems

of arrears of pay for the soldiers at St. Inigo's Fort, just south of St. Mary's. This would seem to indicate the survival of the militia as an integral part of the colony. [194]

Military expansion became necessary in 1647 as a result of new troubles with the Nanticoke and Wicomico Indians on the Eastern Shore. In 1648 Governor Greene appointed Captain John Price "Muster-master General" for "his abilities in martial affairs" and service during the "plundering year." Price commanded what appears to have been a permanent militia force of thirty to forty men. For at least two years he had the authority to impound all weapons brought into the province by outsiders. [195]

In 1648 a body of Puritan radicals, numbering between 400 and 600 people, moved to Maryland. They had been enticed by the liberal religious toleration law in Maryland which required merely that one professed a belief in the Trinity. The Protestant Governor Stone granted them a block of land on the Severn River. There they established a self-governing community, which included an essentially autonomous militia. By 1652 the authorities from Virginia, supported by Puritans within the province and in England, took control of St. Mary's City and removed Stone as governor. Richard Bennett, supported by Claiborne, demanded that Maryland be merged with Virginia and ruled as a single entity.

In 1651 Parliament had decided to become involved in the struggling provinces of Virginia and Maryland. Commissioners were appointed to take control. Virginia readily acquiesced and soon after, in 1652, the Virginia Commissioners came to Maryland to subdue the province. They included Richard Preston and Richard Bennett. Bennett, who had been active in procuring ministers from Britain for the Puritans of Virginia, was one of those who, when driven out of Virginia, came and settled in Providence, eventually Anne Arundel County and Annapolis. Bennett, however, still retained his residence in Virginia when appointed one of the Commissioners for the reduction of Maryland. In his proclamation he proposed "that the settlers should all remain in their places, but only conform to the laws of the Commonwealth of England, and not infringe the Lord Baltimore's just rights. That all inhabitants, including the governor and council, should subscribe to the test called engagement."

Governor Stone and other governmental officials readily assented to a portion of the requirements, but refused to accept the proposition "that all writs shall be issued in the name of The Keepers of Liberty of England." Commissioners Bennett and Claiborne (of Kent Island fame) demanded Stone's dismissal and got it. He was subsequently reinstated with greatly reduced powers. Bennett and Claiborne named Robert Brooke, Colonel Francis Yardley, Mr. Job Chandler, Captain Edmund Winder, Colonel Richard Preston and Lieutenant Richard Banks as commissioners/members of the Council. They were authorized to administer the government of the province in lieu of Stone. The acts of Governor Stone and his Council were declared null and void. The province's capital records and stores of ammunition were moved from St. Mary's to Preston's home, Preston-on-the-Patuxent [River], where the Council was to meet. Bennett and Claiborne returned to Virginia to become Governor and Secretary of State, respectively.

Robert Brooke now effectively headed the province. He had not come from Virginia, as many of his associates had. He had immigrated directly from England with an appointment from the Proprietor to "be commander under us, and our lieutenant of our whole county ... with the power to appoint six or more inhabitants to advise with him." The county created for him was then named Charles, present day Calvert.

Governor Bennett and Secretary Claiborne returned to Maryland to observe the progress of their revolution. Realizing that former Governor Stone was popular with the people, they offered to reinstate him as governor. He accepted their offer. However, friction between the supporters of Parliament (Puritans), primarily located in current Anne Arundel County, and supports of Lord Baltimore continued. In England, as Parliament lost power to the emerging Lord Protector, Oliver Cromwell, Lord Baltimore decided to regain control over his province. He ordered Stone to gather a force, act as Governor-Commander-in-Chief and fight if necessary. Meanwhile, radical Puritans of both New and Old England envisioned extending Puritan domination and control along the American seaboard to Maryland and Virginia.

In January 1653 many of the residents on the Patuxent and Severn Rivers sent Bennett and Claiborne petitions decrying the requirement to swear an oath of fealty to Lord Baltimore on penalty of losing their land. In March 1654 Puritans, now holding a substantial voting bloc in the Assembly, declared Stone removed as Governor, appointing William Fuller in his stead. Since the Assembly had not met since 1651, the Puritans instructed Fuller to call it into session, with the aim of disarming all of those who had borne arms against Parliament and all Roman Catholics, as well as disenfranchising them.

The resistance to Lord Baltimore's rule continued, and on June 22, 1654, the Commissioners issued an order calling for an Assembly on the Patuxent at Preston's home. It met on October 20, 1654 and sat as one house (i.e. no separate

Assembly and Council). It was declared that "henceforth all power in this province is held by protector and parliament." It further stated "that no Catholic can be protected in his faith, but be restrained from the exercise thereof." The next step was war.

Also in 1654 Lord Baltimore again contacted Stone. In a letter Calvert censured Stone for yielding his authority without a struggle and renewed his instructions for actions. Stone was amenable to changing sides again. Calvert directed Stone to issue a proclamation denouncing the Puritan government at Preston; raise a military force; seize the rebellion's records; and force the Puritans into subjection. Stone had little trouble gaining support in St. Mary's and Charles (Calvert) Counties. However, Anne Arundel and Kent Counties ignored his call to swear loyalty to the Proprietor. Stone raised a military force of over 200 men and eleven vessels, primarily from around St. Mary's City. His goals were to capture Richard Preston and overthrow the Puritan stronghold at Providence, near Annapolis. To accomplish both goals Stone split his force. He sent one group, under Josias Fendell, to capture Colonel Preston and the records on the Patuxent. In Richard Preston's absence the red coated troops overcame Preston's wife's defense, took possession of the records and ammunition and ransacked the house. They also threatened what they would do to the people of Providence [Annapolis] and stated that they "would force the factious Roundheads [Puritans – a derogatory term based on Puritan men's general haircuts – a "bowl cut"] to submit ..."

Governor Stone moved the rest of his force north towards Providence. Those who marched overland used his vessels to ferry themselves across the intervening rivers. A portion of his force traveled completely by boat. The Puritan Council sent messengers south and they met Stone's force south of Herring Creek. The messengers/commissioners carried a proposal for a peaceful settlement of the conflict. Stone captured one of the commissioners, but another one fled. Unable to capture him, Stone threatened to hang him upon the door of his house if he didn't surrender. He didn't. Stone, in turn, sent two separate messengers to Providence proclaiming his peaceful intentions. They were ignored and did not return to Stone. He then proceeded to the vicinity of the Severn River where he rejoined his vessels, embarking on them. Stone commanded about 130 men. The Anne Arundel forces were under the command of the Puritan governor, CPT William Fuller. His force numbered about 175. In addition, he had a naval force consisting of two ships, the Golden Lyon out of London and a small trading craft from New England commanded by a CPT Cutts. Fuller had requested assistance from the master of the Golden Lyon, Roger Heamons. Heamons subsequently claimed that he had been "hired," that is paid, for his services.

As darkness approached on March 24th, Stone's flotilla approached the Golden Lyon. After unsuccessfully warning them off, Heamons fired on the ships, diverting them into Spa Creek on the south side of the Severn River, to the east of present day Annapolis harbor. Stone disembarked his troops near Horn Point. Later in the evening, to counteract Stone's apparent intent to fire the "enemy" ships, Fuller directed Cutts to block the mouth of Spa Creek with his small trading vessel to prevent any waterborne attacks by Stone's forces.

On the morning of March 25th Stone and his troops approached the shore with the gold and black flag of Maryland flying and drums beating. As they reached the shore the two ships of Heamons and Cutts opened fire, killing one man and forcing Stone to retire up the neck. Fuller, utilizing boats, had ferried his men six miles upriver from Stone and made a circuit around the creek to get in the rear of Stones forces. After being seen by one of Stone's sentries, Fuller held off, anticipating a parlay. Stone opened fire first killing one man. Fuller's men then charged, shouting their battle cry "In the name of Godfallen; God is our strength." Stone's troops countered with "Hey: for St. Maries" to no avail. They were quickly over whelmed, with only four or five escaping. Forty loyalists were killed and numerous others wounded, including Stone. Fuller's casualties were two killed and two mortally wounded. Upon receiving a promise of quarter, the surviving loyalists surrendered. All of their arms, supplies and baggage were captured, along with their boats.

Two or three days after the battle, despite quarter having been given, ten of the "Papists" were condemned to death, Stone and nine others. Four were executed: William Elton, head of governor Stone's Council, CPT William Lewis, John Legatt and John Pedso. Stone and the remaining prisoners were spared. Stone was ill treated during his confinement. With neglected wounds he and his followers languished in jail. Lord Baltimore was eventually able to convince Cromwell to honor his claims over the southern half of the Province while the Puritans remained in control of the northern portion. By May 1658, with Cromwell's authority fading, the Lords of Trade reconfirmed Baltimore in all of his possessions, i.e. the Province of Maryland. Governor Stone and his fellow prisoners were released. Stone was replaced with another governor and peace returned. However, Baltimore did not regain full control of Maryland until the restoration of Charles II in 1660. [196]

The ongoing dissension in the province had emboldened the Indians. As they seemed to threaten trouble, in 1658 the militia was reorganized. All males capable of bearing arms between sixteen and sixty were mustered. The ablest were enrolled in trained bands and drilled regularly by their respective officers. The entire force was organized into two territorial regiments. The Governor commanded the first, a district extending from the Potomac to the Patuxent. Colonel Nathaniel Utie (Utye) commanded the second, whose district went from the coves of the Patuxent to the Seven Mountains (hills on Gibson's Island at the mouth of the Magothy River), and the Isle of Kent. The regiments were divided into companies, each with its own allocated district. Major Ewen had the company south of the South River; the Regimental commander, Utie, had a special company, from the Severn to the Seven Mountains; and Captain Broadax, Kent Island. There apparently was no other settlement on the Eastern Shore except in the vicinity of the Pocomoke River, despite agreement with the Indians in 1652 allowing English possession between the Choptank and Elk Rivers, i.e. the northern, or upper, two thirds of Maryland's claimed lands on the Eastern Shore. [197]

In 1661 Lord Baltimore appointed his son Charles, then just 24 years old, as governor of Maryland, investing him with full proprietary powers. Among the titles Charles acquired were Commander of the militia, Lieutenant General, Admiral of the Provincial Navy, and Commander-in-Chief of all provincial military forces. He had the power to muster and train the militia, confirm militia appointments, suppress rebellions and seditions, invoke martial law and pardon or condemn any person. In 1665 the Lieutenant General, with the consent of the Council, ordered that there be companies formed which were "diligent in Ranging the woods," who would more easily find the "Skulking Enemy." He also ordered that there be appointed "Smiths who have tooles ... to fix armes for the Soldiers and all other inhabitants of the province." The council authorized the militia to ally with friendly Indians and to offer them a reward in cloth "for every prisoner they shall deliver alive or otherwise." [198]

As discussed above, the original limits of Maryland's charter extended north to the 40th parallel, beyond the Schuylkill River and its confluence with the Delaware. As the region presented many advantages, a party of Maryland colonists settled there in 1642 and began to reclaim and cultivate the wilderness. Further downstream, in Delaware Bay, Swedish colonists had already built a fort on Lord Baltimore's land in present day Delaware. Further, the Dutch of New Amsterdam (New York) laid claim to the whole territory. They fitted out an expedition of two armed sloops to take possession of the fort, as well as the Maryland settlement, and to drive away the occupants. Distance, internal dissension, governmental upheaval and Calvert's inability to completely control the province limited Maryland's ability to offer assistance. The settlers abandoned the region. To add to the confusion, New Englanders were also contending for the region based on its being included in their grants from the Crown. Maryland took no action to assert its claims until the Dutch had overcome the Swedes. Then, in 1659, Colonel Utie, northern regional commander, was dispatched to the Delaware settlements to notify the inhabitants that they were in Lord Baltimore's territory without permission. He required them to leave or submit to the Lord Proprietor. They ignored him.

As more and more settlers had arrived in Maryland open land had grown scarce. Surveyors ventured east from the Chesapeake to explore the land between the Bay and the Delaware River. Their task had been to claim all of the land they were exploring for Maryland. However, there had been one important hurdle to overcome. In Lord Baltimore's original charter his colony included only virgin land, not existing settlements. Small Swedish settlements, and others, had existed along the Delaware long before the arrival of the <u>Ark</u> and the <u>Dove</u> at St. Clements Island in 1634. In England Lord Baltimore continued to press his claim, while the Maryland Assembly established Durham County on the western shore of the Delaware River.

In 1664 King Charles II granted his brother James, Duke of York, all of the territory lying between Connecticut and the eastern shore of the Delaware. In 1673 Baltimore's son, Governor Charles Calvert, commissioned militia under the command CPT Thomas Howell, who marched eastward from Maryland territory, burning a Dutch town. The fighting continued sporadically for several years. English and Dutch soldiers campaigned up and down the Delaware River Valley, burning villages, capturing ferries and merchant chips, and making life miserable for the settlers. Finally, in 1682, the Duke of York granted the western side of the Delaware to William Penn, including in the vicinity of the present day Philadelphia, and half of the Delaware lands, the current state of Delaware. Penn was a better politician than Baltimore, or at least had more influential friends. He became Proprietor of Pennsylvania. [199]

As settlers went inland in search of unclaimed land, moving up the Potomac River and into the surrounding mountains, the Indians saw their land and hunting grounds fast disappearing. Susquehannocks had migrated into the Potomac River region from their lands along the Susquehanna River in 1673, moving away from attacks and harassments from their enemies, the Seneca's and the Cayuga's. Small Indian raids began occurring with greater frequency, small parties attacking isolated farm houses. Among the casualties were Giles Cole and Stephen Corwood of Charles County, killed in fighting the Susquehannocks. The whites fought back by mustering the militia, marching upstream and into the woods, destroying all of the Indian villages in their path. In 1675, as a result of several Indian murders on both sides of the Potomac, full scale war broke out.

Virginia and Maryland called up their militias and ordered a campaign to destroy the hostile Indians. The colonies organized temporary militia units, 500 troops strong. COL John Washington commanded the Virginians. The Governor's council appointed MAJ Thomas Truman as the commander of the Maryland contingent. The force also included a body of Indian allies. Truman marched his units to a Susquehannock fort, or block house, at the mouth of the Piscataway River (On the Maryland side, just upstream and across from the future site of Mt. Vernon, in the vicinity of the mission Father White had been forced to abandon over thirty years previously.). They surrounded the fort despite the Indians' protestations of innocence. To break the stalemate, Truman agreed to meet with a delegation of Indians, promising that any Susquehannocks who came forward to negotiate would not be harmed. Six Susquehannock leaders accepted the offer and walked across the open ground to the militia camp. However, a party of Virginians, enraged at the murder of a group of peaceful farmers, attacked, killing five of the six. One escaped. The militias then laid siege to the fortress. The siege lasted seven weeks, with more than fifty militiamen losing their lives. The siege ended as the weather grew colder and the Potomac River froze. Under the cover of night the surviving Susquehannocks left their fort and crossed the river to safety in the forests and mountains of Virginia. [200]

In 1681 scouts were employed to range on the frontier in order to protect the province from Indians. However, no forts of any importance were built until the royal government was restored. The Governor and Council then directed that three forts be erected on what was then the western frontier: one in Charles County, one in Anne Arundel County and one in Baltimore County near the falls of the Patapsco River. CPT John Addison and COL Nicholas Greenberry were authorized to impress and procure carpenters, ordinary laborers, tools, provisions, and other necessities, with payment to come from the next public levy. Each fort was to be commanded by a Captain, with a force of nine soldiers and four Indians. Their mission was to range all along the line of the frontier, looking for possible trouble. However, early in the eighteenth century the lower house deemed such an expense unnecessary and funding ceased, followed by the cessation of patrolling.

Marylanders had also erected fortifications in the vicinity of the disputed border with Pennsylvania to protect against incursions, but they were never really strong. In 1686 the Proprietor directed that Ft. Christiana, which had been built by the Swedes, should be taken possession of. Accordingly, the fort was garrisoned with five men. The Council determined that the expense should be defrayed out of the Proprietor's revenue, but that he would be reimbursed at the laying, or imposing, of the next levy. While it does not appear that the lower house objected to this, nothing further appears with respect to the fort. [201]

In 1687 the militia was in a poor state of preparedness, despite the many Indian raids on the then frontiers (Charles County in the west, north in the vicinity of the Susquehanna River, and the Eastern Shore, primarily to the north). Men were poorly trained and even worse equipped. The colony's armorer reported that the public arms were in poor condition. The Council ordered that the sheriff of each county was to inventory the arms. They were to confiscate all arms in unserviceable condition and have them repaired. The owner was required to bear the cost of repairs unless he could prove that his weapon had been damaged in actual service to the province. The sheriffs were also charged with improving militia training and discipline. Finally, the Council directed that they make certain that all eligible males were registered with the militia officers of their respective counties. [202]

In 1689 Maryland hosted a successful colonial uprising. The large Protestant majority resented the power of their Proprietor, Lord Baltimore, who reserved the top offices in the colony for his fellow Catholics. Ambitious Protestant planters promoted popular suspicions that the Catholic regime was plotting to betray Maryland to the French and Indians. In 1689 Governor William Joseph, a Catholic, fueled those rumors by refusing to acknowledge the revolution in England featuring Catholic James Stuart and his Protestant daughter and son-in-law, Mary and William of Orange.

Seizing the opportunity, John Goode, a planter, armed and organized a rebel militia known as the Protestant Associators. In a public manifest the rebels promised to "vindicate and assist to defend the Sovereign Dominion and right of King William and Queen Mary to this province; to defend the Protestant Religion among us and to protect and shelter the Inhabitants from all manor of violence, oppression and destruction that is plotted and designed against them." Mustering over 700 armed men, the Associators intimidated the 160 militia loyal to Governor Joseph, who surrendered without firing a shot on August 1st. [203]

In 1694 the Assembly formally created frontier ranger units distinct from other militia, although the general militia served as the manpower pool for the units. The rangers were to scout as far as the falls of the Potomac River, the tributaries of the Susquehanna River and Deer Creek. The units were posted in three frontier forts. Each April two parties, each consisting of a Captain, a Lieutenant and six enlisted men were to cover the areas and report any enemy activity. Each man drafted or volunteering for this service was to be paid 600 pounds of tobacco per month, with pay for the officers slightly higher. Enthusiasm for the program eventually waned and funding was cut off. [204]

While all of this ensued, the colony continued to grow in both territory occupied and in population. As it grew the regiments were reorganized. While still territorial in nature, they increased in number and were broken down by county. By the 1690's the regiments often had troops of cavalry and dragoons alongside their infantry companies. At least one troop of dragoons was equipped with arms and accoutrements imported from England. The colony continued to buy arms and ammunition for many years through a tax on tobacco exports, although the practice became a major cause of contention between the legislative assembly and the governor in the early decades of the eighteenth century. And the seventeenth century drew to a relatively peaceful close in Maryland. [205]

The first half of the eighteenth century continued relatively peacefully in the Province, especially when compared to its sister colonies. The internal dissension and disagreements that had been settled militarily subsided. While there continued to be some conflicts with the Indians as the settlers moved further and further westward, they were , in the main, relatively minor. That is, unless you lived on the frontier and your family were slaughtered and/or your cabin was raided and destroyed. However, armed conflicts involving Marylanders did continue, both with their immediate neighbors and against enemies, both European and Indian, far to the north and the south.

The original area of Baltimore County included a portion of the disputed land also claimed by Pennsylvania. As early as December 1732, Lord Baltimore, who had come to Maryland to settle the disputes, wrote to Governor Patrick Gordon of Pennsylvania. He called Gordon's attention to the fact that "a most outrageous riot had lately been committed in Maryland by a great number of people calling themselves Pennsylvanians." In May 1734, in retaliation, Maryland authorities carried off Pennsylvania settlers from settlements on the Susquehanna and the borders of New Castle County and jailed them in Annapolis.

However, the troubles began much earlier. In 1684 representatives of Lord Baltimore were threatening to turn people out of their homes if they failed to pledge "obedience to Lord Baltimore and Own him to be their [Proprietor], and pay rent to him." Further, they were threatened with the loss of their land. In 1686 the Marylanders were reported to have reinforced their fort at Christiana and acted aggressively against those failing to support the Calverts. In 1711, and again in 1722, complaints of Marylanders surveying and taking up land, especially west of the Susquehanna, surfaced. Also in 1722, Governor Keith of Pennsylvania, in a letter to the Governor of Maryland, refers to a report the "two magistrates ..., with some others, had been taken prisoners by a party of men in arms from Cecil County, and carried before the justices of Kent County, who detained them in custody for two days..."

In 1735 William Rumsey, a surveyor of Maryland, was apprehended by the sheriff of New Castle County and taken before the Governor of Pennsylvania charged with committing and causing others to commit a great abuse and violence against several inhabitants of Chester and Lancaster Counties and for no other reason "than that those persons asserted the jurisdiction of this province [Pennsylvania] in those parts where they live." In 1736 Governor Ogle of Maryland directed Thomas White, deputy surveyor, to lay out two hundred acres of land in the disputed territory of Baltimore County and lying west of the Susquehanna for in excess of fifty people. However, two, Henry Mundy and Edward Leet, were arrested by Pennsylvania authorities and this design to occupy land with debatable sovereignty fell through.

One Thomas Cresap, a citizen of Baltimore County, was given a 500 acre grant of land by Maryland authorities in what is now York County, PA, in the early 1730's. It was situated in the vicinity of the 40th parallel, the northern boundary of land given to Baltimore by the Crown. The land it was located on had also been granted to Penn by a different, later member of the Stuart royal family. Cresap, his family and several in-laws settled in the Conojahony Valley, three miles south of the 40th parallel and in the vicinity of the Susquehanna River. Cresap operated a ferry on the Susquehanna and farmed. Over time he came to strongly object to the presence of what he considered intruders on Maryland land, those who considered themselves Pennsylvanians, with allegiance to the Penns in Philadelphia. The Maryland authorities granted him a Captain's commission in the militia, allowing him to gather a band of about fifty like minded men and push aggressive German Pennsylvania "squatters" out of land believed to be below the 40th parallel and west of the Susquehanna.

Friction between followers of Penn and the Cresap faction increased until open fighting broke out, bringing on border warfare know as Cresap's or the Conojocular War. Cresap led a band into downtown York and stole several items, including a hogshead of rum. In retaliation, Cresap was waylaid and beaten. After complaining to the sheriff of Lancaster, he was informed that Pennsylvania had no justice for Marylanders. This, in turn, evoked a response from Maryland. The Assembly sent an armed militia group to scout the area and make it safe for Marylanders. In 1736 the sheriff of Baltimore County led 300 Maryland militia troops into the vicinity of Wrightsville, PA, with the express purpose of protecting those settlers with Maryland grants. They went so far as to evict several settlers with Pennsylvania grants from their property. They also arrested neighboring opponents of Cresap and took them to Annapolis for trial. They finally stopped when the settlers pledged that they would consult together and give an answer to Lord Baltimore.

The sheriff of Lancaster gathered a posse to capture Cresap. He resisted, mortally wounding a deputy with a blast through his front door. One of his followers, the brother of Richard Lowder, was captured and put into the Lancaster jail. Richard Lowder led a group of sixteen Marylanders who broke him out, along with the others being held there. The Pennsylvania militia then, finally, captured Cresap and four of his followers. Cresap was escorted to Philadelphia where he was imprisoned, but not before exclaiming that Philadelphia was the prettiest town in Maryland. In reporting to both King [the government] and the Proprietor on the situation, Ogle pointed out that the German settlers, who were being subjected to coercion from both sides, had originally applied to the authorities in Maryland for permission to settle in the land in dispute. Considerable quantities of land in what is now York County had been allocated to them. Further, for a time, they had paid taxes to Maryland and in every other way acknowledged its jurisdiction. However, Pennsylvania had lured them away with lower taxes. Ogle's efforts were in vain. In August 1637 the King decreed an end to hostilities and ordered a prisoner exchange. Cresap was sent to Baltimore. He remained there until eventually establishing himself on the western frontier at Old Town on the Potomac, just down river from Wills Creek. It wasn't until 1750 that the dispute was finally settled at the direction of the Chancellor of England. The permanent boundary lines were not completely finalized until the 1760's by Mason and Dixon. Cresap's disputed homestead ended up in Pennsylvania. [206]

The first British military demands on Maryland, made in 1740, were sent in the form of letters from the Secretary of State for the Southern Department, Lord Newcastle, and also in the form of direct war instructions from the King in Council. They specified that the Proprietary Governor should grant commissions to the officers of the provincial troops; that the Council should act on matters pertaining to the enlistment and transportation of troops; that the Assembly should grant such appropriations as necessary; and that the people should be called to volunteer. In making its earliest military demands of a long war period, British authority assumed what it was to continue to assume: namely, that the semi-voluntary system of colonial cooperation would work. In the case of Maryland, this involved the further assumption that the agreement between the Proprietary and the representative elements in the Assembly would furnish the working basis for military cooperation between the Proprietary province and the Crown. Such an assumption was unjustified. [207]

The first instance of a specific royal demand for an appropriation and for Maryland to participate in military activities outside her own borders came on the occasion of the expedition of 1741 against Cartagena, in present day Columbia. On June 29, 1740 the King made the requisition on Maryland to raise and equip five hundred volunteers for service against Spain in the Spanish Main. Spain and England had been at war since the previous year. The Assembly voted the money, but with difficulty. It initially voted 2,560 pounds for support, eventually increasing it to 5,000. 500 men were authorized as requested, but only 390, including a group from Port Tobacco commanded by CPT William Chandler, were mustered, victualled and transported to the West Indies to join the forces under Wenworth and Vernon. There the royal Commander-in-Chief took charge and assumed financial responsibility for maintaining them. It is estimated that 90% of the colonial levies died from the diseases that ravaged the British forces, killing upwards of twenty thousand men. As an historical sidelight, George Washington's half-brother, Lawrence, participated in the expedition. He survived initially, but eventually contracted what proved to be a fatal illness, probably tuberculosis. George accompanied him on an unsuccessful recuperative trip to the Caribbean, during which George contracted small pox, immunizing him against later ravaging attacks while in command during the Revolutionary War. Lawrence's death ultimately led to George's ownership of Mount Vernon, named for Lawrence's commander, Admiral Vernon.

The relatively successful cooperation of King George's War was marked, however, by plain signs of Maryland's independence of decision. When Governor Shirley of Massachusetts requested help for his expedition against Louisburg, the Maryland Assembly refused to appropriate funds. More important was the way in which Assembly relations prevented Governor Bladen from executing certain orders sent him by the Lords Justice. In 1743, on the occasion of France entering the war, they instructed the Governor to have the province put in a sound condition for defense. However, the passing of a duty for the purchase of arms and ammunition was required. That type of duty law was one of the most hotly disputed questions of finance and of prerogative which divided the lower house from the Proprietary element. Not even the pressure of royal authority sufficed to bring the two houses to agreement. The orders of the Lords Justice were disregarded. The situation demonstrated for the first time what was repeatedly to be the case during the SY/FI War: the balance of power between the members of the Assembly and the Proprietor exerted greater influence in Maryland political affairs than any other consideration.

In 1746 a campaign was planned to take Canada from the French. According to Lord Newcastle's orders to Governor Bladen, troops were to be raised and transported to Albany, where they would join others from New York, Pennsylvania and Virginia, under the command of Governor Gooch of Virginia. George Clinton, Captain-General and Commander-in-Chief of the Province of New York, was in overall command. Again, a supply bill was passed; arms and ammunition were ordered taken from the magazines of the province, though with the understanding that the Crown would make compensation; and Marylanders were sent to the royal service.

Three companies went to Albany. Each company, if fully manned, consisted of "One Captain, One Lieutenant, One Ensign, Four Sergeants, Four Corporals, Two Drums and Ninety Four Private Men." In one company the officers, CPT Crofts., LT Brooksby and ENS Frazier, entered "his Majesty's

Service" on June 1, 1746. The NCOs and Privates entered anywhere between June 6th and June 24th. Their enlistment ended June 24, 1747. The companies were provided 300 muskets having slings and bayonets, 300 cartouche boxes with belts, six drums, six halberds for the sergeants and nine half pikes for the officers. While the number of men provided wasn't large, it compared favorably with the number of men sent by Virginia and Pennsylvania. When Maryland made such contributions to the general cause, the tobacco trade occasionally received the security of a convoy supplied without cost by the Royal Navy. [208]

The Seven Years (SY) (European)/French and Indian (FI) (American) War during the 1750's and early 1760's was the longest period of sustained military action in colonial America from the founding of the colonies to the American Revolution two decades later. It also had the most extensive amount of combat, involving not only large numbers of militia troops, both American (English) and Canadian (French), but also an ever growing number of regular soldiers, again both English and French. While provincial troops from all of the colonies were involved in the fighting, the primary participants were from Virginia north, including Maryland.

A developing theme throughout this period was the ongoing dispute between royal authority, as represented by the governors and administrations of the various colonies, and the citizens of the colonies, as represented by the elected representatives in the lower houses of the respective colonial legislatures. This conflict was most often expressed in disputes over funding in support of local troops being mustered, equipped and trained to fight the French and the Indians. Relations in all of the colonies were contentious, with the

Assemblies often not filling the Governors' requests for men and supplies. However, none was more contentious than those in Maryland, where the disputes and disagreements between the popular Assembly, eventually the House of Delegates, and the Proprietor, with his appointed Governor, administration and Council and, eventually, a royal administration, often brought the workings of government to a standstill. These disputes ultimately came to complete fruition in the 1770's.

Maryland's government was very zealous in refusing to spend money to support the British war effort during the SY/FI War. While they were not alone, Maryland's record was bad enough to provoke the wrath of most of the military leaders who came to North America. General Braddock, in a letter to the London administration, stated "I cannot sufficiently express my indignation against the provinces of Pennsylvania and Maryland, whose interests being alike concerned in this expedition and much more so than anyone on this continent, refuse to contribute anything towards the profit." As an example of the results of this conflict, Thomas Cresap, of Conojocular War fame in the 1730's, submitted requests for payment for supplying Indians fighting the French in western Maryland. His request was finally forwarded to General Amherst by Governor Sharpe for reimbursement. The culprit was the Assembly, which had refused to vote the funds for reimbursement. A scathing indictment of the Assembly's ineptitude (In the eyes of many, not all; some came to consider the resistance a growing expression of the power of the populace.) was made by Arthur Schlesinger in 1912. "Maryland's contributions to the war, with one or two exceptions, were made contrary to the wishes of that body and in face of their opposition. Maryland's official participation in the conflict may be characterized as a barren expanse of military inactivity, brightened here and there by the exploits of Lieutenant Governor Sharpe, often at his own expense, and invariably in face of opposition of the Assembly." [209]

There were many reasons for Maryland's overall antipathy to supporting British efforts in addition to the ongoing disputes between the Assembly on one hand and the Governor and Proprietor on the other. Generally, the further south and east a colony's population centers were, the further they were from the danger of French and Indian incursions. This, in turn, lessened their desire to participate. Further, Maryland had some unique circumstances. Its western boundaries were agreed upon and settled, precluding land speculation further west. Those of Pennsylvania and Virginia were still fluid, with the former desiring to expand several hundred miles west of "The Forks" (Pittsburgh) and the latter claiming at least to the Mississippi to the west and the Great Lakes to the northwest.

The wide fighting on the frontiers of Virginia and Pennsylvania gave an unearned relative security to Maryland's narrow frontier and isolated settlements. Those colonies had wide land claims for which to fight and Maryland had few. The fact that trade focused largely in the east and that economic expansion meant the development of grain lands and trade from the Monocacy down to the Bay, rather than a deep penetration in the west, helps explain Maryland's limited enthusiasm and participation in the war. Marylanders asked the obvious question – "Why should we supply money and manpower to save territory for Virginia and Pennsylvania? If the French are a threat to those colonies, let them save their own land." [210]

Prior to Washington's expedition against the French in 1754, Governor Dinwiddie of Virginia had informed London of the necessity of violent action. He had also addressed letters to the other colonies, especially Pennsylvania and Maryland, which were most endangered, asking for their aid and cooperation. Governor Sharpe laid the situation before the Assembly, asking for substantial help, but was met by a dogged reluctance to vote money. He accounts for the legislators' general perverseness on the grounds that the shortness and frequency of sessions made gentlemen of means and standing shun the inconveniences of membership "by which means there are too many instances of the lowest persons, at least those of small fortunes, no soul and very mean capacities, appearing as representatives. He wrote that he had "met the Assembly on the 25th of March [1754] upon the Business that was mentioned in my Letter dated the 10th of Febr ..., but neither my utmost efforts of the example of the Virginians who had first then granted the sum of 10,000 pounds for that purpose could induce them to make the least Provision for the Encouragement of the Ohio Expedition." Another perspective is that it was part of the ongoing and widening rift between Marylanders and the royal government and Proprietor. The Delegates finally were willing to grant 6,000 pounds, with part raised by a tax on ordinary (inn) licenses. However, these were part of the Proprietor's direct revenue, which the Assembly knew when it passed the legislation. Sharpe, therefore, would not consent to that taxation, the bill failed and funds were not provided. [211]

1754 marked a speed up in the engine of war both in Virginia and in England. However, it was not matched in Maryland early in the year, as discussed above, or in other colonies. It was not until after Washington's defeat at Great Meadows that Maryland was awakened to the terrible dangers of frontier raids. Governor Sharpe called the Assembly into special session on July 17, 1754. The next day they were informed of Washington's defeat at Ft. Necessity. Washington's troops were still on Maryland soil. After much prodding by Sharpe, the Delegates proceeded to approve an appropriation of 6,000 pounds to "His Excellency, Horatio Sharpe, Esq., for his Majesty's use, towards the defense of the Colony of Virginia, in support of the Virginians in their Enterprise ... [who] were attacked by the French Indians; and for relief and support of the wives and children of Indian allies that put themselves under the protection of this government." Governor Sharpe immediately notified Governor Dinwiddie of the Assembly's actions.

In a letter to his brother John, Sharpe stated that on "the 17th of July I once more met our Assembly and apprising them of what happened pressed them to grant immediate Supplies for the Service. The Consternation that Washington's Defeat had occasioned inclined many of them to grant a Sum of Money at this time in any manner that the Govt should think proper but some of the Leading Patriots as they stile themselves contrived to insert some Clauses in the Bill which were by no means agreeable and which it was scarcely consonant with his Ldp's instructions for me to pass; However, I was prevailed upon by the Council to Accept the 6,000 pounds on the Terms it was offered but from late instruction that I have received I am a little apprehensive the Substance of the Bill is not acceptable to his Ldp." In a letter to Lord Baltimore, Sharpe complains that "the Incursions of the French on His Majesty's Dominions oblige me to push them on the disagreeable Business of granting money for that purpose at this time and it is too notorious that they always shew greater Backwardness in every last session to do anything generous, lest it should induce their Electors to reject them when they offer themselves Candidates at the ensuing Election." [212]

Another result of Washington's defeat at Ft. Necessity was the construction of a fort at Wills Creek. COL Innes, who commanded several companies of North Carolina troops, was ordered by Governor Dinwiddie to march to Wills Creek and erect a fort, which would serve as a rallying point and a defense for the frontiers. It was built by Rutherford's and Clarke's Independent companies of foot from New York, Demerie's Independent company from South Carolina, and the three Independent companies from North Carolina under COL Innes. They were assisted by a company from Maryland which arrived in November. The fort was ultimately named Cumberland in honor of the Duke of Cumberland, Captain-General of the British Army.[213]

Despite his dissatisfaction with the Assembly's reluctance to act in 1754, Governor Sharpe quickly took advantage of Maryland's war-like spirit. He issued a commission to CPT Thomas Cresap, late of Pennsylvania, to raise a company of 100 riflemen to operate beyond the Alleghany Mountains. They soon began to earn enviable reputations as Indian fighters. In August Sharpe directed that other companies be raised in eastern Maryland to be sent west to join the forces at Wills Creek. On August 15th the Maryland Gazette announced that "we are now raising recruits to go against the French on the Ohio." The privates were to receive eight pence a day, clothes, arms and accoutrements. They were to be armed with muskets, "slings, cartouch boxes, and bayonets." On September 23rd part of a company left Annapolis under the command of LT John Forty, on their way to Frederick. On September 30th another detachment headed in the same direction under John Bacon. CPT John Ross raised another company. They were all to serve under the command of one CPT John Dagworthy of Worcester County. Sharpe described Dagworthy to Charles

Calvert as "a gentleman born in the Jerseys who commanded a company raised in that province for the Canada expedition ..." Dagworthy was considered an officer with military experience. More importantly, he had been given a royal officer's commission while on that Canadian expedition. This would have serious repercussions in the future. Upon their arrival at Wills Creek they professed their willingness to join forces with the Virginia and North Carolina troops in an expedition against Ft. Duquesne. Maryland eventually contributed troops to General Braddock's expedition, but the exact number is unknown. [214]

As a result of new orders from England on the precedence given regular British officers over their provincial counterparts, George Washington was, in effect, reduced in rank from Colonel, albeit in Virginia's provincial military, to Captain; whereupon he resigned his commission. The Duke of Newcastle subsequently appointed Governor Sharpe as Commander-in-Chief of all British forces on the western frontier. Sharpe received his commission at Williamsburg and, with it, instructions to make his headquarters in Virginia. His deputy, COL Fitzhugh of Virginia, endeavored in vain to get Washington to resume his command. Despite these additional responsibilities, Sharpe's main concern continued to be the difficulties in convincing the Assembly to support the Maryland troops in the field. Eventually, he was replaced by Major General Braddock as Commander-in-Chief. The Crown opted for experience over enthusiasm. [215]

During his tenure as C-in-C, Sharpe traveled west to Wills Creek to inspect the ongoing construction of the fort. He brought a company of troops with him. He then returned to Annapolis, all the while supervising the vigorous preparations for the spring campaign. Military stores and ordinance were collected in Frederick, MD and Alexandria, VA. The militia were properly organized and disciplined. Finding the existing militia law defective, Sharpe convened the Assembly on December 24th. They passed a law for the levying of troops for the coming campaign against the French and Indians. As an inducement for men to enlist, they directed "that if any citizen be maimed in the service as to be incapable of maintaining himself, he should be supported at the Public expense." In an ensuing session, in February 1755, the Delegates regulated the rates of transportation of military stores and the mode of quartering within the province. They also prohibited any inhabitant from supplying the French or their Indian allies with stores, ammunition or provisions, levying severe penalties for any violations.

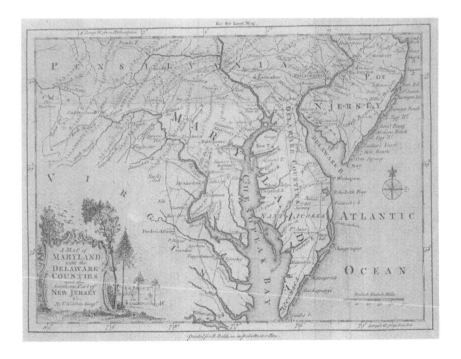

Governor Sharpe did not have difficulty in procuring volunteer soldiers. He had more applications than he could provide billets for. As noted in the <u>Maryland Gazette</u> of February 6, 1755, "We are assured that at Chestertown in Kent County, several men enlisted immediately on the arrival of the officer in that town, before the drum was beat, and that officer who wanted 30 men, got his compliment and marched with them.... They are gone to Wills Creek."

Despite the exuberance, Governor Sharpe was somewhat skeptical. In a letter to Lord Baltimore of January 12, 1755 he said: "As to levying a number of men, I conceive we will not find it difficult, ... but the difficulty will be to get money from the Assemblies to support them after they are raised; indeed this I look upon as impracticable, or not to be expected without the legislature of Great Britain shall make a law to be binding on all these several colonies, and oblige them to raise such a fund as may be thought expedient for the support of their own troops." Concerning Maryland's legislature, at least, he was prophetically accurate. [216]

Although Maryland was facing its first severe and extensive military threat the Assembly continued its ongoing dispute with the Proprietor and his government. They did, at least, authorize some troops to be called up. Some volunteer units were raised, notably at Ft. Garrison, where CPT John Ristou mobilized men of the Baltimore County militia in 1755. In July, 1755 the Assembly authorized 80 men to serve on the frontier for four months, a normal term of enlistment in those days for similar forays. The Bladensburg Independents were issued "55 new flintlocks, slings, cartouch boxes and bayonets." In September "the inhabitants of Baltimore" purchased "by subscription, a quantity of Carbines, Bayonets and Cartouch Boxes," which were preserved in a "Publick

Repository, for the Defense of that flourishing place" as reported in the <u>Boston Evening Post</u>, September 1, 1755. Some men were clearly preparing for duty, as 20 firelocks were issued to the Baltimore Volunteers in October. [217]

After Braddock's defeat and death on the Monongahela, his deputy, COL Dunbar, assumed command of the remnants. He withdrew to Maryland and kept on going, arriving at Philadelphia on August 1755, where he established "Winter Quarters" several months early. And there he sat, leaving Maryland and its neighbors in a precarious position. Lacking troops trained to the standards of regular soldiers, fortifications or military supplies, they were not prepared to withstand the onslaughts of the French and their Indian allies. Virginia reacted by ordering out the militia, raising three independent militia companies and reinforcing Ft. Cumberland, even though it was in Maryland.

As we have seen, Maryland's initial, in fact ongoing, response was more fragmented, less organized and, to some extent, less effective. Governor Sharpe had perceived the need for action well prior to receiving word of Braddock's defeat. However, his attempts at action had often been stymied, as we have seen, by the Lower House. The Assembly did respond to Sharpe's letter of June 28, 1755, outlining Indian attacks in the western areas and detailing the proclamations and instructions he had issued to deal with the attacks. He stated "[h]owever, I find neither the proclamation nor instructions will be effective unless the militia can be assured that they shall receive satisfaction and pay for the time they shall be on duty. I should consider it highly proper for us to have about a hundred, or at least a company of sixty men, posted or constantly ranging for some time on the frontiers, for our protection." He also asked for funds for couriers he had engaged to convey correspondence to and from Wills Creek. On the same day the House passed two resolutions stating that it would make "suitable provision" for maintaining eighty men, including officers, for four months on the frontier and to pay for the couriers. As we have seen, they funded the eighty men in July.

It was not very long before reports began to arrive from the frontier with accounts of horrible atrocities. At the same time, Governor Sharpe continued to struggle to get the Assembly to provide adequate funds for defense. He had limited success. They insisted that money raised for the protection of Maryland should come from the issuance of paper money, taxes on the Proprietor's estates, and taxes on licenses for haulers, peddlers and ordinaries. The Proprietor, on the other hand, wanted a tight lid on the amount of paper money issued and refused to sign bills which included taxes which he considered an invasion of his proprietary privileges. Meanwhile, the frontier was left unprotected.

As Thomas J. C. Williams stated in A History of Washington County, almost the first news of the defeat of Braddock western Frederick (now Washington) County valley residents received was the onslaught of Indians. They kept up steady warfare upon the settlements, scalping and burning and carrying white settlers into captivity, while being themselves hunted like beasts for more than a decade.

Forts on the frontier began proliferating at an astounding rate. In the Potomac watershed no less than twenty four forts and stockades of various descriptions were built or improved to stem the tide of Indian devastation along the Potomac and its tributaries. As the attacks became more frequent, the pleas for protection took on a quality of hysteria. All were aware of the many reports of atrocities coming from almost every frontier outpost.

Typical of these accounts are letters which appeared in the <u>Maryland Gazette</u>. "We are in the greatest distress here. Besides a shortage of our crops, we are full of people who have been obliged to leave their plantations to avoid falling into the hands of the savages. Last Friday the Indians killed three men in the gap to the mountains, and we have certain accounts that there is a large body of Indians who expect to fall on this settlement. This day we have an account that three or four persons have been killed by the savages near the State line." Also, "it is necessary to arm and fortify, for the French and Indians are making raids within 100 miles of Annapolis."

The alarm inspired by Braddock's defeat and the advance of the French and Indians was so great that many inhabitants of the western settlements fled to Baltimore. Preparations were even made to place the women and children on board vessels in the harbor and send them to Virginia. At an earlier period the inhabitants of Baltimore had erected a wooden stockade around the town as a defense against Indian attacks. None were ever made. The fence survived only a few years, succumbing to the need for fuel during an especially hard winter. The general terror level continued to increase. By September 1755 the country up to 30 miles east of Cresap's Fort at Old Town was virtually deserted. Sharpe estimated to Calvert "that all that part of Frederick County that lies beyond Frederick Town will be abandoned before this time twelvemonth at farthest."

In the fall the people of Baltimore raised money to purchase fire arms and ammunition, as well as establish a public armory. Upon receipt of what turned out to be an erroneous report of a large body of French and Indians approaching from Frederick in early November, several companies of volunteers in Baltimore and vicinity mustered and marched without delay. On November 6th, receiving a report that the French and Indians were within thirty miles, about two thousand volunteers assembled for defense. While the rumor proved to be unfounded, Baltimore did furnish men and supplies for the protection and support of the ravaged frontiers. By the spring of 1756 raids were occurring within thirty miles of Baltimore. In April 41 people abandoned their homes near Conococheague and came to Baltimore.

The increased activity of marauding Indians eventually compelled Governor Sharpe to protect Maryland's western borders. As he told Cecilius Calvert, he had assured the settlers that he "would take proper Measures to prevent the Inroads and Incursions of any French or Indian parties which I hope will be effectually done by the Small Forts that I have ordered to be built, one on Tonoloway Creek and three under North Mountain in each of which I shall place a small garrison with Orders to them to patrol from one to the other and to Fort Cumberland." Several blockhouses and stockades had already been started on the plantations of Allen Killough, Thomas Mills, Evan Shelby and Isaac Baker. At that time any private dwelling which served as a place of protection for a surrounding population took the name of "fort." Ft. Tonoloway, also called Stoddert's Fort, was located on the property of Evan Shelby in the vicinity of present day Hancock. It was one of the first small stockades built in western Maryland. Sharpe, in a letter to Cecilius Calvert, mentions that Lieutenant Stoddert and 15 men have built a "Staccado Fort" on his orders at North Mountain. [218]

As soon as the news of Braddock's defeat reached Annapolis, Sharpe set out for Ft. Cumberland via Bladensburg, Frederick and Conococheague Creek. As he wrote Lord Baltimore, "I was on my way to Fort Cumberland with a number of gentleman volunteers who had entered into an association to bear arms and protect our frontiers ... I shall now halt a little and expend a sum of money (which the Council and the gentlemen of the country had subscribed upon the Assembly's refusal at their last meeting to grant any supplies) in purchasing a quantity of fresh provisions and such things as I think necessary for the troops, and then escort them with such men as I can persuade to join men at Fort Cumberland." He departed westward on July 17th at the head of his hastily assembled troops, apparently after the Assembly session. As he told Lord Baltimore, volunteer subscriptions were opened to defray their expense because of the Assembly's refusal to provide funds. Annapolis and the immediately surrounding area raised one thousand pounds. The militia was called up, and, in October, was relieved by a force of volunteers raised to meet the emergency.

Such was the effect of the panic caused by marauding Indian bands on the militia that when MAJ Prather tried to assemble them on the frontier for the purpose of pursuing one of the hostile bands he found it impossible to do so. Each man dreaded to leave his own house unprotected lest, in his absence, his family should fall prey to the enemy. These problems were not exclusive to Maryland. For this and other reasons Virginia had trouble mobilizing its militia at this time also. However, Maryland was not completely unresponsive. From the lower part of Frederick County (now primarily Montgomery County), which was generally secure from attacks, 30 volunteers under CPT Alexander Beall and LT Magruther, joined by 30 men under COL Ridgely from Anne Arundel County and 60 men from Prince George's County traveling at their own expense, and several from Frederick

Town itself, hastened to the site of the attacks. They arrived too late to punish the Indians and could only remain to protect the survivors from further assaults. [219]

In August 1755 Governor Sharpe reported to Lord Baltimore that he had ordered small forts to be built at proper distances from one another in the western portion of Frederick County (present day Washington County) and that each fort was garrisoned with "a few men" who were ordered to patrol between the places, as he had also pointed out to Cecilius Calvert. On October 24th Calvert wrote advising Sharpe that Lord Baltimore approved of the plan for Tonoloway Creek and hoped that the Assembly would appropriate the necessary funds so that the three forts planned for North Mountain might be built. The plan to garrison each fort was also approved by the Proprietor.

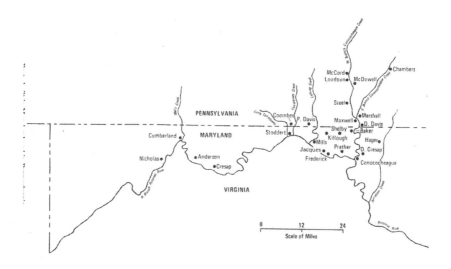

The defenses built by the settlers on the frontier, and by the military in the Potomac River Valley, regardless of style or type, were all known as forts, the terms embracing stockades, block houses, forts, stations, posts, log cabins, stone houses, cellars and, in fact, any and all positions or buildings that could be strengthened and fortified so as to offer protection from enemy attack. The military authorities in Maryland, Virginia and Pennsylvania generally only constructed forts or stockades, as these installations furnished the greatest protection to the largest number of people in a given region. The settlers usually erected stockades or blockhouses, but they were not adverse to the use of any other position that might furnish a haven in time of danger.

Of all of the various defensive structures constructed on the frontier, the fort was the strongest. It was built by the armed forces (militia and/or regulars) according to plans formulated over many years by leading military engineers. It usually consisted of a double outer wall made of heavy palisades closely fitted together. The space between the two perimeter walls was then filled with dirt, gravel and stone, making a solid, bullet-proof obstruction. If the nature of the ground allowed, the fort was generally surrounded by a deep ditch, with a rampart and parapet. It was usually square in form with diamond shaped bastions at each corner. Some had redoubts and all had sally ports. The former is a breastwork (a low wall put up quickly as a defense in battle) outside the fortification to defend approaches; the latter, a gate or opening to allow defenders to rush out (sally) and attack besiegers. Sometimes the outer wall was constructed of stone, like Ft. Frederick. All of the forts were defended by artillery, consisting of howitzers, from four to eighteen pounder cannon (the weight of the ball), and several guns capable of firing clusters of lead balls (grape shot), comparable to a musket firing buckshot, only significantly larger balls.

A fort was a staunch position and, if resolutely defended, could only be taken by a strong force with artillery. Cumberland, Frederick and the two Loudons (one in Winchester, VA and one on the West Branch of the Conococheague in Pennsylvania) were the only true forts erected in the Potomac River Basin during the Indian wars period. Benjamin Chamber's home in Pennsylvania (Chambersburg) was so strong that it nearly attained the status of a fort. Because it was built of stone, Ft. Frederick was considered the strongest position in the Potomac Basin.

Within a fort, barracks were constructed capable of housing, in some instances, up to five hundred men. Store houses, stables and other structures were erected as needed. A well was sunk within the enclosure to furnish a constant supply of water. There was also room for a parade ground, officers' quarters and, sometimes, cabins to house settlers who might be gathered in the place during dangerous times. Cumberland and Frederick each enclosed approximately one and one-half acres.

The stockade was the most common defense. It was favored by both the settlers and the military and had been since the landing at Jamestown. It consisted of a square or rectangular wall made of upright logs called palisades, which were planted in a trench three to four feet deep. The logs extended from twelve to eighteen feet above the ground and sometimes enclosed as much as one acre of land. The palisades were generally shaved to a sharp point on top to make any attempt to climb over them uncomfortable and hazardous. A cat walk was constructed on the inside of the wall four to five feet below the crest to permit riflemen to fire over the stockade or through loopholes at any point on the perimeter. Within the enclosure barracks, storehouses, cabins, stable and other structures were built for the use of the garrison and any settlers who had congregated there. Two to four blockhouses, sometimes called bastions, were built at the corners of the stockade. Their purpose was to provide the defenders an opportunity to shoot at any enemy that might have gained a position close to the stockade walls. The corner blockhouses were two stories high, the upper story projecting about two feet beyond the palisades, enabling the garrison to fire along the outer wall. The stockade had the added advantage of offering a haven for the settlers' livestock when the Indians were about. In rare cases artillery was mounted in and around the stockade. [220]

Conococheague, located in the vicinity of present day Williamsport, MD, at the mouth of the Conococheague Creek, was the easternmost anchor of a line of defensive positions established for the protection of Maryland's and Virginia's frontiers. The fortifications then extended in a line westward up the Potomac for nearly one hundred miles. Across the Potomac, Virginia established Ft. Maidstone. Conococheague and Maidstone both operated as supply depots; both were generally referred to as Conococheague by both Marylanders and Virginians; and both were located on the Great Warrior Trail, running from New York, through Pennsylvania, across Maryland and up the Shenandoah Valley (generally south - southwest) to western Carolina, eastern Tennessee and northeastern Georgia. Ft. Conococheague became a supply depot for General Braddock. Flour and other materials, primarily obtained in Pennsylvania, were moved there preparatory to being ferried up the Potomac. When that proved unfeasible, the supplies were moved to Wills Creek by wagon and pack animals. There was a ford over the Potomac which was used extensively by British and

American forces. Over 100 years later General Robert E. Lee used the ford when moving in and out of Maryland, to include in June 1863, prior to Gettysburg.

Maryland maintained a military base at Conococheague throughout the entire period of Indian trouble. At Governor Sharpe's direction, a stockade was constructed and CPT John Dagworthy was placed in command. Initially the Assembly would not vote for troops and supplies. The Governor had to raise funds through public subscriptions. Eventually, however, the Assembly began to cooperate. Conococheague soon became an important supply base for the troops being sent west to Forts Frederick and Cumberland. [221]

Ft. Cresap was a stockade surrounding the house of COL Thomas Cresap at Old Town, in present day Allegany County. It was on the north bank of the North Branch of the Potomac, at or near where the Shawnee Trail crossed the Potomac. It was also on the New Road, leading from Winchester to Wills Creek. As such, it was well located to do business with the various Indian tribes moving through the area and the white settlers moving west. It had been built several years before the outbreak of the hostilities that became the SY/FI War, because it was in existence when Braddock's army came through in March, 1755.

Although never a public fort, it provided protection for the inhabitants of the area from the numerous Indian raids and attacks that went on during the war. At times Governor Sharpe ordered troops to be stationed there. In early October 1755 the fort was besieged by a French and Indian force and COL Cresap requested that troops be assigned to the area. On November 22, 1755 60 militiamen were stationed there for several weeks. It also served as a depot/stopping point during Forbes' expedition in 1758. [222]

Ft. Cumberland was located near the point where Wills Creek flows into the Potomac River at present day Cumberland, MD. Its site was selected by Governor Sharpe, while its initial construction was directed by Governor Dinwiddie operating under the authority of the British government. The fort was situated on Walnut Bottom, a site surveyed by COL Cresap in 1745. Although in Maryland, the fort was considered a King's establishment, a source of later contention between Maryland and Virginia. At different times of its existence, it was garrisoned with different combinations of troops from Virginia, Maryland, New York, North Carolina, South Carolina and even British regulars.

It began as a magazine or storehouse built by Christopher Gist on the west bank of Wills Creek for the Ohio Company in 1750. It was located in the "Cumberland Narrows," regarded as the front door of the Allegany Mountains. Its strategic location made it useful as a base of operations against the French in the Ohio Valley. The Ohio Company reportedly stocked the first store with 4,000 pounds worth of goods to be traded. Wills Creek received its name from a friendly Indian who lived near the future site of the fort. In 1752 the Ohio Company, whose stockholders, as we have seen, were primarily upper-class Virginians, built another trading post in Virginia, across the Potomac from the mouth of Wills creek. Joined by another building and then both being converted into blockhouses, it became known as Ft. Ohio or New Store.

On September 1, 1754, after Washington's defeat at Great Meadows in July 1754, Governor Dinwiddie appointed COL James Innes as commander at Wills Creek. He directed Innes to build a fort to be used by the British Army. Innes had companies from New York, North and South Carolina and Maryland. He used them to begin construction in mid-September. The new fort was completed in mid-October. The stockade was 20 feet square, situated near the foot of "Fort Hill," in the vicinity of the first storehouse. Innes named it Mount Pleasant. Barracks were completed by Christmas.

Governor Sharpe, recently made a Lieutenant Colonel in the Royal Army and appointed Commander-in-Chief of colonial troops in America, arrived to inspect the fort in late November. Based on his previous military experience, he determined that the new fort was too small for its potential future missions. He ordered that another fort be constructed, adjacent to the original stockade on a nearby ridge. He directed the assembly of materials to begin construction. Governor Dinwiddie, meanwhile, had received instructions from London. While the initial efforts were ongoing to comply with Sharpe's directions, Innes received new orders from Dinwiddie, implementing the King's instructions. Innes was to build a fort at Wills Creek of sufficient size to be used as a base of operations in the upcoming struggle against the French in the Ohio country. Using the site Sharpe selected, Innes completed construction and the fort was ready for occupancy in the spring of 1755. It was completed in time to be used by Braddock's forces as they passed through. At General Braddock's suggestion, the fort was renamed for his mentor, the Duke of Cumberland, Captain-General of the British Army.

Ft. Cumberland's stockade was 400 feet long and 160 feet wide, enclosing about 1 ½ acres. It was a palisade work, except the bastions at the corners. The palisades were eighteen feet long, planted in the ground to the depth of six feet, held together with strips and pinned on the inner side. The walls were pierced for muskets. There were also embrasures for large guns, stocks for swivels and loop holes for small arms. There were four cannon on each bastion. At the west end of the stockade a fort was constructed with bastions, ditches and parapets. It was a smaller version of the soon to be constructed Ft. Frederick on the Potomac and Ft. Loudon in Winchester.

There were enough barracks to house a garrison of about two hundred men. Housing included a dwelling for the commander, five smaller officers' quarters, and four store houses for provisions. There were also barracks, a commissary and a hospital. The water supply was initially secured by digging trenches from the eastern end of the stockade to Wills Creek. After Braddock's defeat it was considered too dangerous to get water from the creek. Also, there was the possibility that the flow from the Creek through the trenches could be cut off. To alleviate the problem, an eighty foot well was sunk in the fort.

FORT CUMBERLAND 1755.

Ft. Cumberland became a gathering point for scouting partied sent out to probe Ft. Duquesne, as well as an assembly point for the Virginia troops joining the Forbes expedition, subsequently moving north into Pennsylvania to meet him. It was ineffective as a protection for settlers living along the North Branch of the Potomac and contiguous areas because the garrison was never large enough or strong enough to defend the fort and the settlers at the same time. Being on the Braddock Road to Ft. Duquesne, the enemy was almost continuously around or about it. However, the fort never had to withstand a siege and it was never in any real danger of being taken by the enemy. Washington used Ft. Cumberland as his headquarters only infrequently, as he appeared to prefer Ft. Loudon as a place from which to direct the war effort on the Virginia frontier. His stays were rare and generally of short duration. However, important councils of war were held there and decisions were made that affected the frontier as far south as North Carolina. The two primary places from which the war in Maryland and Virginia was directed were Forts Cumberland and Loudon. Washington subsequently recommended that Cumberland be abandoned, but it was manned until 1766.

More troops were assembled in the vicinity of Ft. Cumberland at various times than any other place on the Maryland/Virginia frontier; and more events relating to the Indian War occurred there. In 1753 Washington had stopped at Wills Creek, hiring guides for his trip to Ohio. In 1754 Washington's troops, as well as those of CPT Mackay and LTC Joshua Fry, concentrated there during the campaign that resulted in Washington's defeat at Ft. Necessity. In 1755 General Braddock led nearly 2,100 troops through the area enroute to his defeat at the Monongahela, suggesting the new name as he passed through. In 1758 Washington assembled nearly 1,000 men at Ft. Cumberland preparatory to joining

General Forbes in his campaign against Ft. Duquesne. In 1763 COL Adam Stephens led 400 men to Wills Creek to be in position to aid COL Bouquet in his attack on the Indians besieging St. Pitt (nee Duquesne).

In 1755, after Braddock's defeat on the Monongahela, Washington was appointed commander of Virginia's forces with the rank of Colonel. He set up his headquarters in Winchester and appointed Adam Stephens (Stephenson) as Lieutenant Colonel, serving in the other major post in his command, Ft. Cumberland. Even though it was in Maryland, Virginia contended that it was a "King's Fort" and that command and control of the fort and the area was not a cut and dried question. Specifically, Virginia contended that it was theirs to command and proceeded to do so. Governor Sharpe, in the meantime, assigned a company of 30 troops under the command of CPT John Dagworthy to the fort.

When COL Innes departed on personal leave to North Carolina in November 1755, he turned command over to Stephens, who commanded into 1756. Stephens was accountable to Washington, a Virginian. CPT Dagworthy was still there. As previously noted, he had been given a British Army commission of some type (the exact type he received is vague, but it was not a traditional commission) while serving with New Jersey militia troops in support of an expedition against the French and Indians in New York. He claimed that his commission was still valid. He further claimed that under the British Army rules of precedence existing at that time a British Army commission gave him seniority over any officer whose commission had been issued by a colonial government. He insisted that it gave him rank over all other provincial officers, including COL Washington. Dagworthy's claims caused much hard feeling and concern among the Virginia officers, as well as confusion as to who could give orders to whom. The conflict caused significant morale problems, including refusals to share supplies, and affected the operations of the fort. It would take a major effort on Washington's part to clear up the confusion. [223]

Ft. Shelby was in Upper Frederick (now Washington) County, three miles south of Pennsylvania, seven miles north of Conococheague (Williamsport). It was situated on a grant of 1,000 acres conveyed to Evan Shelby by the governor in August 1739. It was on, or near, the road constructed in 1755 between Conococheague and Ft. Frederick. In early 1756 Governor Sharpe made Shelby a Lieutenant in the militia and instructed him to raise twenty men. On March 6th the Assembly authorized the governor to use public money for activities during the period March 4 to May 20, 1756, in effect paying for Shelby's actions among others. By 1758 Shelby was a Captain of Volunteers in Forbes' army. The fort consisted of a strong log structure where Shelby, an Indian trader, stored his goods, and which he later fortified. It burned in 1763. [224]

Ft. Frederick, named for Frederick Calvert, sixth Lord Baltimore and Proprietor of Maryland, was one of the largest and most elaborate of all of the defenses constructed by the American colonists and the English government any place in North America during the SY/FI War. Immediately after Braddock's defeat Governor Sharpe petitioned the Assembly for funds for the construction of forts and blockhouses along the Upper Potomac, as we have already seen. On March 27, 1756 the Assembly appropriated 40,000 pounds for the defense of the colony, eleven thousand of which were to be used for the erection of a strong fort and several smaller blockhouses (stockades) along the Potomac, and for the costs of maintaining a body of troops to garrison the fortifications.

On August 9, 1756 Sharpe purchased 150 acres on North (Fairview) Mountain, overlooking the Potomac and equidistant from Conococheague and present day Hancock. The largest single portion of the site, 56 acres, had been purchased from Lancelot Jacques, a French Huguenot merchant in Annapolis. Jacques had been granted, for practically nothing, an immense tract of fifteen thousand acres. To this were added other parcels which made up the total which were connected with the fort's operation. Sharpe directed construction to begin before the actual date of the deed transmitting the land to Maryland, August 29th. At his direction it was built of stone to preclude the French or Indians from burning it. It was situated on a hill overlooking the Potomac, about 100 feet above it and about 500 yards away. In the present day it is difficult to ascertain the significance of the fort's location. In the intervening years the Chesapeake and Ohio Canal was constructed running through the land between the fort and the Potomac. Further, foliage has grown up inhibiting the sight lines and limiting the potential effectiveness of direct fire weapons, which would have been used in the seventeenth century. This, in turn, makes it difficult to determine the fort's effectiveness in controlling traffic on the Potomac, one of its primary purposes for being sited where it was.

Governor Sharpe informed Lord Baltimore, in a letter dated August 20, 1756, that the French and Indians had burned Ft. Granville in Pennsylvania. He further stated that his decision to build Ft. Frederick of stone was justified, despite the additional cost, in view of the stark reality that wooden forts could not easily withstand the onslaughts of the French and Indians. He wrote that "the accident has a great deal alarmed the Inhabitants of Pennsylvania while it makes our people see the expediency of my building Fort Frederick of Stone, which alone (tho it is expensive) is the only one that can secure a Garrison against the Savages conducted by European officers as it certain these Indian parties are."

Sharpe was serious about the speedy construction of the fort. Soon after the original six thousand pounds was appropriated in May, 1756, he informed Governor Dinwiddie that he was "… about to proceed to the North Mountain which is our extreme limit, to put our frontiers also in a better posture of defense and to have a fort constructed there, agreed to by an act of the assembly. My presence there will, I apprehend, be absolutely necessary until the work is pretty far advanced." The Governor's continued support is evidenced by the fact the he remained at the site and personally supervised construction until the end of July 1756. The fort was not completed by early fall, as noted by Sharpe when he reported to Dinwiddie on October 10th that the Assembly had just approved an appropriation on money to finish the work and recruit another one hundred men for the garrison. However, by late autumn 1756 construction was far enough along to allow troops to be stationed there. Thereafter it was manned by Maryland militia during much of the course of the war. It provided refuge in time of Indian raids, not only for Maryland settlers, but also for many Virginians living on Back and Sleep Creeks in what is now West Virginia. The fort is located midway between the mouths of those streams on the Maryland side.

Following the style of designs developed by renowned French military engineer Sebastian de Vauban, the stone that constituted the outer wall was impregnable to small arms and all but the heaviest cannon. The perimeter wall was about 1660 feet in length. Its limestone walls average 17 ½ feet in height, with a thickness that tapered from 4 ½ feet to 3 feet. It enclosed 1 ½ acres. At each corner was a bastion filled with dirt which would allow for the positioning of cannon. Two six pound cannon, so called because of the weight of the cannon balls, were mounted in two of the bastions. Cat walks were constructed to allow the troops to see and fire over the walls at any intruders. The single portal in the south wall was twelve feet wide. Facing the Potomac River some five hundred yards away, the gates were so cumbersome that they required hinges weighing forty-two pounds each to make them serviceable. There was at least one well within the fort, possibly more. There were originally two double story barracks within the walls which were intended to house two hundred troops. There was another building used as officers' quarters.

Ft. Frederick was manned at different times by a variety of forces. Over time there were a number of different British regiments stationed there. The one which saw the most service was the 60th Regiment of Foot (The Royal Americans/ Royal Rangers) whose troops were recruited primarily from the many German-Americans already living in the area in Virginia and Maryland. Next were Maryland Forces or Provincial regulars (Maryland State Troops) and then volunteers from the state militia. The latter were only used for temporary periods in case of emergencies. After the crisis or need subsided they were released to return to their homes. Each company of Maryland Troops or militia was authorized one Captain, two Lieutenants, one Ensign, four Sergeants, four Corporals, one drummer and 88 privates. The original Maryland Troops commander was now COL John Dagworthy. Dagworthy's company served from October 9, 1757 to April; 26, 1779; as did those of CPT's Alexander Beall (lower Frederick [Montgomery] County, Joshua Beall, Francis Ware (Charles County) and Richard Pearis. Rezin Beall served as an Ensign and then Second Lieutenant in Ware's Company.

While the newly arrived units started out in colorful uniforms, life on the frontier brought about attrition and adaptation forced by the realities they faced. Pictures of various units display a remarkable lack of uniformity in military attire. Frontier garb of necessity became functional. The most distinctive frontier garment to emerge in eighteenth century America was the fringed hunting shirt. It became a uniquely American military garment during the SY/FI War and, later, during the Revolutionary War. The hunting shirt was an outer garment, usually made of cotton or linen, but occasionally of leather. It was an adaptation of the loose farmer's smock that had been commonly worn in Europe since the Middle Ages.

In May 1757 Ft. Frederick was the site of the signing of a treaty with a group of Cherokees who had decided to ally with the British against the French. In 1758 it was an assembly point in the area for troops and supplies needed to capture Ft. Duquesne (Forbes' expedition). Governor Sharpe, George Washington and Thomas Cresap, among others, were there while COL Dagworthy trained the Maryland contingent. Ft. Frederick never came under sustained attack during the war. Once it took fire from hostile Indians, but it had no significant effect. After the conquest of Ft. Duquesne the need for the fort declined. In December 1762 the property was leased. The land was finally sold by the state in 1792.

Ft. Frederick was an important haven for settlers and a staging area for Maryland troops being sent west. Since there was no wagon road on the Maryland side of the Potomac connecting Forts Frederick and Cumberland in the early years of the war, soldiers with wheeled vehicles were required to cross into Virginia to reach the Braddock Road. They would go west to a small stockade in the vicinity of the mouth of

Tonoloway Creek, Ft. Stoddert or Tonoloway (Hancock). The route wound through present day West Virginia until recrossing the Potomac back into Maryland at Old Town (Ft. Cresap) and hence to Ft. Cumberland on Wills Creek, a distance of eighty-one miles. The straight line distance was forty miles, but impassable for wheeled vehicles. The longer route was faster.

The need for a road on the Maryland side became obvious. However, it was not until July 1758 that COL Bouquet directed Washington, then at Ft. Cumberland, to have three hundred men, including all of the Maryland troops under his command, begin cutting a road already blazed eastward towards Ft. Frederick. They were to continue until they joined the five hundred men coming westward from Ft. Frederick. However, construction quickly halted and in December, 1758 the Assembly appointed a Commission that included COL Cresap, to study the project. The Commission reported that a road could easily be built between Forts Frederick and Cumberland, covering a distance of sixty-two miles for about 250 pounds. It was completed in 1759 and then used by traffic to and from Conococheague, Ft. Frederick and Ft. Cumberland. [225]

As noted above, John Dagworthy of Maryland was originally from the Jerseys (New Jersey). Serving with the militia from there in support of expeditions against the French and Indians in New York he was given some type of royal appointment which equated to a British Army commission. Ordered to Wills Creek by Governor Sharpe, he arrived with a contingent of 30 men and took command of the Maryland levies. When he had entered Maryland's service he still laid claim to precedence of rank under his old commission. Emanating from the King, under existing regulations of the day governing the relationship of the British army officers with Provincial officers, a royal commission in the British army was considered to confer superiority over all colonial commissions, regardless of rank.

Shortly after Dagworthy's arrival the commander, COL James Innes, needed to return home on personal business. He designated LTC Adam Stephens as his replacement as commander. At this point Dagworthy asserted his right of precedence over the other colonial officers at Ft. Cumberland, challenging Stephen's right to command. He was supported by Governor Sharpe, who claimed the post as a Maryland fort and subject to his jurisdiction. Governor Dinwiddie claimed that it was a King's fort, built at Crown direction, and that Dagworthy could not outrank the officers of the Virginia regiment. General Braddock, when he was passing through enroute to the Monongahela, decided in favor of Dagworthy, and there the matter rested.

On Braddock's death the dispute was revived. The conflict simmered on, with a negative effect on the garrison's morale. Stephens of the Virginia forces was ordered to ensure that none of the provisions sent to Ft. Cumberland by Virginia were distributed to the Maryland or Carolina troops. Dagworthy refused to permit any interference in his command. He even claimed to outrank COL Washington, commander of the Virginia Regiment and overall commander of the combined colonial effort on the Maryland/Virginia frontiers.

Finally, at the direction of Governor Dinwiddie, Washington took a leave of absence and traveled to Boston in February 1756 to see Governor and Major General William Shirley of Massachusetts, successor to Braddock as Commander-in-Chief of British forces in North America, to get the dispute resolved. Washington carried a letter from Dinwiddie that said, in part, "This Fort was built by virtue of His Majesty's instructions to me … It's true that it happens to be in Maryland, but I presume His Majesty had a right to build a Fort where he pleases in any of his colonies; and the guns mounted are guns sent by His Majesty for service in Virginia; it cannot reasonably be suggested that His Majesty intended them for the Proprietary of Maryland."

In March, 1756 Shirley issued an order definitively settling the ranks of the various claimants. Dagworthy was reduced to a Provincial Captain, holding a commission from the Governor of Maryland, subordinate to all colonial field grade officers. Washington was given command of Ft. Cumberland. In a letter to Governor Sharpe, Shirley said "I would be extremely unwilling to do anything that might appear in the least disagreeable to any gentlemen who had the honor of bearing His Majesty's Commission … . But as the Command … from his Majesty obliges me upon all occasions to act for the best of his service, I must desire that Capt. Dagworthy may be removed from Fort Cumberland; or acquainted that if he remains there, he must put himself under the command of Col. Washington." Sharpe moved Dagworthy, putting him in command of the newly completed Ft. Frederick. [226]

Governor Sharpe authorized Major Prather to organize all of the forces on the frontiers, except those at Ft. Cumberland, and to operate between the Potomac and the Pennsylvania line. While experiencing difficulties in raising a force due to the reluctance of potential members to leave their families and homesteads unguarded, by March 11th Prather had under his command one hundred and fifty backwoodsmen skilled in fighting. CPT Alexander Beall of Lower Frederick (Montgomery) County, commanding a company of volunteers, was also authorized to raise a force of one hundred men and join MAJ Prather. [227]

Indian raids continued through the first half of 1756 on the Maryland frontier, reaching as far east as Emmitsburg, 20 miles north of Frederick. However, the several bands of Indian fighters that had been raised were fighting and raiding with varying degrees of success. Among the most successful was COL Thomas Cresap, whose home, as we have seen, was almost as far west as Ft. Cumberland. However, even his success was relative. Writing in August 1756, Washington said that the "whole settlement of Conococheague (on the east bank of the creek of the same name, roughly at its confluence with the Potomac) in Maryland has fled and there remains only two families from thence to Fredericktown." [228]

In early 1756 Governor Sharpe had appointed Isaac Baker a Lieutenant of militia with instructions to raise a body of twenty men for the protection of the inhabitants of the frontier. In a March 1756 message to the Assembly Sharpe confirmed this, saying "I ... gave Lieutenants Baker and Shelby Commissions and Instructions to raise each of them a Party of Twenty Men for the Protection of such Inhabitants, till I could recommend their deplorable case to your Consideration, and until more effective Measures could be taken for their Preservation." The Assembly authorized five hundred pounds to support Baker's troops and also those of Evan Shelby. Baker was paid 218 pounds 19 shillings for pay and provisions for his troops for the period February to May 20, 1756.

Troops were stationed at Ft. Baker from time to time and military stores were often stored there. On February 9th muskets, powder, musket balls and lead were delivered to the fort by order of the Governor. On August 18th the Indians attacked settlers in Baker's vicinity, killing two. They were pursued by a detachment of thirteen militiamen led by LT Luke Thompson. The pursuit yielded inconclusive results, except for rescuing a previously captured settler. On August 23rd COL Hall, in command of the Baltimore County militia, was ordered to send an officer and 30 men to Ft. Frederick to join two other parties of militia. They were to go by way of Ft. Baker, receiving supplies either from there or at Ft. Frederick. In April, 1758 a company of militia from Queen Anne's County was ordered stationed at Baker's. This unit "remained on the frontier for a considerable time." [229]

Only twice during the entire course of the SY/FI War could the Assembly be brought to pass tax laws for His Majesty's service. Both were enacted in the early years of the war, and resulted from fear caused by military defeat so near as to place Maryland in danger. The Assembly refused to make any contribution to COL Washington's 1754 expedition, which departed from Wills Creek. After his surrender at Ft. Necessity, as we have seen, the Assembly quickly passed a bill raising 6,000 pounds for the defense of the Province. The Governor signed it, even though the appropriation of certain fees violated his instructions from the Lord Proprietor.

Braddock's defeat and the subsequent withdrawal of his surviving regular troops to Philadelphia left Maryland and its adjoining colonies open to imminent attacks from the French and Indians. This impelled a second tax law, passed in the spring of 1756. When exactly is open to question. James McSherry, in 1904, and William Ansel, in 1984 (using McSherry?), stated that it was passed on March 22, 1756. Alan Powell, in 1998, contended that the Assembly haggled with the Governor and Council from early March until May. Regardless, the legislation that was finally passed provided for raising 40,000 pounds. It was the strongest Maryland action during the war. However, even under the desperate conditions of 1756, when the people of the back country were being killed and driven from their farms, the Assembly almost balked. Governor Shirley of Massachusetts, North American Commander-in-Chief, had ordered recruiting officers for regular units to enlist indentured servants without regard as to whether or not their masters gave their consent. This caused serious resentment in Maryland. Though the Assembly did not take action to prevent this type of recruiting, it threatened to. It did lead to the jailing of the recruiting officer and to a minor quarrel of jurisdiction between Crown and Proprietary officials.

The forty thousand pounds included twenty-five reserved for a proposed joint expedition planned against Ft. Duquesne. It also included eleven thousand pounds for the erection of a large fort and several other forts/stockades/blockhouses (Ft. Frederick, et. al.). Further, it was also to be used for levying, arming, paying and maintaining a body of troops, not to exceed two hundred men. They were to "Garrison this Fort and raise on the Frontier two companies of 100 men; each are to be raised and kept up until next February." The men raised were to be armed, provisioned, and, a new feature, clothed by the province, while being required to serve until February 1757. [230]

Ft. Cumberland, lying nearly sixty miles beyond the Maryland frontier, although within Maryland's boundaries, was found to afford no protection from the Indians. The settlers had been compelled to fortify their homes, erecting stockades and blockhouses on the verge of settlements as places of refuge and security in case of sudden danger. To remedy this defect, Sharpe determined to build a fort within the vicinity of the then existing frontier to provide both a place for troops to work from when patrolling the area and as a refuge for settlers under threat of attack. He wanted it to be a stone fort because there were reports from Pennsylvania that wooden forts were being burned by attacking Indians. As previously discussed, he selected a site on North Mountain, overlooking the Potomac River west of Conococheague, on the creek of the same name, and the location of present day Williamsport. He purchased one hundred and fifty acres of land and initiated construction with a planned capacity of three hundred troops

In June 1756 Sharpe traveled to then western Maryland to expedite construction on the new Ft. Frederick. He reported "[t]his journey of mine I think the more necessary as Engineers or persons of Military Experience and Skill are not to be found in this part of the world as Ft. Cumberland and the little places of defense that have been built in the two neighboring counties are by no means such as I would have built on the Frontier of this Province." He returned to Annapolis by August 16th. The fortifications were far enough along to accommodate troops in August 1756, according to McSherry, and in early 1757 per Powell. The recently promoted COL Dagworthy commanded the first garrison of two hundred men. [231]

In August 1756 Governor Sharpe issued recruiting instructions for the Maryland Forces, the province's "regular" militia. "You are not to enlist any Roman Catholics or Dissenters, knowing them to be such ... You are not to enlist any Persons that are ill-limbed, sick weak, pot bellied, or who have any aliments, particularly such as have their Legs Frostbitten; but you may enlist any other Man between 18 and 40 years of age, if he is not less than 5 Feet 7 Inches High [This was generally ignored. The average height of the soldiers was 5'6".]. You may also enlist any lad under 18 years of age, if he be 5 Feet 4 Inches high, or upwards … You are to endeavor to Recruit as Cheap and on as good Terms as you possibly can; but you are, on no Account whatever, to give to, or expend more, on one Man, than Five Pounds Currency." [232] Also in August, on the 30th, Sharpe ordered a company of militiamen from Prince George's County and Baltimore to Ft. Frederick for one month's service. They departed in late October, "well equipped" and at their own expense. [233]

Ft. Baker, west of Hager's Fort (Hagerstown) on the west bank near Conococheague Creek, on Baker's Ridge, was eleven miles east and north of the site of the future Ft. Frederick. It was built and named for Isaac Baker, an Indian scout operating in western Maryland during the early days of the war on the frontier. As noted, Baker had been made a Lieutenant in the militia early in 1756 by Governor Sharpe and eventually provided funds to pay for the men he had recruited.

Baker's garrison was not included among the defenses ordered built by the Governor, so it appears to have been in existence before the order was issued. On September 21, 1756 Sharpe reported to the Lower House that several blockhouses and stockades had been built on or near North Mountain (Ft. Frederick was built on the southern lower slope of the mountain.), particularly on the "plantations" of Allen Killough, Thomas Mills, Evan Shelby and Isaac Baker. He further stated that these places had been constructed before he had made his first trip to the frontier. If he meant his trip to Wills Creek, they could have existed as early as mid-1754, but no later than mid-1755.

On October 27, 1757, Baker acknowledged receipt of the sum of twenty pounds paid him by Governor Sharpe "out of subscription money as a reward for building a log fort on a hill near my house for the security of the neighborhood." On September 29, 1761, he received from the Governor, on behalf of the Proprietor, a deed to 200 acres on a tributary of Conococheague Creek. He occupied the land for several years before the grant and it was on this land that the fort had probably been constructed. [234]

The neighboring colonies having failed to cooperate with Maryland in the proposed joint expedition on Ft. Duquesne, and the season for any such attempt having passed, the legislature convened again in September 1756 for the purpose of reallocating the previously reserved 25,000 pounds for other purposes. Five thousand pounds were appropriated to raising and maintaining men for the Royal American (60th) Regiment and to furnish a supply of wheat for troops in New York under Lord Loudon, the new Commander-in-Chief. Three thousand five hundred pounds were designated for forming a company of one hundred men to serve until April 1757 and to be incorporated into the battalion at Ft. Frederick under COL Dagworthy. One third of this force was required to be constantly on duty on the frontier as rangers for the protection of the settlers. To increase their activity, as well as their pay, each soldier who took a scalp or a prisoner was allowed a bounty of thirty pounds. Additional appropriations were made toward completing Ft. Frederick, for purchasing arms and ammunition and erecting a magazine. Further, the Governor was reimbursed the expense of maintaining the rangers, whom he had employed on the frontier the preceding spring. [235]

In October 1756 another company of 100 men was added to the troop strength, to serve until April 1757. In February 1757 the two companies originally authorized in May 1756, and serving at Ft. Frederick, were ordered kept in service until April of that year. On April 17th the Assembly convened at Baltimore and made other provisions for the security of the frontiers. Applying some of the unspent monies from the previous September, they appropriated a total of ten thousand pounds. The forces in the west were increased to 500 men, divided into four companies. To promote recruiting, those who enlisted were exempted from the levy and promised an annual pension for their support. Finding that every effort at a combined operation had failed the previous year, the government now sought only to defend its own frontier.

During the year a combined force led by CPT Richard Pearis out of Ft. Cumberland and LT Shelby out of Ft. Frederick ranged as far away as Raystown (today's Bedford, PA). On this expedition they were accompanied by an estimated sixty Cherokee warriors who had made an agreement to fight for Maryland. They reported that they had encountered enemy Indians, killing four and capturing two. The captured Indians were carried to Ft. Lyttleton for questioning.

The 500 man force must have been judged too expensive. As a result, after heated debate, the legislature finally agreed to a compromise and approved a force of 300 men to serve during 1758. Some would serve with Forbes' army marching against Ft. Duquesne. About 100 were with MAJ Grant's force which was routed by the French and Indians near that fort in September. Maryland troops also helped to defend Ft. Liganier when it was raided on October 15th. The 300 man force level for the Maryland frontier was renewed until 1759, stationed at Ft. Frederick and ordered to "act as rangers for the Security and Protection of the Frontier Inhabitants." Thereafter the colony did not raise provincial troops. However, two companies of Maryland volunteers in Pennsylvania's pay were with COL Bouquet's expedition against Pontiac's Indians in 1764. [236]

In June, 1757, in response to reports of oncoming Indian assaults, the Frederick County militia companies of Captains Butler, Middogh and Tuckett were ordered to relieve the garrison at Ft. Frederick, then under the command of CPT Alexander Beall. During their tour of duty they prevented the attacks of three different parties of Indians. Besides furnishing the garrison of Ft. Frederick, the people of Frederick County raised another two hundred men. In August they marched under Governor Sharpe to strengthen and garrison Ft. Cumberland. In September they were joined by a company of volunteers from Cecil County, under the command of CPT Jesse Hollingsworth. [237]

Lord Loudon, successor Commander-in-Chief to Governor Shirley, incurred the resentment of Marylanders very early in his command. In addition to his instructions to recruit indentured servants, in the winter of 1756-1757 he sent men to be billeted with inhabitants in a none too flourishing section of the Upper Eastern Shore. There was no particular objection at first. However, when he sent five more companies the next year, this time to Annapolis, the Governor himself complained. The city council made what provision it could, but the burden was a heavy one and seemed quite arbitrary, although it was common practice in England. The Assembly lodged a serious protest. [238]

Loudon raised the ire of the Maryland leadership again over the control of Maryland troops. As the supreme British military commander in North America, Loudon assumed that he would control all military forces in the colonies, including the militia. He did not reckon that the control over the militia was a prerogative that the colonial legislatures guarded jealously. He met with the southern governors to plan the defense of their colonies, including Maryland. Loudon assigned Maryland a quota of 500 select militiamen. Maryland would be required to pay, equip, and supply these men at the province's expense. They were not required to serve outside the colony, but, rather, would garrison Ft. Cumberland. The Assembly initially voted a small sum for recruits that happened to equal an amount that was in the treasury. They did so on the condition that they were to be used where and how the Assembly itself directed. General Loudon was precluded from having even indirect control over them either inside or outside of Maryland.

Later in the year the Assembly passed a supply bill for 200 men. They insisted that the men remain in Maryland. However, the members decided that Ft. Frederick represented the western edge of what it could defend. Consequently it declared that Ft. Cumberland lay to the west of the provincial boundaries and that the supply bill would not be amended to include any post west of Ft. Frederick. Under the circumstances, the supply bill could not be finalized. The dispute was finally settled when Loudon eventually capitulated. To prevent the fort from falling to the French, he agreed to cover the expense of maintaining the garrison with his own funds. He enlisted, payed and commanded the men stationed at Ft. Cumberland.

Loudon reported to the future Prime Minister, William Pitt, that Governor Sharpe and the Assembly were conducting their own battle over "the Provincial Troops raised by them, the Command of which Troops, the Assembly insist on wresting out of His hands as Governor, and indeed out of the King's hands, and would take into their own hand the Sole Command and destination of them." When, as noted, Sharpe asked the Assembly to pay the garrison at Ft. Cumberland with provincial funds it refused. Loudon reported that it "not only insisted on our Troops being withdrawn from Fort Cumberland, but likewise" that none of them "should be subject to any account whatever to the Commands of the Earl of Loudon [himself] or any other of His Majesty's generals." Brigadier John Forbes subsequently informed Pitt that "I can have but very little dependence on Maryland doing any Good for the Service." In writing to the Duke of Cumberland, Captain-General and ranking officer of the realm, Loudon said that "if there is not an effective stop put to that precedent now begun in Maryland, the king will at once lose the command of all troops raised by the provinces." [239]

The Assembly's refusal to support a garrison at Ft. Cumberland was not completely arbitrary and, in fact, was logical from their parochial point of view. Lord Loudon, as Commander-in-Chief, ordered Ft. Cumberland, being maintained and, hence, paid for, by Virginia, to now be maintained by Maryland. This was perfectly logical to him because it was located within Maryland's boundaries and, he felt, the colonies needed to collectively support the Crown's military efforts to protect them. In the fall of 1757 Governor Sharpe applied to the Assembly for means to support the garrison which he had placed there. The Assembly refused, being averse to maintaining a force too far beyond the frontier to protect the inhabitants. Ft. Cumberland was perceived to be a weak fort for several reasons. It was far beyond the frontier settlements and individual plantations under the protection of Maryland. Further, the route of the Indians making their incursions was between Forts Cumberland and Frederick, but out of range of the former. The garrison of Ft. Cumberland had, in the Assembly's opinion, been stationed there contrary to the intention of the act by which they had been raised. All of this combined to give the Assembly its justification for refusing funding. It even recommended that the artillery and stores of the fort be removed to a place of greater safety. Then the members self-righteously ended the disagreement, from their point of view, by stating that any blame for "evil consequences" must rest with those who had acted without "warrant of law." Loudon took offense and said so pointedly, as we have seen, but to no avail. [240]

The Assembly's strong disagreement with the policy of supplying Ft. Cumberland using funds they did not feel they had authorized, combined with its desire to be a uni-cameral legislature (i.e. absorb the Council) continually made it unwilling to vote for military troops and supplies. This was especially true for military activities which they felt would not contribute to Maryland's immediate safety. When the Assembly elected in September 1757 had met in four sessions without voting funds for military supplies the Governor determined on August 21, 1758 to dissolve it and call for new elections. However, the elections failed to solve the problem. The Assembly which met in October 1758 contained most of the anti-Proprietary group that had been in the previous Assembly.

The long standing controversies between the Governor and the Assembly, including the locus of power between the executive and legislative branches, and the philosophy of separation of powers, had all ended inconclusively when the legislature had been prorogued in August. The Assembly had returned to the fray in the spring of 1758. This time the argument stemmed from the power, unsupported by legislative act, to order out and make dispositions of the Provincial militia.

On April 1st, in a message to the Governor, the House requested "the Favour to be informed explicitly by what law and Authority the Militia of Kent and Queen-Anne's County were ordered out and compelled to march." The question also extended to the militia of Calvert County which, the House understood, was about to be ordered out. The Governor's reply, on April 4th, was that previously, with the assent of the House, he had ordered out units of county militia to protect the settlements in the Conococheague area and "to range on the Western Frontier." These enlistments were about to expire and the Governor believed the orders for the Kent and Queen Anne's militias were covered by the earlier authorization. Immediately the House determined to bring a "Remonstrance" on the subject.

The ground work for the "Remonstrance" was laid with care and precision. The House sent the Governor an "Address and Remonstrance" detailing its complaints. Next, it passed a series of seven propositions, formed as resolutions, each being recorded with a separate roll call. Finally, it combined the seven resolutions into one document, which was entered into the Journal as the "Resolves" of the House. All of this was done with the ceremonial trappings of the time.

In the "Remonstrance" the House's core complaint was the sending of two militia companies toward the western frontier. They then disputed the Governor's claim that he was supported by law in calling out the two companies of militia, saying that the law covered only the mustering and training of troops in counties of their residence. In this instance, the province was not experiencing any invasion. "We really are at a Loss to conceive what would induce your Excellency to be of Opinion, that you had a Power, under that Law, to march the Militia before mentioned, unless you supposed you had an Authority under it, to march the Militia of this Province whenever and wheresoever you pleased."

The resolves, all approved by large majorities, contested the Governor's action and limited the employment of the militia without legislative approval to a "Foreign Invasion." Given this continuing stalemate and controversy, Sharpe hoped that a new group of Delegates would yield better results. However, most of the same "dissenters" were returned, with predictable results. [241]

In 1757 command of British forces in the middle and southern colonies passed from Lord Loudon to Brigadier General John Forbes. Early in 1758 another expedition against Ft. Duquesne was decided on, with Forbes in command. The expedition had been promised at least 3,000 Provincial troops from Pennsylvania, Maryland, Virginia and North Carolina. Maryland's contribution, as agreed to by Governor Sharpe in Philadelphia in March 1757, was to be 500 troops. In 1758 Virginia already had one regiment in the field and had directed the formation of another. Maryland had troops under COL Dagworthy at Ft. Frederick.

In March 1758 efforts were made to appropriate funds for a large Maryland force. However, they fell prey to the ongoing disputes between the Assembly on one side and the Council, Governor and Proprietor on the other. The Assembly appropriated funds for the supplies to raise one thousand men. However, to provide the funds, they imposed taxes on, among other things, the Proprietor's quit rents. The Council refused to agree and the Assembly remained adamant. The government abandoned all hope of further supplies being funded and ordered Dagworthy and his troops to join the expedition as Maryland's quota. However, the number of troops fell way short of the number agreed on in Philadelphia. According to a return of July 17, 1758, the Maryland troops consisted of 4 Captains, 8 Lieutenants, 4 Ensigns, 8 Sergeants, 4 Drummers, and 248 Privates, totaling 276 men; significantly less than the promised 500.

There were further problems. The Maryland Forces, the units sent on Forbes' expedition, had been formed in response to Braddock's defeat in 1755. They were volunteer militia companies whose missions had been to protect the frontier settlements from Indian raids, while raiding the Indian settlements themselves. Further, they had not been paid since October 8, 1757. It was difficult for the officers to keep their companies from disbanding. BG Forbes wrote William Pitt that "as there were only 300 men [Maryland Forces] and have been used to woods and Indian manner of fighting, I thought it would be a great loss to allow them to disband themselves." As a result, Forbes took the Maryland Forces into Royal pay, with the understanding that the Maryland Assembly would reimburse the Crown.

The problems being encountered were, as detailed above, a direct result of the ongoing struggle between the Assembly and the Governor, representing the Proprietor. The legislators were attempting to tax items that the Proprietors had traditionally considered theirs, and not subject to local tax, such as income from their estates. To add to the confusion, the Assembly included a clause in a bill which forbade troops from Maryland from going west of Ft. Frederick. This, then, precluded the possibility of troops leaving the Province in support of Forbes. It also was the basis for the refusal of support for Ft. Cumberland. To supply garrisons for the forts left vacant by the departure of Dagworthy's force, Governor Sharpe called out the western militia and marched at their head to Ft. Cumberland. While under his command, a magazine at the fort blew up, with a serious loss of ammunition.

Maryland was not alone in providing little, if any, support for Forbes' expedition. The Assemblies of the other southern colonies would provide little or no support to the military in general and the British Army in particular, except for the defense of their own territory. The southerners were not cowards, they were just being provincial. Assemblies did not care to support the Crown's battles when they saw no advantage to themselves. [242]

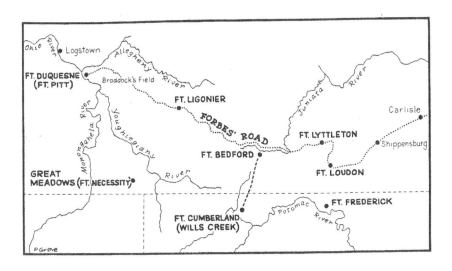

There were, however, Marylanders with Forbes' troops. While estimates vary, there were at least 100. In July, 1758, CPT Shelby, late of Ft. Shelby and Indian fighting in Maryland, and his "Volunteer Company" arrived in Pennsylvania to join General Forbes' army. By August he and his company had joined the advancing troops at Ft. Loudon, located about as far west in Pennsylvania as Ft. Frederick in Maryland and Ft.

Loudon in Virginia. There is some indication that Shelby's company of volunteers had been raised and equipped at his own expense. They stayed with the army for over a year and were in numerous skirmishes with the Indians. Shelby also became involved in blazing and building a road to the former Ft. Duquesne (Pittsburgh). He received a commission in the Pennsylvania militia. When his unit disbanded he returned home to Maryland in the spring of 1760. [243]

In September, 1758, with Forbes' expedition approaching the vicinity of Ft. Duquesne, MAJ Grant, a British regular, with a force of well over 800 men, was detached to conduct a reconnaissance. His force consisted of three hundred and thirty Highlanders, one hundred and fourteen Royal Americans (60th Foot) and about four hundred colonial troops from Pennsylvania, Virginia and Maryland (95). He approached and established a position on a hill about 80 rods (almost 450 yards) from Ft. Duquesne, unobserved by the French. The next morning Grant's troops beat revile and sounded their bagpipes in several places. The Indians, sufficiently alerted, then proceeded to attack and severely punish the English. The English were defeated with a loss of two hundred and seventy three killed, forty two wounded and numerous captured, including MAJ Grant. The Maryland troops covered the retreat of the survivors in the direction of Loyal Hanning and COL Bouquet's troops, but at severe cost to themselves. Out of ninety five men, they lost twenty three enlisted men and one officer, Lieutenant Duncan McRae, killed and missing, and seventeen wounded nearly half their number. CPT Ware, (Francis Ware?) LT Riley and ENS Harrison, probably from Charles County, with fifty privates, made good the retreat.

On October 12th, still awaiting BG Forbes' army trudging westward from Carlisle, COL Bouquet's force at Loyal

Hanning was attacked by over one thousand Indians. The attack was repulsed after four hours, although the English works remained under sporadic fire all night. The Marylanders lost one officer, LT Prather, and two privates killed, ENS Bell and six privates wounded, and eleven missing, about one-seventh of the English losses.

Due to the lateness of the season, as well as the attacks and losses he had taken, Forbes began to plan a withdrawal to friendly areas to the east until spring. Then, Maryland's CPT Ware took an Indian prisoner who revealed the departure of the French's Indian allies from Ft. Duquesne. They too felt the oncoming winter and disliked the French's odds of success. COL Washington was placed in command of a mixed band of colonial troops to reconnoiter the fort. On November 22, 1758 they reached Ft. Duquesne, finding it abandoned and still smoldering. They and the British regulars quickly repaired the fort, renamed it Ft. Pitt, and garrisoned it with a force of two hundred troops from Pennsylvania, Maryland and Virginia. [244]

Governor Sharpe, by proclamation, appointed a day of public thanksgiving and praise for the capture of Ft. Duquesne/Pitt. The Assembly appropriated fifteen hundred pounds to be distributed to the participating soldiers. LTC Dagworthy received 30 pounds, each captain 16, each lieutenant 12, each ensign 9, and non-commissioned officer 6. The remainder was devoted to the purchase of clothing and suitable necessities for the privates. After this Maryland had little concern in continuing the war, although its rangers, numbering two hundred and thirty men, were engaged in an expedition against the Shawnee towns. [245]

In December 1758 General Jeffrey Amherst informed Governor Sharpe that he had been appointed

Commander-in-Chief of British forces in North America. He expressed hope for cooperation from Maryland in the upcoming summer's campaign. On January 26, 1759, Sharpe informed Amherst of his failure to provide the requests for men and supplies. "Within the last Year I met the Assembly of this Province on four separate times and used my utmost Endeavors to induce them to comply with the Requisitions of His Majesty's Generals but I am sorry to say that all my Endeavors proved fruitless and that I have little reason to hope the Assembly will be now prevailed on to act a better part." In the spring another attempt was made to persuade the Assembly to meet Maryland's obligations to assist in the upcoming summer campaigns. It was unsuccessful. At the same time, the legislatures in Virginia and Pennsylvania designated funds to provide military support for the campaigns.

The Maryland Assembly continued its obstinacy. In a letter to General Amherst, Sharpe reported "[t]hey did indeed, in order to save Appearances, express Readiness to comply with His Majesty's Requisition and there upon voted a thousand Men for the Service of the ensuing Campaign, but they resolved at the same time that the money necessary for Levying and Supporting such Men should be raised by a Bill which they were morally certain the Upper House would not pass since they had already rejected it five times and Mr. Pratt the King's Attorney General in his Opinion given thereupon had declared it to be unjust and unreasonable and such a one as could not be enacted into Law without a Breach of Public Faith and Violation of our Constitution ... ." [246]

The perennial issue of supply and assessment bills continued without substantial abatement until the end of the SY/FI War in 1763. The Assembly remained wary of expending the men and the capital of Maryland for what it regarded as a frontier war waged by and for England, except when the close interest of Maryland were concerned. It proposed something very like an income tax in order to meet what it considered the necessary expenditures. The King, the Proprietor, and the Governor, joined by the Upper House (Council) took a broader view of the interests of the province and the way to impose the extra taxes. [247]

Contrary to the commonly held view, some authors have felt that the Maryland Assembly was, in fact, willing to vote funds for the prosecution of the SY/FI War, and did so appropriate them. However, the bills containing the appropriations were rejected by the Governor and the Council because the legislators insisted that the extensive lands and special privileges of the Lord Proprietor should share in the cost of maintaining the war for the good of the Proprietary as well as of his tenants. Hence, Maryland's reputation with British officials, including William Pitt, and military leaders for not providing their fair share towards the war effort. [248]

During the winter of 1765-66 Benjamin Franklin was asked by a committee of Parliament whether Maryland had refused to furnish a quota for the defense of the province during the SY/FI War. He replied that "Maryland has been much represented in this matter. Maryland, to my knowledge, never refused to contribute or grant aid to the Crown. The assemblies, every year during the war, voted considerable sums, and formed bills to raise them. The bills were, according to the constitution of that province, sent to the Council, or Upper House, for concurrence, that they might be presented to the Governor, in order to be enacted into laws. Unhappy disputes between two Houses arising from the defects of that constitution, principally, rendered all the bills but one or two abortive. The proprietary's Council rejected them. It is true, Maryland did not then contribute its portion, but it was, in my opinion, the fault of the government, not of the people." [249]

The taking of Ft. Duquesne and the victory over the French and their Indian allies in 1758 essentially ended the threat to Maryland. While there were minor incursions and the frontier settlers remained vigilant against raids and attacks, the colony as a whole generally ignored the fighting elsewhere. Attempts to get troop support and/or funding support for subsequent expeditions elsewhere were essentially unsuccessful. Requests for aid fell on deaf ears. As time went on, the condition of the militia as a trained, fighting force deteriorated. The organizations existed, but as the threat lessened and, to a major extent, ceased to exist near the population centers in the east, interest waned. Funding dried up and then equipment deteriorated in quantity, quality and condition. In 1768, a special committee was appointed by the Assembly to inspect the State's arms. Their report detailed the low levels of on hand munitions and weapons. There were 785 muskets, old and new; 420 bayonets; 262 swords; 35 pistols; 47 pikes; 2 halberds; 97 kegs of shot and musket ball; 80 ½ barrels of powder; and 15 artillery pieces. Lexington and Concord were less than seven years away, the Battle of Long Island less than eight. [250]

On paper the seventeenth century militia fostered an illusion that the colonies had a well trained and armed civilian population that could defend itself against any enemy. Most colonial leaders by mid-century knew the facts were otherwise and sought alternatives. The Dutch of New Amsterdam, with no militia tradition to fall back on, relied chiefly on negotiations and diplomacy in dealing with the powerful Iroquois

Confederacy. Pennsylvania did the same and it worked well until the eighteenth century. New England experimented with garrisons, in effect, like the blockhouses that Governor Berkeley had had built along the Virginia frontier, to create a buffer zone. Berkeley was forced to try them after the settlers baulked at the expense of his proposed force of five hundred professional soldiers in the colony's pay. [251]

Notwithstanding their frequent lack of their enemies' forest skills, the colonial militias served reasonably well to guard the westward moving edge against Indian counterattacks. When the Indians retaliated for the loss of their lands with terrorizing raids against the fringes of settlement, the whites took up arms and assembled their militia companies to defend themselves, driving off the raiders in hundreds of skirmishes. The militia proved less useful when they were not fighting directly and obviously in defense of their homes. Although there were exceptions, e.g. the siege/capture of Louisburg in 1745, the colonial militias were generally not a reliable instrument of offensive war distant from their own firesides. Few men came to America to be soldiers; rather, they came, in part, to escape soldiering. They would fight when they had to, to preserve homes and farms and a way of life they had crossed the ocean to find. But they did not wish to abandon homes and families for months, or a season, to go off soldiering in pursuit of objects only remotely connected with their own operations and security. [252]

Europeans, judging by what they said about muster days, had only disdain for the American militia. In 1680 in New York, one commented "[t]here was a training and muster today. Some were on horseback, and six small companies were on foot. They were exercised in military tactics, but I have never seen anything worse of the kind." Some years later, in Virginia, another ridiculed the "diversity of weapons and dresses, unsizeableness of the men [In regular units the men were arranged by size, from tallest to smallest, from right to left. The regimental companies were paraded in a straight line. The tallest men were in the right hand company through the shortest in the last one on the left. Over time the company with the biggest men became Grenadiers and that with the shortest became the Light Infantry or skirmishers. Within each company, the men were again arranged from tallest to smallest. In current U.S. Army units the troops are "sized" the same way within their companies in formation. If there is a mass battalion formation they are sized from tallest to shortest from right to left. They then begin to march with a Right Face and the tallest are in the front.], and want of the least grain of discipline in their officers or them" exhibited on muster day. However, they should have sensed that every one regarded muster day as a holiday and judged it as such. They should also have realized that the men they were watching were farmers, merchants and mechanics who only occasionally gathered and drilled as a unit, not professional soldiers.

The quality of their performance depended on the quality of their leaders. Further, not everyone was "mobilized", or chosen to go, when a crisis arose. Commanders tried to select the steadiest soldiers and best marksmen. If they chose well, the troops performed well. The militia was an adequate solution, for a time, to an American dilemma: how could a people unable to support a standing army defend itself against an omnipresent enemy that fought wars by its own rules.

No colony during the seventeenth century developed an informed, forceful command to direct operations over its various self-centered companies. Nor did any produce experienced quartermasters to keep troops on the march supplied. Inter-colonial cooperation rarely materialized, not unique to the seventeenth century. Massachusetts in 1691 refused to join New York in a joint assault on Canada, despite the fact that the French direction of Indian raids on both colonies was obvious to all. Rhode Island and Connecticut, in turn, later refused to aid an oppressed Massachusetts. [253]

In 1709, during Queen Anne's War (War of Spanish Succession), the British planned to take Montreal and Quebec, utilizing British regulars and militia troops. New York with 800, the Jerseys with 200, Pennsylvania with 150 and Connecticut with 350 were to furnish a total of 1,500 men to attack Montreal by land. They were to be mustered at Albany by the middle of May. The Jerseys, far removed from the fires of border warfare, gave no men at all. Pennsylvania, ruled by pacifist Quakers, supplied only 300 pounds, with the quaint proviso that the money should not be used to kill people. [254]

While the threat from the French in Canada provided the impetus for the New England and Northern colonies to conduct joint military operations, they more often met with failure than success. The capture of Port Royal, Nova Scotia in 1690 and 1710 and Louisburg, Cape Breton Island in 1745, were rare successes. Failed expeditions were the norm. There is no one reason for these dismal showings, but certain factors occurred with almost predictable regularity: bickering between colonial leaders, accusations of nonsupport directed at various provinces, epidemics of small pox and dysentery (bloody fluxes), shortages of provisions, ill discipline and desertion. Even at Louisburg the provincial army could not be held together for a long period. Once the élan of victory had subsided, the troops complained of orders against plundering and of Connecticut men, for example, receiving higher pay than men from other colonies, of hard labor, cold weather, illness, and the need to return home to protect their homes from Indian incursions. [255]

The universal training mandated by law in each colony portended the concept of a nation in arms. However, in reality, interest in mastering the manual of arms soon waned. Learning the seventeenth/eighteenth century manual of arms or evolutions required the discipline of endless repetitions, consuming time the colonists found themselves unwilling to sacrifice. Weekly militia drills gave way to monthly, then bi-monthly, then bi- and tri- annual musters. Further, the number of occupational exemptions from duty increased steadily. Muster days became community social events, reminiscent of medieval fairs, with speeches and sermons, games, copious refreshments and even some drill; although one participant describes his drill as an "admirable burlesque of everything military." The militiamen at muster often seemed more interested in drinking than in drilling. Even on the rare occasions when sobriety was the order of the day, little of military value could be accomplished at such infrequent, haphazard drilling. Every generation of colonists experiences a renewed enthusiasm for militia training, usually in response to a crisis. When the crisis passed, however, so did the enthusiasm. As a part-time citizen army, the militias were naturally not well disciplined, cohesive forces like the professional armies of the day. Criticism of the militia was frequent. Its efficiency varied, even for Indian fighting, from colony to colony, and even from locality to locality within the same colony. It all depended on the ability and determination of the commanders and the presence or absence of a threat. [256]

The militia was everywhere in being throughout the seventeenth and eighteenth centuries: farmers, shopkeepers, professional men, all giving their spare time to train in the rudiments of soldiering. Most of them used firearms as a part of their daily life. However, by the latter part of the eighteenth century none of the men in the settled areas actually lived by their weapons; nor did they depend for them for their lives. The riflemen of the frontier did, and that is why they used rifles, not muskets. A rifle had two to three times the range of the musket and it was infinitely more accurate when used in the frontier way.

Colonial youths did not exactly make good soldiers, chiefly because they were free men who hated the iron discipline of armies and did not believe that they had sacrificed their freedom when they "listed" in the "milishy." For the most part, they were willing farm boys, fishermen, mechanics, sailors, clerks, handy-men, carters and jobless drifters. Their only military experience was at monthly meetings of the "milishy," which, as noted above, were actually more like social gatherings or picnics with refreshments, cider or beer for the adults and sweet meats and hot chocolate for the children. After a half hour of leisurely drill with the drums rattling gaily and the fifes playing away, the true purpose of the gathering became apparent, paraphrasing Yankee-doodle, with the girls be handy.

Because many of them were hunters, especially in the seventeenth and early eighteenth centuries, they did fairly well in battle. But the Colonial Wars were never periods of constant contact. Rather, they had a few military episodes in which few Americans were killed or wounded. Battle was only occasional, separated by long intervening months of indolence and ennui. These might have been used to make better soldiers of the troops by weeks of drill, target practice, and the building of roads, forts and camps. Instead, they were often allowed to degenerate into dirty, lazy loafers.

They were also very aware of the differences between themselves and regular soldiers. For decades American troops could not, or would not, stand against the European bayonet charge. One glimpse of the regulars in white or scarlet coats and pipe-clayed criss-cross belts, yelling loudly, charging out of the black clouds of smoke from their discharged muskets, was like an immense and horrifying starter's pistol sending them sprinting to the rear.

However, despite their inadequacies, the American militia often made the British authorities nervous. An indication of what the militia would really do in the event of an Anglo-American rupture was revealed in 1747. Bostonians became thoroughly outraged by continued illegal impressments of seamen into the royal navy. A mob assaulted a sheriff's deputy and seized hostages to bargain for the release of the sailors. Governor William Shirley reported that the Boston militia "refus'd and neglected to obey my Orders ... to appear in Arms for quelling the Tumult, and to keep a Military Watch at night ... ." Another royal governor, Bennington Wentworth of New Hampshire, encountered a similar problem during the Stamp Act crisis. In fact, no colonial governor, he confessed, could call out his militia, who were "the very People of the other Side of the question." [257]

The system of territorial militia with call ups as required was admirable for reactive defense against Indian raids on individual communities. Unless they were conducting patrols in response to previous attacks, the militia invariably failed to anticipate surprise attacks, the Indians favorite and most successful weapon. Once alerted, however, the militia could react swiftly. Massachusetts Bay put twelve hundred men in the field within an hour or so after Indians raided a town thirty miles inland. From its very nature and makeup, severe complications arose when a militia force was involved in protracted operations. To be called from home to cope with a sudden emergency was one thing. But to spend weeks or months in the field at the expense of one's family and livelihood was quite another matter. An inadequate supply system which never evolved, leaving the troops regularly low on, if not without, food ammunition and other critical supplies, added to the difficulties of maintaining and sustaining a force in the field.

The militia system did better in wars during the earlier periods of settlement, when its members responded to attacks on their homes. But in the "Great War for Empire" (the SY/FI War), part-time soldiers demonstrated that they felt no inclination for extended campaigns that did not involve their own interests and aspirations in any direct way that they could understand. The militia system had shown it could be useful when the citizenry felt involved in a military crisis. It was not a fit instrument for prolonged warfare on distant frontiers.

For a war such as the SY/FI War, remote from the interests of most inhabitants of the colonies, insufficient numbers of colonists volunteered for duty. Further, the assemblies proved unwilling to impose sufficiently vigorous drafts on their militias to permit colonial forces alone to fight effectively. After the French overran Virginia's outpost at the Forks of the Ohio in 1754 and defeated Gorge Washington's force at Ft. Necessity, Governor Dinwiddie secured supplementary appropriations for defense from his Assembly and proposed to raise a regiment of 2,000 volunteers. Poor recruiting results quickly lowered the goal to 1,000 and then 800. Those coming forward failed to approach even the lower goals. Dinwiddie then suggested that one in ten of the militia be drafted. The Virginia Assembly did not comply.

Some writers have argued that the militia was not a system at all. In reality, they contend, it was a concept of defense; the idea of universal obligation for a defensive war, a people in arms to ward off an invader. The function of the militiaman was to protect hearth and home, nor to engage in regular warfare. Pervasive localism was at the heart of the concept. Those who were expendable in society, the down and outers, were deemed to be the appropriate persons to be sent off to engage in full scale combat at some distant point on the map. That was the reality, in their view, of the American participation in the SY/FI war, if not in earlier colonial wars. [258]

George Washington, with extensive experience with militia troops from the 1750's on, was generally dismissive of their capabilities. Writing about his experience with them, he said that "[m}ilitia ... will never answer your expectations, no dependence is to be placed on them; They are obstinate and perverse, they are often egged on by the Officers, who lead them in acts of disobedience, and when they are ordered to certain posts for the security of stores, or the protection of the Inhabitants, will, on a sudden, resolve to leave them, and the united vigilance of their officers cannot prevent them." [259]

By its very nature the militia system reinforced the provincialism that was a salient characteristic of the colonial period. The county court, the town meeting, the church congregation, and military unit consisted of local people under local leadership meeting local needs. Some of the obstacles in coming together to form a cohesive force and, later, to the creation of a genuine Continental Army, are illustrated in the rejection of Benjamin Franklin's Albany Plan of Union in 1754. Difficulties in bringing men together, problems of expense, and fears of leaving one's own country/colony bereft of adequate strength all militated against the concept that one province would be sacrificed in favor of the interests of another. [260]

In addition to lack of unity, or maybe instrumental to it, the provincial troops lacked discipline (Washington's feelings in different words.) and this deficiency was harmful to their units and, more importantly, to themselves. Men pitched their tents where-ever they pleased. They located latrines for convenience rather than sanitation, right in the midst of camp. Then they would dig their wells close by. The natural result was sickness. Many more men sickened and died in the midst of their own filth in camp than were struck down in battle. The casualty lists were the strongest imaginable argument against military democracy. The same lack of discipline prevailed on the march and in combat. Although the higher commanders were appointed by the Assemblies, the troops often elected their company officers or influenced their selection. These elected or locally appointed officers were never allowed to forget that another election could displace them or that they served at the sufferance of local leaders who were susceptible to influence from their "constituents." The consequence was that orders took on qualities of persuasion and cajolery rather than command. [261]

Because the militia was largely untrained, the troops often lacked military proficiency. British officers had assumed that back country settlers would possess important skills that would make them good soldiers. However, they were mistaken. These men often lacked "woods skills." Few seemed to have been familiar with the use of guns, especially in the eastern portions of the colonies (longest settled, longest period of time since in actual danger of attack). Although by law all members of the militia were supposed to provide their own weapons, fewer than half of those who mustered possessed any sort of arms. Many of those who carried arms had weapons that were too ancient for use; or they had different bores (were of many different calibers), which made the provision of ammunition all but impossible. Even if they could be supplied with ammunition, few militiamen were experienced marksmen.

The militia officers were the source of just as many problems as their men. The officers were often elected and, hence, reluctant to execute an order that might prove to be unpopular. As the election of an officer was more often a reflection of social status than military prowess, militia officers were especially sensitive about rank. Washington complained several times that "every petty Person must assume Command, direct and advise." Many militia officers saw their commissions more as opportunities for profit than as a service to their country. [262]

A persistent myth attached to the militia was that every American was well versed in small arms and above every hearth hung a musket or rifle. However, the popular idea of the parlor citizen-sharpshooter born to the gun was not accurate. During his command of Virginia's provincial troops in 1756, Washington reported that the militia turned up invariably minus weapons. He makes the point of having to drill men in basic firearms use – not something one would have thought necessary with men well versed in their use. "One contingent of two hundred Culpepper County men reported with a total of only eighty firelocks." However, all of the militiamen were not unskilled. Colonial era militia muster rolls indicate that some had been involved in military activities against the Indians, and then the French, and that many of their weapons were relics of that era. Perhaps the truth is that with the increasing settlement, cultivation, and even urbanization, of the older colonies, men had become less reliant on the forearm and more reliant on the ledger book. [263]

By the middle of the eighteenth century there were thirteen different militia systems. Each of them sprang from and reflected a different culture and operated under different laws. The units of the several colonies were in no way interchangeable, making it difficult for them to amalgamate into larger units if there was a need. The New England militia was generally superior because the political township provided a compact base upon which military organization could rest. In addition, the Puritan congregation provided strong spiritual support. In the Chesapeake Bay colonies of Maryland and Virginia the militia traditions were deeply rooted and the quality of their systems was about equal. Their counties were larger than the New England townships and offered a less compact base for military organization. Moreover, their Anglican and Catholic parishes did not provide a spiritual support system equal to the Puritan congregations.

As a part-time citizen army, the militia was naturally not a well disciplined, cohesive force comparable to the professional armies of the age. Moreover, its efficiency, even for Indian fighting, varied from colony to colony, depending on the ability and determination of commanders and the presence or absence of any threat. When engaged in eliminating an Indian threat to their own community, militiamen might be counted on to make up in enthusiasm what they lacked in discipline or formal training. However, when the Indian threat was pushed westward there was a tendency for people along the seaboard to relax. As the frequency of training days decreased and the participants focused more on festivities than military matters, the efficiency of the militia declined.

On the frontier, where Indian raids were a constant threat, training days were held more frequently and the militia had to be ready for instant action.

Colonial weakness in the military struggles after 1754 arose out of a justified lack of a sense of urgency. The inhabitants of the densely populated, prosperous seaboard region of the colonies mostly had little reason to worry about events on remote frontiers. The struggle was not for their survival, or even safety, but for territory and prestige useful only in the long term. Coastal America, when it thought about the SY/FI War, considered maritime trade and conquest. On the whole the struggles on the frontier caused little disruption to everyday life or external trade. [264]

In the mid-1750's Virginia expected the militia force to form the backbone of their defense against French and Indian attacks. However, the militia soon proved itself inadequate for such a demanding task. Eighteenth century militia musters had become social events rather than opportunities for inculcating military discipline, especially the further east the musters were held. Local gentry sought rank in the militia as a symbol of their social status, rather than as an opportunity of proving their martial prowess. Consequently, county militia Captains were reluctant to risk their lives during Indian assaults. The commanders refused to muster their troops. On occasions where they could be persuaded to muster, the unit would neither hurry to its station nor remain in service for any length of time. As they expected to be on duty for only a month at a time, when units arrived at their posts they often felt that they had served long enough and would disband immediately. On several occasions entire militia companies decided that they had served a sufficient length of time and abandoned their posts, leaving important positions unmanned. They also refused to march out of their own counties. The Virginia House of Burgesses further increased the difficulty by specifying that the militia could not march more than five miles beyond the furthest settled part of the colony, a restriction that prevented the militia from garrisoning the advanced frontier posts. [265]

After Braddock's defeat, in September 1755, of the eleven militia companies that were part of his force (nine from Virginia and one each from North Carolina and Maryland), only 198 soldiers and a dozen officers remained fit for duty at Ft. Cumberland. In another attempt to enhance recruiting efforts, in August the Virginia Assembly had granted immunity from civil process for debt as an inducement to recruits. The law also provided for a draft of unmarried men if an adequate force was not recruited within three months. It did, however, allow for substitutes. If neither the draftee nor the substitutes appeared, the draftee was liable for a fine not to exceed ten pounds. The results are negligible. These and other legislative inducements yielded relatively few results.

The local militia officers were slow in implementing the provisions of the draft. When they did so a sizeable portion of the draftees failed to appear, with minimal consequences. Officers were hesitant to call for militia assemblies to help provide the needed soldiers because they knew that many of their members would not comply. When the militiamen did report for duty, there was no assurance of their remaining to face danger. Washington dispatched 121 Prince William County men to an outpost of the upper Potomac in 1756. On the first night a sergeant and 14 privates deserted. On May 13th a messenger galloped into Winchester shouting that he brought news of a strong Indian foray in the area of Patterson's Creek and the South Branch of the Potomac.

Much of Washington's military strength evaporated. By dusk on May 13th four of the county detachments numbered 299 men. By morning their combined strength was 76, a reduction of almost 75%. [266]

The enlistment period for the volunteer colonial forces was only for the duration of a campaign, at best a year or so, not for longer periods as in the European regular armies. Colonial assemblies had to vote money for pay and supplies. The assemblies were usually parsimonious as well as unwilling to see volunteer forces assume the status of a standing regular army. With short enlistments, inexperienced officers and poor discipline, by European standards, even the best of these colonial volunteer units were, like the militia, often held in contempt by British officers. [267]

The militia and provincial troops served mostly as support to the British regulars during the SY/FI War period. Their rangers and light troops could, to an extent, check the marauding frontier raids of the French and Indians, but could not consistently make forays deep into the wilderness. Robert Rogers in upstate New York, Canada and northern New England was an exception. American provincial infantry regiments were generally not as disciplined nor as well drilled, nor as steady in action, as British regular troops. Provincial officers lacked military education and experience in the field. All of this surprised no one as these were temporary units best suited for support or garrison duty. The majority of Americans at that time resided safely in the extensively settled farming areas, fishing villages and towns found along the Atlantic seaboard. Most did not venture into the primeval forest wilderness where the majority of the fighting was to take place.

Volunteer units could, and did, perform well under certain circumstances, but generally suffered from low morale and slack discipline. Major General Abercrombie, if no one else, understood that there were two kinds of provincial troops: those levied from among the militia on the basis of a legal military obligation; and those who were recruited for all of the wrong reasons: money, escape and the assurance of easy discipline.

The generally low opinion of the American fighting man acquired by most British officers originated with the kinds of provincial units they saw in the SY/FI War. Even when resorting to drafts to fill their quotas, the colonies first provided for the impressment of "strollers" and "idle, vagrant, or dissolute persons." Most of the provincial units were relegated by the British command to an auxiliary function, becoming, toward the end of the war, "hewers of wood and drawers of water." This was demeaning and back breaking work, often on short rations, contributing to even lower morale and worse discipline. Compounding the problems was the frequency of epidemics among the Americans, caused, at least in part, by low to nonexistent standards of field sanitation. Even if officers had understood such standards, they would have been unable to enforce them. [268]

On the positive side, the militia did provide a necessary pool of manpower from which men could be drawn by volunteering, by calling up units, and even by draft if need be. The poll performed a useful function even though the men drawn from it were insufficiently trained. The colonies took a medieval and communal institution and adapted it to new conditions. The adaptation made it possible for a loose society of acquisitive individuals to carry out military actions with a minimum dislocation of the economy. Donald Leach stated that "much credit must be given to the system of compulsory military training that provided the colonies with an ever

available reservoir of manpower. The fundamental sound-
ness of the old militia system, one of England's important
legacies to America, was tested and proved in the Indian wars
of the seventeenth century;" and of the eighteenth century
as well. However, there is no question that the militia system
was flawed. Troops on active duty showed slack discipline,
poor camp sanitation, chronic shortage of weapons, and a
propensity to opt out at the most critical moments. Further,
their training, especially that of the easternmost units in the
eighteenth century, did not prepare them to fight Indians. [269]

The most vexatious question for the militia was that of
command in any joint colonial effort, a problem foreign to
the English militia system, a homogenous force. In America,
as we have seen, each colony had its own little army whose
allegiance was to its colony, not some amorphous temporary
arrangement. Accordingly, any joint effort was on a temporary basis only, an association of equals. Not only did the
militiamen resent being commanded by officers of colonies
other than their own, their respective colonial governments
showed themselves to be equally jealous of command and
procedure. At the rare times when troops from several colonies were actually assembled to act together, there was invariably a squabble over whether officers from one colony would
be obliged to take orders from those of another. An added
conflict never failed to develop when an officer of the Crown
was placed over the colonials. This normally was resolved by a
compromise. During peacetime the several militias remained
subordinate to their respective governors. However, in time
of declared war, the British government might name an overall commander. [270]

On June 16, 1745 the French citadel at Louisburg was
captured by a combined force of a fleet of the Royal Navy

and provincial soldiers from New England. New England, especially the press, was highly critical of Maryland's governor and legislature for failing to support the Louisburg expedition with troops and money. The newspapers argued that Maryland's reluctance was the fault of the 16,000 Roman Catholics in the province who secretly wanted the French Catholics to win the war. This despite that by 1744 Catholics in Maryland had been systematically disarmed and thus barred from militia service.

In the mid-eighteenth century the Maryland militia had fallen into a state of disorder. The militia had not drilled or practiced and the equipment was deteriorating. A significant portion of the legislative sessions between 1748 and 1752 were devoted to arguing over raising money to buy new arms for the militia. Some political officers of the colony inspected the provincial arms in 1748. They were horrified to discover them to be in a deplorable state of repair. The Assembly charged the colonial armorer, Henry Walls, with dereliction of duty.

By May 18, 1750 Governor Samuel Ogle received a further report on the colony's store of militia arms. There were, in one armory 72 old muskets and carbines much out of repair, 144 swords, 25 bayonets, 16 cutlasses and 14 pistols, all nearly useless. Another armory contained 386 muskets and carbines, 71 pistols, 74 swords, 44 halberds and pikes, 50 sword blades, and 18 daggers, most of which were in poor condition. On May 19th Ogle wrote to the Speaker of the Lower House, calling its attention to the deplorable state of arms of the colony. Utilizing a tax on tobacco exports enacted in 1748, by June 6, 1751 the government had raised only 383 pounds, 19 shillings, 1 pence, a sum insufficient to buy arms for even one select or ranging militia company. The militia lists contained about 14,000 names, although not more than 10,000 were effectively mustered, equipped, armed and trained. Governor Sharpe subsequently reported that the "militia is far from formidable." Moreover, "a good militia act our Assembly will not make."

In 1755, at the outset of the SY/FI War, Maryland had approximately 26,000 citizens capable of bearing arms. However, the Militia Act of 1715 was so encumbered by amendments and supplements that its effectiveness was considerably reduced. At least 10,000 citizens were excused for various reasons. Of the remaining 16,000+ eligibles, one third had no arms. Many of the others were poorly equipped and ill-trained.

On May 5, 1756 Governor Sharpe, disgusted with the lax discipline and irregular training of the militia, ordered major exercises "at least once every month during the summer" months and regular musters in other seasons. He also ordered an accounting of the numbers enrolled in the provincial militia. Sharpe was asked to report on Maryland's militia to the Lords of Trade. He enumerated "about 26,000 able to bear arms" out of a white population of 107,693. Of the 26,000, about 10,000 were exempted by law or custom or were Roman Catholics who were forbidden by law to keep or bear arms. "The Militia does not exceed 16,000, one third of whom are entirely destitute of Arms and many of Musquets." Many of the arms are "very bad and scarcely fit for use." He reported that Maryland needed "a proper Militia law which the Assembly have in vain been frequently solicited to make. The people are undisciplined as well as badly armed." On August 23rd Sharpe supplemented his report at the Lords' request, reporting that "the number of militia is 16,500, but as they are for the most part unprovided or very ill supplied with arms and for want of a good militia law not properly regulated, they are not very formidable." Sharpe also reported that one reason for the lower than anticipated numbers in the militia was that "12,000 men enlisted in His Majesty's Service." He is referring to the British regular regiments that had either been deployed to or formed in America to combat the French and Indians. America, especially the corridor from north of Frederick MD to the Potomac River, with a heavy concentration of German settlers, was a fertile recruiting ground. [271]

The different colonial forces bickered regularly. Maryland and Virginia are typical examples. At Ft. Frederick the officers of their respective forces repeatedly disputed each other's command. The situation at Ft. Cumberland was even worse. When Washington was defeated at Ft. Necessity in 1754, Maryland was able to do no more than to muster a company of 100 men to take station at Wills Creek, even though it was within its borders. By 1756 Maryland refused to provide any men or resources for the garrison and the now Ft. Cumberland, arguing that it protected Virginia more than Maryland. An accurate statement as far as it went. Maryland's frontier settlements did not generally extend as far west as present day Hancock, much less to the Wills creek area. There were individual exceptions, like the Cresaps at Old Town, but they were the exceptions. Further, difficult terrain precluded traveling west in Maryland from the current settled areas to Wills Creek for any wheeled vehicles or large bodies of men. The normal route was through Virginia territory (current northeastern West Virginia). Finally, the conflict started in the first place when Virginia was trying to project and protect its territorial claims in western Pennsylvania and eastern Ohio regions to benefit, primarily, a private commercial land development company, The Ohio Company, whose major "stockholders" were Virginia's leading government and military figures (including Washington) and land owners. Virginia had used Maryland's territory for its own ends and then called for an expected assistance. Maryland's assembly was not impressed. However, failure to act helped cost Maryland territory granted in its original charter that became part of Virginia.

In the interim, between 1754 and 1756 there Maryland troops were present at Wills Creek. They helped build Ft. Cumberland. As noted above, Governor Sharpe had, in fact, given instructions on how to construct it, after reviewing the site. The Maryland officers felt the fort's location in Maryland gave them the authority to command all of the provincial force present. CPT Dagworthy's claim to overall command based on a previously held royal commission of some kind added to the confusion. The Maryland officers claimed that they had precedence over the Virginia officers and had a right to consume the Virginia stores as they saw fit. However, over three quarters of the forces present were from Virginia, which had been the primary force in constructing the fort and supplying it. The Virginia officers refused to cooperate and countermanded any orders of the Maryland officers. Virginia's Governor Dinwiddie directed that none of Virginia's stores would be shared with the Marylanders. During the height of Indian assaults and threats, internal bickering paralyzed this key frontier post. [272]

The SY/FI War brought significant changes to the Maryland militia. Units were called into extended periods of duty. Previously, volunteers or recruits were solicited, but the militia companies had not been called out. Maryland Provincial Troops were recruited and were engaged in full scale actions with British regulars against French regular troops. Full-time Provincial troops were raised for garrisons on the western frontier. As a legacy, Maryland entered the revolutionary era with a nucleus of experienced officers and men, and with experience in mobilization. [273]

Necessity had forced the original American settlers to create a universal militia. The military dangers they faced were very real, both from the native Indians, other European foes (the French, Spanish and Dutch), and random marauders. To protect themselves they determined they needed military forces of some kind. The initial settlements were all commercial ventures, sanctioned by the Crown, but not government sponsored. As such, they really had no access to government troops who could be sent over to protect them. Further, even if it wanted to, the government did not have any troops available. The only regular standing forces at the time guarded the King and manned some garrisons defending ports and other sensitive areas. There were no regular troops to send. The colonists were essentially on their own.

To protect themselves, the first settlers did three things. They required all free men to become involved in the settlements' defenses; they organized a military system based on one they were familiar with and the only available English military system at that time, the militia; and they hired professionals to organize their first landings' defenses and train the settlers (e.g. John Smith and Miles Standish). This system worked initially. The settlers were generally protected, the Indians gradually defeated and pushed ever westward, and the colonies were able to develop agriculturally, commercially, socially and politically.

There were different levels of conflict throughout the colonies during the pre-Revolutionary period. In New England, due to close proximity to French settlements in Canada and subsequent agitation of the Indians, there was a higher and more intense level of warfare throughout the seventeenth and early eighteenth centuries than in most of the other colonial areas. Maryland's military activity during this period, while involving fighting with the Indians to some extent, was primarily inter- and intra- colonial. This ranged from the fighting with the Kent Islanders and others on the Eastern Shore within a decade of the first landings, to the conflict between the Puritans and Calvert supporters for control of the colony in the mid/late seventeenth century, to disputes and fighting with Pennsylvanians over their mutual boundary in the 1730s. The pain and suffering inflicted by Indian raids on individual homesteads and settlers cannot be minimized. However, overall Maryland had significant periods of peace that let prosperity flourish.

This, in turn, impacted on the militia's military capability. As it became more peaceful, interest in military activities and training waned. The troops, or potential troops, weren't interested in training, the leaders lost interest in leading, to some extent, and the government didn't see the need to spend a lot of money on military supplies, equipment and soldiers. Over time the authorities had figured out that universal mobilization wasn't really effective. They had evolved their military system into a generally universal training base with ad hoc volunteer units drawn from it serving a limited time, for the duration of the campaign or for a set period of time. As an example, during the SY/FI War period Maryland's Assembly generally would authorize funding for volunteer companies only for a period of four months. Separate legislative action was necessary to extend their service.

As the locations of conflicts where the governments wanted to use the militias moved further and further away from the settled areas, the militias, or at least their ability to be effectively used, deteriorated. The distance from home, the periods of time required, the general growing lack of interest in serious military affairs and the increasing struggles for political control as expressed by the growing conflicts between popularly elected lower houses of the colonial legislatures and the royal government and/or proprietors and their appointed governors, all combined to produce a generally ineffective fighting force by the mid-eighteenth century.

The internal disputes between the British Army and the militias and between the various colonial militias contributed to the overall dysfunction. The uproar caused by CPT Dagworthy's claim of the supremacy of a company grade British Army commission over all colonial commissions regardless of rank highlights several issues that continued to impede American and British military efforts through the SY/FI War period. The feeling of inferiority by American officers, further exacerbated by the British precedence regulations, combined with British haughtiness, actual in some cases and perceived by overly sensitive colonists in others, made cooperation and joint operations difficult. The colonists also had problems working together, each considering the needs of his "country," i.e. his colony, as the primary concern. Precedence of rank, seniority and superiority among colonial officers was also a thorny issue.

The militia generally accomplished that which it was designed for, protecting the colonists from immediate attacks. However, by the mid-eighteenth century, it was not up to the demands being placed on it. The government needed and wanted a military force with the discipline, steadiness and military capabilities of a regular force. The militia as configured and organized was incapable of providing this. The British government, at least, had recognized this and determined that regular British troops were going to be required to defeat the French in America. An unstated benefit was that, ultimately, they planned to have the Americans bear the cost for the troops, thus relieving the Crown of that burden.

The militia system that arose in the American colonies found its roots in the lore and traditions of England, while adapting to the unique environments of the New World. Over time the contributions of the militia units in America surpassed the limited roles that English militiamen had performed in the British Isles. The creation of a minuteman was a novel innovation that gave the American militia far greater capabilities.

The American militia system developed its own unique traits and characteristics. It was a geographically based local defense force designed for limited service during short term emergencies. It served as both a training base and a reservoir for manpower. During local emergencies entire militia units responded to alarms. For more ambitious and extended operations the militia provided a pool of trained manpower from which colonial leaders raised provincial units.

More than anything else, the militia insured the success of English colonization in America by protecting nascent settlements and colonies from attacks by Indians and other colonial powers. In a new and hostile land, the militia gave structure and security to settlements and became a critical, stabilizing element in colonial social life. As the Indian threat receded, the militia allowed the creation of provincial units for more ambitious and long-lasting operations during disputes with France and Spain. [274]

After the conclusion of the SY/FI War in the 1760s, British Army units remained in America to defend the colonists from the Indians. The demands for payments to cover their costs, the perceived slights, and the selective imposition of martial law by the British Army continued in the 1770s. It all helped to mold the colonists' attitudes and fuel the fires of Revolution. What is most remarkable is that given the general low level of military capability of the militia, and the disunity and inter-colonial conflicts at the beginning of the SY/FI War, within twenty years, the period of time since the election of George H. W. Bush to the present, the Americans were uniting to take on the British regulars. They had not completely resolved their conflicts over military precedence (see Benedict Arnold and Horatio Gates) and loyalty to the whole, as opposed to any of their parts, nor would they. However, they were able to work well enough together, with some outside help, to win.

4. The Regulars

Militia training did not prepare the citizens for extended campaigns, nor was the militia organization designed for or capable of sustaining long expeditions. A long campaign to distant fields that also involved meeting Indian tactics of stealth and ambuscade was a campaign for which colonial militia, except units recruited from frontiersmen, were especially unsuited. When the SY/FI War demanded such campaigns, the militia system did not suffice. Therefore, regiments of the British Army appeared in America to fight the French and their Indian allies.

The SY/FI War or, as some have titled it, the Great War for Empire, primarily was a war of military offensives reaching far and beyond the existing limits of British settlement. The militia system was not designed for such a war and governmental officials both in Great Britain and in America soon decided that they had to call for professional soldiers to fight it.

The authorities in London had been developing the thought that to carry the fight to the enemy in the remote American forests, and in Canada itself, was a task for regular regiments, adapted to long offensive campaigns as the militia could not be. They had also concluded that a unified British command had to be imposed upon the American war to overcome one of the major impediments to success in the militia system, the separateness of each colony's armed forces from the others. The militias' political masters, the governors and assemblies, were also remarkably jealous of each other and slow to cooperate. The royal governors were the commanders of the armed forces of the royal colonies. Charter limitations required British command of the troops of the proprietary and corporate colonies in war emergencies. The Commander-in-Chief in North America would simply abrogate to himself the military authority to which officers of the Crown were already entitled. Major General Edward Braddock was chosen to fill the position. [275]

Contrasting the significant differences between the French colony in Canada and the British colonies on the American eastern seaboard were their respective abilities to organize and execute military actions. A Canadian governor, usually a veteran military commander, had only to issue his order to send canoes and bateaux swarming down the rivers to the Ohio country. A British colonial governor had no such power over people extremely sensitive of their liberties and their right of self rule. Abhorring war and waste, loving peace and gain, they could rarely be made to see that in the America of that day war was only slightly less avoidable than the continent's twin scourges of small pox and malaria.

The colonies were a welter of races and creeds, a mosaic of differing interests and forms of government. Only New York and the New England colonies, under the guns and hatchets of the French and Indians, could be made to see that England's war with France was also their war. Virginia refrained from becoming involved until France began to invade those western lands which she considered her own. Even then, the response was conflicted. The Burgesses gave Governor Dinwiddie a most frugal grant of money, and then, jealous of their prerogatives, placed it in the hands of a committee of their own. Of the other colonies to which Dinwiddie appealed for help only North Carolina, also claiming western lands, replied with men and money.

The French victory over Washington at Ft. Necessity on Great Meadows had brought almost all of the wavering western Indians to their side. Flanked by the Spanish of Florida and the French of Louisiana in the south, by the French in the west and north, with the sea at their backs, divided and disorganized, the thirteen colonies at last resolved to act. A Congress was convened at Albany, NY in 1754. However, neither the colonies nor the Crown could or would overcome their mutual distrust. The famous plan proposed by Benjamin Franklin was rejected by both sides because they felt that it gave too much power to the other. Neither side was willing to relinquish governmental functions to the central council proposed by Franklin. While the colonies continued to flounder along their separate ways, France began naval and army preparations. The English learned of the French efforts and quickly made plans to forward two regiments of regulars to America and to initiate naval actions to disrupt French activities. [276]

After the flintlock had replaced the firelock and the subsequent development of the socket bayonet, infantry tactics had been simplified. Four kinds of infantry – pike men, musketeers, fusiliers and grenadiers – were amalgamated into one general type of foot soldier, armed with a flintlock and attachable bayonet. He was drilled incessantly and subjected to barbarously rigorous discipline that made him, in effect, a battlefield automaton. He fought in the open; was taught to wheel and dress ranks amid the smoke and screams and chaos of battle; to load and advance, fire and reload – and to drive home the assault with the bayonet under the smoke of the final volley.

A musket's killing range was only a few hundred paces and firing was not very accurate. In fact, the British fire drill of the period did not include the order "Aim" before the order "Fire." The object was not so much to riddle the enemy as to frighten him and pin him down for the shock action of the cavalry. Such tactics, adjusted to terrain and weapons, were almost the complete opposite of American wilderness fighting, in which the forests imposed a premium on dispersion, cover and accuracy. [277]

The British Army of the mid-1750s was in pitiful condition, down to less than 20,000 men. A large number of the battalions had been disbanded in 1748 after the War of Austrian Succession. The disbanded regiments were mainly the least senior. However, some less senior units were retained due to their quality, including the 54th to the 59th Foot, subsequently reflagged the 42nd to 48th Foot.

In 1740 the Duke of Argyll had remarked that, for the most part, soldiers of the British army were "too stupid or too infamous to learn to carry on a trade." But recorded behavior rarely bears out the expressed contention that the army was the refuge of the desperate and criminal classes. The most basic motivation for enlistment was probably economic, i.e. a more secure source of food, shelter and clothing. Successful recruiters made a military life of relative ease and glory more appealing than laboring from dawn to dusk on a farm. In times of crisis, however, Parliament often authorized conscription. The "vestry men" could include every petty criminal for miles around, ridding local authorities of potential problems.

Regular infantry regiments usually only mustered a single battalion, although several were authorized to raise a second during the early years of the SY/FI War. In peacetime infantry battalions could sometimes muster as few as eight companies, but in active service (i.e. wartime conditions) usually mustered ten. In wartime some regiments also had "Additional Companies," which functioned as recruit depots. [278]

In the seventeenth century the English military proved of little benefit to the American colonists. Most of the English military resources were used to protect England from France and other European foes. The first British regulars appeared in America during the Dutch War in 1664. Also, some British regulars were sent to Virginia in the 1670's to quell a rebellion among the colonists. The resources that were sent to the colonies overwhelmingly went to the English West Indies. In the valuable Sugar Islands the local British inhabitants, fearful of slave revolts, willingly contributed to their upkeep. Considered less valuable and less vulnerable, the mainland colonies were largely left to defend themselves. Even as late as the mid-eighteenth century there were no regular British regiments stationed on the mainland.

Although relations between the colonists and the Crown and its regular forces were often strained, the colonists consistently requested additional troops when confronted by Indians, the French or the Spanish. They likewise requested that regulars garrison the frontier forts. This was a duty the militia disliked and performed badly. It was also deadly. One regular Independent Company that was eventually stationed on the Carolina frontier, with an initial strength of 94 soldiers, lost 130 men and five officers to disease in four years.

New York was the only one of the mainland colonies to have redcoats present during most of the era of British control. After 1682 the English Crown maintained a small, underfunded garrison of four Independent Companies at

New York; about 150 badly trained and poorly equipped men. They were generally forgotten or ignored by the home authorities as were the occasional Independent Companies in South Carolina and Georgia. These troops experienced a series of horrors, miseries, frauds, stupidities and sheer neglect rare in either colonial or military annals. Officers had small chance for advancement and there were no provisions for rotating enlisted men in American service. In a sense they were sent to rot and die in a strange land. Their ranks were replenished with vagabonds and criminals. As a consequence, the British regulars dreaded American duty. [279]

In 1754, as the French advanced to secure the Ohio Valley, there were only a few British regulars in the Eastern Seaboard colonies. The four Independent Companies in New York were meant to defend Lake Champlain, Lake Ontario and the city itself. There were three more companies in South Carolina to guard against potential Spanish and Indian forays. Nova Scotia and Newfoundland had three regular regiments with artillery and ranger companies. They were stationed there as a counterpoint to the powerful French naval base and fortress of Louisburg on Cape Breton Island.

There were, however, no British line regiments stationed in the thirteen colonies. The settlement pattern and politics of what became the British North American colonies did not favor much involvement from the royal government in Britain. The colonists were not eager to have royal troops in their new homes. There were some royal troops in garrisons following the 1713 Treaty of Utrecht between England and France, but, as noted above, these troops were largely posted on the northern and southern frontiers to watch the French and the Spanish. [280]

The British Army, which would do little for the American colonies, was one which was recovering from an "anti-army" attitude which had followed the great European wars of Marlborough. Its regiments, still bearing their Colonels' names, although numbers had been assigned to them in 1751, were stationed wherever a British flag flew. Some were building roads in Scotland; a few freezing in the wilds of North America; some living in tents on Gibraltar; still more sickening in the tropics.

This geographical spread led to differences in dress, habits and even drill between regiments. James Wolfe, commanding the 20th Regiment of Foot, automatically expected to find differences between his and other regiments, and did. At the direction of the Colonel of the Regiment, Lord Bury, the 20th copied another regiment's "platoon exercise" because they had been able to fire more quickly than the 20th. Wolfe may have commanded the 20th in the field, but Lord Bury would decide what drill would be used. The appointed Colonel rarely served with his regiment, being given the post largely as an honor for past services. He also expected to profit from what money was left over from the government's allocation after he met the regiment's annual expenses.

The regiment Lord Bury commanded was typical of all British regiments with one grenadier and eight battalion companies. The 15th Regiment of Foot, in America in 1760, had a Lieutenant Colonel, a Major, four Captains, sixteen Lieutenants, 8 ensigns, a chaplain, an adjutant, a surgeon and his mate, a quartermaster, thirty three sergeants, fourteen drummers, two fifers, and 455 Privates, totaling 539 officers and men. It had left England with 858 officers and men. There were also six women per company, officially soldiers' wives, to do washing and mending. [281]

In a letter dated October 26, 1754, Sir Thomas Robinson, Secretary of State, informed the colonial governors of the impending arrival of two regular British regiments. In a letter to Lord Baltimore, Governor Sharpe reported that "it is thereby signified to me that His majesty for the Defense of his just Rights and Dominions in those parts has been pleased to order over to Virginia two Regiments of Foot consisting of 500 men each besides Commissioned and Non-commissioned Officers to be augmented by us over 700 men each …" [282]

In January 1755 an expeditionary force was assembled in Ireland and shipped to America where, after sailing up the Potomac, it debarked at Alexandria, Virginia. It was commanded by Major General Edward Braddock, an officer of the Coldstream Guards, a duelist, a veteran of the War of Austrian Succession and, to his contemporary, Horace Walpole, "a very Iroquois in disposition." Braddock's authority permitted him to deploy colonial troops as he wished, although he would remain dependent upon the American assemblies to raise and support them. In fact, however, the colonial troops primarily passed into an auxiliary role, providing logistical and engineering support to the regulars.

On his arrival Braddock conferred with the governors of Virginia, Pennsylvania, Massachusetts and Maryland. They mutually agreed on a strategy so aggressive as to make the official peace between the kingdoms of Britain and France appear a fiction. As he assembled his force Braddock saw some results from his meetings with the governors, but not what he had anticipated. Virginia, despite recruiting problems, managed to contribute nine companies, although manned at distinctly less than their authorized strength of 100 men each. North Carolina and Maryland only contributed a company each. On June 21, 1755, Braddock, his two regiments and his force of colonials, including George Washington, set out for the fort at Wills Creek, Maryland, soon to be Ft. Cumberland. [283]

In a letter to Lord Baltimore, Governor Sharpe reported on his tour of inspection to the scenes of anticipated operations, in the vicinity of Wills Creek. He returned down the Potomac, conducting a route reconnaissance for Braddock's force and securing provisions on both sides of the river, i.e. Maryland and Virginia. With Braddock's approval he hoped to quarter five companies in Maryland for a month or so: "one company in Marlborough, one at Bladensburg, a third at Rock Creek and three towns in Prince George's County, and two at Fredericktown ... Besides the Maryland Company, which I have before mentioned to your Lordship, I had raised 80 more recruits in this Province, have reason to fear they will be so much approved of that 150 men from the company and them will be drafted into /English regiments. In that case I will form two companies each consisting of 56 men, in your Lordship's government, for the honor of the Province, even though the Assembly should determine to grant no further supplies." [284]

In anticipation of Braddock's summer campaign, recruiting had been actively conducted in all parts of Maryland. The province had been the recruiting ground for most of the regular regiments, both those transported from Ireland and those originally raised in America. This was owing to the fact that there was no regular organization in the pay of the province. Thus, the services they rendered were credited to other organizations. In this, the zeal and energy of the Maryland volunteers surpassed the expectations of the English officers. They found that their regiments were mainly kept full by recruits obtained from Maryland. The regiments, not content with receiving volunteers and levies, enlisted a large number of indentured servants, which upset the merchants and farmers.

Governor Sharpe said that "I shall not be much surprised if [the Assembly] express dissatisfaction of the behavior of the troops before they left the province, and mutter at their enlisting and taking away a good many servants from the inhabitants of Frederick, Prince George's and Baltimore Counties, as well as impressing their carriage ponies." In February 1756 several of the recruiting officers of "General Shirley's regiment" enlisted a large number of indentured servants on the Eastern Shore. The planters of Kent County became indignant. They attacked the recruiting officers, upon which a conflict ensued "in which blood was spilt." The farmers were successful.

Despite their notoriously low pay and harsh discipline, British regiments enlisted about 7,500 Americans after Braddock's arrival. Some of these recruits may have been Indians and Negroes. Many of the white men were second class citizens of one sort or another. It wasn't until Prime Minister William Pitt promised to reimburse the colonial governments for recruiting and military expenses that the colonies were able to pre-empt the recruiting market with high pay and enlistment bounties. Only in this way were they able to compete with the regulars for troops for their militias and volunteer units. [285]

As an immediate reaction to Braddock's defeat the British government sought to recruit even more regulars in America to fight the war. This followed the precedent set in the Cartagena expedition in the 1740s; the difference being that then the colonial troops were recruited for units which did not become the responsibility of the Crown until they arrived in the Caribbean. Several regiments were raised, the most famous among them COL Henri Bouquet's Royal Americans (60th). On the whole, however, the effort was a failure. Most Americans preferred short service in the militia to the long term service and rigid discipline of the British Army. After 1757 the British government under Pitt, now convinced that America was the area in which the SY/FI War would be won or lost, dispatched increasing numbers of regulars from England – a total of 20,000 during the duration of the war. This was a vastly significant number. The British Army's end strength was less that 20,000 at the beginning of the 1750s. [286]

Even though the British government ultimately funded colonial units, they had to rely on colonial governments to fill the ranks. In the end the British government's tactic was successful, with the colonial governments providing more soldiers than before in 1758 and 1759. The constant need for soldiers and supplies from the colonies was a continual source of friction between British military officials and the colonial assemblies. Both sides accused the other of not carrying its share of the load and of being autocratic. The debate became so acrimonious that even the end of the war did not resolve it. The argument continued through the financial crises of the postwar period. [287]

The chief American contributions during the SY/FI War were in logistics, an area to later plague Britain during the Revolution. In the colonies, the troops of Braddock, Loudon and Amherst procured large quantities of food stuffs, making it unnecessary to transport many provisions from Britain. However, American militiamen and workers provided much of the muscle power to construct roads and to carry supplies over those roads. To the consternation of Lord Loudon, British Commander-in-Chief in America during 1756-1757, however, the colonial assemblies dallied over raising troops and held fast to their purse strings. The legislatures viewed Loudon, the Crown's supreme military authority in the colonies, to be as much of a threat to their constitutional position as the governors had been. Noting the impotence of the colonial executives, whose "[p]redecessors sold the whole of the King's Prerogative to get their Sallaries," Loudon urged the ministry to furnish the governors with funds independent of the assemblies; "if You delay it till a Peace, You will not have force to Exert any British Acts of Parliament here ..." [288]

The regular European troops deployed in the SY/FI War were not trained to think or fight as individuals. Their role was to stand in tightly packed ranks and exchange close range volley fire with the enemy. Traditional battles, therefore, required flat, open terrain where these tactics could be used to good effect. However, such places were rare in the dense forests and rugged uplands of North America. They were forced to change. By late 1755 they had begun to adapt to the "ranging and wood service" in America by lightening their equipment, docking their full skirted coats, cropping their hair, and relinquishing their swords in favor of hatchets and tomahawks. They were taught to fire from a prone position; to take cover in the forest ("tree all" was the command for doing so); and to aim and fire independently.

Rifles made their tentative appearance in the Army in 1757, most likely for shooting game for the pot rather than Indians or Frenchmen. In December 1757 a light infantry battalion, armed with shorter and lighter flintlocks, was formed under officers and men skilled in ranger duties. From the 1758 campaign onwards one company per battalion was detached as light infantry, an innovation which lapsed at the end of the war until its reinstatement on an army-wide basis in 1771. In 1759 Major General Amherst, then Commander-in-Chief in America, authorized the use of a two-deep line as, in his view, the paucity of French regulars made the traditional third rank unnecessary. A two-deep line in open order continued to be the norm throughout the Revolution. [289]

As recorded in <u>The Annual Register; or a View of History, Politics and Literature for the year 1763</u> (London 1796), Edmund Burke, writing on the SY/FI War in 1763, said that "[t]hose who have only experienced the severities and dangers of a company in Europe can scarcely form an idea of what is to be done and endured in the American War.

To act in a country cultivated and inhabited where roads are made, magazines are established, and hospitals provided; where there are good towns to retreat to in case of misfortune, or, at worst, a generous enemy to yield to, from whom no consolation but the honour of a victory can be waiting – this may be considered as the exercise of a spirited and adventurous mind rather than a rigid contest where all is at stake and mutual destruction the object, or as a contention between rivals for glory rather than a real struggle between sanguinary enemies.

But in an American campaign everything is terrible – the face of the country, the climate, the enemy. There is no refreshment for the healthy, nor relief for the sick. A vast, unhospitable desert, unsafe and treacherous, surrounds them, where victories are not decisive, but defeats are ruinous, and simple death the least misfortune that can befall them.

This forms a service truly critical in which all the firmness of the body and the mind is put to the severest trial, and all the exertions of courage and address are called out. If the actions of these rude campaigns are of less dignity, the adventures in them are more interesting to the heart and more amusing to the imagination than the events of a regular war." [290]

From the time of their arrival the British regulars annoyed, exasperated and, finally, enraged the colonials. Benjamin Franklin, commenting on the precipitate retreat of Braddock's retreating army, said that the retreating commander "was requested to afford some protection to the inhabitants; but continu'd his hasty march thro all the country, not thinking himself safe until he arrived at Philadelphia, where the inhabitants could protect him" Even before the disaster, Braddock had treated the Virginia regiment so arrogantly that "no person of property family or worth has since enlisted in it, so Governor Dinwiddie has been obliged to fill up new companies with Scots."

Franklin was far from enamored with those British regulars even at their pre-battle bravest and showiest. "In their first march, too, from their landing till they got beyond the settlements, they had plundered and stripped the inhabitants, totally ruining some poor families, besides insulting, abusing and confining the people if they remonstrated. This was enough to put us out of concert of such defenders if we had really wanted any." Such conduct was not permitted to troops in Britain except when putting down rebellion. Franklin's remarks reveal that Braddock's regulars conceived themselves to be in an alien land, officers and men alike. The inhabitants saw in such troops a confirmation of their traditional fear of standing armies. [291]

In 1754 the British mainland colonies had seven regular units in Independent Companies posted in parts of New York and South Carolina. The "Independent" in the title meant that it was separate from and not an integral part of its "home" regiment, from which its troops had probably been drawn. The American colonies were looked on as extensions of the British garrison and fort system, whereby each garrison town or fort had its own permanently attached company of men; part soldiers, part caretakers of the facility. These Independent Companies were often made up of drafts from regiments. This often meant exile for life, as there was no policy of rotating enlisted men, making the drafts unpopular with the troops. It is also an indicator of the quality, or lack thereof, of the soldiers who were "drafted." No unit in any modern day army willingly sends good troops to fill such a numerical requirement. It would fulfill the quota with its problem soldiers. It was the same in the eighteenth century.

Some lieutenants were encouraged to submit letters of proposal to raise companies "for rank." Each would become the company captain, who would appoint lieutenants from officers then in the service and ensigns from among their civilian friends. The new captains would continue to be listed on their regimental rosters while recruiting, as on leave. They would not receive their new commissions until the companies were completed and mustered. By this method, never tried before, some sixty two Independent Companies were raised by November 1760. The companies were divided into divisions of six companies each with the senior captain acting as division commander. The first two divisions sent to America landed in New York and some were subsequently sent to South Carolina.

The Independent companies of foot (infantry) were virtually ignored by the British home government, with the result that they merged year by year with their host communities. They were frequently dependent upon them for the basic necessities. They developed ties in the community. They had women and children, starting families, both formal and informal. Ironically, the disbanding of these companies in 1764 after their undistinguished performance in the SY/FI War, by depriving upwardly mobile colonial gentlemen of their chance to wear the King's red coat, became a minor contributory factor in the Revolution.

In 1754 Governor Dinwiddie of Virginia corresponded with his fellow governors in the Carolinas, Maryland and New York to secure additional troops and munitions for the expedition against the French and Indians in the Ohio country. Governor Glen of South Carolina was the first to respond favorably. Three Independent Companies had been formed in South Carolina from the disbanded Oglethorpe's Regiment of Foot. Through Glen's efforts, detachments from the three South Carolina companies were formed into a temporary Independent Company numbering 100 men under the command of CPT James Mackay. The company arrived in Hampton, VA on May 1st. Traveling through Winchester and Wills Creek, picking up horses and wagons along the way, they joined Washington at Great Meadows on June 4th.

Mackay asserted his right to command the entire force, regulars and provincials, based on the existing British Army precedence procedures giving British regular officers superiority over any colonial officer, regardless of rank. Washington refused to concede and they ended up with a split command, contributing to the confusion. Further, there were too few of them to engage the French regulars in any meaningful way that could have an impact. The British troops contributed little to the battle except to participate in the defeat and surrender of Ft. Necessity. They were also present with Braddock at the Monongahela in 1755.

In November of that year the remaining men were drafted into Shirley's 50th Regiment, while the officers and NCOs returned to South Carolina to recruit. By 1757 the three companies were back to normal strength.

The South Carolina companies continued to raise garrison forts, man them, and fight the Cherokees until they disbanded in 1764. Two companies from New York under CPTs Clarke and Rutherford joined Braddock in Virginia in 1755 and were also at Monongahela. It was their first combat action and they were badly mauled. Further detachments from the New York Independent Companies served through the War. Following service in the West Indies, in 1763, when their strength fell from nearly 300 to 101 fit for duty, and recruitment had become impossible, they were disbanded.

The Independent Companies were a good method for raising troops quickly, but they turned out to be not very useful combat company sized units. By the early 1760s the divisions were disbanded and all of the companies were placed into new regiments numbered 95 to 120. The two divisions, disbanded as noted above, were designated the 95th Regiment of Foot. [292]

During 1740-1741 thousands of American colonists (including George Washington's half-brother Lawrence, as we have seen) were recruited locally to form Gooch's 61st Regiment, a unit on the regular British establishment (i.e., part of its regular standing army). It was sent to serve against the Spanish in the West Indies and Cartagena, Columbia. Only 10% of the men returned. This had an understandably negative impact on the future enlistment of Americans in the British Army. In 1745 William Shirley and William Pepprell, heroes of the capture of Louisburg, were each commissioned to raise regiments of 1,000 men, the 65th and 66th respectively. While neither reached its authorized strength, they were sent to garrison Louisburg. Disputes over treatment of the men and the low number of officers' commissions granted to Americans led to their being disbanded in 1749.

In the fall of 1754 Shirley, by this time Governor of Massachusetts, and Pepperell were again appointed by the Crown to each raise an infantry regiment on the regular British establishment, the 50th and 51st. Again there was discontent over the low number of officers' commissions granted to Americans, as well as various financial difficulties. Both regiments did muster enough recruits to be formed by early summer 1755, though neither had more than half of its establishment strength. They were ordered to garrison the forts at Oswego, NY on Lake Ontario. In August 1756, after a short resistance, they surrendered to the French and Indian forces under Marquis de Montcalm. Two companies of the 51st managed to escape. The remainder of both regiments was taken to Canada and, eventually, to France for exchange. Both units had practically ceased to exist and were formally disbanded on March 7, 1757. [293]

The first British regiments to arrive in colonial America were the men of COL Sir Peter Haskett's 44th Regiment of Foot and COL Thomas Dunbar's 48th Regiment of Foot. They had been ordered to sail in September 1754. They were to be General Braddock's primary military force when he engaged the French and Indians on the Ohio. Both regiments had been present, and fled from the field, at Prestopans during the 1745 Rebellion, so neither could have been considered the best the country had to offer. There were reasons other than military prowess or competency for their selection. They were stationed in Ireland, which was required to defray most, if not all, of the expense of maintaining them and thus relieve the British government of the costs. They were selected, ultimately, to save transportation costs. The regiments were on a peacetime footing and were, therefore, over officered and undermanned. Their strengths were from 310 to 350 men each (historians disagree on the totals), so they didn't take up as much space as full strength regiments and were, hence, cheaper to move. They were supplemented by drafts from six other regiments enroute, so that when they arrived in Alexandria, VA in early 1755 their combined strength was about 1,000 soldiers.

Crack outfits or not, the regiments' appearance should have been enough to strike fear into the bravest Indian and courage into the most scared of colonials. They wore brick red wool coats, with yellow cuffs, lapels and linings for the 44th and buff for the 48th. The coats were made without collars. Liberal portions of worsted lace, with different colored designs for each regiment, were sewn around their buttonholes, pockets and cuffs. Waist coats were also laced. Battalion men (in the line companies) wore large black felt tricorns, pointed equally on all three sides, and bound up with white wool worsted tape. Grenadiers wore wool caps about a foot tall. Some regiments wore traditional designs on them, but most were standard with embroidered designs.

All of the men carried large cartridge boxes (cartouches) with a wood block inside pared out to hold twenty four cartridges as well as tools to clean and clear their weapons. They also carried bayonets, small swords, or hangers, a water bottle, extra clothing and personal supplies. In August 1762 a Lieutenant in the 60th Regiment (Royal Americans) determined that the average soldier's load exceeded 63 lbs. Steps were taken to reduce the load by mandatory turning in of uniform items and supplies deemed unnecessary.

The plan was to bring the 44th and 48th toward full strength by recruiting Americans to fill their ranks. However, to escape inter-colonial jealousies and to assure European (regular), not American (militia) proficiency, the British military would do the recruiting and training. In addition, two new regular regiments would be raised entirely in America, but with primarily British officers and under British auspices rather than those of any individual colony. These became the 50th and 51st Regiments of Shirley and Pepperell of Massachusetts. Recruiting for the 44th and the 48th was conducted primarily in southern Pennsylvania, Maryland and Virginia. The area from Lancaster and Reading, PA down through Frederick, MD to the lower Shenandoah Valley around Winchester, VA was a fertile recruiting area with many German settlers who were interested in joining up. The recruiters were somewhat successful prior to Braddock's departure west. They had brought both regiments up to 1454 men when they left Wills Creek (Ft. Cumberland) for Ft. Duquesne at the forks of the three rivers.

Braddock's forces were divided into two columns – one on each side of the Potomac – for part of the journey west. COL Dunbar's 48th proceeded to Frederick. They then crossed South Mountain at what is now Braddock Heights. After passing through Boonsboro and fording Antietam Creek at the Devil's Backbone, the regiment proceeded to Conococheague, at the mouth of the creek of the same name, present day Williamsport. The original plan was for the regiment to proceed west through Maryland to Wills Creek. However, there was no existing road through the mountains and the route was deemed impassable. Therefore, the 48th crossed the Potomac and joined the 44th at Winchester. The combined force then proceeded to Wills Creek through Virginia territory (now primarily northeastern West Virginia), cutting a road through the forest as they went.

Braddock was a veteran soldier and commander. Despite his depiction as choleric and often unwilling to listen to advice, a quite accurate description, he was aware of the dangers of operating in the wilderness. He was fully cognizant of the manner in which he might be attacked and attempted to prepare for it. He had spent some time in training, or attempting to train, his men to deal with the unusual threats of wilderness warfare. However, he had not had sufficient time to get his units fully trained, keeping in mind that they were integrating a large number of new men into their units, one third of the original force, while moving through the wilderness creating a road enroute to Wills Creek. Braddock was supported by a battery of the Royal artillery under the command of CPT Ord. To supplement his force and increase their "woods wariness" Braddock also had twelve independent companies of regular and provincial troops from Virginia, Maryland, North Carolina and South Carolina. When he left Wills Creek his force numbered nineteen hundred men.

As the fighting went on and losses among the regulars mounted through combat casualties and disease, the recruiting among American continued. The 44th and 48th lost 372 men during Braddock's campaign. By June of 1756 they were up to 1,700 men. A report of August, 1756 credited them with having enlisted 1,562 men in America in eighteen months. The two new regiments, the 50th and 51st, had a total of 1,300 men by the fall of 1755. A severe winter reduced them to half strength, but by June, 1756 it was up to 1,260 again. Three

British regiments already in Nova Scotia, the 40th, 45th, and 47th, enjoyed similar recruiting success in the New World. This success led to the decision, in 1756, to recruit still another regiment in America. However, it was to be an oversize regiment with four battalions of 1,000 men each. It became the Royal Americans, originally the 62nd, later the 60th. [294]

There can be little doubt that Braddock's defeat set the stage for a concerted effort on the part of the Indians to devastate white settlements which were steadily pushing westward. Goaded and bribed by the French, the Indians were relentless in their drive to stop this encroachment into their tribal lands. The British colonials were a threat because they intended to stay on the land as homesteaders; in contrast to the French who were, primarily, traders, and as such, no threat to the life style of the natives. [295]

Braddock's defeat, however, also had some favorable consequences for the British Army in America. The broken and wooded terrain of the colonies demanded that small unit warfare be the norm. Furthermore, it was an army that did not suffer so acutely from the problems that beset other armies in Europe. In the colonies, the regiment was turned in on itself. The officers were cut off from the blandishments of home society and devoted their paternalistic attentions to the welfare of their men. Moreover, the effect of local troops, in particular the militia, was to bring in individuals of higher intelligence used to local ways. All of the strands were pulled together rapidly. On Christmas Day, 1755, the year of Braddock's defeat, the first steps were taken to raise four battalions of American provincials, to combine the qualities of the scout with the discipline of the trained soldier. Many of them were Swiss and German émigrés, brought up to use a rifle rather than a smooth bore musket, and trained in the ways of the woods from their earliest days.

James Campbell, Earl of Loudon, succeeded Braddock as Commander-in-Chief in America. He brought replacements with him: the 35th and 42nd Foot (the Black Watch of the kilted Highlanders), and a contingent of Royal Artillery. He was given command of the 50th and 51st. He also had orders to raise what became the 60th (Royal Americans) and to strengthen the provincial corps of militia. With the remnants of Braddock's regiments, the 44th and 48th, which were rapidly recruiting new men to replace those lost on the Monongahela, Loudon would command ten battalions (the 35th, 42nd, 50th, 51st, 44th, and 48th were one battalion regiments; the 60th was to have four) and a powerful siege field and siege artillery team.

The training of the 60th Royal Americans reflected, in particular, the thinking of COL Henri Bouquet, who commanded the 1st Battalion and, in effect, the regiment. The men were inspired by kindness and emulation, by awards of prizes rather than the lash. They were instructed in shooting, swimming, and running, rather than in the formalism of Prussian drill. They were trained as skirmishers in the back woods and their approach to discipline smacked more of Comte Gilbert and his citizen soldiers than of Frederick of Prussia.

COL Bouquet trained his men in the conditions of broken forested country, making them run individually and in formation and even swim; to load and fire with great rapidity and accuracy while using available cover. He also trained them in self-sufficiency in the wilderness, which involved finding food, making shelter, and building bridges. The men's uniforms were made more convenient and the best marksmen were given rifles. When attacked by Indians, Bouquet would form his column into a square. His light troops would then push out towards the encircling Indians, forcing them back so that their fire could no longer have an effect on the square. Simultaneous charges on a number of points would puncture the Indians' cordon and expose them to attacks on the flanks.

The Royal American Regiment was raised during New Castle's ministry, Pitt's predecessor. Originally planned as a four battalion regiment raised exclusively in America, as previously noted, it ran into severe recruiting problems. Only one quarter of the regiment ended up being Americans. British and European recruits were used to fill out the remainder. Despite these early issues, the battalions of the 60th participated with distinction throughout the SY/FI War. In 1756, 15,000 additional men were authorized to form the second battalions of the line regiments, becoming separate regiments themselves in two years. After becoming chief minister in December, 1756, Pitt ordered seven regiments to America for Lord Loudon. However, they arrived in July, 1757, two to three months after they were needed. [296]

During the SY/FI War the light infantry, trained as scouts and skirmishers, became a permanent part of the British regimental organization. When engaged in operations in the forest the troops were clad in green or brown clothes instead of the traditional red coat of the British soldier. Their heads were shaved (instead of the long, traditional ques) and they sometimes painted their skin, especially their faces, like the Indians. Special units, such as MAJ Robert Roberts' Rangers, were recruited from among the skilled woodsman in the colonies and placed in the regular British establishment. When Lord George Howe, older brother of Richard and William of Revolutionary War renown, brought his regiment, the 55th Foot, to America, he immediately fell in with the new ideas and consulted experienced Americans, including MAJ Rogers. In showing a willingness to take lessons from American leaders George Howe was unusual. His death at Ticonderoga in 1758 was a serious loss. Parenthetically, the regard in which he was held by Americans and the respect shown him after his death had a great impact on his family, especially his brothers William and Richard. Some historians have conjectured that this greatly influenced the Howe brothers' attitudes during the Revolution, where they appeared to strongly prefer a negotiated settlement with the American rebels over a harsh military victory. [297]

The British regulars, both those transported from England and those recruited in America, were deployed in conjunction with short term militia (i.e., militia units with enlistment terms of only several months, if that long) and longer term voluntary forces raised in the service of the various colonies. The British never determined any effective device to assure the sort of colonial co-operation they desired. The burdens of the war were unequally divided since most colonies did not meet the quotas for troops, services or supplies the British government had set or that the governors had agreed to. Massachusetts, Connecticut, and New York furnished about 70% of the total colonial force employed. The British found it necessary to shoulder the principal financial burden, reimbursing individual colonies for part of their expenses and providing the pay and supply of money to the colonial volunteer units in order to ensure their continued services. [298]

In a report to Lord Baltimore on April 19, 1755, Governor Sharpe reported on the current status of Maryland troops with Braddock. "Of the 180 men that I had raised only 60 are left (the rest being drafted into the regiments) which compose one company from this Province; ... At present two Virginia and the Maryland company are engaged in opening a road to Will's Creek, and then towards the Juniata River, in Pennsylvania, which flows into the Susquehannah. Two of the independent companies will, I believe, remain at Will's Creek during the campaign; and the third will march westward with the other forces."

As Braddock assembled his forces at the newly renamed Ft. Cumberland prior to heading west, they represented a mixture of regular and colonial forces that prevailed throughout the war. They totaled about two thousand effectives. Halket's and Dunbar's regiments now totaled fourteen hundred strong after an influx of volunteers and conscriptions, primarily from Maryland. There were also two Independent Companies of regulars from New York; five companies of rangers and two of carpenters and pioneers, principally from Virginia; one company of rangers from Maryland; one company of rangers from North Carolina; a contingent from the Royal Artillery and thirty seamen to help move and fire the cannon. [299]

By 1758 the British Army in North America consisted of some 20,000 regulars, a force larger than the entire British Army in the early 1750s. They were nearly independent of provincial aid in provisioning, transport and scouting. Provincials had fought in the campaigns, starting with Braddock's and continuing into the latter stages of the war. However, for the most part, they had acted as a workforce, mainly building and repairing forts and roads. The war brought the provincials into greater intimacy with the British regulars and they were unimpressed. They claimed that the colonial troops had been the prime mover in driving the French from North America. Colonial troops also had little desire to work with the regulars. The Independent Companies, which they had most often observed, were frequently ragged, ill-fed and badly sheltered. Moreover, they were controlled by a discipline so brutal that it repelled the colonists, who themselves were capable of much brutality. Englishmen, on the other hand, believed that the colonials had often been delinquent in their duty. They were convinced that colonial cooperation had been bought and that without British effort North America would have become French. As they saw it, the American soldiers had been ineffective. [300]

Antagonisms prevailed not only between the regulars and the civilians they were quartered with and initially intermingled with, but also between the regulars and provincial troops. The regulars were contemptuous of provincial slovenliness. The provincials were aghast at the cruelty of disciplinary measures used on the enlisted regulars. Disgusted British officers would not trust the provincials with responsibility. As one Lieutenant Colonel explained, the Americans were "sufficient to work our Boats, drive our Waggons, to fell trees, and do the Work that in inhabited countrys are performed by peasants." Such treatment did not contribute to cordiality between Britons and Americans.

The planners in England had assumed that American recruits generally would be good marksmen, with experienced skill in woodland warfare. However, the provincial recruits turned out to be mostly farm boys and drifters, younger sons and recent immigrants who had never spent a night in the woods. In an ambush they panicked disastrously. To do the job for which the regular colonial troops had proved incompetent, rangers were recruited. However, the rangers understood only too well how necessary they were, so they did as they pleased without fear of retribution.

There were some British officers, Governor Shirley and then Major Gage among them, who valued the colonials and their soldiers and worked well with them. However, they were the exceptions. The majority rebuffed provincial officers, derided wilderness warfare tactics and ridiculed the motley appearance of the militia. On the other hand, the provincial governments, while loyal in principle, resented and opposed what they considered to be inordinate British military demands. Colonial officers sulked, provoked by their "second class" status. Even after the British adjusted their regulation on the precedence of officer commissions vis a vis regular and provincial, the colonists were still subordinate to regular officers of equal rank regardless of their dates of rank, as well as the appointed British commander, regardless of the colonial officers' ranks. [301]

It did not take MG Braddock long after his arrival to condemn most colonials as a crowd of ignorant sloths, reserving special contempt for colonial troops. Describing the contemptible "blues," the 450 some odd militia, primarily Virginian, accompanying him on his campaign against Ft. Duquesne, he said that "their slothful and languid disposition renders them very unfit for military service." When Lord Loudon came to America, he initially harbored under the misconception that all colonial militiamen were skilled woodsmen and Indian fighters. However, he discovered, to his chagrin that the average provincial soldier knew less what to do if he fell into an ambush than a British regular. The overwhelming majority of the militiamen had never been trained, either in the discipline of arms or in frontier warfare.

Braddock and Loudon were not alone in finding fault with the colonial troops. James Wolfe, conqueror of Quebec, but a known misanthrope, condemned provincial soldiers as "the dirtiest, most contemptible, cowardly dogs you can conceive. There is no depending upon them in action." Jeffrey Amherst, Wolfe's superior, castigated the colonials thusly: "if left to themselves [they] would eat fryed Pork and lay in their tents all day long." John Forbes, who chased the French from Ft. Duquesne, complained that his Pennsylvania and Virginia officers [and, presumably, those from Maryland] were a "bad collection of broken Innkeepers, Horse Jockeys and Indian traders, while the [m]en under them is a direct copy of their officers."

The charges contained elements of truth. Americans steeped in individualism, localism and fighting on their own generally performed poorly whether as enlistees in the British army or as militia units acting in conjunction with regulars. The colonial farmer or artisan appeared out of place in a war that ever more became a European conflict in a New World setting. However, something unknown, or forgotten, by subsequent British leaders contemplating actions against colonial armed resistance was that many of the unimpressive Americans of the SY/FI War were servants, apprentices, and transients who had been drafted from outside the militia system. [302]

Of course, all of the American troops weren't militarily inept. Both sides, the French initially more so, used local forces, colonial militias, volunteers and Indians, to wage a guerilla-type war of swift marches, ambushes from cover and attacks on the enemy's weak and isolated garrisons. While the colonials from the more settled areas lacked "woods savvy" and, even, marksmanship capabilities, the frontiersmen didn't. They were hardened fighters, men with the skills needed to live off the land and move stealthily through the forest. Most, being hunters, were excellent shots. The British did not make the best use of such men, especially at first, believing them to be too wild and undisciplined to be of much use. But, when they recognized their value, various units were raised from the backwoodsmen, including the most famous, Rogers' Rangers. [303]

The disputes between the British Army officers and Provincial officers were often bitter. COL Henri Bouquet of the 60th described Provincial officers as "without Knowledge and Experiences ... They are all a cruel Incumberance upon us." He found they "haven't an idea of service, and one cannot depend on them to carry out an order." Quoting General Wolfe again, he thought that "there never was a people collected together so unfit for what they were set upon [as provincials] – dilatory, ignorant, dissolute, irresolute, and some grains of a very unmanly quality and unsoldier-like or unsailor-like." To another correspondent: "The Americans are in general the dirtiest, the most contemptible, cowardly dogs you can conceive. There is no depending on them in action. They fall down dead in their own dirt and desert by battalions, officers and all." Their animosity was reciprocated by the Americans. They constantly sniped at Bouquet and others while complaining of the haughty, imperious behaviors of the British officers. [304]

Even before the Treaty of Paris in 1763 ending the SY/FI War, the London ministry had made the decision to maintain regular forces in North America. Thus, amidst all of the bravado of victory came the startling announcement from London that there would be a peacetime lodgment of 8,000 to 10,000 royal troops in America. The decision was enough to make any conspiracy minded provincial suspicious about the ministry's true intentions, especially with the French menace removed from the landscape.

The red coats, actually, were to form a frontier constabulary to stand between aggrandizing white settlers and angry Indians being systematically exterminated or pushed off tribal tracts. The goal was to have the regulars keep the peace and to prevent the kind of general uprising that Pontiac's Rebellion of 1763-1764 turned out to be. The Royal Army was not being brought in through the back door with the ulterior purpose of deploying it against the recalcitrants in eastern settlements who might resist other imperial bodies.

The task of maintaining frontier harmony could not be entrusted to provincial militia because most units were in a state of general disrepair, if they were still functioning at all. Colonial militiamen were as likely as anyone to spark a general conflagration, based on their traditional support of white claimants. Regular troops were the only alternative, the ministry concluded, even if that necessitated a standing army present in the American colonies during peacetime. [305]

It is doubtful that any important British politician subscribed to the view that military forces should remain in America to guarantee colonial subordination or cooperation. Rather, the outcome of the SY/FI War made some kind of army absolutely necessary. With the need to maintain a sovereign presence over the newly acquired territories in Florida, in Canada, over the French forts of the Illinois, Great Lakes and Michigan-Wisconsin regions, and in Nova Scotia and Newfoundland, there could be no return to the position of a few years before when there were few regulars in the colonies. Further, the consensus of opinion among Indian agents like William Johnson and among informed military commanders was that some means had to be found to prevent white settlement west of the mountains which would "infallibly irritate and provoke the Indians, and might be attended with fatal consequences" as well.

From these views came the assumption in British circles that troops should be used to control trade and to police white activities in the interior. Decisions that regiments should be maintained in North America were made in late 1762 and early 1763 when the only discussion was over the size of the American garrison. The orders to the Commander-in-Chief in America in October 1763 for the use of regular troops in peacetime referred to the prevention of illegal settlements on Indian land, the regulation of the fur trade and the assistance of Custom Officers. [306]

The decision to keep a standing army in North America ran contrary to the British government's normal policy. Such forces were expensive to maintain. The East Indian Company, for example, provided what troops were necessary at that time in India. Further, the British public was, at best, uninterested in and, at worst, strongly opposed to, funding standing armies in faraway places. The new policy met with strong opposition in the colonies. While the brunt of the fighting had been borne by the British Army (in their view due to the military incompetence of the Americans and the recalcitrance of the colonial governments in providing troops and funds), the colonists strongly felt that they had made a significant contribution. They felt ill rewarded to be told that an army would now stay in place. It was there, they felt, to cow them, not to protect the frontier. [307]

After the Treaty of Paris the British Army was reduced in size. Some of the new knowledge and techniques of wilderness fighting declined in the twelve years of peace. For one thing, the reduction in 1763 eliminated the tenth companies of the marching regiments of foot. It was the light companies that were disbanded. Peacetime manpower was organized on the model of the classic European battle. Most officers seem to have taken little interest in new ideas. However, the light companies did reappear in 1770. In 1774 General William Howe, brother of George, who, like his brother, had been an enthusiast of light tactics, supervised the new training of light companies at a camp outside Salisbury. By contrast, in the overseas possessions of the Crown much less was achieved in training. Boredom and sickness succeeded the drama of wartime.

In 1765 Welbore Ellis, the Secretary at War, began a system of rotation of overseas regiments which was partially successful. He proposed replacing five regiments in North America in 1765, 5 in 1766 and three in 1768. However, there were some problems and delays, with some regiments remaining in overseas garrisons for years. The 8th Foot remained in Canada from 1768 to 1785. The 16th, dispatched from Ireland to America in 1767, stayed there until 1782. The regiments had a home base and the area surrounding it served as their primary recruiting location. The regiments overseas for long periods of time sent recruiting parties home to the British Isles to supplement what they were able to do locally in North America. This was expensive. Discipline was sometimes relaxed because officers feared that their troops might desert or mutiny. When relieved the regiment would return to Britain in shattered condition, its ranks much thinned with disease. The surviving soldiers might also be quite elderly. It would take a year or two to rebuild it.

The SY/FI War was Britain's most successful war of the eighteenth century. However, overseas possessions, particularly American, involved the expenditure of far greater sums of money. After 1763 schemes to reduce expenditures back to the pre-war 1754 level were discussed and attempted; but the efforts were in vain. Fifteen regiments were now needed to police North America. By 1771 it had risen to seventeen, and in 1775 to twenty six. However, some felt that the presence of an increasing number of soldiers was itself provocative when the population was in a volatile state. The Adjutant General, Edward Harvey, in 1766, recommended withdrawing the Army from its vulnerable and scattered posts in the colonies so that they could be concentrated in Canada, Nova Scotia and Florida. He renewed his recommendation as war seemed to approach, but it was again ignored. [308]

The defeat of the French eliminated the danger of French and Indian attacks on the colonies frontiers. It opened up safer trade with the interior; and, it eliminated the strategic, if not yet the legal, obstacle to settlement across the line of the Appalachian Mountains. This all sharply diminished, in the eyes of the American colonists, the value of the continued red coat presence in their territories.

The British concerns were significantly different. The victory over the French had been paid for almost entirely by Great Britain. Hers was now the huge financial burden. In addition, in 1764 the peacetime Army establishment, although reduced in size, had been fixed at seventy regiments, 45,000 troops; more than twice the size of the Army in the early 1750s. These included 17,000 for Great Britain and 10,000 for the vastly increased colonial empire, including North America. From George Grenville's Stamp Act of 1765 forward to 1775, when the first shooting took place, the slide towards a breach between Britain and the American colonies was impelled by British attempts to get the Americans to pay for the expenditures in the SY/FI War and for the costs of their current security. [309]

Military reality underlay the fiscal disagreements which are usually charted as the steps by which the colonists and the Crown proceeded to conflict in the Revolution. Victory had a price, as every empire has discovered. The defeat of the French, though resolving a crisis, thereby devolved on Britain a responsibility which its enemy had hitherto largely discharged single-handedly – control the Indians of the interior. In response the British made two decisions which ultimately became sources of further conflict with the settlers. One was the Proclamation of 1763, in response to Pontiac's Rebellion, which reserved the land west of the Appalachian crest line to the Indians, limiting colonial expansion. The other was the decision, necessitated by the strategic burden that domination of Atlantic America imposed, to maintain a large military garrison in the region. The response of the British landowning and mercantile representatives on whom this additional tax burden for the continued military presence in America would fall was predictable. Since it was in America that the heaviest military costs were incurred, the colonists should make an appreciable contribution to what ultimately was a benefit supplied to them without charge by the Crown. Hence, the Sugar and Stamp Acts of 1764. [310]

The provincial troops had tended to view British officers as aristocratic snobs and their men as mere puppets who marched impressively at the word of command, but who had no feel for the kind of fighting that prevailed in the deep wilderness of North America. Of course, the majority of those who lived in the eastern areas of their colonies had no feel for the woods either. One other aspect of the military consequences of the war was the continuing presence of a standing army after the fighting had stopped. When they were brought back from the frontier the British soldiers were housed in cities in the east. The colonies where they were maintained were required to supply barracks and supplies as part of their support. The colonists took little consolation from the fact that this was common practice for British soldiers wherever they were stationed, including England, even if they ever knew it. The various pieces of legislation taxing the colonists to support these troops as well as to help defray the costs of war, among them the Quartering Act and the Sugar Act, along with the Stamp Act, contributed to the growing unrest. [311]

Contrary to modern day perceptions, and even those of the American colonists, by the beginning of the Revolutionary

War British common soldiers were not typically beggars or criminals; they were, on the contrary, men of respectable origins who volunteered for the Army, accepted privation, and became – as much through motivation as through discipline – effective fighting men. Twice during the American War the British government did sweep men from poorhouses and jails into the Army. However, because opinion was against impressment (used much more extensively by the Navy), the government usually relied on volunteers. Most of the rank and file were solid, productive members of society who, thrust out of work by industrialization or temporary shifts in the economy, entered the Army to get bounties and permanent employment. The typical soldier was a farmer, weaver, shoemaker, carpenter, gamekeeper, or farm laborer. He was unmarried, about 30 years old with ten years of service. And, he was no sicklier than any other British subject.

The soldier's day was filled with manual labor, marching, enforcing the law, and, occasionally, preparing for war. He learned, during periods of training, how to keep cadence, deploy from column into line and from line into column (both critical skills in battlefield maneuvering and fighting), load and fire his musket on command, and use his bayonet. If he sometimes deserted or mutinied, he was far more often an obedient soldier and formidable enemy. His collective strength lay in long, common service; years of living in the same regiment (possibly with other members of his family or with men from his hometown or county), years of being isolated from society at large, of wearing a scarlet coat and regimental facings, of honoring his regimental colors, of enduring battle, and of acknowledging duty to King and country. Such shared experiences made ordinary, solid Englishmen into disciplined, determined soldiers. [312]

The British experience in the American colonies during the war strongly influenced British policy after it. It seemed to have taught them lessons that proved costly in the post-war period. One was that the colonies could not be depended on to defend themselves, even in the greatest danger to their own safety and well being. Another was that every colony was interested only in its own self interest and could not be persuaded to unite with the others whatever the extremity. Only a British initiative, it was believed, could make the colonies act together. Although there was truth in these lessons learned, the British were in for quite a few surprises when they tried to apply what they thought they had learned before and during the war to the struggles that arose between them afterwards.

The failure to understand exactly the makeup of American provincial forces served to confuse the British army officers about American fighting prowess. As we have seen, General Wolfe described provincial soldiers as "the dirtiest, most contemptible, cowardly dogs you can conceive. There is no depending on them in combat." To another officer they were "nastier than anything I can conceive." Army officers repeatedly characterized American soldiers as lazy, shiftless, and hardly fit for latrine duty. However, these provincial soldiers were not the militia, but rather outcasts from the middle class society; unfortunates who had been lured or legally pressed into service through promises of bounty payments, decent food and clothing. New England supplied the vast bulk of the provincial troops engaged in conquering Canada. As John Shy stated, "It was the Yankee who came to be regarded as a poor species of fighting man. This helps to explain the notion of the British government in 1774 that Massachusetts might be coerced without too much trouble."

General Gage, a SY/FI War veteran, did not distinguish between militia and expeditionary service, or those who made up the respective rank and file. At Lexington and Concord, and at Breed's Hill, Gage's regulars were not fighting against unfortunates who had been dragooned into service and whose primary goal was to stay alive. They had run into propertied freeholders operating locally, actually defending hearth and home, an historical reason for their militia's existence. This was the unique strength of the militia system. [313]

In the 1760's the home grown American, and Maryland, military forces were not capable of fighting the British Army on equal terms. While the volunteer units that served with the regulars were not necessarily representative of the militia units, the militia itself was actually only good at its traditional role, the defense of the homeland. Most Americans took that to mean the immediate area around where they lived, not somewhere over the horizon, two colonies, and maybe not two counties, over.

The British army was on its way to becoming one of the best in Europe and a major part of the British military establishment. However, it was a flawed organization, relying on fear and overly harsh discipline to make its troops effective. Another problem was that the type of warfare they were effective at was not always applicable to American battlefields. Finally, they, or at least their senior officers, greatly underestimated the potential capabilities of their future foes.

Simply put, neither the Americans nor the British were overly impressed with each others' military capabilities. Both thought they could easily defeat the other. The Americans felt, initially, that woods style fighting and then a positional strategy would be effective. They quickly evolved into thinking that they could defeat the regulars at their own game, open landscape warfare. The British completely underesti-mated their American opponents. They considered them "rabble" and incapable of standing up to the British forma-tions. After the severe rebuffs of the retreat from Concord and Breed's Hill, the British were initially correct (see the battles around New York in 1776). However, the Americans eventually learned how to fight the European way and sur-vived using something that the British hadn't factored in, patience and long suffering.

5. The Maryland Continentals

The conflicts and disagreements highlighted during the SY/FI War between the British and the American colonists were exacerbated by the continuing presence of the British Army. Actions and reactions on both sides drew them ever closer to armed conflict. The colonists developed virtual parallel governmental organizations that, in some cases, controlled and ran the colonies; or, at least, significant portions of them. The actual governing power of the royal and proprietary governors steadily declined. The colonists developed Committees of Correspondence which shared information, helping to bring the disparate colonies, ever slowly, together. The principles of collective action and the need for it philosophically, politically and militarily, continued to be accepted more readily. Few, if any, of the moderate colonial leaders were actively considering war; but their more radical brethren were. As tensions grew in Massachusetts and the other colonies began to become more involved with its problems, an unplanned action at Lexington and Concord ignited the combustibles that had been building for years.

The key question then began to revolve around the colonists' military arm, the militia. Could the militia units engage in combat with the regulars and survive? How would they be organized? Who would lead them? Who would pay and supply them? As hostilities approached most American patriots (i.e. the approximately 1/3 of the colonists who actively supported armed conflict) simply accepted that the militia could stand up to the regulars and thereby secure a republican polity. Public virtue and moral commitment were all that were necessary for the militia to enjoy success. While many, if not most, of the people of Maryland held this inflated view of their militia's military prowess, they also held a contrary view that a strong militia would be a hindrance to liberty. It wasn't until they had come to feel their supremacy over the Lord Proprietor, until it had become possible to keep a militia force under their control, and until they felt that such a force was needed to resist the oppression of England, that they came to feel that a strong militia would be a protection. [314]

In response to the news of the closing of the port of Boston until the tea destroyed earlier in the "tea party" had been paid for, and a subsequent call for support from Massachusetts, a meeting was organized and held in Annapolis in May, 1774. Its purpose was to consider possible courses of action. It appointed a committee to engage Baltimore Town and the counties in an association for securing American liberty. The counties were galvanized into action. Within two weeks they were selecting their representatives to an extralegal Provincial Congress. Many simply chose their current representatives to the House of Delegates. Despite the increasingly strident rhetoric, Governor Eden had not postponed a planned four month business trip to England. Prior to his departure he had called for what turned out to be the last meeting of the Assembly for a three week session. The Provincial Congress met on June 22, 1774. Its ninety two delegates were experienced politically, with the majority having served in the General Assembly. They called themselves the "Convention" and, among other things, called for a Continental Congress to meet in Philadelphia in September. Anticipating events, they also appointed delegates to represent them.

When the second Convention met in November, 1774 the membership again closely corresponded to the roster of county party delegates to the now defunct Assembly. The members unanimously approved the recommendation of the Continental Congress for strict cessation of trade with Britain. Then, again unanimously, the Convention "recommended" recruiting and arming a militia unit for each county. Further resolutions established a Committee of Correspondence for the province and appointed delegates to the next Continental Congress. They concluded by calling for a "provincial meeting of deputies" chosen by the counties to meet in December, 1774. The Convention had institutionalized itself. It met a total of nine sessions: June 22-25, 1774; November 21-24, 1774; December 8-12, 1774; April 14-May 3, 1775; July 26-August 14, 1775; December 7, 1775-January 18, 1776; May 8-25, 1776; June 21-July 6, 1776; and August 14-November 11, 1776.

In actuality, the designations of these meetings as sessions, indicating successive, consecutive, separate gatherings of one activity (comparable to the first and second session of each U.S. Congress) is not accurate. Each Convention, although called by the one immediately preceding it, was a uniquely separate meeting, with the members being elected/selected for each one separately. However, the vast majority of the same members kept being returned for each Convention. There was not a significant amount of turnover. This indicated that the "people" continued to be represented by, essentially the same political elite (modern day politicians). It also helped provide continuity to the successive sessions. Subsequently, the delegates also established a much smaller

Council of Safety to, in effect, govern the Province when they were not in session.[315]

In order to protect themselves from alleged encroachments of British tyranny upon American liberties, Maryland politicians found it necessary to form, train and equip a military force. The emergence of this force, originally designed to provide armed opposition to parliamentary and royal oppression, resulted in the creation of a potent political instrument. When the Maryland Convention met for the third time since June in Annapolis in early December, 1774 one of the most important concerns was the establishment of a militia. The militia structure of the province had deteriorated since the end of the SY/FI War in 1763. The loyalty of many of its officers to the revolutionary cause could not be trusted. Just like in many of the other colonies, the militia officers, especially the senior ones, were members of the upper classes and landed gentry, many, but not all of whom (see George Washington) strongly supported the status quo, i.e. the royal government. In response, the convention created a rudimentary militia force. [316]

In September, 1774, at the behest of Marylanders, among others, the First Continental Congress met in Philadelphia to discuss the perceived British presence. Following the advice of the Congress, Maryland, along with other colonies, established Committees of Observation and Correspondence. In November the Maryland Convention approved all of the Congress' resolutions. The following April another Convention established a smaller Council of Safety to govern Maryland when it, the Convention, was not in session. To all intents and purposes the body, although entirely extra-legal, now became the executive, as well as the legislative, government of Maryland.

Two weeks after its conclusion in November, the Convention reconvened from December 8th through the 12th. One of the first resolutions it passed dedicated Maryland to supporting Massachusetts or any other colony against illegal taxation or its execution by force – to the "utmost." The next resolution, adopted unanimously, began "[a] well regulated Militia, composed of the gentlemen, freeholders, and other freemen, is the natural strength and only stable security of a free government." The two together could only mean that the people of Maryland would meet force in kind. They continued: "such militia will relieve our mother country from any expense in our protection and defence; will obviate the pretence of a necessity for taxing us on that account, and render it unnecessary to keep any standing army (ever dangerous to liberty) in this province." The Convention thereupon recommended that the inhabitants proceed with haste to organize themselves: "that those between the ages of sixteen and fifty form themselves into companies of sixty-eight men [the standard size for a militia company], to choose a Captain, 2 Lieutenants, an Ensign, four Sergeants, four Corporals and a drummer for each company; and use their utmost endeavors to make themselves masters of the military exercise; that every man be provided with a good firelock and bayonet fitted theron, half a pound of powder, two pounds of lead with a powder horn and bag for ball, and be in readiness to act in any emergency." No military structure was established over the individual militia companies. The Convention further recommended that funds be raised for "equipment of the militia," to be used for the purchase of arms, ammunition and military equipment and accoutrements by the county committees. The assessment was 10,000 pounds, levied to each county proportionally, and based on its population. The allocations were: St. Mary's – 600; Charles – 800; Calvert – 360; Prince George's – 833; Anne Arundel (present day Anne Arundel, Howard and parts of Carroll Counties) – 866; Frederick (present day Washington [upper], Frederick [middle], and Montgomery [lower] Counties) – 1333; Baltimore – 933; Harford – 406; Cecil – 400; Worcester - 553; Somerset – 533; Dorchester – 480; Caroline – 358; Talbot – 400; Queen Anne's – 533; and Kent – 566. [317]

The Convention, reinforcing the requirement that the militia be formed of gentlemen, free holders, and other freemen, appointed recruiting officers and sent them detailed instructions for enlisting men into the militia companies. They were "to enlist no man who is not able bodied, healthy, and a good marcher, nor such whose attachments to the liberties of America you have any cause to suspect. Enlist young hearty robust men, who are tied by birth, or family connection or property to this country. Enlist men who are well practiced in the use of firearms, are by much to be preferred. You are not to enlist any servant imported, nor without leave of the master, any apprentice."

The recruiting officers, normally sergeants, were to seek out men of good character and the instructions mentioned sobriety specifically. The Convention was diligent in gathering recruits. As soon as they had ten recruit, it instructed the recruiting officers to send them to the local county inspector for his approval. As a temporary expedient, the sergeants paid each recruit twenty shillings in lieu of regular pay and fifteen pence in lieu of rations. Since there were no enlistment bounties, this measure indicated the good faith of the Convention and perhaps served as an inducement to service. [318]

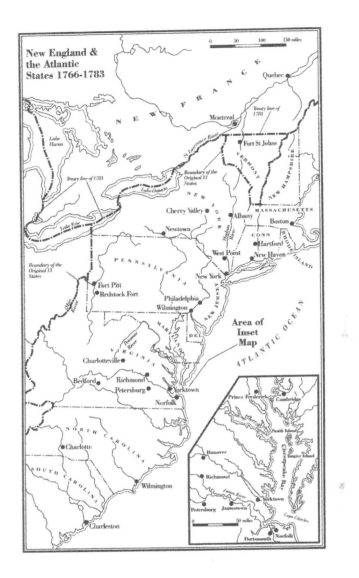

One of the first groups to respond to the Convention's call was the "The Baltimore Independent Cadets." In fact, the founders anticipated the December Convention's resolution and on December 3, 1774, organized themselves under the leadership of a 34 year old merchant named Mordecai Gist.

The 60 original members of this unit were wealthy enough to purchase their own arms, equipment and uniforms. They were intent on learning military drill on par with the British regulars. [319]

The non-importation system developed in response to the Intolerable Acts had rendered the colonies destitute of the necessities of either peace or war. It was now found almost impossible to provide the hastily collected troops with ammunition or clothing. Throughout the upcoming war the scarcity of these articles, and of the necessary hospital stores, crippled the Americans and caused greater loss of life than the enemy. The arsenal at Annapolis was almost devoid of supplies. The leaders perceived almost at once the necessity of providing for a permanent supply of military stores. The Convention allocated monies for the manufacture of salt-pe-tre to be used in making gun powder. To encourage a general production of this indispensable material, a bounty of two pence was offered on every pound made in private factories. Powder mills were also erected. The growth and processing of wool, flax and hemp was encouraged. The making of gun barrels and munitions were undertaken. However, the colonial troops were still very deficient in artillery. This was partially remedied by a citizen of the state contracting to supply the province with cannon. [320]

New England did not have all of the radicals. In fact, Samuel Chase exceeded them in militancy. In a message to John Adams he said that he thought that the British were soon going to invade the colonies. He proposed to immediately outfit ships to war on the British merchant marine. Initially they were, in essence, to be American privateers, following the lead of the English privateers Drake and Hawkins, as well as their successors in the British Navy, who preyed on the Spanish in the seventeenth and eighteenth centuries. He also favored the destruction of the British Army in Boston. "In short," he stated, " I would adopt every scheme to reduce G[reat] B[ritain] to our terms." [321]

Remarkable in the December, 1774 resolutions was the requirement that officers should be elected. Hitherto, the appointment of offices had lain in the hands of the Governor. This first preparedness call had many inadequacies. There was no hierarchy of officers above Captain. There was no provision for placing the newly created force under the command of the Convention, Council of Safety, or the Committees of Observation. The lack of any enforcement powers and the lack of any centralized control of militia companies resulted in the establishment of only a few companies. The lack of an adequate supply system insured that the militia would not be an effective fighting force. [322]

The Convention was in session in April, 1775 when it learned of the hostilities at Lexington and Concord on April 19th. On April 27th, 8 days after the fighting, but before the members knew of it, they resolved "that it is earnestly recommended to the inhabitants of this province to continue the regulation of the militia, as recommended by the last provincial convention, and that particular attention be paid to forming and exercising the militia throughout this province, and that subscription of this purpose by the said convention recommended be forth with completed and applied." On the same day a committee of the Convention asked Governor Eden to place some of the province's arms and ammunition "in the hands of the people," ostensibly for fear of a servant or slave uprising. Consider an extra-legal body asking the royal governor for arms for whatever reason; or a self-appointed group of people from around the state meeting in Annapolis asking the Governor for arms from the National Guard armories to be distributed to citizens' groups around the state, ostensibly to help protect them from potential attacks by hoodlums. Remarkably, after initially resisting, Eden gave weapons to the four counties whose Colonels had "made a regular application," on the presumption that they would share them with the counties that had not yet applied. Actions such as this played a large part in the relatively amicable relations that the Maryland "rebels" maintained with Eden until he was allowed to leave peacefully. Contrast them with those of Virginia's royal governor, Lord Dunmore. Following the engagements in Lexington and Concord, a definite increase in military activities occurred in Maryland. To meet the needs created by the beginnings of hostilities, the military system would have to be more rigidly organized, and funds for its support more rigorously solicited, if Marylanders were to back the New Englanders in their hour of need. [323]

In May, 1775, some time prior to the fighting at Bunker/ Breed's Hill, the Massachusetts Provisional Congress, aware of the necessity of enlisting the support of all of the colonies in the struggle against the British, appealed to the Continental Congress, then meeting in Philadelphia, to adopt the New England citizens' army currently laying siege to Boston. Although there is no formal record of action, Congress evidently did vote to adopt that army on June 14, 1775, down to the present considered the U. S. Army's "birthday." In order to provide additional assistance, on the same day it voted to raise ten companies of expert riflemen, six from Pennsylvania, and two each form Maryland and Virginia. On June 15th Congress chose George Washington to be Commander-in-Chief of American forces, specifically, those around Boston.

In voting to raise the rifle companies Congress specified the manner of enlistment and the tables of organization. Each company was to enlist a Captain, three Lieutenants, four Sergeants, four Corporals, a drummer or trumpeter, and sixty-eight privates (The standard size of a militia company.). Together these companies, the standard size of a regiment, but with a different weapons mix, became the 1st Continental Regiment. Congress' votes of June 14th to adopt the New England militia around Boston and to raise the ten rifle companies, in effect, created a Continental Army, at least on paper. On June 15th they solidified their actions by putting in a new command structure, hence George Washington. [324]

Before its adjournment on August 2, 1775, the Second Continental Congress accomplished a number of significant tasks. It:

- approved a Continental Army of 20,000 men;
- appointed George Washington as Commander-in-Chief, formally expanding his authority from the troops around Boston to include the entire newly authorized Army. It also selected four Major Generals, four Brigadier Generals and a number of support officers;
- called for the ten rifle companies from the middle colonies (PA, MD, VA) to go to Boston for one year's service;
- recommended that each state make provision for sea coast defense;
- accepted a plan for a military medical service to support the 20,000 man force;
- arranged for financing the Army by the issuing of paper money;

- modified the Association rules it operated under to permit the importation of arms and ammunition and the non-exportation rules to permit the export of sufficient produce of the states to pay for the imported munitions;
- recommended that each colony appoint a Committee of Safety and Security during the recesses of their provincial assemblies. [325]

The Maryland Convention reconvened in Annapolis from July 26-August 14, 1775 to consider the reports of the delegates from the 2nd Continental Congress. It accepted the principle that it was necessary and justifiable to repel force with force, and approved the opposition by arms to the British troops employed to enforce obedience to acts of the British Parliament. The first day of the session a resolution establishing an Association of Freemen was introduced. It was debated, amended, and ultimately, signed by the members of the Convention. The Association outlined the reasons for their dissent, supported the Convention's acceptance of the use of military force and began the process of refining and strengthening the military actions taken and arrangements made in prior Conventions.

The Association noted the delegates approved of "the opposition by arms to the British troops employed to enforce obedience to the late [Intolerable] [A]cts and statutes of the British Parliament, for raising a Revenue in America, and altering and changing the Charter and Constitution of the Massachusetts Bay, and for destroying essential securities for the Lives, Liberties and properties of the Subjects of the United Colonies." It undertook the "maintenance of good order and the public peace, to support the civil power in the due execution of the laws … and to defend, with our utmost power, all persons from every species of outrage to themselves or their property." It directed that the County Committees of Observation appoint people to procure the "subscription" [signed approval] of every freeman. Members of the Governor's household were exempted. Those who refused to subscribe were to be reported to the next Convention for possible retribution.

The formation of the Association formalized the passage of supreme governing power in Maryland to the Convention. For interim periods between meetings of the whole body that governing power was vested in a Council of Safety of sixteen members, eight from each shore elected by the Convention. The Council was to direct and regulate "the operations of the minutemen and the militia, grant all military commissions, appoint the field grade officers, and, during the recesses of the Convention, as required, call out the minutemen for service within the province, or neighboring colonies, or the militia within the province."

The Convention established a regular organization for the militia. Every able-bodied freeman was again called upon to enroll himself in a militia company by September 15th. Clergymen, physicians, the Governor's household, minutemen (just being established), artillery men and objectors to the war on religious grounds were exempted from serving. The militia was designed strictly for the defense of Maryland within its borders; preferably within its home county, if possible. Extensive rules and regulations were promulgated for the organization of the militia units, for training and equipping them. The soldiers' monthly pay rates were established. Provision was made for the purchase and manufacture of arms and ammunition; articles of war were prescribed for the colony's armed forces; and paper money was issued to defray the cost of these preparations.

Each county Committee of Observation received authorization to form its companies into battalions of approximately eight companies each. The companies were to drill one day a week, including one day a month as part of one of the newly forming battalions. For the first time artillery companies (batteries) could be formed if enough men volunteered. While the company officers continued to be elected, the Convention reserved to itself or the Council the right to commission the battalion, or field/field grade, officers, reverting, at least partially, to a previous method of central governmental control of the state's military forces.

The members of the Convention also realized that the militia system was incapable of quick reaction to the threats imposed by Lord Dunmore's (royal governor of Virginia) naval and military force that was operating from the mouth of the Chesapeake Bay. To counteract this actual threat, and other potential ones, it authorized the recruitment and organization of 40 companies of minutemen, i.e., units capable of very quick response to sudden threats of danger. It directed that "there be forty companies of minute men enrolled ..., as soon as may be ... and that the said forty Companies be enrolled in the Counties and proportions following: Worcester 1, Somerset 1, Dorchester 2, Talbot 1, Caroline 1, Queen Anne's 2, Kent 1, Cecil 2, St. Mary's 2, Calvert 1, Charles 3, Prince George's 3, Anne Arundel 4, Baltimore 5, Harford 3, Frederick 8." Once "enrolled" (enlisted) the minutemen were to serve until March 1, 1776, "to march to such places either in this or the neighboring colonies, as may be commanded ... and fight ... for the preservation of

American liberty." As with the militia, the senior officers were to be appointed by the Convention or Council. Each minuteman was to drill a minimum of twice a week.

Three battalions were organized for some of the companies on the Western Shore. One battalion was established in Frederick County (8 companies); one in Baltimore and Harford Counties (8 companies); and one in St. Mary's, Charles and Prince George's Counties (8 companies). The companies in Cecil (2), Calvert (1), and Anne Arundel (4) Counties, as well as those on the Eastern Shore, were, presumably, to be left independent. The battalions were to establish light infantry companies, drawing 8 men from each of the 8 "battalion" companies. Each battalion (regiment) was authorized one Colonel, one Lieutenant Colonel, 2 Majors (all four, along with the Light Infantry Company officers to be approved by the Convention or council), a Quartermaster, and an Adjutant. The minutemen were to be equipped from "the public arms" held by Colonels in Prince George's, Dorchester, Talbot and Kent Counties.

On August 14th, the last day of the session, the Convention ordered:

> "That the Rules and Regulations established by the Continental Congress for the government of the Continental Army, be published with the proceedings of this Convention (NO 1,)." This, in effect, meant that these rules and regulations would govern the conduct of Maryland's military forces.
>
> "That the Gentlemen appointed to receive monies for the purchase of Arms and Ammunition, return a list thereof to the treasurer of each shore."

"That the Treasurer of each shore pay the sums of money advanced, agreeable to such List, to the residents of their respective Shore."

"That out of the public Arms in the possession of Colonels John Beall, Richard Lloyd, Edward Lloyd and Henry Hoyser, a quantity of arms with a proportion of Lead and Ammunition sufficient for a Company, be by them delivered to such Captain of Minute-Men, as a Council of Safety shall direct." [326]

This summer session of the Convention continued the process in enhancing Maryland's military structure and capabilities, while, in effect, moving at an ever faster pace. Its actions were a mixture of old and new. The delegates took steps to resuscitate the moribund militia organization, starting to return it organizationally to that of the SY/FI period. They reinforced and, actually, restated the requirement for mandatory service for most freemen, while lowering the upper age limit from sixty to fifty. The Convention recognized the need for a rapid response force and also for one whose service was not restricted to the bounds of Maryland. It took the major step of realizing that military conflicts do not pay attention to arbitrary boundaries and that commanders need flexibility in deciding where to deploy their troops. They should not be limited by arbitrarily established political boundaries. The minutemen weren't completely "free." They were only authorized to deploy and fight in the neighboring colonies, but this still represented a significant attitudinal change. The minutemen's enlistments were limited to about 6 months, assuming they would be enlisted in late August/ early September. While this was a severe limitation, the limit of the term of service was consistent with past practices for volunteer units and, in fact, was somewhat longer than those for other similar units. Moreover, nationally, the other colonies, as well as the Continental organization, were only slowly coming to the realization that longer periods of service than had traditionally been used were necessary. Eventually the enlistment periods covered multiple years and, in some instances, were "for the duration of the conflict."

The most significant problem facing Washington as he assumed command in 1775 was how to create an effective Continental fighting machine in the face of the colonial militia tradition and so many ideological pronouncements about the inherent tenacity of virtuous citizen-soldiers. He knew that he could not abandon the militia tradition; he would have to work with it. However, he and his aides/military family (modern day staff) hoped to modify it by employing militia on the periphery while developing a core of trustworthy regulars, combining the best of both the amateur and regular traditions. Washington recognized that he would have to depend largely on scratch units and that he could not hope for more than a nucleus of seasoned Continentals. His aim was to make this nucleus as large as possible and to enlist battalions for as long as Congress would allow and Americans would consent to serve. Upon taking command in Massachusetts, his immediate objective became that of turning the citizen-soldiers into well trained and well disciplined fighters; functioning cogs in the machinery of war rather than the strutting individualists of militia muster days. Sustaining the rebellion depended upon thorough training and good order, as much as anything else, in Washington's mind.

Nathaniel Greene, soon to become one of Washington's most capable and most trusted subordinates, described the human material that Washington had to work with and the problems that it caused. He wrote that militiamen represented "people coming from home with all the tender feelings of domestic life." As such, they were not "sufficiently fortified with natural courage to stand the shocking scenes of war. To march over dead men, to hear without concern the groans of the wounded. I say few men can stand such scenes unless steeled by habit and fortified by military pride." Only training, discipline and combat experience (qualities setting off the regular from the amateur soldier) could make for an effective army.

The new commander and his most trusted aides aspired to an army of regulars. Washington's personal involvement in the SY/FI War had convinced him that heavy reliance on amateur citizen-soldiers in long term campaigns was folly. As he once stated: "To place any dependence upon militia is assuredly resting upon a broken staff." He did not question the inherent character of the citizen-soldier; but past experience had convinced him that virtue and moral commitment were not so important in sustaining soldiers in combat as rigorous training, regimen and discipline. Militiamen, with their short term enlistments, could come out, fight, and go back home when they pleased. They could be, and often were, erratic and prone to run in battle. Their very independence made them an unsteady base on which to lean for a commander charged with combating His Majesty's red coats. [327]

The growing antipathy towards the British and their allies did not, of itself, produce an identification of interests among the colonists. Though many of them were convinced that they were not British, very few of them went beyond this to regard themselves as Americans. Though the enemy had been indentified, there was no cohesive sense of solidarity amongst the colonists that could create an effective organizational base. In the absence of such political machinery, there was no way in which the more enthusiastic patriots could begin to remedy the deficiencies in national feeling. They found themselves caught in a vicious circle: regional diversities and divisions fed upon themselves to create an atmosphere of political apathy and helplessness.

The most immediate and desperate result of this lack of genuine nationalism among the Americans was the widespread neglect of the Army that was being created by almost all of the state legislators and local assemblies. On the face of it the Americans moved quickly to establish a national army, with the Congress adopting the New England militia around Boston in late spring 1775. However, the significance of many, if not all, of the Congressional initiatives was rhetorical, and this was no exception. Throughout the war the various regional assemblies never fully acknowledged that their main responsibilities were to the creation of a supra-state military establishment. The politicians of the state legislatures and the ordinary people in the states generally limited their military horizons to the state boundaries, and in many cases to the confines of their own county or town. Within such circumscribed areas both legislators and ordinary people were most zealous in assembling hastily mustered bodies of militia to fight against the British. But once they had left the immediate vicinity of the militiamen's hearth and home, the militia units would break up and the men would return home. They were remaining consistent with many, if not most, members of the regular, not the volunteer, American colonial militias throughout the late seventeenth and entire eighteenth centuries. Congress' remedy was to authorize a Continental Army and allocate quotes for soldiers to the individual states. [328]

While establishing discipline in the existing army he was commanding around Boston, Washington, at the same time, had to form a new army in the Continental service, in effect regulars. Washington and his closest advisers, as we have seen, mistrusted the militia because of its lax discipline and its member's refusal to serve for more than brief, appointed times. However, many Americans wanted to rely primarily on the militia, supported by a minimum of state and Continental troops, to defeat the British. Would not the militia, inspired by a love of liberty and a sense of divine providence, be able to overcome regular British forces? Would not courage and simple tactical skills offset discipline and the most intricate maneuvers? This philosophy, strongly held in England from the late seventeenth to the mid-eighteenth centuries, had seen its influence overcome, or at least strongly dissipated, by the latter part of the century, if it ever really had any. However, in America it had taken hold among the classically educated elite and still held sway. The concept of the virtuous citizen soldier, Cincinnatus, defeating the regimented foe and then returning to the land, coupled with a fear of a standing army's potential for oppression, continued to have a strong hold among America's self-proclaimed intellectually elite into the twenty first century.

Washington, however, did not espouse these views. He was not a believer. Conversely, he believed that only a regular army, an army with discipline and cohesive enough to fight effectively in open country, not behind barricades like at Bunker/Breed's Hill, could defeat the British. Out of conferences with a Congressional committee that visited the camp in Cambridge in September 1775 emerged a plan for such an army. Although he did not have time to completely create such a force, by the Battle of Long Island, Washington did succeed in making some Continental and state troops more like regulars than militiamen.

During this period most of the "new Americans" generally expected a short war, obviating the need for soldiers with terms of enlistment longer than those of the militias and short service volunteers. Congress, however, had collectively come to the sense that a semi-regular force, free of the limitations of state armies and militias, was needed. After receiving the reports of the conferees outside of Boston they began considerations for a national, or Continental, army. Washington recommended that the Continentals be enlisted for the duration of the war. Congressional thinking, while changing, did not yet go that far. Further, they felt that such long, indefinite terms of enlistment would discourage all but the most impoverished men. Being unwilling to rely on such men in a standing army, they authorized enlistments for just one year. The Army would be subject to Congress and to the Commanders appointed by Congress. Since much of the time Congress, despite its lofty ambitions and statements, could not sustain the regiments it had authorized, it promised to pay the costs if the states would take care of them.

The Army Congress authorized was to be composed of 26 regiments of 728 men each, plus one regiment of riflemen and one of artillery; 20,732 men in all. They were to be uniformly paid, supplied and administered by the Continental Congress. They were to be enlisted to the end of 1776, the expected duration of the war. Except for the short term of enlistment, it was an excellent plan. However, Washington soon found out that he couldn't carry it out. Among his current troops, both officers and men resisted a reorganization that cut across locally organized units in which they were accustomed to serve. The men saw their families and farms or businesses at home as their first obligation, and they were reluctant to enlist for another year's service. The short term enlistees around Boston were departing in December 1775, being replaced by militia from Massachusetts and New Hampshire. Washington found that he had just over 8,000 enlistments on January 1, 1776, instead of the 20,000 + planned when the Army became "Continental in every respect." By March only 1,000 or so more had been added to the rolls.

In the spring of 1776, however, there was some progress made in enlisting soldiers and forming units for what became the Continental Army. Despite Congress' attempts to limit the inclusion of men from the lower, impoverished class, many, if not most, of the men enlisted were among the most desperate economically and socially. In Massachusetts, Virginia and Maryland the officers committing to serve in the Continental units were from the "best people," the upper political, economic and social reached of colonial society. However, the privates who were enlisting were often poor farmers or artisans and their sons, crudely educated with few opportunities for advancement. They were almost totally indifferent to the cause of independence. They had been enticed into service by promises of a bounty, land, steady employment and easy discipline. With such young men, similar in social origins and motivation to the British soldiers, Washington sought to build a regular army. He emphasized respect for rank, discipline, cleanliness and order, as well as tactical skills and loyalty to regiments and the Revolution. By August 1776 he had had modest success with some regiments; enough to form the nucleus of what would be the regular army, the Continental Army. [329]

In response to the call of the Maryland Council of Safety in late October 1775 the Convention reconvened in

December, meeting from December 7, 1775 to January 18, 1776. At its opening sessions the delegates selected by the counties included John Allen Thomas, one of two from St. Mary's County; William Smallwood and Francis Ware, two of five from Charles County; and Nathaniel Ramsey, one of five from Cecil County. All four were to play significant military roles in the near future. Throughout most of 1775 Maryland's new leaders had not felt that the province was in any specific danger. However, the growing threat from the forces controlled by Lord Dunmore, the royal governor of Virginia, to the Chesapeake in general, and Maryland's long shoreline on both sides of the Bay and up the Potomac in particular, raised concerns and drew a vigorous response. In its session the Convention took a number of significant actions to improve Maryland's defensive posture.

The Convention approved the concept of raising full-time regular, or what they called state, troops. Subsequently, they disbanded the 40 militia companies authorized in August 1775 and replaced them with the force of state troops. The obligation for all able-bodied men between 18 and 50 to participate in a universal militia was restated. However, the militia's services were only obligatory with the boundaries of Maryland. The state was divided into five military districts, each commanded by a Brigadier General, to expedite the recruiting and drilling of troops. Militia battalions within the districts, normally county specific, were established. Officers were named for the state troops and the militia. Regulations were drawn for the administration of the forces, including techniques and procedures for selecting and drafting men from the manpower pool into the regular units, the line. Provision was made "for raising clothing and victualling the forces to be raised." Several manufacturing projects were funded for generating military supplies, including the establishment of a gun factory in Frederick. [330]

On December 13th the Convention appointed a committee to examine and report the returns by the county Committees of Observation of "the companies of artillery, minute and militia men, enrolled or formed into battalions, and of the persons who have enrolled themselves … according to the directions of the last Convention." It also elected Francis Ware of Charles County and two others to a committee to "examine and report the quantity of arms and ammunition belonging to this province, and the state and condition of such arms and ammunition." All were prudent actions to determine the province's existing state of readiness. [331]

On January 1, 1776 the Convention "resolved itself into a Committee of the Whole" and recommended resolutions that were subsequently agreed to by the Convention. The Committee of the Whole is a parliamentary device where all of the members of the legislative body become members of the Committee. They are then able to more freely discuss and debate an issue or issues because the normal restrictions on debates, what issues can be raised when, time limits, etc. don't apply. The rules of a committee govern, not those of the legislative body. When they are finished their business, the Committee members close the Committee meeting, reconvene the normal legislative session, in this case the Convention, and formally present a report of the Committee's findings/ actions to the body. This resulted in the following:

"Resolved, That the Province be put in the best state of defence.

> Resolved, That a sufficient force be immediately raised and embodied under proper

officers, for the defence and protection of the province.

Resolved, That 1444 men, with proper officers, be immediately raised in the pay and for the defence of this province.

Resolved, That 8 companies of said troops, to consist of 68 privates [a standard militia sized company], under proper officers, be formed into a battalion.

Resolved, That the remainder of said troops be divided into companies of 100 men each.

Resolved, That two companies of said troops, to consist of 100 men each, be composed of matrosses [privates of an artillery battery], and trained as such."

"Francis Ware, along with Messirs T. Johnson, Carroll Barrister, Stone and Rumsey were elected to a committee to report resolutions for "Raising, Clothing and Victualing the Forces to be raised in this Province." A second committee consisting of Mr. T. Johnson [again], Mr. Carroll of Carrollton, Mr. Stone and Mr. Rumsey [both again], and Mr. Tilghman was elected to draft rules and regulations for "the government of the forces to be raised." [332]

The Convention continued to work on Maryland's new military force structure. On January 14th it considered the report of the Committee appointed to develop procedures for raising, clothing and victualling the regular forces to be organized and then approved the following: "That one battalion of regular troops of one colonel, one lieutenant-colonel, two majors, one adjutant, one quarter-master, and nine companies, one of which is light infantry [This is based on the Continental Army structure, with the addition of one major and the light infantry company.], and also seven independent companies of regular troops, two companies [batteries] of matrosses [artillery], and one company of marines, be immediately raised, paid and supported at the expense of this province, for the defence of the liberties thereof." The independent and artillery companies were to have 4 officers, eight NCOs, 2 musicians and 92 privates. The battalion companies, less the light, were to have 4 officers, 8 NCOs, 2 musicians and sixty privates. The officers and musicians apparently did not count against the originally authorized strengths of 100 and 689 men, respectively. The light company was to have 4 officers (with a third lieutenant instead of an ensign as the junior), 8 NCOs, 2 musicians and sixty four privates.

The Convention specified the pay for each rank, as well as the daily ration allocation. The field officers were named. William Smallwood and Francis Ware, delegates from Charles County, were elected Colonel and Lieutenant Colonel, respectively. It then listed the officers by company and rank for the battalion and repeated the listing for the Independent Companies from their previous actions of January 4th. The battalion of state troops was to be officially organized as the Maryland Battalion. They followed with detailed instructions for enlisting soldiers and then for the stationing of the regular and Independent Companies. One month's pay was to be advanced to each person enlisted in the regulars, Independent Companies, artillery or marines. Yearly they were to be issued a new hat, short coat, waist coat, pair of breeches and hunting shirt. The expenses of shoes, stockings and shirts would be deducted from their pay. The uniform of the forces came to be hunting shirts. The marines' would be blue. The land forces' would be other colors.

The Battalion's ultimate organization of eight infantry companies and one of light infantry was identical to the organization of the militia battalions authorized in July - August, 1775. It was ordered to divide its men between Annapolis and Baltimore, the province's principal ports. It was formed primarily with companies from the northern portion of the province and the western shore. The artillery batteries were also split, with one in Annapolis and one in Baltimore. Of the seven Independent Companies, five were to be stationed, and presumably raised, on the Eastern Shore, one each in Worcester, Somerset, Dorchester and Talbot Counties. The fifth was divided, with one half in Kent County and the other in Queen Anne's County. On the Western Shore, one company was stationed/raised in St. Mary's County and the other split half and half between Calvert and Charles Counties. [333]

On January 15th the Convention outlined the rank structure for the Maryland military forces, both regular and militia. More specifically, it established an order of precedence for the officers being incorporated from previously existing units, as well as those commissioned or promoted to fill vacancies. It also clarified the seniority of officers in the regular and militia forces, attempting to preclude the difficulties encountered during the SY/FI War. Militia rank was to be incorporated into the regular rank structure only if they were acting together. Then the order of precedence was: regular field grade officers (Colonels - Majors), militia Brigadier Generals and Colonels, regular Captains, militia Lieutenant Colonels and Majors, regular Lieutenants, militia Captains and Lieutenants, regular Ensigns, and militia Ensigns. As long as their units existed, minutemen officers superseded militia officers of comparable rank. However, they were considered militia officers when acting in conjunction with the regulars.

On January 17th, the day prior to its adjournment, the Convention outlined some of the powers of the Council of Safety, which was to meet and, in effect, govern Maryland when the Convention was in recess. The Council could direct and regulate Maryland's military forces (regular, militia and minutemen [until their dissolution on March 1st]) as well as deal with all personnel matters for officers and enlisted men. The regular forces and the minutemen could be deployed within Maryland or in the neighboring colonies of Virginia, Delaware and Pennsylvania. The militia could only be deployed within Maryland. [334]

Coincidentally, following the Continental pattern, Maryland's new defacto government had no executive to execute the legislature's directions and acts. This was accomplished by a combination of action by the Convention and the Council of Safety, with the latter assuming a greater and greater role as time went on. Maryland's journey towards a viable military force continued. The legislators were still primarily focused on Maryland's defense and, beyond philosophical concern, not much else. The regular, or state, units they authorized were positioned to defend Maryland and, more specifically, to defend it against British incursions up the Chesapeake Bay, their current area of greatest exposure. However, some feeling for collective involvement was beginning to be felt, as evidenced by the approval for the regulars to be deployed in the surrounding colonies. The politicians were still thinking in terms of companies, or small units, which was how even the state troops had been deployed as late as the early 1760s. Regimental structures within the counties theoretically existed, but were rarely, if ever, utilized tactically. Compared to what would be done in the next eighteen to twenty four months, the Convention's efforts were not particularly dramatic in terms of the number of units authorized. However, given Maryland's past military history and, more particularly, the resistance of the Assembly to attempts to organize military forces, especially standing forces, the Convention took a significant step forward. Just as important as the newly authorized units, if not more so, was the development of the administrative and logistical infrastructure necessary to support their troops. At both the Continental and state levels these organizations had to be created and staffed, new manufacturing had to be initiated, and existing operations enhanced, all to create, stockpile and distribute military supplies. The success of the military units was dependent on the functioning of their logistical "tails." As is well known, efforts in these areas were often unsuccessful and/or ignored throughout the war, to deleterious effect. However, the Convention was making a good beginning.

In the late spring of 1776, after forcing the British out of Boston and moving his remaining troops to New York, Washington faced numerous major problems. The most significant was his shortage of troops. He asked the Continental Congress to provide for more troops to help him defend New York. Specifically, he requested a reserve of 10,000 men. Congress obliged on June 3, 1776, tasking the middle colonies. It authorized a Flying Camp, under the command of Brigadier General (BG) Hugh Mercer of Virginia. The camp was established at Amboy, now Perth Amboy, New Jersey. It was to be comprised of militia units from New Jersey, Delaware (600), Pennsylvania (6,000) and Maryland (3,400). The term "Flying Camp" had been used by the British Army at least as far back as the sixteenth century. It was a term used to describe a body of armed men available for quick movement. The force was expected to perform a number of vital functions in New Jersey while Washington's army focused on the defense of New York. Its duties would include guarding the vulnerable Jersey coast, protecting the Continental Army's supply lines, suppressing roving bands of Tories and acting as a ready reserve should Washington need some reinforcements.

On June 25, 1776, the Maryland Convention resolved "[t]hat this province will furnish 3,405 of its militia to form a flying camp and to act with the militia of Pennsylvania and the Delaware government in the middle department: that is to say, from this province to New York, inclusive, according to the request of the Congress of the 3rd day this instant June." These companies were to serve within the stipulated limits until December 1, 1776, unless sooner discharged by the Continental Congress. None were to be compelled to serve out of these limits or beyond December 1st. The "flying camp" was to consist of four battalions/regiments and one company. Each battalion was to consist of nine companies, with four officers, eight NCOs (Sergeants and Corporals), one drummer, one fifer and seventy six privates per company.

Warrants were to be issued by the President of the Convention to persons appointed by the Convention to enroll noncommissioned officers and privates. A Captain was to enroll 30 men, a Lieutenant 20 and an Ensign 16. Enrollments, even if not all completed, were to be returned to the Convention, or Council of Safety, by July 20th. If any enrollments were not complete, the Convention, or Council of Safety, could commission the person to whom the warrants were directed, or any other persons, "as would but promote the service." Enrollments were to be of those who voluntarily offered themselves. The intention was for the units of the Maryland Flying Camp to move to and become part of the Continental Flying Camp in New Jersey. This happened to some extent. However, New Jersey provided little support for the Flying Camp. Pennsylvania sent some 2,000 troops, many of whom were quickly transferred to Washington's army. Additional troops did arrive from Maryland and Delaware. But the difficulty of running the command overcame its benefits and it was disbanded in the late fall of 1776, shortly after the fall of Ft. Washington on the Hudson above New York. [335]

The Convention adjourned on July 6, 1776, and the responsibility for supervising the gathering, organization and deployment of Maryland's military forces, both to join and assist the Continental Army, as well as providing for the state's defense, fell to the Council of Safety. It had its first meeting on the day of the Convention's adjournment, July 6th, in Annapolis. Daniel of St. Thomas Jennifer, Charles Carroll, Barrister, and James Tilghman attended. Jennifer was elected President and Carroll Vice President. On July 12th John Nicholson, Jr. was administered the required oath and joined. On the 15th John Hall joined the Council's deliberations, and they were joined by George Plater on the 16th. [336]

In the lead up to the war and, then, throughout it, the Convention's and Council's manpower and fiscal "levies" were subdivided by County, with the ones with the largest populations and/or territory receiving the largest allocations. In 1775 the boundaries of the counties were different, in many cases, than those in the present day. Frederick County had upper (Washington), middle (Frederick) and lower (Montgomery) districts. Anne Arundel included its present territory, plus all of Howard and part of Carroll Counties. Frederick's middle district included the western portion of Carroll. Baltimore County included part of eastern Carroll. Baltimore Town was often, but not always, included in Baltimore County's allocations. On the Eastern Shore, Wicomico County had not been formed. [337]

Throughout the counties war preparations were being made, primarily in response to the Convention's resolutions/directives, although some citizens anticipated the Convention. In the early 1770's Caroline County had no militia units. In response to the Convention's resolutions in 1774, Caroline, along with the other counties, began raising money and enrolling men in the militia. After the Convention's action in January, 1776 Caroline established two militia battalions, east and west. Baltimore's share of the ten thousand pounds requested by the Convention in December 1774 for the purchase of arms, munitions and military supplies was 930 pounds. The County, in turn, further divided the request among the districts throughout the county.

The News of Lexington and Concord in April 1775 found the best part of Maryland ready to arm. In Baltimore County, William Buchanan, County Lieutenant, collected a body of older citizens for home defense. Their unmarried sons and others organized themselves into two companies. These were in addition to the Baltimore Independent Cadets. The Cadets "donned an excellent scarlet uniform," and chose Mordecai Gist as their leader. Many of these young men eventually joined one of the companies of Smallwood's Regiment. By November 13th, implementing a recommendation of the Continental Congress, a committee was established in Baltimore for procuring arms and ammunition. Its members included Samuel Purviance, John Smith, William Buchanan, organizer of the older home defense, Benjamin Griffith, Isaac Guest Thomas Gist, Sr. and Darby Lux. They all took an oath to keep their proceedings secret. Their actions were being duplicated throughout Maryland. [338]

Marylanders, and other colonial Americans, used the existing European and British military organizations as guides when they, in turn, began to develop their own military units. While they had adopted a structure for their then current military organizations, the militia units' organizational structure was more geographically driven than the number of people involved would normally dictate. Often times the companies in each county had been grouped into regiments without consideration for the varying number of troops in each company and companies in each regiment. Congress, in organizing the Continental army during the Revolution, and the individual states in organizing their militias, attempted to follow a more consistent Eurocentric model.

At the time a British regiment consisted of one or more battalions authorized a strength of a thousand + officers and men. It was not unusual to have one battalion on active service while another, or a smaller portion of it, served as a recruiting and training unit. While there were some regiments with multiple battalions on active service (this was the goal of the 60th, Royal Americans), they were rare. The regiment was the instrument through which men were recruited and supplies were distributed. The subdivision of the regiment was the company. It was usual for a regiment to form one battalion, but sometimes regiments were so small that the effective men from two or more of them had to be pooled to form one combined battalion. On rare occasions a stronger regiment might form two battalions.

When British regiments had ten companies, the flank, or end, companies came to be considered elite units. For uniformity and appearance sake units were internally organized from the largest man to the smallest in a line. So, the men on the flanks were, respectively, the largest and the smallest. The Grenadiers were the largest men in the regiment, usually outfitted in uniforms and accoutrements designed to make them appear bigger and, hence, more fearsome. The Light Infantry, the smallest men in the regiment, were used as flank guards and skirmishers to annoy and upset the enemy. During the Revolution the British organized units utilizing the Light and grenadier companies of their regiments to form ad hoc battalions that were often deployed away from the main body of the regiment(s).

The normal tactical unit of the infantry was the battalion. In the overwhelming majority of regiments with only one battalion on active service, the tactical battalion designation and the administrative designation were actually one and the same. Hence, early in the war, the terms were used synonymously and interchangeably. A battalion was the smallest unit of men that maneuvered and fought together. Usually a battalion was divided into four divisions of two platoons each. The divisions and platoons were to facilitate fire control and existed only within a battalion formation, as they were not permanent subdivisions.

The standard Continental battalion in 1776 was authorized 1 Colonel, 1 Lieutenant Colonel, 1 Major, 1 Adjutant, 1 Surgeon, 1 Surgeon's Mate, 1 Chaplain, and eight companies with 1 Captain , 2 Lieutenants, 1 Ensign, 4 Sergeants, 4 Corporals, 1 Drummer, 1 Fifer, and 76 Privates each, totaling 728 officers and men. However, most, if not all, regiments were considerably below strength. The typical infantry battalion would likely consist of 250 officers and men.

Under the Articles of Confederation that became the ruling documents of the American government during the Revolution, the states were responsible for raising troops for the Continental Army, for organizing and equipping them, and for appointing officers through the rank of Colonel. The states maintained an interest in supplying and administering the troops of their own "lines" as well as their militia. In addition, the Continental agents had to continually enlist state assistance in their own efforts. Lines of authority crisscrossed at every turn. [339]

In accordance with the Maryland Convention's resolution in the spring of 1774, it was not long before companies were formed in several towns and hundreds, as we have seen. A royalist observer, W. Eddis, wrote: "The inhabitants of this providence [Maryland] are incorporated under military regulations and apply the greater part of their time to the different branches of discipline. In Annapolis there are two new companies; in Baltimore seven. And in every district of this province the majority of the people are actually under arms. Almost every hat is decorated with a cockade." [340]

Anti-British feeling in Maryland was strong enough that after the 2nd Convention's militia resolution several companies were formed by the end of 1774. However, probably due to the extra-legal nature of these activities, only a few related documents survive. Just a few names of militia members prior to January 1, 1776 are available. By the spring of 1775 one of the Proprietor's officials wrote in a letter to England that "every appearance indicates approaching hostilities," and that "large sums have been collected for the purchase of arms and ammunition; and persons of all determinations are required to associate under military regulations, on pain of the severest censure."

There is little surviving about the "official" royal militia in Maryland during this period. The governor had expressed reservations about its loyalty, although there were numerous military titles among the gentlemen of the Province (once given or earned, perpetually used). From the alacrity with which the revolutionary companies were formed, it seems likely that most, if not all, were reorganized units of the royal militia, possibly retaining the officers most sympathetic to the colonists' cause and ousting royalist supporters, as was done in New England. Some support for this theory is given by the fact that one of the artillery batteries raised in Annapolis called itself the Royal Artillery Train for a short while. [341]

One of the first companies was organized in Baltimore. It was significant because it was the first unit organized of what was to become the Maryland Line. It continues in existence to this day. One of the units of the Maryland National Guard, the 175th Infantry Regiment of the 29th Infantry Division, traces its lineage back to this Baltimore unit, making it one of the oldest in the U. S. Army, predating its official creation. In December 1774 Mordecai Gist, a young Baltimore merchant from a prominent family, "at the expense of his time and hazard of his business," acted on what he perceived as the coming storm. On December 3rd he formed a militia company of "gentlemen of honor, family and fortune," to be ready for any emergency. They called themselves The Baltimore Independent Cadets. He did so in response to an ever growing feeling that resistance to British force was necessary. The articles of incorporation stated that the company was formed in response to the "Alarming conduct of General Gage and the Oppressive Unconstitutional acts of Parliament to deprive us of Liberty ..."

After sixty men had been enrolled they would meet to elect officers. Gist was subsequently elected Captain. They would be "ready to March to the assistance of our Sister Colonies ... in the space of Forty Eight Hours" of being notified. Under the provisions of its articles of incorporation, the Cadets were required to arm and equip themselves, as well as buy their own uniforms. They "firmly resolve[d] to procure at our own expense a uniform suit of clothes, viz.: Coat turned up with buff (i.e. buff cuffs and lapels [facings]) and trimmed with yellow metal or gold buttons, white stockings, pouch, a pair of pistols, belt and cutlass, with four pounds of powder and sixteen pounds of lead, which shall be ready to equip ourselves at the shortest notice."

The Independent Cadets apparently were drawn largely from Baltimore's upper social classes, as they were willing and able to pay for their own equipment and uniforms. Further, several of them later accepted commissions in the Continental Army at a time when normally only those who were at least moderately well-to-do could afford the long military service. The term Cadet was quickly dropped and Independent Company or Independent Infantry Company was used. The company drilled throughout 1775. However, this was an amateur body, composed purely of volunteers and, as such, enjoyed no legal recognition. After futile appeals for legal incorporation, the Independent Company virtually dissolved. Many of its members, as individuals, either volunteered for the rifle companies going to Boston or enrolled in the newly formed Maryland militia. Some also probably formed the corps of one of Smallwood's companies raised in Baltimore. [342]

By the spring of 1775 the Independent Company was no longer a unique corps, for Maryland was quickly developing an adequate militia. Even before the fighting at Lexington and Concord on April 19th, numerous Baltimore companies were under arms and drilling intensely. Gist's men had their own drillmaster, Richard Carey, a former adjutant from Massachusetts who had been a member of the Ancient and Honorable Artillery Company of Boston, lately commanded by John Hancock, the first president of the Continental Congress. On May 6, 1775 George Washington reviewed Gist's company enroute to the Continental Congress in Philadelphia. It was either the most accomplished of the Baltimore units, had the best looking uniforms, or possessed the best political connections; possibly all three. Less than two months later Washington was elected Commander-in-Chief.

On December 30, 1775, in a letter to Matthew Tilghman, Chairman of the Maryland Convention, Gist requested appointment as an officer. He claimed, correctly, to have raised the first military company in Maryland in preparation for the upcoming conflict. He said, in part, that "[p]rompted by the regard I owe my country, I did at the expense of time and hazard of my business, form a company of militia early in December 1774 - a company composed of gentlemen of honor, families and fortune ... Unanimously approved by this company, I have been appointed to the honor of being their commander ... [not having been confirmed as an Independent Company by the Council of Safety] I have entered my name among the number of applicants who are soliciting preference from the Convention."

His request may just have been a formality, but possibly not. The Convention had been in session since December 7th. Two days later, January 1, 1776, it announced, in a resolution, the units of state troops, regulars, that were going to be formed and their organization. While the officers were not formally announced until two weeks later, presumably there had been ongoing, detailed discussions, in the Convention and in its committees, whether or not to create new units; if so, what composition and organization; and who would fill the officers' positions, especially what became the four field grade officers. The implication is that Gist had been under consideration before his request. Possibly not, but it presumably was a spirited discussion. Gist had a strong desire to serve Maryland and combat the British. As mentioned above, his Independent Cadets had virtually ceased to exist. They had twice requested to be established as an Independent Company by the Council of Safety, but had received no response. However, as we shall see, Gist's request was not denied. He, and over a quarter of the Cadet's officers and non-commissioned officers, enrolled in Smallwood's battalion/regiment when it was organized in early 1776. In fact, Smallwood's 8th Company was drawn from Baltimore and had at its core the Independent Cadets. Until 1777 the terms regiment and battalion were used interchangeably in the Continental Army because regiments were usually one battalion units. Smallwood's Regiment was the nucleus of the soon to be famous body of men known as the Maryland Line.[343]

On December 8, 1774 Frederick County passed an act enabling citizens to begin organizing companies for military use. During 1775 several regiments were raised in the Tom's Creek - Mechanicstown area, in the northern portion of the County's central district. A regiment consisted of two companies ready for military use. The Game Cock Company, so called because of the plum colored feathers in their hats, was commanded by CPT William Blair. A second company was formed under CPT William Shields. There were two other companies raised in Frederick, outside of Tom's Creek that also collectively numbered over 100 men. They were commanded by CPTs Jacob Ambrose and Benjamin Ogle, respectively

The companies from Tom's Creek were initially attached to a Flying Camp Battalion, which was organized in the spring of 1775, a synonymous term for the original regimental designation. As previously noted, the term "flying camp" had been used in the British Army at least as far back as the sixteenth century when Holinshead used it in <u>History of England</u>. Chamber's Encyclopedia of 1729 gave the description as a body of armed men available for quick movement. Thomas Jefferson and, presumably, other well read and educated gentlemen in America had copies of the Encyclopedia in their libraries and were familiar with the term. The Continental Congress used the term for several different situations, but most prevalently as a reserve force of units, regular and/or militia, ready to be deployed where needed when needed. In the summer of 1776 they also used it to designate a specific location, in that case New Jersey. At the state/local level, as in Maryland's case, it designated a group of militia or Home Guard units whose duties were to serve and protect the community in case of invasion, the traditional purpose of both English and American militias. In this case it did not necessarily indicate a specific geographic location, but, rather, a specific state of readiness. They acted like a police force, guarding barracks, government buildings and other important structures and positions. It had been organized in response to the act calling for independent companies for home service. However, by July, 1776 there were at least four regiments called the Flying Battalion that were called to active service.

John Miller in "The Flying Camp Battalion" stated that Blair's, Shields' and Ogle's companies, along with two or three from Montgomery County became part of Smallwood's Regiment. In "The Forgotten Patriots of Tom's Creek Hundred" he contends that several militia companies from Frederick County were allocated and attached to Smallwood's Regiment and accompanied it to New York. Further, he said that when CPT Blair was mortally wounded on Long Island, he was succeeded by CPT Henry Williams. Miller is the only source I found that states this. There was one company in Smallwood's Regiment from Frederick County, but it was commanded by George Stricker initially. There also was one company from Prince George's and Frederick's Lower District (Montgomery). None of the Independent Companies were from either county. Blair, Shields and Ogle are not listed in Steuart's The Maryland Line, drawing from the Archives of Maryland, Vol. 18, or in Hertman's Register of the Officers of the Continental Army, or in McSherry's History of Maryland as Continental Army officers from Maryland. Neither Blair, Shields nor Ogle appear on any muster rolls for Smallwood's Regiment, the Independent Companies, the Maryland Flying Camp in New Jersey or any subsequent unit's rolls, all of which are listed in Muster Rolls and Records of Service of Maryland Troops in the American Revolution, 1775-1783, originally Volume 18 of the Maryland Archives, published in 1972. S. Eugene Clements' and F. Edward Wright's The Maryland Militia in the Revolutionary War, published in 1972, has a number of probable references to the three officers. A CPT William Blair is listed as a member of the 35th Battalion (one of Frederick County's Militia Battalions) on November 29, 1775. Subsequently, a LTC William Blair is listed in the Scharf Collection of the Maryland State Archives with an original commission date (presumably to LTC) of January 3, 1776. He is listed again in

The Proceedings of the State Convention on October 7, 1776 (page 53). Benjamin Ogle, Jr. is listed as a Captain in Frederick County's 2nd Battalion in the Maryland Magazine, 11:50, and James Ogle is listed as an Ensign in CPT B. Ogle's Company in the same citation. Benjamin Ogle is subsequently listed as First Major of the 37th Battalion of the Frederick County militia on January 6, 1776 (page 108). In the Proceedings of the Convention William Shields is listed as a Captain in Frederick County's 3rd Battalion on November 29, 1775 in Maryland Magazine, 11:50. He is subsequently listed as 2nd Major of the 35th Battalion, with a date of rank of January 6, 1776. Later in the Proceedings he is listed as 1st Major of the 35th, with a date of rank of October 7, 1776 (180). Hence, it is doubtful that the three officers and their companies were part of Smallwood's unit, or that they fought with it or any part of it at Long Island; or were ever in the Continental Army. It is possible that they were in the Flying Camp in New Jersey as part of Griffith's Frederick Battalion/Regiment and fought on Long Island and, subsequently, Manhattan, with him under Smallwood's overall command. However, there is no record of their being there and their battalions, the 35th and 37th, did not deploy out of Maryland. [344]

William Richardson was named a Caroline County delegate to the Convention in 1774-1775. In the summer of 1775, when the Convention called for more militia and created the minutemen, Richardson resigned his legislative post and returned to the Eastern Shore. He was elected Captain of Caroline County's East Company of militia. Each company consisted of 50 - 75 privates, plus lieutenants, an ensign, and several non-commissioned officers. The companies were to drill weekly at a location designated by the commanding officer. However, circumstances often dictated that commanders such as Richardson divide their companies into smaller groups and drill them separately once a month. Militia units in Maryland were organized and capable of being deployed by September 1775, but they still needed significant training.

In August 1776, after the minuteman units had been disbanded, including Caroline County's, Richardson was appointed Colonel of the Eastern Shore Battalion/Regiment of the Maryland Flying Camp. Again, Flying Camp designated a reserve force ready to be deployed. It could be at a fixed place, like the Continental Flying Camp at Amboy (Perth Amboy), New Jersey; or, as in this instance, designate a reserve force ready for defense, but not necessarily colocated. Richardson's unit was one of four Maryland Flying Camp Regiments/Battalions in 1776: Smallwood's (regulars, enroute to, if not already in, northern New Jersey/New York) Ewing's, Griffith's and Richardson's. The seven regular Independent Companies were not included, although they were assigned to the Continental Army during this period.

Richardson's Regiment consisted of seven companies from the various Eastern Shore counties, about 650 men in all. At first the troops were provisioned mostly from local stores. However, he also recruited supplies, including arms, from Annapolis and Baltimore. Richardson may have used the landing and storage facilities at Gilpin Point, and possibly his own sailing vessels to import supplies for his regiment at this time. Provisioning the troops was difficult and caused delays before Richardson and his 4th Maryland Battalion/ Regiment could join the Continental Army at Elizabethtown, N.J on September 8, 1776. [345]

After the outbreak of hostilities in April 1775 and after the fighting at Bunker/Breed's Hill, the Continental Congress enacted measures providing for a "Main Army" to add to the New England forces besieging the British in Boston. As previously noted, these measures included authorizing ten companies of riflemen on June 14, 1775. They were to come from Pennsylvania (6), Virginia (2), and Maryland (2). The riflemen were to serve until the end of 1775, a term commensurate with normal practices when authorizing volunteer forces. Some sources state that the term of service was one year, i.e. to June 1776. However, the earlier date appears more accurate. Each company was to form and march independently to Boston. The companies were to have four officers, eight NCOs, a drummer or trumpeter, and 68 privates, a normal company compliment in Maryland at that time.

The Maryland Convention assigned the two companies to Frederick County, the county closest to the frontier. On June 21st Frederick County's Committee of Observation announced the organization of two "companies of expert Riflemen to be furnished by this [Frederick] County, to join the Army near Boston, to be there employed as Light-Infantry under the command of the Chief Officer of the Army ..." The soldiers were to "find their own arms." The officers selected by the Committee were: CPTs Michael Cresap and Thomas Price; and LTs Thomas Warren, Joseph Cresap, Jr., Richard Davis, Otho Holland Williams, John Ross Key, and Moses Rawlings. Michael Cresap was the son of COL Thomas Cresap. Rawlings and Price eventually commanded regiments, Price in late 1776. Williams also commanded a regiment in late 1776, served as General Gates' Adjutant General in 1781 and was promoted to Brigadier General in 1782.

The Committee selected both officers and enlisted volunteers for the two rifle companies from frontiersmen, hunters and trappers, some of whom were said to have come hundreds of miles from beyond Maryland's western boundaries.

The two companies' 130 men were armed with rifles and tomahawks, adorned with Indian face paint and dressed in hunting shirts and moccasins. A letter written by an eyewitness describes the appearance of the riflemen: "I have had the happiness of seeing Captain Michael Cresap marching at the head of a formidable company of upwards of one hundred and thirty men from the mountains and backwoods, painted like Indians, armed with tomahawks and rifles, dressed in hunting shirts and moccasins, and though some of them traversed near eight hundred miles from the banks of the Ohio, they seemed to walk light and easy, and not with less spirit than at the first hour of their march."

They left Maryland on July 18th, arriving at the Flying Camp at Cambridge on August 9th. They traversed 550 miles of difficult terrain without losing a man. Cresap and Price's companies were the first from the south to reach Cambridge. The Virginia troops came in soon afterwards. Their presence, along with the eight other frontier companies, helped persuade the British to evacuate Boston. They were stationed on the south side of Boston. They were described as "remarkably stout and hardy men; many of them are exceeding six feet in height. They are dressed in white frocks, or rifle shirts, and round hats. These men are remarkable for the accuracy of their arms; striking a mark with great certainty at two hundred yards distance … They are now stationed on our lines, and their shot have frequently proved fatal to the British officers and soldiers, who expose themselves to view, even at more than double the distance common musket shot."

Washington considered them a mixed blessing. They were outstanding field soldiers, woods wise and excellent shots. However, their benefits were often outweighed by their outrageous conduct in garrison: ill disciplined, unsanitary and in constant brawls with other units and among themselves. The problem was only partially eliminated when some of them were detached for duty with the Canadian expeditions. The companies' enlistments expired at the end of 1775, along with those of a significant portion of Washington's other troops. Many went home, but some chose to stay on and reenlist.

Cresap and Price started their units southward towards Maryland. In October 1775 Michael Cresap died and was buried in New York. He was succeeded in command by his First Lieutenant, Moses Rawlings. After arriving back in Maryland, the remnants of the companies and many, if not most, of the officers were absorbed into the newly forming units. Rawling's/nee Cresap's men were mostly incorporated into Smallwood's Battalion/Regiment in January 1776. CPT Thomas Price was elected by the Convention as Smallwood's First Major. Price's men were absorbed by the later forming Rifle Regiment.

On June 17, 1776 the Continental Congress decided that the rifle companies from Maryland and Virginia serving with the Continental Army should be formed into a regiment. On June 27th Congress resolved that in addition to the three companies of riflemen from these states serving at New York, four more companies should be raised in Virginia and three in Maryland. Together they formed the 1st Continental Regiment or, more commonly, the German Battalion, so called because the men were raised primarily from among the German settlers in Frederick County and the northern end of the Shenandoah Valley. The men were to be enlisted for three years, making it one of the first units with enlistments longer than one year. CPT Joseph Cresap commanded one of the companies. COL Stephenson of Virginia was placed in command of the regiment. His field grade officers included his deputy, LTC Moses Rawlings and 1st MAJ Otho H. Williams. All three, freshly promoted, were from the original Maryland Rifle Companies. Most of the riflemen were captured at Ft. Washington in November, 1776, effectively ending their war. [346]

By December 1775 Maryland's militia had been reorganized as a defensive body. On January 14, 1776 a new military code was set forth by the Convention sitting in Annapolis. It clarified punishable offenses, established court-martial proceedings, required a monthly reading of the militia rules to the troops, and set an enrollment deadline (i.e. the date all able bodied men had to be enrolled in a militia unit) of March 1st. The militia, newly revitalized and, in essence, recreated by the Convention, gave unsettling evidence of the dangers inherent in extralegal, self appointed government resting on popular goodwill. At first the militia elected their junior officers, the ensigns, lieutenants and captains of company units. The rank and file, many of them men with no property, had a kind of franchise for the first time. Shortly they were demanding a voice in selecting field grade officers, battalion commanders with the rank of major and lieutenant colonel, whose appointments the Convention had specifically reserved for itself. In Queen Anne's County the 20th Battalion refused to acknowledge field officers appointed by the Convention and elected its own colonel and lieutenant colonel, neither of whom was from the elite of the county, where such officers normally came from. [347]

The hope in 1775 and 1776 was that the Continental Army could be recruited from volunteer units already possessing some military organization and discipline. Much of the Continental Army would be roughly comparable to modern day National Guard units. They would be sufficiently "Congressional" or "Continental," however, that the regiments of the 1776 Army would be designated not by their numbers in their respective forces, but by a Continental nomenclature. In mid-January 1776, along with the military code discussed above, the Maryland Convention formally created an armed force, in effect ratifying an organization that had existed for two weeks. It was to be maintained by the state, but was, according to the act that created it, available for service not only for the state of Maryland, but also for the Continental cause.

The initial regiment was created as a unit of eight line companies and a company of riflemen, following the then British infantry regimental structure of nine companies, eight infantry and one light infantry. Each infantry company's strength was authorized at 4 officers, 8 NCOs, a drummer and 60 privates. The light infantry/rifle company had a third lieutenant instead of an ensign. It also had 64 privates, four more than the line or battalion companies. The total number of privates in the regiment was the same as in a regiment of with eight 68 man companies, a normal militia configuration.

In July 1776 the regiment was directed to leave the Maryland Flying Camp (The state's mobile reserve and, in this case, a status, not a location, because the companies were in several different locations.) and to join the main Continental Army under Washington in New York. Part of the regiment made the march to New York mounted, but during the New York campaign the regiment served exclusively as infantry. Although there is an absence of any existing legislation, the Maryland regiment was regarded as Continental from the time it joined Washington, if not earlier, when it arrived in

Philadelphia or the Amboy Flying Camp. On January 8, 1777 it was paid off by Congress, implying Continental service. After the one year men left, those who remained founded the core of the 1st Maryland Regiment of 1777 of the Maryland Brigade (Line) in the reorganized Continental Army. [348]

On January 1, 1776, the Maryland Convention reconvened, having been in virtual continuous session almost four weeks through Christmas. They almost immediately designated themselves as a Committee of the Whole, as we have seen, possibly to review the recommendations of their committees for creating and staffing military units to protect Maryland and serve, potentially, with the Continental Army. After voting themselves back into session, they authorized a battalion of state troops of eight companies, with no light infantry.

On January 2nd the Convention resolved that "the acceptance of any office in the regular forces to be raised in this province, shall be a disqualification of the officer accepting the same, from and after the making out and acceptance of his commission, to be a delegate to serve in convention, or to be of the council of safety, or a member of any committee of observation, or of any other civil office under the authority of the convention, during the continuance of his said commission." This was specifically designed to assert and maintain civilian control over the military. The classicists among the Convention delegates were very aware of what Caesar, Pompey, Crassus, Sulla, Gaius Marius, et al did to the Roman Republic. Further, they were attempting to avoid problems that their British opponents did have with military officers, some senior, also being members of Parliament and opponents of the governing administration and/or its policies. As noted previously, several of the officers about to be given commissions in the units of state troops being created were delegates to the Convention, including the Commander and Deputy Commander, William Smallwood and Francis Ware, respectively.

The Convention then proceeded to elect by ballot the field grade officers for the battalion - Colonel William Smallwood, Lieutenant Colonel Francis Ware, 1st Major Thomas Price (previous commander of one of the Frederick County Rifle Companies in the summer/fall of 1775), and 2nd Major Mordecai Gist (organizer of the Baltimore Independent Cadets). The Convention's Journal does not show the specific results of the election, so it is unknown whether they "competed" individually for each rank/position (The 1st and 2nd Majors' titles designated both a position and a rank.) or were appointed in the order they finished in the election. The men selected were extremely capable. COL Smallwood was subsequently promoted to Brigadier General in October, 1776, taking command of the Maryland Brigade (Line). He was promoted to Major General in 1780. After the war he was elected to three terms as Governor of Maryland. 1st Major Price was promoted to Colonel and command of the 2nd Maryland Regiment in late 1776. 2nd Major Gist commanded the 3rd Maryland Regiment as a Colonel in late 1776 and was promoted to Brigadier General in 1779. Ill health forced LTC Ware to retire from active military service. However, he remained active in local militia activities.

After electing the field officers, the Convention elected seven Captains for the Independent Companies, which will be discussed in detail below. Next, they elected Captains for the Battalion: John Hoskins Stone - 15 votes; William Hyde - 11 (Resigned January 20, 1776; replaced by Patrick Sims); Barton Lucas - 10; Thomas Ewing - 10; Nathaniel Ramsey - 8;

Peter Adams - 8; John Day Scott - 8; Samuel Smith of John [?] - 8; George Stricker - 7. The formal designation of the companies for the battalion was in the order of the election results. So, for example, Thomas Ewing commanded Smallwood's 4th Company and George Stricker commanded the 9th, or Light Infantry. The order of the companies may have indicated the respective order of rank for the Captain Company Commanders, a matter of potential significance in the future in the absence of the field grades. The total number of votes cast or, at least, listed for the Independent Captains was 82, for Battalion Captains was 88. 48 Delegates were listed in the December 7, 1775 opening session. It is unknown exactly how the voting was conducted. Further, there is no indication of where the names of those elected came from. There were committee hearings in December. The men elected, especially to the senior positions were, as we will see, prominent men in their communities. The delegates doing the final selections were not only revered founders of the state of Maryland, but also working, serious politicians. Consequently, the process had to have been a political one, at least to some extent. However, until further documentation is found nothing can be said about the process with any assurance of accuracy. [349]

This was followed by an election of the Lieutenants and Ensigns for all of the Companies being authorized. Those for the Independent Companies will be discussed below. Note that the numerical Lieutenant designations, i. e. 1st, 2d, 3rd, indicate both a rank and a position, like those of the Majors. For the Battalion they were:

1st Lieutenant
Daniel Bowie - 13, Benjamin Ford - 12, William Sterrett - 12, Joseph Butler - 11, Levin Winder

- 10, Nathaniel Ewing - 10, Thomas Harwood - 6, Joseph Campbell - 6, Thomas Smyth - 5 (Light Infantry).

2nd Lieutenant
John Kidd - 11, John Beans - 11, Alexander Roxburgh - 10, Joseph Baxter - 10, Alexander Murray - 9, David Plunkett - 9, Thomas Goldsmith - 8, Joseph Ford - 8, James Ringgold- 8 (Light Infantry).

Ensigns
Benjamin Chambers - 14 (The highest vote count of any Lieutenant or Ensign), Henry Gaither - 12, William Ridgely - 12, Edward Praul - 12, Walker Muse - 12, John Jordan - 12, James Peale - 11, Bryan Philpot - 9, Hatch Dent - 8 (Third Lieutenant of Light Infantry).

These Battalion officers appear to have been generally assigned to companies in the order of finish; i.e., the Lieutenant and Ensign who received the most votes were in the 1st Company, those who had received the least were in the 9th (Light Infantry). The Company officers were responsible for recruiting the soldiers for their respective units. As will be seen, many, if not most, of the enlisted men came from the vicinity of the Captains' home locales. There is no indication that the Lieutenants and Ensigns were similarly tied to those locations. [350]

The original officer staffing for the Regiment follows. These were the officers originally elected in early January, as well as the specialists. As with any military unit, especially one that is being organized and prepared for employment, and more especially one in the midst of a rapidly changing and extremely fluid military environment, there were numerous changes, which will be highlighted and discussed below.

*-Former Baltimore Independent Cadets

Regimental Headquarters

COL William Smallwood; LTC Francis Ware; 1st MAJ Thomas Price; 2nd MAJ Mordecai Gist *; Surgeon - Dr. Charles Wisenthal; 1st Surgeon's Mate - Dr. William Wallace; 2nd Surgeon's Mate - Dr. William Dashiel; Quarter Master - Mr. Joseph Marbury; Clerk to COL - Mr. Christopher Richmond; Acting Adjutant - Mr. Jacob Brice; Chaplain - Rev. Daniel Sire

First Company

CPT John Hoskins Stone; 1LT Daniel Bowie; 2LT John Kidd; ENS Benjamin Chambers

Second Company

CPT William Hyde (Resigned January 20, 1776)) replaced by CPT Patrick Sims; 1LT Benjamin Ford; 2LT John Beans (Beanes); ENS Henry Gaither

Third Company

CPT Barton Lucas; 1LT William Sterrett; 2LT Alexander Roxburgh; ENS William Ridgely

Fourth Company

CPT Thomas Ewing *, 1LT Joseph Butler, 2LT Joseph Baxter (resigned); ENS Edward Praul (promoted to 2LT)

Fifth Company

CPT Nathaniel Ramsey, 1LT Leven Winder, 2LT Alexander Murray, ENS Walker Muse

Sixth Company
CPT Peter Adams, 1LT Nathaniel Ewing, 2LT David Plunkett *, ENS John Jordan

Seventh Company
CPT John Day Scott, 1LT Thomas Harwood, 2LT Thomas Goldsmith, ENS James Peale

Eighth Company
CPT Samuel Smith *, 1LT James Campbell, 2LT Joseph Ford, ENS Bryan Philpot

Ninth Company Light Infantry
CPT George Stricker, 1LT Thomas Smyth, Jr., 2LT James Ringgold, 3LT Hatch Dent, Jr. [351]

The Regimental companies were overwhelmingly drawn, by design, from the Western Shore and, more specifically, from the northern and western counties of the state; i.e. from Cecil, Harford, Baltimore (town and County) and Frederick (now Washington, Frederick, Montgomery and part of Carroll) Counties. However, Prince George's and Charles Counties also provided troops, as did other Western Shore locales. Normally, the companies were recruited and organized in the area where the Company Commander, Captain, was from. Traditionally a commander's ability to recruit men to serve with him had been a major factor in his selection. His subordinate officers usually were also from the same area as the Captain and assisted him in recruiting. While they did assist in recruiting, organizing and training the new troops, it is unclear whether the Lieutenants and Ensigns were primarily from the locations where their respective companies were forming.

The men of the First Company (John Hoskins Stone) were primarily from Charles County. It had been subject to raids and sorties directed by Lord Dunmore, erstwhile royal governor of Virginia, as he and his forces moved up and down the Potomac River and Chesapeake Bay. Dunmore and his marauding fleet had landed on their shores multiple times, burning and looting. This inevitably helped American recruiting. Most of the men of the Second Company (Patrick Sims) were from Prince George's County. It had been established in 1695 from portions of Calvert and Charles Counties. It originally included that territory plus all or parts of Frederick and Montgomery Counties and the District of Columbia. The former two had been subsequently combined in 2/3's of Frederick County. There were also some from Frederick's Lower District (Montgomery). The men of the Third Company (Barton Lucas) were primarily from Prince George's and Montgomery Counties. Montgomery was organized from Frederick's Lower District, and part of Prince George's Counties. The Fourth Company (Thomas Ewing, former Independent Cadet) was from Baltimore, Cecil and Harford Counties. Determining the home locations of the Fifth Company's (Nathaniel Ramsey) troops is more problematic. Ramsey was from Cecil County. The limited available documents (applications for land warrants and pensions for three men after the Revolution) are for men from Prince George's and Montgomery. While accurate, they may not, and probably do not, reflect the home area of the majority of the company. The Sixth Company (Peter Adams) troops were from the Eastern Shore, primarily Queen Anne's, Kent and Caroline Counties.

The Seventh Company (John Day Scott) drew primarily from Anne Arundel County. The Eighth Company (Samuel Smith, a former Independent Cadet) recruited in Baltimore Town and County. It was a direct successor to Gist's Baltimore Independents, while also including men from other militia companies that had been organized in that region. The Ninth Company (George Stricker) were almost all from Frederick County. They were predominantly of German ancestry. The County, created in 1748, shortly before the SY/FI War, was the actual Maryland frontier during that era, not the western boundary in the mountains west of Ft. Cumberland. Many of the soldiers in the Ninth, and in the rifle companies formed the previous summer, as well as their fathers and uncles, had fought during the SY/FI period and had become known for their superior ability to fight "Indian Style" and their superior marksmanship. [352]

The pay for a Private in the Regiment was $5.50 per month; a Sergeant $6.50; a Lieutenant received $18.00; a Captain $26.00; a Lieutenant Colonel $40.00, plus $20.00 for expenses; and a Colonel received $50.00 per month, plus $30.00 for expenses. The daily rations consisted of: 1 pound of beef or ¾ pound of pork,; 1 pound of flour or bread; 3 pints of peas per week or other vegetables; 1 quart of Indian meal per week; 1 gill of vinegar or 1 gill of molasses per day; 1 quart of cider , small beer or rum per day; three pounds of candles per week each hundred men; and 24 pounds of soft soap or 8 pounds of hard soap per week per 100 men. [353]

After establishing Smallwood's Regiment of State troops, the seven Independent Companies, two artillery companies (batteries) and one marine company, the Convention dictated where they would be stationed. The primary focus was still on protecting Maryland from attacks and raids and, more specifically, the two largest ports in the state, Annapolis and Baltimore. On January 14th the Convention directed that the "ordinary station[s] of the land forces [not the marines]" were to be as follows: five companies of the Battalion, together with the Light Infantry (Ninth) Company, one battery of artillery and the Regimental Headquarters under COL Smallwood were to be stationed at Annapolis. The other three companies of the Regiment and the other artillery battery were to be at Baltimore Town. The officers of the Baltimore battery were CPT Nathaniel Smith, 1LT William Woolsey, 2LT Alexander Furnival and 3LT George P. Keeports. LTC Ware and 2nd MAJ Gist were also stationed there, but both were frequently away from Baltimore. [354]

In any military unit there are regular changes in personnel for a wide variety of reasons. Smallwood's was no different. On July 9, 1776, after the Convention had ordered the unit to Philadelphia and points north, the Council of Safety issued commissions promoting a number of officers in the Regiment to fill vacancies, as well as adding some new officers. In many, if not most, cases these probably formalized what had already taken place. In the 1st Company, 2LT John Kidd was promoted to 1LT to replace Daniel Bowie; ENS Benjamin Chambers was promoted to 2LT and Walter Brook Cox was commissioned Ensign. In the 2nd Company 2LT John Beans was promoted to 1LT, replacing Benjamin Ford; ENS Henry Chew Gaither was promoted to 2LT and James Fernandis was commissioned Ensign. In the 3rd Company, 2LT Alexander Roxburgh was promoted to 1LT replacing William Sterrett; ENS William Ridgely was promoted to 2LT and Peter Brown was commissioned Ensign. In the 4th Company ENS Edward Praul was promoted to 2LT replacing Joseph Baxter who had resigned and John Gassaway was commissioned Ensign. In the 5th Company ENS Walker Muse was transferred to the 9th Company as 3LT and was replaced by newly commissioned William Courts. In the 9th Company Muse filled the vacancy created by the promotion of 3LT Hatch Dent to 2LT, replacing James Ringgold. [355]

In January 1776, as part of its legislation dealing with military matters, the Convention also authorized two artillery batteries, as mentioned above, and seven Independent Companies. These companies, even more so than Smallwood's Regiment, were designed to defend Maryland as an independent entity. They were not part of Smallwood's unit and were not under his command. They were also larger than the Regimental Companies, having 92 privates and a total strength of over 100 men if fully manned. They subsequently were referred to as "ready" companies. On January 2nd the Convention elected the Companies' officers. This was the same day they had elected the officers for the Battalion/Regiment. In fact, for each rank (Captain and Lieutenant 1,2,3) the Convention voted on the officers for the Independent Companies before it voted for the Battalion officers of comparable grades. Note that the lowest ranking officer of the Independent companies was a 3rd LT, comparable to the Light Infantry, not an Ensign as in the Battalion companies. Further, as with the battalion, the title 1st, 2nd and 3rd Lieutenant designated both a rank and a position. In the morning they voted for the Captains: Rezin Beall - 15; John Gunby - 14; John Watkins - 11; James Hindman - 10; John Allen Thomas - 9; Lemuel Barrett - 7 (resigned February 16th, replaced by 1LT Thomas Woolford); Edward Veazey - 6. In the afternoon they voted on the Lieutenants and Ensigns:

<u>1LT</u>

Thomas Woolford - 11; Moses Chaille - 11; William Harrison - 10; Uriah Forrest - 10; Bennett Bracco - 10; John Stewart - 6; William Goldsborough - 5

<u>2LT</u>

John Eccleston - 11; John Halkerston 10; John Davidson - 10; Solomon Long - 10; William

Bowie - 7; Archibald Anderson - 7; Samuel Turbutt Wright - 6

3LT
Edward Hindman - 12; Hooper Hudson - 12; Edward DeCourcy - 11; Henry Neale - 10; Ely Dorsey - 8; Daniel Jennifer Adams - 8; Benjamin Brooks - 8

As stated previously, the company grade officers for the Battalion appear to have been generally assigned to companies based on the results of the elections. The officers with the highest vote totals were assigned to the First Company and those with the lowest to the Ninth. This was not completely the case in the Independent Companies. On January 4th the Convention considered making out the commissions, i.e. designating seniority and determining the assignments, of the officers of the Independent Companies in the order in which they stood on the list "As balloted for." This was rejected. A comprehensive list was then offered and approved. As a result, while the Captains companies of assignment were numerically designated in the order of balloting (e.g. Beall in the 1st Independent Company [IC] and Veazey in the 7th), which presumably also indicated relative seniority, the Lieutenants were assigned based on some other method, possibly geographically. Given the dispersion of the companies, they might have been originally assigned to the ones being raised closest to their homes. [356]

On January 14th, after dictating the locations of the Battalion and artillery companies, the Convention did the same for the Independent Companies. Five were allocated for the Eastern Shore: one company in Worcester County, one in Somerset, one in Dorchester and one in Talbot. The remaining company was split equally between Queen Anne's and Kent Counties. On the Western Shore, one company was to be in St. Mary's County and the other split between Calvert and Charles Counties. The original officer staffing follows, along with the primary county (ies) of assignment for recruiting and initial deployment. Even more so than Smallwood's, the Independent Companies, also Maryland State Troops were intended for the specific defense of Maryland. Also listed is each company's formal date of organization, although, as noted above, the location assignments weren't finalized until January 14th.

> 1st Independent Company ((IC), Charles and Calvert Cos., January 2nd
> CPT Rezin Beall, 1LT Bennett Bracco, 2LT John Halkerston, 3LT Daniel Jennifer Adams
> On August 16, 1776 Rezin Beall was promoted to Brigadier General of the Flying Camp, with Jennifer Adams being promoted to be his Brigade Major (principal staff officer; the military staff organizations of recent times did not exist; the position of Brigade Major in the British Army existed as the Brigade's primary/only staff officer at least through World War II). Bracco and Halkerston were promoted to the vacancies above them. In addition, Thomas Beall was appointed 2LT and Calmore Williams 3LT.
>
> 2nd Independent Company (IC), Somerset Co., January 2nd
> CPT John Gunby, 1LT Uriah Forrest, 2LT William Bowie, 3LT Benjamin Brooks

3rd Independent Company (IC), Worcester Co., January 5th
CPT John Watkins, 1LT Moses Chaille, 2LT Solomon Long, 3LT Ely Dorsey

4th Independent Company (IC), Talbot Co., January 5th
CPT James Hindman, 1LT Archibald Anderson, 2LT Edward Hindman, 3LT William Frazier

5th Independent Company (IC), St. Mary's Co., January 2nd
CPT John Allen Thomas, 1LT John Steward (Stewart), 2LT John Davidson, 3LT Henry Neale

6th Independent Company (IC), Dorchester Co., January 5th
CPT Thomas Woolford, 1LT John Eccleston, 2LT Harper Hudson, 3LT Lilburn Williams

7th Independent Company (IC), Queen Anne's and Kent Cos., January 2nd
CPT Edward Veazey, 1LT William Harrison, 2LT Samuel Turbutt Wright, 3LT Edward DeCourcy [357]

The Independent Companies became the core of the 2nd Maryland Regiment, formed during the reorganization conducted in the winter of 1776-1777. In its history, the origins of the 2nd Regiment are traced to the formal authorization of the Independent Companies by the Convention in January 1776. From March 7th to March 14th they were formally organized, although the actual recruitment, organization and initial

training had been going on for two months. It is also probably erroneous to think that these companies, Smallwood's
unit or the other companies started from scratch, that is were
created from willing, but unorganized inexperienced volunteers. While that may have been true to some extent, in all
probability the companies being formed had a core of already
existing militia companies that were absorbed enmass, or, at
least, had a large number of their soldiers, in effect, transfer
into the new unit. Further, many of them probably continued
to serve under the same officers. As will be seen, many, if not
all, of the senior officers were prominent members of their
communities. It is also interesting to note that the Convention
continued to think in terms of companies, raising companies, assigning individual companies. This mind set would
continue into the summer of 1776. To fulfill the requirement
for troops levied on them by the Continental Congress, the
Maryland Convention assigned the Independent Companies
to the Main Continental Army on July 6th. However, they
were not officially adopted until August 17th, 10 days prior to
the Battle of Long Island. They fulfilled part of Maryland's
requirement by allowing the Convention to state that it had
assigned a second battalion/regiment's worth of state troops
to the Continental Army. They just didn't assign a second
command group comparable to Smallwood's. [358]

The Maryland Convention's organization of military
forces during its December 1775 - January 1776 session was
not limited exclusively to State Troops. As discussed above, it
also took actions concerning the militia. In the midst of electing officers for the Battalion/Regiment and the Independent
Companies, dictating their initial deployment locations and
establishing logistic and administrative frameworks and
primitive support organizations, the Convention dealt with

the militia. As indicated above, the minutemen companies were to be paid off by March 1st, with their equipment going to the local committees of observation. Further, all able-bodied freemen between 16 and 50, who had not already done so, were to enroll in the militia by March 1st. Those who failed to do so were subject to fines.

On January 6th the Convention "elected by ballot" officers for the militia throughout the state (Majors through Brigadier Generals). Benjamin Ogle was elected 1st Major of the 2nd Battalion, Middle district (Frederick County). William Blair was elected Lieutenant Colonel of the 3rd Battalion, Middle District. William Shields was elected 2nd Major of the same battalion. The Middle District was, approximately, present day Frederick County where the Game Cock and the other two companies had been formed, in the vicinity of the Tom's Creek Hundred. For a more detailed discussion involving these three officers see above. [359]

In response to Britain's use of German (Hessian) troops the Continental Congress determined to form its own "German" units. Germans were presumed to make good soldiers. As discussed above, the rifle companies formed in 1775 had been staffed overwhelmingly with German immigrants, especially those from Virginia and Maryland. For the Americans of that time, rifle companies equated to companies of frontiersmen, men who used the Pennsylvania long rifle. The southwestern frontier area of Pennsylvania, the Maryland frontier and the northwestern frontier of Virginia all had a heavy concentration of German settlers. There was a steady flow of German immigrants coming west from Philadelphia up the rivers, then across country and southwest down through Frederick County, MD, across the Potomac and continuing southwest down into Virginia to the upper reaches of the Shenandoah

Valley in the vicinity of Winchester. These areas, especially in Maryland and Virginia, had proven fertile recruiting grounds for the British regiments which had accompanied General Braddock almost 25 years previously, as well as at least one regiment (60th Foot, Royal Americans) that was organized in America.

On May 25, 1776 Congress authorized a German Battalion/ Regiment that was to be assigned to the Middle Department, i.e., from New York to Maryland. Men of German descent and immigrant Germans were recruited from Maryland and Pennsylvania for three year terms. Each state was to provide four companies. They came primarily from the Lancaster, PA region, south and south west through Maryland in the vicinity of Frederick and further west. On June 17th a ninth company was subsequently raised in Pennsylvania. The regiment was organized from July 6th through September, 1776 and assigned to the Main Continental Army on September 23, 1776. Congress appointed MAJ Nicholas Hausegger of the 4th Pennsylvania Battalion as Colonel, CPT George Stricker of Smallwood's Light Company as Lieutenant Colonel and Ludwig Weltner of Maryland as Major.

On June 17th Congress decided on another joint unit to be known as the Maryland and Virginia (or Virginia and Maryland if you were from the latter) Rifle Regiment. On June 27th they formally authorized it. The original premise was that the rifle companies from Maryland and Virginia already serving in the Continental Army would form the core of the unit, providing a cadre force. Of the four companies originally raise three had moved with Washington's army from Boston to New York. The fourth, Daniel Morgan's Virginia Company, had been captured in Quebec, along with other American troops. The troops from the three remaining companies were reenlisted on the same terms as the other companies that were forming, i.e., for three years. These "German" Battalions/Regiments were some of the first Continental troops to enlist for that long a period.

Four more companies were to be raised in Virginia and three in Maryland. CPTs Hugh Stephenson of Virginia, Moses Rawlings and Otho Holland Williams became the regimental officers, as Colonel, Lieutenant Colonel And Major, respectively. Some of the companies had still not joined the regiment before it was captured at Ft. Washington, New York in November 1776. A previously noted, this effectively ended their war. [360]

On July 6, 1776, in response to the Continental Congress' "requisition" of June 27th, the Maryland Convention determined to raise still another German Battalion/Regiment, this time exclusively using Maryland troops. The Convention directed that "two companies of riflemen and four companies of Germans" be raised. One company of riflemen was to be from Harford County, two companies of Germans from Baltimore County, and one company of riflemen and two companies of Germans from Frederick County. To expedite the raising of troops, the respective committees of observation were directed to recommend officers, except for the rifle company in Frederick. The Convention wanted Lemuel Barrett to command if he was willing. The German companies were to consist of four officers, eight NCOs, two musicians and 76 Privates. The rifle companies had the same authorized strength, with one exception. They were authorized a 3rd Lieutenant, instead of an Ensign, to help ensure more experience in the command group. The officers, as with the other military units being formed in Maryland, were to be appointed by the central government, in this case the Council of Safety, and not locally appointed or elected. Hence, Maryland's German soldiers and their units. [361]

On June 3, 1776, the Continental Congress resolved that a Flying Camp of 10,000 men be immediately established in the middle states, Pennsylvania, Maryland and Delaware. Maryland's allocation was 3,400 soldiers. As will be seen, they filled their allocation with a mixture of their state troops, who became part of the Continental Army, i.e. regulars, and militia. On June 25th, in response to Congress' resolution, the Maryland Convention resolved unanimously that Maryland would furnish 3405 militia for the Continental Flying Camp. Although they distinguished between state troops and militia within the state, for the purposes of fulfilling their quota all of the troops were considered militia. They were to act with the militia of Pennsylvania and Delaware in the "middle department, that is from this province to New York inclusive ..." and to serve until December 1, 1776 unless sooner discharged by the Continental Congress. Washington's views on the necessity of long term enlistments to help establish stability in his force was starting to take hold in Congress, as evidenced by the three year enlistments for the German and Rifle regiments authorized in May and June, 1776. However, they hadn't filtered down further, or, at least, to the Maryland convention. The six month enlistments were actually longer than what had been used previously in almost all instances as recently as the SY/FI War period. It was what the legislators were used to. Further, it displayed a mind set and belief that was then prevalent among the patriots, namely that it was going to be a short war. With the successes at Concord and then Bunker/Breed's Hill, and the subsequent forced departure of the British from Boston, they strongly felt that the

American troops were going to defeat the British when they met again and do so quickly.

The Convention directed the raising of four battalions/regiments of nine companies each and an independent company. A battalion company was to have four officers, eight NCOs, two musicians and 76 Privates (90 total). The independent company was to have 110 men. The battalions were to be staffed with 3 field grade officers, a quartermaster, an adjutant, and a surgeon with two assistants. The men were to provide their own weapons, if serviceable, but would be furnished other supplies and equipment as required. The four battalions subsequently, in whole or in part, moved to the New Jersey Flying Camp and participated in the battles around New York. The Flying Camp was dissolved on December 1, 1776 with many of the officers and men joining the newly organized Continental regiments in the Maryland Brigade (Line).

On June 27th the Convention designated the force for the Flying camp with greater specificity, allocating out the requirement to provide companies to the counties. In doing so they only specified thirty five companies: St. Mary's - 1; Charles - 2; Calvert - 1; Prince George's - 3; Anne Arundel - 5; Frederick - 9; Baltimore (County) - 4; Harford - 2; Cecil - 2; Kent - 2; Queen Anne's - 2; Talbot - 1; Caroline - 1. The Independent Company, with strength of 110 - 112 men, was to come from Dorchester County. The Convention also elected senior officers for the Flying Camp: Thomas Johnson, Jr. as Brigadier General; Battalion Commanders (Colonel) Otho Holland Williams (Frederick), James Dent (Eastern Shore); John Dent (Western Shore, lower district battalion); and John Carvil Hall (Western Shore, upper district battalion).

For a variety of reasons, none of these officers remained in command for long. By the time the units were close to being ready to move north an entirely different command group was in position. On July 4th the Convention elected deputies to represent Maryland in the Continental Congress, including Thomas Johnson, just elected as the senior officer of the Flying Camp. Preferring that Johnson represent Maryland in the Congress, the Convention proceeded to elect John Dent, the just elected Colonel of the Western Shore lower district battalion. He was replaced by CPT Thomas Ewing.

Officer changes continued. On July 22nd one of the Continental Congress' Maryland delegation, in Philadelphia, informed the Council that CPT George Stricker (9th Co/LI) of Frederick had been appointed Lieutenant Colonel of the German Regiment being raised, a Continental Army unit and, hence, a Continental, not Maryland, commission. Stricker went directly to Frederick County to assist in raising the Regiment's companies. On July 23rd Otho Holland Williams informed the Council that he was reluctantly declining their commission as Colonel of the Frederick County Battalion of the Flying Camp, a short term (six months) state commission. Instead, he chose to accept a Continental commission for 3 years as a Major in the German Regiment. On July 30th Samuel Chase, at the Continental Congress, forwarded a letter from now COL Stricker requesting permission to enlist into the "German Battalion from the companies raised for the Flying Camp [militia]." Chase recommended that the Council approve the request despite potential problems caused by the disparity of enlistment periods, i.e. three years in Continental service versus now less than six months for the militias.

On August 16th the Convention ordered the Council of Safety to direct that the militia units which had been raised for the Flying Camp which were already armed and equipped march to their assigned physical location in the Jerseys (Amboy). It also resolved that the Brigadier General (senior officer) of the Flying Camp (i.e. the militia), if acting in conjunction with the regular troops, would be "subject to the command" of Colonel Smallwood. Rezin Beall was elected Brigadier General of the Flying Camp, replacing John Dent. Beall was a Captain commanding the 1st IC (Calvert/Charles Counties). William Richardson was elected Colonel of the Eastern Shore Battalion, replacing James Kent. William Whitely was elected Lieutenant Colonel. Richardson, as we have seen, had been a delegate to the Convention from Caroline County.

By mid-August, then, the changes to the Flying Camp's command structure appeared complete. As just mentioned, the commander of Maryland's portion of the Flying Camp was newly promoted Rezin Beall. His Brigade Major (Executive/Staff Officer), as previously noted, was Daniel Jennifer Adams, formerly 3LT of Beall's company. The First Battalion was commanded by COL Charles Griffith with companies from all parts of Frederick County. COL Josias Hall commanded the Second battalion, with companies primarily from Baltimore and Harford Counties. COL Thomas Ewing commanded the Third Battalion, with companies primarily from St. Marty's, Charles Calvert, Prince George's and Anne Arundel Counties. As previously noted, COL William Richardson commanded the Fourth battalion, with companies primarily from Cecil, Kent, Queen Anne's, Caroline and Dorchester Counties. [362]

The extra-legal governmental bodies of Maryland, the Convention, the Council of Safety, and local Committees of Observation, were well on their way to establishing viable military units by the summer of 1776. They had evolved in their thinking and understanding of the military requirements and had progressed from authorizing short service militia to long service regulars, or Continentals. As will be seen, they were starting to develop logistical and personnel support programs and organizations and their pace was accelerating. However, before reviewing how the units developed and how they were employed locally before being released to the Continental Army, it is important to learn more about the leaders of these newly created military units.

Colonial America, although more socially dynamic than the Old World, was still hierarchical. This balance was reflected in its officer corps, a very mixed bag indeed. In the New Jersey Line 84 per cent of the officers were drawn from the wealthiest one-third of society, many of them coming from the wealthiest ten percent. The Maryland Line was similar. Senior regimental officers came from the colony's political and social leadership. COL Smallwood, LTC Ware and several of the company commanders had been members of the Maryland Convention prior to their election. Thomas Price had commanded one of the early rifle companies in 1775. Mordecai Gist had organized the Baltimore Independent Cadets in 1774. The session of the Convention that created the Regiment and the Independent Companies opened on December 1, 1775 with four of the soon to be senior military leaders listed as delegates: William Smallwood and Francis Ware from Charles County, Nathaniel Ramsey (5th Co) from Cecil County and John Allen Thomas (5th IC) from St. Mary's County . [363]

Actual combat military experience among the newly elected military officers in Maryland was limited. Most, if not all, had been active members of the militia for a combination of reasons: patriotism, a sense of obligation and the status conveyed both within the local communities and the province as a whole. Militia titles once earned were used forever, unless a higher rank had been subsequently awarded. A few had been involved in actual fighting, or at least had been in units exposed to it, primarily in the SY/FI War era. But even among those, there was no one who had been involved in a battle against European troops fought in the European, not frontier, style. In this they were not alone. Although some of the senior Continental Army officers had seen combat (Washington is a good example), the only ones who had been directly involved in European style war fighting against comparable foes were the former British officers, like Horatio Gates and Charles Lee, and they had only been relatively junior officers. This absence of experience, however, while contributing to some of their initial poor performance, did not deter them.

Why, or even how, these particular officers were initially selected for the Regiment and the Independent Companies is unclear. They were elected, with vote totals shown for the company grade officers. However, there is no clear record of how their names surfaced in the first place. Subsequently the Convention rank ordered the senior militia officers throughout the state. However, if something comparable was done in the selection of the field officers for the state troops, Smallwood et al, there is no record of it. Most, if not all of the first officers selected were locally prominent men. The more senior, especially Smallwood and Ware, had been involved at the provincial level for a decade or more and must have been well known to their colleagues. This is especially true since the overwhelming majority of the Convention delegates had been members of the Assembly for years. The Convention had been meeting periodically for 18 months prior to the officers' election. It had been gradually increasing the military posture of Maryland. It now appeared ready to react to changing circumstances and take serious steps in Maryland's defense. The session in question lasted 6 weeks (December 7, 1775 - January 18, 1776), through the Christmas and New Year's holiday period, and was significantly longer than any of the previous sessions. Committees were appointed to deal with various military matters and, presumably, reports were made to the Convention, but there is no record of these reports in the Convention's journals. At the meeting on January 1st the Convention almost immediately voted itself into a Committee of the Whole to, presumably, review committee reports and more freely debate what they wanted their new military to look like. By January 2nd they had confirmed a structure and started to announce the results of officer elections and unit assignments, which they concluded on the 5th. Then, on January 14th, four days prior to the end of the session, they confirmed what they had done two weeks earlier.

Moving with this relative legislative rapidity implies prior ground work and discussions. Lists must have been presented, delegates ensuring that prominent men from their counties were considered and championed. While they were Maryland's honored Founding Fathers, they were also politicians, not in the modern sense of the term necessarily, but as men of their times. While they would have bridled at the suggestion, the leaders, while presumably honorable men, were astute politicians, sensitive to the needs of their fellow delegates and conscious of the necessity of balancing the various requirements for military defense with the political needs of the delegates to have their men selected. The desire to spread the wealth did not completely dominate their selections. Although the company grade officers were from throughout the Maryland, primarily from the Western Shore in the Regiment and the Eastern Shore in the Independent Companies, the field grade officers were all from the Western Shore. Further, the most senior, William Smallwood and Francis Ware were from the same county, Charles.

Military backgrounds must have played some role. Mordecai Gist was from a prominent Baltimore merchant family, had organized one of the initial militia companies and had been deemed capable enough and popular enough to be elected the unit's commander. Thomas Price, from the more frontier and remote region of Maryland, Frederick County, had impressed his fellow enlistees sufficiently enough to have been selected as one of two commanders of the rifle companies that went to Boston in 1775. His performance must have been considered noteworthy, because he was selected as the Regiment's third ranking officer. Ware had a militia background, to include service during the SY/FI War. Smallwood's military background and experience is more obscure. Tradition states that he led a unit during the SY/FI War and had a military background. Some sources state that he had a military career. However, as will be seen, there are no existing records to document this, or, at least, none have been found to date. While it is an assumption, or implication, Smallwood's experience and background must have provided some justification for his selection in addition to his willingness, availability and political prominence. He was elected to what was, de facto, the highest military position in the state of Maryland (When serving together he superseded the militia generals.). Smallwood must have possessed and shown military acumen and experience at least equal to, and possibly exceeding, that of his fellow delegates.

William Smallwood was a member of a highly respectable family. He was in the fourth generation of a family that had become prominent and wealthy land owners in Southern Maryland. His great-grandfather, James, had arrived in Maryland in 1664. He was of sufficient importance to provide for his own transportation. He apparently arrived unmarried. However, by 1666 he was married to Hester (Ester/ Esther). On May 24, 1666 he requested land (as payment) for his transportation in 1664, as well as for his wife who had arrived in 1650, presumably as a child, with her parents or other relatives. He was granted 100 acres for himself and, for some unknown reason since he had not been involved in it, 50 acres for his wife's transportation. One possible explanation is that neither she nor her parents had ever claimed the transportation payment and James was exercising his husband's rights over his wife's property. James and Hester had eleven children, including Pryor, born in 1680. Hester died some time prior to March 20, 1703. That's the date of her son James' will in which she is not mentioned. James was active in the community, to include being a justice of the Charles County Court. He had numerous real estate transactions, accumulated a large amount of land, and became the owner many plantations (farms). This was both a sign of , and an avenue for, the accumulation of wealth and social advancement in his society. He was appointed the appraiser of numerous estates in the late seventeenth century to help in the probation of wills. He also served as an overseer and trustee of several wills, an indication of his growing prominence and perceived trustworthiness.

In 1676 James was appointed "Post" to convey all public intelligence in Charles County to the Governor and his Council. In 1683 he was a Charles County Commissioner. In 1694 he was the County High Sheriff, as well as contributing 800 pounds of tobacco for the support of a free school. During almost the entire period of the royal government in Maryland, 1692 - 1715, he represented Charles County in the Maryland Assembly. In 1689 he had been appointed Major of Foot in the militia and was named as one of a number of men to regulate civil affairs in Charles County. Being acquainted with most of the County's Indians, in 1692 he was appointed to deal with them. More specifically, in that same year he was authorized to raise a company (some sources say a regiment) to fight the Indians. A unit was to be raised on the east side of Port Tobacco Creek and on the north side of the Potomac River, within the bounds of the Port Tobacco Parish. The boundaries would support him raising a company. However, as a field officer (a Major since 1689) a regiment is more likely. It was probably a small regiment of maybe two companies totaling 65 - 100 men. 65 years later, when raising units in the mid-1770s, the initial militia regiments in Frederick County had only two companies. On June 9, 1700 James is referred to as Lieutenant Colonel in a document. From then until his death in late 1714/early 1715 he was referred to as Colonel. [364]

James' son Pryor was born about 1680. He continued the Smallwoods' upward mobility through the continued accumulation of land and wealth. He and his wife Elizabeth had five children. His oldest son, Bayne was the executor of his estate on his death in 1734. Bayne was born about 1711. Although no contemporary records exist, according to tradition, he was married to Priscilla Heabard of Virginia, a woman of prominent family and fortune. During this period it was easier for the residents of Charles County, especially those with water access to the Potomac River, to maintain contact with Virginia than with Anne Arundel and Annapolis. Much of the overland "road" was a blazed trail through the woods. Travel by water meant going down to the mouth of the Potomac and then north up the Chesapeake Bay. It was quicker to just cross the river. Bayne and Priscilla had seven children: William, Priscilla, Lucy, Eleanor, Margaret, Heabard and Elizabeth. Heabard served during the Revolution as a Lieutenant with a Virginia unit.

Bayne Smallwood, Esquire, was both a merchant and a planter on a large scale. He grew primarily tobacco on his land, with his main estate being on the Potomac River, in the vicinity of Mattawoman Creek. As with most plantations in Maryland and Virginia, the Smallwood's cash crop was tobacco. George Washington, across the river, later in the century, was one of the few who turned to other crops. Through his extensive record keeping Washington tracked his land's declining productivity when growing tobacco and its consequent declining profitability. His cash flow was decreasing and his debts were increasing He subsequently turned to wheat, corn and other grains and produce as less deleterious to the land and more profitable.

Bayne filled the various offices of the Justice of the Peace in Charles County. He served at least one term as the presiding officer in the Court of Common Pleas. He represented Charles County as a delegate to the lower house of the Assembly for almost 20 years, from 1738 to 1756. As he grew older his son William took over the management of the family estates. He died in 1768. [365]

William Smallwood was born in 1732, the exact day unknown. He was one of Bayne's and Priscilla's seven children.

Rieman Steuart claims that he was one of ten children, but all of the other sources state seven. It could be that ten children were born, but only seven survived into adulthood, a favorable ratio for that period. Where he was born is also open to some speculation. J. D. Warfield, among others, states that he was born in Kent County on the Eastern Shore. However, Margaret Klapthor and Peter Brown, among many others, disagree and strongly assert that he was not born in Kent County, but in Charles County. Although his father Bayne owned land in Kent County, there is no record to indicate that William was born there. The record of his life in Charles County is almost continuous and there is no record of William ever having lived in Kent County. He was probably born at "Smallwood's Retreat," Bayne's plantation in Charles County. The plantation was in the Chickamuxon District, on Mattawoman Creek, in western Charles County. By 1760 William was referred to as a Gentleman, a specific title and status during that era. Also in that year he built his own house on the family estate, to become Mattawoman Plantation. By 1777 he was being referred to as Esquire, denoting rising social status. He was an Anglican, the state religion of the upper classes. He was probably a Freemason. In 1763 his occupation was listed as planter. According to tradition, he became a career military officer, albeit part-time in the militia. [366]

Again according to tradition, Smallwood was sent to England at an early age to be educated. The first school of record was that of Thomas Rebank's Grammar School in Kinsdale, Western Cumbria, Kendal School. It subsequently became known as the Quaker School. However, Steuart maintains that the school has no existing records prior to 1770, so Smallwood's attendance cannot be confirmed. Ross Kimmel also states that the Kendal School records are too sparse for the period of his potential attendance to confirm it. When William was qualified he was "received to Eton" near Windsor, where, it is believed, he completed his education. Again, there are no existing records at the school for that period to confirm his attendance. Continuing with tradition, Smallwood became a career military man, until the Revolutionary War, confined within the boundaries of Maryland. Upon returning from his schooling in England he performed military service during the SY/FI War (1756-1763). He was 24 - 31 during that period, the right age for a young officer. Many of his local contemporaries saw active military service in units in the frontier regions. It normally is stated that his military service or career began during the SY/FI War, with the implication being that it continued after that. However, again no hard evidence of such service can be found. It is possible that, like his great grandfather before him, William held a commission as a militia officer during the war and that his unit may have been called up, with no record surviving. In fact, some sources claim that he was in the British Army, again with no surviving records. [367]

Despite the lack of records documenting William Smallwood's military service, there are strong indicators the he had, in fact, served, had significant military service relative to his social peers and fellow military veterans, and that he was a strong military leader. The first can be documented. After the organization of the state troops in January 1776 and the designation of their officers, the Charles County Committee of Observation met on February 26, 1776. The members requested the "honourable Council of Safety ... to inquire of Colonel William Smallwood for a recommendation of officers for the Company he commanded." They had already selected officers for the other eight local companies whose

Captains had been promoted or selected for other positions during the ongoing reorganizations, or had died. With the militia structure having fallen into disrepair in the preceding decade, command of a militia company would have been deemed a significant military, social and political position. By implication, the commanders would almost surely have to have had well known, successful military experience. Further, Smallwood is the only company commander accorded the privilege of recommending and, in effect, selecting his successors. Some of this deference may have been accorded him because of his selection as the highest ranking officer of the state troops and, essentially, the senior military officer in Maryland. But, it might have also been in recognition of his previous military stature.

The second indicator is determined by implication, his selection as the senior commander and highest ranking Maryland officer. He was selected for a variety of reasons: availability, social and political standing and prominence, and the perceived perception of superior abilities among them. However, military skills and leadership capabilities, or the perception thereof, had to be a factor. By implication therefore, his contemporaries, who would have known, must have considered him a superior military leader and, again by implication, this would probably have included some kind of combat experience. The only time he could have gained such experience was during the SY/FI War. The only other possible place he could have exercised leadership in combat would have been with the British Army during fighting in Europe, the Caribbean, India, or the East Indies. Although he and his troops would subsequently confront British officers and soldiers who had done just that, there is absolutely nothing to suggest that Smallwood did so. [368]

William Smallwood's name first appeared in official documents during the late 1750's in Charles County land records, where he recorded a deed for a land purchase. In 1761, at the age of 29, he was elected to represent Charles County in the 3rd session of the 1758-1761 Assembly, in the Lower House. He was elected to the seat previously held by his father Bayne. He served, with some breaks, through 1776, both in the Assembly and in the extra-legal Convention which succeeded it. He served in the Assembly's Lower House in 1761-1763, 1765-1766, 1768-1771, and 1773-1774. He also served as a Justice in Charles County in 1762 and again in 1770-1773, and on the Durham Parish Vestry from April 1775 to April 1776.

During his service in the legislature, he became one of its leaders, speaking and voting on important questions with Thomas Johnson and William Paca. He began his career serving on the Assembly's Arms and Ammunition Committee in 1762-1763, then again in 1765-1766 and 1768-1770. Also in 1765-1766 he served on the Grievance Committee; and in 1773-1774 on the Public Offices Committee. In addition, at various times he served on the Courts of Justice and Examination of Agents Committees. In 1769 Smallwood joined the Maryland Non-Importation Association, a group of merchants and planters protesting the English tea tax and Townsend Acts. [369]

As he became more involved in the Assembly's activities into the 1770s, as well as serving in local offices, Smallwood gained a reputation for decisive leadership. He became an active advocate of the anti-British position in the Assembly as it became the focal point of Maryland's resistance to royal authority. Although sometimes an outspoken individual with regard to his beliefs, Smallwood saw himself as a dutiful subject of the King. As such, he originally defended the old, cherished order of things. This stance was changed dramatically, however, by the events leading up to the Revolutionary War. When the Maryland Convention began to consider the Continental Congress' request for soldiers for a Continental Army, Smallwood, by this time favoring revolution, offered his services to Maryland. He was selected to represent Charles County in many of the sessions of the Maryland convention: 1st (June 23-25, 1774); 2nd (November 21-24, 1774); 4th (April 24-May 3, 1775 (elected, but the records indicate that he did not attend); 5th (July 26-August 14, 1775); 6th (December 7, 1775-January 18,1776); 7th (May 8-25, 1776); 8th (June 21-July 6, 1776). He did not attend the 7th and 8th sessions. In addition to being busy with his new command, he was precluded from holding civilian office while serving with the state troops by legislation passed by the Convention in January, 1776. [370]

On May 22, 1774 Smallwood was reappointed as a Deputy/ Delegate to represent Charles County at any "General Convention to be held by this Province." He was reappointed in the sense that he had been a Delegate to the Assembly as had been most of his soon to be colleagues at the Convention. He was among sixteen appointed, any five of whom had the power and authority to act for and bind the county. In 1774 he had joined the Charles County Association of Freemen, signing another non-importation agreement, this time protesting Parliament's Boston Port Act. In June he joined a group of county residents at Port Tobacco to draw up the agreement.

On June 14, 1774 they gathered at the Court House in Port Tobacco to "deliberate on the effect and tendency of the Act of Parliament for blocking up the port and harbor of Boston." Smallwood was one of eighteen men named to the county's

Committee of Correspondence "to answer and receive all letters" from similar committees throughout the colonies. Any seven of the eighteen could act as the Committee. In addition to dealing with correspondence, they were authorized in an emergency "to call a general meeting of the county." He was listed second after William Hansen who had been chosen chairman of the meeting. He was also one of nine men, all also on the Committee of Correspondence, who were appointed as Deputies for Charles County to attend the general meeting scheduled in Annapolis for June 22nd. The Charles County meeting had resolved that "[d]eputies should be sent from this County to meet at the City of Annapolis on the 22nd instant, and join with the Deputies appointed by the several counties in a general, rational, and practicable Association for this Province, and to appoint Deputies to attend a Congress of those nominated by the several Colonies, and to adopt any other Measures for the relief of the people of Boston, which to them seems reasonable." He was among the Charles County Deputies at the Convention's June 1774 session. [371]

On November 18, 1774 there was a meeting in Port Tobacco of the inhabitants of Charles County "qualified to vote for Representatives" to the Continental Congress in Port Tobacco. It elected a committee of 100 men, the best known citizens of Charles County, to "act and represent" the county "and carry into execution the Association agreed on by the American Continental Congress." Seven of the one hundred members acting together had the power to act for the entire group. Smallwood was selected for the committee, being listed second after Walter Hansen, the chairman of the meeting. He was also one of eleven (Klapthor and Brown state twelve) Deputies selected to represent Charles County at the next Provincial "Meeting on the 21st instant ..." He again was second, after Samuel Hansen. Smallwood was not reappointed to the Committee of Correspondence. [372]

At a meeting on January 2, 1775, again in Port Tobacco, Smallwood was reappointed as a Deputy to the next Provincial Convention. He was one of 13, any three of whom could act for and bind the county. He was also appointed to the committee to manage and conduct a general subscription to raise funds to satisfy what remained of the "sum of money appointed to be raised in this County by the last Provincial Convention," 800 pounds. They were to offer subscriptions "to every free person in each Hundred." Smallwood had the Upper Hundred in Durham Parish, while CPT Joseph H. Harrison had the Lower Hundred. Six months later he was recorded as present at the opening session of the Convention on July 26, 1775, one of six Deputies representing Charles County. He was one of the subscribers/signers of the Association of Freemen of Maryland, proposed on the session's opening day. The Association is outlined in full as Report No. 13 appended to the Journal of the Convention's July-August proceedings. It advocated "opposition by armes to the British troops, employed to enforce obedience to the late acts and statutes of the British parliament, for raising revenue in America." [373]

In August 1775 Smallwood was one of 100 citizens of Charles County petitioning the Convention to restore the citizenship of one Patrick Graham of Port Tobacco. Graham had gotten into trouble helping John Bailie smuggle in and sell banned British goods. On September 12th Smallwood was selected, along with 31 other members of Charles County's Committee of Observation, to serve for a period of one year. He was also elected as one of five Deputies to represent the County at the Provincial Convention for a term of one year.

On September 27th he chaired a meeting of the Committee for Charles County electing himself and six others to license suits in the County, "agreeable to an order of the late Convention [the July-August session]." The Committee also elected a five man Committee of Correspondence. As previously noted, Smallwood was listed as one of five Deputies to the Convention in the record of its opening session on December 7, 1775. [374]

Although, as will be discussed, Smallwood did not lead his unit on August 27th, he was actively involved in the rest of the fighting in and around New York in 1776. In October he was promoted to Brigadier General and, ultimately, appointed to command the Maryland Brigade (the "Maryland Line"). In 1780, while in South Carolina he was promoted to Major General and placed in command of a division. He is mentioned several different times in the journal of a teenage Quaker girl, Sally Wister, whose family was living near Smallwood's headquarters in the vicinity of Wilmington, Delaware in the winter of 1777-1778. She first mentioned him on October 20th: "The General is tall, portly, well made; a truly martial air, the behaviour and manner of a gentleman, a good understanding and a great humanity of disposition constituted the character of Smallwood." On October 17th she wrote: "We had the pleasure of the general and his suite at afternoon tea. He (the General, I mean) is most agreeable: so lively, so free and chats so gaily that I have quite an esteem for him." And on November 1st: I declare this General is very, very entertaining, so good natured, so good humour'd and yet so sensible. I wonder he is not married. Are there no ladies formed to his taste?" [375]

After the war, in 1784, he was elected as a Maryland Delegate to the Continental Congress. However, he did not serve. He chose, instead, to serve as Governor of Maryland from 1785-1788. As Governor he called the Maryland Convention that ratified the U. S. Constitution. About that time, in the 1790 census, Smallwood was recorded as having 56 slaves at Smallwood's Retreat on Mattawoman Plantation. According to the records of Durham Parish from the same period, his yearly crop of tobacco was 3,000 pounds. By 1791 he was in the Maryland Senate, being elected Senate President for the first session. He died in 1792, before the opening of the second session. [376]

William Smallwood became a major figure in Maryland during the Revolutionary War era. He was a prominent, successful plantation owner, merchant, community member and political figure in the pre-war period. His involvement in the political activities of the day at the local and provincial level increased over time. He was esteemed by both his neighbors and his provincial peers, as evidenced by his selection to numerous important positions leading up to the outbreak of the fighting. His political prestige grew during the war, and after it, as indicated by the high offices he was selected to. He appears to have been an excellent organizer and trainer, as shown by the performance of his soldiers in their first battle on August 27, 1776. They were generally accorded to have been instrumental in the survival of Washington's Army and did so without Smallwood. Due to circumstances beyond his control, his Regiment was commanded by the third ranking officer present in New York and the fourth in the chain of command. The absence of the commander can be extremely deleterious to a unit in a crisis situation. That it wasn't is indicative of well trained, motivated soldiers and a cohesive, organized unit; in almost every instance the results of the efforts of a good commander.

However, Smallwood also had his negative side and it often overshadowed his outstanding contributions in Continental service. According to a biographer, Smallwood "made himself disagreeable by repeated complaints that he was not promoted as rapidly as he deserved; by complaints that his state was not accorded recognition in proportion to its service; and by his offensive attitude towards foreigners. The sacrifices of his men during battle seemed not to disturb him. His greatest service in the war was as a drill master, in raising men and supplies, and in administering other military affairs in his state." [377]

Francis Ware of Charles County was appointed Lieutenant Colonel in the Maryland Battalion in January 1776, the second ranking officer to COL Smallwood. As with Smallwood, there is no record to indicate why or how he was selected except a general statement to the effect that he had been elected. The Battalion was primarily recruited on the Western Shore, but there was some geographical and political dispersion of the field officers, except for Ware and Smallwood, both from Charles County. Given the social, political, economic, and geographic circles they were involved in, they must have known each other and, possibly, been close colleagues and/ or friends. It is probable that Smallwood approved of Ware's appointment, at a minimum, if not outright recommending him. However, no conclusive record exists either way.

Born in Charles County, probably in 1732, Francis Ware was the son of Francis Ware, one of five children, four sons and a daughter. Given his subsequent involvement in political activities in the colonial, pre-Revolutionary and Revolutionary periods, he came from a family of some distinction and, probably, wealth. He was married by 1764. He was literate, but no record of his schooling exists. Possibly it was a combination of family taught and a tutor, often used by the well-to-do of that period. He was considered a gentleman in 1764 and Esquire in 1776, like his fellow Charles Countian, William Smallwood. His occupation was listed as planter. Unlike Smallwood, there is a record of Ware's military service, which probably commenced during the SY/FI War. He was in his twenties and early thirties during that period. He commanded a company of Maryland Troops from October 9, 1757 - December 30, 1758, probably at Ft. Frederick. Those troops were the next step up from the militia, comparable to the Virginia Provincial Regiment of George Washington. Command of them implied some previously acquired military skill and experience, as well as political connections, the way of the mid-eighteenth century upper class world. He continued to serve in the militia and was listed as a Captain in 1775. At the February 16, 1776 meeting of the Charles County Committee of Observation the slate of officers proposed to be commissioned to fill vacancies in the County's militia companies included one for the company of now "Colonel [Lieutenant Colonel] Francis Ware." [378]

Ware was elected to fill a vacancy in the Lower House of the Assembly for 1765-1766, a co-member of the Charles county delegation with Smallwood. He served on the Arms and Ammunition Committee with him during that session. Subsequently, they served together on the Grievance and Arms and Ammunition Committees from 1768-1771. Ware again served on the Arms and Ammunition Committee from 1773-1774. He was elected to represent Charles County at the Maryland Convention in 1774 and, with one exception, was re-elected through early July 1776. He was elected to attend the first and second sessions in 1774, the fourth and fifth in 1775 (although he did not attend the latter), and the sixth - eighth in 1775-1776. He did not attend the seventh and eighth sessions because his military appointment to the Maryland Battalion precluded holding political office. [379]

Eighteenth century electioneering involved more than behind the scenes maneuvering, election day speeches and a few real issues. Candidates willingly "treated" electors before and after balloting in a convenient tavern. Liquor flowed freely on election day, but many came to consider it bribery for candidates to "treat" the voters. It had become so common that in 1768 Maryland's Lower House prohibited any person from "giving any money, meat, drink, entertainment, or provision or [making] ... any promise, agreement, obligation or engagement ... in order to be elected." Nonetheless, the practice continued. The elections of one Josiah Hawkins and Francis Ware to the Lower House were challenged for "treating." On October 14, 1771 the House of Delegates considered a petition charging both of them with "treating." The objection was sustained and they were both dismissed from the House, the Speaker signifying that "their attendance was no longer required." In the election called to fill their seats they were both re-elected to represent Charles County and qualified on November 18, 1771, one month later. [380]

In 1774 Ware was a member of the Board of Trustees of the school at Charlotte Hall in St. Mary's County, serving as the Charles County representative. The school was funded by St. Mary's, Charles and Prince George's Counties. On June 14th, at the meeting at Port Tobacco, Ware joined Smallwood in being one of eighteen men named to the Charles County Committee of Correspondence. He was the fourth name listed. He was also one of the nine from the group selected to attend the meeting in Annapolis in June, representing Charles County, to discuss the British closing of the port of Boston, what became the first session of the Maryland Convention. Again, he was listed fourth. He was listed among the eight Charles County Deputies who attended the June 22-25 session, On November 18, 1774, at an emergency meeting; he was also selected to the 100 man Charles County Committee to act for and represent Charles County and to execute any association agreed upon by the Continental Congress. He was, again, the fourth person listed. He was selected to attend the November 21st Convention session. Similarly to Smallwood, he was not reappointed to the Committee of Correspondence. [381]

On January 2, 1775, Ware joined Smallwood in being selected as a Deputy for the next Convention session. He was also selected as a member of the Committee to raise, manage and conduct a general subscription to raise funds to fulfill the County's quota to the Convention to cover the costs associated with creating the military. While Smallwood was in Durham Parish, Ware joined Josiah Hawkins in the East Hundred of Port Tobacco Parish. On September 12th he and Smallwood joined 29 other members of the county Committee of Observation. Their terms were set at one year. He was also one of five deputies selected to represent Charles County in the Convention. Their terms were also set at one year, eliminating the requirement for elections each session. On September 27th a Committee elected Ware, Smallwood and 3 others to license suits in the County, "agreeable to an order of the late Congress (July ... August, 1775)." He and Smallwood were listed as two of the five Charles County Deputies at the Convention's opening session on December 7, 1775. [382]

On January 1, 1776, Ware and Thomas Stone, also of Charles County and future Mary- land Delegate to the

Continental Congress and signer of the Declaration of Independence, along with others, were appointed to a committee "for raising clothing and victualizing forces in the Province and to report regulations on governing troops." The next day he was elected Lieutenant Colonel of the Maryland Battalion and, in effect, the second highest ranking military officer in Maryland. On January 17th he was still listed as a member of the Convention, although he was absent. This indicated that he had not yet accepted his commission, because doing so would have precluded him from holding civil office under the provisions of the law passed January 2, 1776. As will be discussed, he wasn't present for the Battle of Long Island on August 27th. However, during the reorganization in December of that year he was promoted to Colonel and given command of the 1st Maryland Regiment in Smallwood's Maryland Brigade. Illness and infirmity forced him to resign his commission and he returned to Charles County. From July 1, 1777 to at least January 17, 1782, he served as a Colonel in the militia and as the County Lieutenant (senior officer) for Charles County. He was listed as a resident of the Port Tobacco East Hundred in 1778. He also held other local County positions, including sheriff, through 1782. He represented Charles County again in the Lower House from 1783-1784. He died after 1798. [383]

Thomas Price was born on September 3, 1732 (the same year as Smallwood, Ware and Washington), possibly in Philadelphia. By 1754 his family had immigrated to Frederick County. His father was John Price, his mother Rebecca King. By 1765 he was married to Mary, with whom he had numerous children. He was privately educated, listed as a Gentleman by 1764 and an Esquire by 1788. He was a planter and owned a hat shop in Frederick Town. He held several public offices in Frederick County during the 1760s and 1770s, including justice, public school visitor and coroner. He also held local offices in Frederick in 1780 and 1781.

At a meeting on June 20, 1774 Price was one of nine men selected to be a "Committee to attend the General Congress at Annapolis." This group, plus 6 more, was designated a Committee of Correspondence with any six having the power to act. He was recorded as one of 12 Deputies from Frederick County attending the Convention from June 22-25. On November 18, 1774 at a meeting of Frederick County inhabitants, Price was appointed to a large Committee to "carry into execution the Association agreed on by the American Continental Congress." This was the same date as the Charles County meeting that selected a comparable group for the same purpose. This may not have been coincidental, because exactly the same verbiage was used in describing the purpose of the Committees in both counties. It's possible, if not probable, that the Convention dictated the dates of the meetings and the language to be used. Price was selected again as a member of the Committee of Correspondence and to attend the November session of the Convention. He attended three sessions in 1774.

On January 24, 1775, Price, along with many others, was selected to serve on a Committee of Observation to enforce the Association and Resolves of the Continental Congress (This may actually have taken place in the previously referred to meeting on November 18, 1774.). He was subsequently appointed to a more compact Committee of Correspondence whose term ran through October 1775. Finally, he was selected to help administer a subscription in the Frederick Hundred to help raise 1,330 pounds throughout the County. This was Frederick's share of the 10,000 pounds the Convention had directed to be raised to purchase arms and ammunition. His Hundred was one of 33 some odd hundreds/areas throughout Frederick County. Two other future members of the Rifle Companies, Otho Holland Williams and Richard Davis, were also selected to aid in the subscription.

Price had some, and possibly extensive, military experience; most, if not all of it, on the frontier. In 1759 he was listed as a Captain in Pennsylvania, after his family had moved to Frederick. In June, 1775 the Frederick County Committee of Observation selected him as one of the two Rifle Company Commanders. He was politically, as well as, probably, economically and socially, prominent in the community. He must have exhibited strong leadership and woods lore to have been given command of a group of frontiersmen. As noted above, his and the other rifle companies from Maryland and Virginia contributed significantly to Washington's success in Boston. In January 1776 he was selected First Major (third in command) of the Maryland Battalion. Duties assigned him by the Convention to protect Maryland effectively precluded him from joining Smallwood in time for the battle on August 27th. He and the companies he commanded rejoined in September and participated in the fighting around New York. In December 1776 he was promoted to Colonel in the Continental Army and subsequently given command of the 2nd Maryland Regiment in the Maryland Brigade. He served until April 1780. Returning to Frederick County, he died in 1795. [384]

Mordecai Gist was the member of a prominent Baltimore County and Maryland family. Born in 1743, possibly in Reisterstown, he was the fourth child of Thomas and Susannah Cockey [Cockeysville] Gist. Thomas Gist's father, Captain Richard Gist (1684 - August 28, 1741) was the surveyor of the Eastern Shore and one of the commissioners who laid out Baltimore in 1729. Richard's father, Christopher Richard (1655 or 1659 - 1690) was an English immigrant who arrived in Maryland prior to 1682 and settled in south Canton on the south bank of the Patapsco River. He married Elizabeth Cromwell (1660 - 1694), believed to have been a relative of the Lord Protector, Oliver Cromwell. One of Mordecai's great-great- grandfathers was Lawrence Washington (1602 - 1655), also George Washington's great- great-grandfather. Hence, he was Washington's third cousin. He was also the nephew of Christopher Gist of western Maryland. Christopher Gist was a frontier settler, explorer, scout and trader. In 1753 he accompanied Washington on his expedition into the Ohio country. On that journey he saved Washington's life on two separate occasions. Mordecai's formal schooling was at St. Paul's Parish school, and he was educated for commercial pursuits.

In the pre-Revolutionary years Gist was a sea captain and became a prosperous and wealthy merchant, operating on Gay Street. He became a member of the Baltimore non-importation committee which attempted to implement the non-importation resolutions of the Continental Congress. In October 1774 he represented Baltimore Town in a meeting in Annapolis to determine what should be done with a ship-load of tea at the Annapolis docks. On November 12, 1774 Gist was one of 29 men appointed to the Baltimore County Committee of Observation representing Baltimore Town. In December of the same year he helped organize the Baltimore Independent Cadets, a company-sized, volunteer, military unit, and was elected its commander (Captain). The Independent Cadets were the immediate predecessors of the 8th Company of Smallwood's Regiment. In August 1775 Gist was one of two Captains commended, along with their companies, for assisting the sheriff of Baltimore County in capturing a debtor who had been arrested and, subsequently, freed by "some disorderly people," and for restoring order.

On September 25, 1775 Gist was elected to Baltimore County's Committee of Observation, one of thirty-five. In January 1776 he was elected/appointed Second Major, fourth in command, of the Maryland Battalion of State Troops. On August 27th, on Long Island, 1st Major Thomas Price had still not joined the Regiment. COL Smallwood and LTC Ware were on court martial duty in New York. Gist was left in command of the Regiment. It was his first experience in combat. By all accounts he performed brilliantly. In the reorganization of late 1776 he was promoted to Colonel in the Continental Army and then given command of the 3rd Regiment in Smallwood's Maryland Brigade. He joined Ware (1st Reg.) and Price (2nd Reg.) in command. In January 1779 he was promoted to Brigadier General and commander of the Second Maryland Brigade. He and his unit fought in the south under Nathaniel Green. Gist was subsequently given command of the Light Corps during the reorganization of Greene's army in 1782. He was present at and witnessed Cornwallis' surrender at Yorktown. He died in 1792. [385]

William Truman Stoddert, nephew of William Smallwood, was born in 1759. His boyhood home was "Southhampton Enlarged" on Pamonkey Creek. He was left an orphan at the age of nine, inheriting the estates of his mother and grandfather. Smallwood was appointed executor of the estate and it seems likely that he played a large part in rearing Stoddert. He attended Philadelphia College until 1776 when, at age 17, he enlisted in the Continental Army. He eventually served as Brigade major (The primary, and sometimes sole, staff position in both British and American Brigades.) for the Maryland Brigade under his uncle. [386]

John Hoskins Stone was born in Charles County in 1745 (several sources state 1750). His parents were Thomas Stone and Elizabeth Jennifer. His brother, Thomas Stone, was a member of the Continental Congress. His uncle, Daniel St. Thomas Jennifer, was a member and then president of the Council of Safety, president of the Maryland Senate, and a member of the Continental Congress from 1778 - 1782. He was educated in a private school in Charles County and later studied law. He was an Anglican, the religion of the upper classes, a well known attorney in Annapolis and Charles County, and a merchant in Charles County. In 1774 he was elected a member of the Charles County Committee of Correspondence. He was elected to represent Charles County at the 5th Maryland Convention from July 26 - August 14, 1775, joining Smallwood and Ware, among others. He was also a signer and member of the Association of Freemen of Maryland.

By 1775 Stone commanded a militia company in Charles County and continued as a Captain in the militia until January 1776 when he was appointed Captain and commander of the 1st Company of the Battalion of Maryland troops. He was one of at least 8 Charles County militia company commanders for whom the Committee of Observation recommended replacements in February 1776. Edward Papenfuse states that Stone was quickly promoted to Major on January 14, 1776, probably in the militia. He also stated that Stone helped form the Maryland Flying Camp and fought at Long Island, in New York and, later, at Princeton. During the reorganization in late 1776 he was promoted to Lieutenant Colonel of the 1st Regiment of the Maryland Brigade (Line) under Francis

Ware. Upon Ware's resignation in February 1777, Stone was promoted to Colonel of the Regiment. He was severely wounded at Germantown in October 1777. He was eventually permanently incapacitated and resigned his commission on August 1, 1779. He subsequently served in numerous local and state positions, culminating in being Governor of Maryland from 1794 - 1797. He died in 1804. [387]

Daniel Bowie was born in 1754 in the Lower District of Frederick County, now Prince George's County. His parents were Thomas Bowie and Hannah Lee. She was the granddaughter of COL Richard Lee, the immigrant ancestor and progenitor of the Lee family of Virginia and West Virginia. He was selected 1st Lieutenant and appointed to the 1st Company of the Maryland Battalion in January 1776. In February he was promoted to Captain and command of the 1st Company to fill the vacancy created by John Hoskins Stone's departure. He was replaced by 2LT John Kidd, while ENS Benjamin Chambers replaced Kidd as 2LT. Bowie organized, trained and commanded the company through August 27th on Long Island where he was wounded and then captured. He died in captivity. [388]

Other 1st Company officers included the following. Cadet William Courts enlisted on January 14, 1776. He was promoted to Ensign in the 5th Company on July 9th. He was wounded and taken prisoner on August 27th. He subsequently was exchanged in December 9th and promoted to 2nd Lieutenant in the 1st Maryland Regiment on December 10th. Cadet James Fernandis enlisted on January 30, 1776. In July 19th he was promoted to Ensign in the 2nd company. Taken prisoner on August 27th, he wasn't exchanged until March 24, 1777. In the meantime he had been promoted to 2nd LT in abstentia on December 10, 1776. He was subsequently promoted to 1st

LT on April 17, 1777 and Captain Lieutenant on March 1, 1778. ENS Samuel McPherson enlisted on January 14, 1776. He remained in the Continental Army for the duration of the war, eventually achieving the rank of Captain. Cadet Charles Smith enlisted on January 24, 1776. He was promoted to 2nd LT with the 1st Maryland Regiment on December 10, 1776. He subsequently was promoted to 1st LT on February 20, 1778 and Captain Lieutenant on August 2, 1779. [389]

Patrick Sims (Sim) was the son of COL Joseph Sims and his wife Catherine Murdock. He was commissioned Captain and appointed as commander of the 2nd Company of the Maryland Battalion. He replaced CPT William Hyde, the original commander, who had resigned on January 20, 1776. He was promoted to Major in the 1st Maryland Regiment in January 1777, and then to Lieutenant Colonel in March. Sims resigned for unknown reasons on June 20, 1777. On March 10, 1778 he was appointed Colonel of Prince George's County's Middle Battalion of militia. His father Joseph commanded the Lower Battalion. After the war Sims resided on his plantation, Sims' Delight. In his application for a military pension in 1818 Sims stated that "he was appointed Captain in the fall of the year 1775 in the regiment Commanded by Colonel Smallwood of the regulars, was on recruiting service until February and joined the regiment in Annapolis ..." Sims probably merged his militia and regular service together when he applied 40+ years after the event. [390]

Other 2nd Company Officers included the following. Benjamin Ford was commissioned 1st LT on January 14, 1776. He was promoted to Captain in May 1776 and assumed command of the 9th (Light Infantry) Company. He was promoted to Major in the 2nd Maryland Regiment on December 10, 1776. On April 17, 1777 he was promoted to Lieutenant

Colonel of the 6th Maryland Regiment. He transferred to the 5th Maryland Regiment in January 1781, dying of his wounds on June 15, 1781. Ensign Henry Gaither, son of Henry Gaither and Martha Ridgely, was born in 1751. Commissioned on January 3, 1776, he was promoted to 2nd LT on July 9th and by August 27th he was a 1st Lieutenant. Serving until the end of the war, he was a Breveret Major. He remained in the Army after the war and was appointed Lieutenant Colonel of the 3rd Infantry Regiment in 1793. He served until 1802. Cadet Walter Brooke Cox, son of John Cox and Sarah Brooke, was in the company, but no enlistment date was given. He was promoted to Ensign on July 9, 1776 and by April 1777, the date he resigned, he had been promoted to 1st LT. [391]

Barton Lucas, son of Thomas Lucas and Ann Hungerford, was born in Rock Creek Hundred, then in Prince George's County, in 1730. He served as a soldier with Maryland forces and also in Virginia units during the SY/FI War. He was commissioned Captain and assigned to command the 3rd Company of the Maryland Battalion. Lucas was ill during the Battle of Long Island and did not participate on August 27th. He was apparently distraught over the loss of the overwhelming majority of his company during the battle. This, combined with, and probably enhanced by, his illness, caused him to resign on December 1, 1776. (Some sources say October 1, 1776.) However, he continued to serve in the militia. He was listed as a Colonel of the 25th Battalion in Anne Arundel County on March 10, 1778. He was subsequently shown as the Colonel of the Lower Battalion of Prince George's County in April 1779. [392]

Other 3rd Company officers include the following. William Ridgely was commissioned Ensign on January 14, 1776. He was promoted to 2nd LT on July 9th. Ridgely was captured on

August 27th. He was appointed 2nd LT in the new 1st Maryland Regiment on December 10, 1776, but never joined the unit. Alexander Roxburgh was commissioned 2nd LT on January 3, 1776. Promoted to 1st LT on July 9th, he was promoted to Captain in the 1st Maryland Regiment on December 10th and to Major in the 2nd Maryland Regiment on April 7, 1780. He continued to serve in the Army until November 1783. William Sterrett was commissioned 1st LT in January 3, 1776. 2LT Roxburgh was promoted to 1st LT on July 9th, but there is no indication where Sterrett went. He was captured on August 27th and initially it was believed that he had died during the battle. [393]

Nathaniel Ramsey was born on May 1, 1741, the second son of James Ramsey and June Montgomery of East Drumore Township, Lancaster County, PA. James was a farmer who had emigrated from Ireland and served in the Pennsylvania Assembly. Nathaniel was one of three brothers, including David who represented South Carolina in the Continental Congress from 1782-1786. Nathaniel graduated from Princeton (then the College of New Jersey) in 1767 and then read law. By 1781 he was an Esquire. By 1771 Ramsey had settled in Cecil County, in Charlestown on the banks of the North East River. There he bought a house from John Ross Key, father of Francis Scott Key, and settled down to practice law. He married a widow, Margaret Jane MacMordea, sister of Charles Willson Peale. He became a planter and continued to practice law in the Maryland Provincial courts as well as those of Cecil and Harford Counties.

Ramsey became a political leader of the local Scots and Irish. He was a member of the local Council of Safety and he was also active militarily, being listed as a Captain and Company Commander of one of Cecil County's militia companies on August 1, 1775. Ramsey was elected to represent Cecil County in the Maryland Convention during the 4th (April/May 1775) through 8th (June/July 1776) sessions. On July 28th, 1775 he is shown as joining the 5th Maryland Convention, already in session. He subsequently subscribed to and signed the Association of the Freemen of Maryland, which had been initially introduced on July 26th. In January 1776 he was elected to be a Captain of Maryland Troops in the Maryland Battalion. On January 14th his appointment as commander of the 5th Company was confirmed by the Convention.

Ramsey was not only involved with recruiting and training his own company, he also had regimental wide responsibilities. On February 10th the Council of Safety gave him permission to purchase linen to make rifle frontier shirts for the troops. When the Regiment departed for Philadelphia each company wore linen hunting shirts of different colors. In December 1776 Ramsey was promoted to Lieutenant Colonel of the 3rd Maryland Regiment under COL Gist. He survived Valley Forge and fought heroically at Monmouth, NJ in 1778 before he was wounded and captured. He was on parole until he was exchanged in December 1780, retiring in January 1781. Ramsey subsequently served in numerous local, state and federal positions. They included: a Delegate to the Continental Congress 1786-1787, U. S. Marshal 1790-1798, and Naval Officer, Port of Baltimore 1794-1817. He unsuccessfully ran for Congress as a Federalist in 1789. He died in 1817. [394]

Another of the original officers of the Fifth Company was Alexander Murray, son of Dr. William Murray and Ann Smith. He was born in 1754 in Chestertown. Murray was commissioned a 2nd LT on January 1776. His appointment to Smallwood's unit as the 2LT of the Fifth Company under Ramsey was confirmed on January 14th. He was promoted to 1st LT in August. On December 10th he was promoted to Captain in the 1st Maryland Regiment under Colonel Ware. On June 10, 1777 he resigned and joined the forming American Navy. He commanded at least three privateers. Murray continued in the Navy after the war. He was appointed the first commandant of the Philadelphia Navy Yard in 1813, serving until his death in 1821. [395]

Peter Adams, a resident of Great Choptank Hundred, Caroline County, was commissioned Captain in the Maryland State troops on January 3, 1776. Later in the month he was confirmed as the commander of Smallwood's Sixth Company, from the Eastern Shore. He was sick on August 27th and did not lead his company during the battle. In December 1776 he was promoted to Lieutenant Colonel and he served until April 1, 1783. John Jordan, son of John Jordan and Eleanor Dent of St. Mary's County, was commissioned Ensign on January 3, 1776. Later in the month he was confirmed as Ensign in the 6th Company. He was promoted to Lieutenant in the 1st Maryland Regiment on December 10th. On December 20, 1777 he was promoted to Captain in the Second Maryland Brigade, where he served until the end of the war. [396]

Samuel Smith was born in Lancaster, PA in 1752. He was a member of the Baltimore Independent Cadets. When Mordecai Gist was elected 2nd Major in the Maryland Battalion, Smith was elected one of the Captains for the unit, finishing tied for seventh with John Day Scott with eight votes. After his commissioning, his appointment as commander of Smallwood's Eighth Company was confirmed later in January. Thieman Offutt stated that Smith commanded the Sixth Company. However, virtually every other source states the Eighth. This, combined with his tie for 7th in the election of Captains, and the fact that the number of their companies corresponded to their order of finish in the election (e.g. Stone in the First Company and Stricker in the Ninth) would indicate that Offutt is incorrect. The Baltimore Independent Cadets formed the core of the Eighth Company and Smith, in effect, succeeded Mordecai Gist in command.

Smith was promoted to Major in Gist's 3rd Maryland Regiment in December 1776. In February 1777 he was promoted to Lieutenant Colonel of the 4th Maryland Regiment under Colonel John Carvel Hall. He was wounded at Ft. Mifflin later in 1777 and resigned on May 22, 1779. However he continued to serve locally and was listed as a Colonel of the Baltimore Town militia on September 25, 1780. Smith's post-war career was extensive on the local, state and federal levels. He served in the Maryland House of Delegates, as a member of Congress, as a Senator and as Secretary of the Navy. He became a Major General in the state militia, commanding Maryland state troops in the defense of Baltimore during British attacks in 1814. He also served as Mayor of Baltimore from 1835-1838. He died in 1839 in the fullness of his age. [397]

George Stricker was born in 1732 in Winchester, VA. His parents were Swiss immigrants who had originally settled in North Carolina. He, in turn, moved to Frederick County, MD by 1774, and probably much earlier. Stricker was self educated. By 1770 he was an inn keeper along with possibly being a planter/farmer. He was elected to the Frederick County Committee of Observation. On September 2, 1775 he was elected a Captain in Frederick's militia. He is listed as in command of a Minuteman Company on October 4, 1775. In January 1776 he was elected Captain in the Maryland troops and selected to command Smallwood's Ninth Company drawn from Frederick County. In July 1776 he was promoted to Lieutenant Colonel of the newly forming German Regiment. He was succeeded in command of the Ninth Company by Benjamin Ford, 1LT of Second Company. He resigned April 29, 1777 after George Washington wrote Maryland's governor that Stricker's character did not justify his promotion to a command a battalion (regiment). Stricker later served in the Lower House of the Maryland Assembly from 1779-1780. [398]

Thomas Smyth was commissioned 1st LT and appointed to the Ninth Company in January 1776. In July 1776 he was promoted to Captain in the Fourth Battalion in the Maryland Flying Camp. Hatch Dent was elected Ensign and assigned to the Ninth Company in January 1776. In March he was promoted to 2LT and July 9th he was promoted to 1LT to fill the vacancy created by Smyth's departure. He was captured on August 27th and not exchanged until April 20, 1778. In the mean time, he had been appointed a 1LT in the 1st Maryland Regiment in December 1776. This was followed by his promotion to Captain in the 2nd Maryland Regiment on April 17, 1777. After being exchanged he resigned seven months later in November 1778. Hence, some of the officers of the Maryland Battalion. [399]

Rezin Beall was born in 1723, making him nine years older than William Smallwood and Francis Ware. He served as Ensign and then as 2LT in Francis Ware's Company of Maryland Troops from October 9, 1757 to December 30, 1758. He was elected Captain of the 1st Independent Company (IC) on January 2, 1776, receiving the highest vote total of the Captains elected. As discussed earlier, the company was based in Charles and Calvert Counties. Beall was severely wounded in an engagement with Lord Dunmore's fleet at

St. George's Island off St. Mary's county, nine to ten miles up the Potomac from Point Lookout at the river's mouth. He was elected Brigadier General of Maryland's Flying Camp that deployed to Amboy, NJ, joining troops from Delaware and Pennsylvania. However, he never saw action with those troops. He refused to come under Smallwood's command because he considered himself Smallwood's superior in rank. This was specifically contrary to Maryland law that gave regular Colonels seniority over militia Brigadier Generals and Colonels when they were serving together. He continued serving until December 1776 when he resigned. He died in 1809. [400]

John Allen (Alleyine) Thomas was born in Talbot County in 1734, son of William Thomas and Elizabeth Allen. He moved to St. Mary's County by 1771. He was listed as a Gentleman by 1768. He had read law and was a practicing attorney in Talbot, Queen Anne's Frederick and Charles Counties and the Provincial Courts. He was elected to represent St. Mary's County in the Maryland Convention during the 3rd to the 8th sessions. He did not attend the 7th and 8th sessions in the spring and summer of 1776 because his regular military appointment precluded the individual simultaneously having a civil office, as we have seen. Thomas filled several different offices in St. Mary's County in the pre-war period. He had also served as clerk of the Lower House of the Assembly in 1761-1762. In the summer of 1775, during the Convention's session, he had subscribed to and signed the Association of the Freemen of Maryland. In January 1776 he was elected Captain and appointed commander of the 5th Independent Company, drawn primarily from St. Mary's County. In August 1777 he reverted to militia service and was promoted to Major of the St. Mary's County Upper Battalion of militia. After the war he again served in several local and state offices, dying in 1797. [401]

Officer turn-over was not just limited to the Battalion companies of regulars. The same happened in the Independent Companies. Rezin Beall (1st IC) was promoted to Brigadier General of the Flying Camp (a militia position) taking his 3LT Daniel Adams as his Brigade Major. Bennett Bracco and John Halkerston were promoted to Captain and 1st LT, respectively. On February 6, 1776 CPT Lemuel Barrett (6th IC - Dorchester County) resigned. This resulted in the promotion of Thomas Woolford, John Eccleston and Harper Hudson to CPT, 1LT, and 2LT, respectively; as well as the commissioning of Leburn Williams as 3LT. In the 5th IC, 1LT John Stewart (Steward) received a Congressional naval appointment. In August 1776 John Davidson and Henry Neale were promoted to 1LT and 2LT, respectively, and Robert Chesley was commissioned 3LT. [402]

The Private Men of Smallwood's Regiment, today's enlisted soldiers, showed a typical pattern for Continental regiments. They had very little taxable wealth; many were unskilled laborers; and their median age was twenty one. Forty per cent were foreign born. The evidence suggests that the remaining sixty per cent were native born men, single, from a variety of backgrounds. For the 7th IC, at least, they were primarily in their twenties and single. Many of the recruits were farmers (or their sons) and/or artisans (blacksmiths, brewers, bakers, coopers, carpenters, etc.). There is also evidence to suggest that military service was a family affair. Smallwood's muster rolls show multiple (two, and in some cases three) members of the same family (or, at least with the same last name from the same general area), enlisting, normally in the same company. This is not surprising because the recruitment for each company, Smallwood's and the Independents, was generally very specifically regionally based. There were also some among the recruits who were of at least moderate means.

While most of the recruits for the Maryland state troops, the regulars, emerged from the lower portion of the socio-economic spectrum, they were by no means from the very bottom. In fact, they probably fluctuated somewhere on the margin separating the lower and the lower middle classes. Regardless of where they fit in the society around them, all appear to have been willing to serve and had minimal attachments to the wider society around them. This made them attractive candidates for military service. [403]

A sampling of some of the 1776 enlistees would include the following. John Adams, probably from Prince George's County, enlisted in CPT Patrick Sims' 2nd Company on April 6th. Josias Holton, born in 1756, enlisted in CPT Barton Lucas' 3rd Company on January 30th. He survived the war and died at 42 in 1798. Richard Watts of St. Mary's County enlisted as a Private in CPT Thomas Ewing's 4th Company, drawn primarily from Baltimore, Harford and Cecil Counties, on January 3rd. He was joined by John Carberry who enlisted as a Private under Ewing on January 29th. John Baptist Kerby, born in 1750, enlisted in CPT Peter Adams' 6th Company, primarily from Queen Anne's, Kent and Caroline Counties, on February 24th. He also survived the war and died at the age of 78 in 1828 in Prince George's County. [404]

Some of Smallwood's enlisted men went on to successful careers as officers, both in the regulars and in the militia. Samuel Baker was a Sergeant on January 20th, 1776, implying previous military service. He was appointed Adjutant in the 1st Maryland Regiment on May 5, 1777. Michael Burgess, a Corporal on February 3, 1776, was promoted to Ensign in the

3rd Battalion, Flying Camp, Anne Arundel County on July 23rd. Edward Edgerly was listed as a Sergeant in the 6th Company on February 15, 1776. He was promoted to Captain in 1779 and killed in action in 1781. John Gassaway, born in 1750, was a Sergeant on January 3, 1776. He was a Captain when he was captured in 1780. George Hamilton enlisted as a Private on January 31, 1776. He served until 1783, achieving the rank of Captain. Robert Morrow was a Sergeant on January 23, 1776. He was discharged on May 3rd. By July 12th he was an Ensign in the 2nd Battalion, Flying Camp, Baltimore County. He joined the Dragoons in 1777 and served until November 1782, achieving the rank of captain. [405]

Maryland's initial efforts to create effective regular forces yielded an overall outstanding group of men. Subsequent comments of others from outside of Maryland on the troops and their officers, especially those in the Regiment, referred to them not only as "dandies," because of their appearance, but also as the elite of the province. It is a natural progression as military units expand in size for experienced men and, especially, officers, to be selected from the "core" unit and advanced to positions of greater authority. That so many of the originally selected group was so militarily effective at increasingly higher ranks is a testament to the success of the selection process in identifying the best men available. It also was a significant factor in the unit's initial early, and, frankly, surprising, success.

Maryland made several crucial decisions that would affect the quality of its soldiers. Among them were the requirements that the Maryland state troops, at least, be trained, well equipped, well fed and paid. The Maryland troops displayed soldierly conduct that rivaled or exceeded the best in the Continental Army. The performance and conduct of the troops was the product of their time spent drilling before joining the ranks of the Continental Army - training that differentiated them from other state's troops. While many other states responded to Congress' call for recruits with untrained militia, in January 1776 the Maryland Convention, working on the assumption that paid soldiers furnished with rations and suits of clothes would be better soldiers, established two regiments worth of regular soldiers, men whose jobs were to be full time soldiers, not part-time. The Convention's assumption proved correct as the Regiment, supplemented with the Independent Companies, exemplified a cohesive, disciplined unit, especially in contrast to the throngs of untrained militia that formed the bulk of the Continental Army of that time. [406]

Unlike the militiamen, who would muster in their own clothing and carried a personal weapon, each of Smallwood's soldiers received a full set of clothes, among to wit: a pair of shoes, a pair of buckles, a pair of stockings and garters, a coat, a waistcoat, a pair of breeches, two white linen shirts, a hunting shirt, a pair of linen overalls, a pair of woolen overalls, a hat, a comb, a blanket and a knife. Each soldier required 1/6 part of a tent, a camp kettle, and would need both a knapsack and a haversack, among other items. Each would be issued a musket (or rifle), a bayonet and scabbard, a gun sling and bayonet belt, a canteen and sling, a cartridge box "filled with Powder and Ball," cartridge paper, flints, and bullet molds. The clothing costs exceeded nine pounds per man, while each musket cost five pounds. [407]

The officers, especially the field officers, were actively involved in equipping and clothing the soldiers. Tradition says that the Marylanders killed on Long Island were buried in their scarlet and buff uniforms. The officers may have been, but the enlisted men were in their hunting shirts, which had become the Regiment's prescribed uniform. In letters in January and May, 1776 to the Council of Safety and Thomas Johnson, respectively, COL Smallwood discussed the use of hunting shirts as the uniform for his soldiers, as well as the absence, or lack of authorization for, "splatter dashes" to complete the uniform. Splatter dashes were, in essence, leggings used to protect the men's pants or breeches during the march. The British and Hessian soldiers cringed at the sight of the soldiers wearing hunting shirts, based on their previous experience and subsequent tales about the excellent marksmanship of the rifle companies in 1775, all outfitted in hunting shirts. [408]

Smallwood's Regiment and the Independent Companies were created to defend Maryland from British attacks and to act as a countervailing force against loyalist sentiments. To protect the two most likely targets of any British expedition up the Chesapeake, six companies were stationed at Annapolis and three at Baltimore Town. Each location had one of the artillery companies/batteries. To protect the rest of the Chesapeake's shoreline, the Council of Safety spread the Independent Companies out in two rough semi-circles on the Eastern and Western Shores. Defense of key villages which were commerce distribution points was of primary importance. CPT Beall's 1st IC divided itself between Port Tobacco in Charles County and Drum Point in Calvert County. CPT Thomas' 5th IC was stationed at Leonardtown in St. Mary's County. CPT Veazy's 7th IC was split between Kent Island in Queen Anne's county and Chestertown in Kent County. CPT Hindman's 4th IC was at Oxford in Talbot County, and CPT Watkin's 3rd IC at Snow Hill in Worcester County. CPY Gunby's 2nd IC was at Princess Ann in Somerset

County. Hence, the ICs were defending the areas they were most familiar with and from which they had generally been recruited. [409]

COL Smallwood's Headquarters (HQ) was initially stationed in Annapolis. It consisted of himself, 1st MAJ Thomas Price, Paymaster Charles Wallace, Clerk Christopher Richmond, 1st Surgeon's Mate Dr. Michael Wallace (sick when the muster roll was prepared), Quartermaster Joseph Marbury, and Acting Adjutant Jacob Brice. The 1st (Stone - Charles County), 2nd (Sims who had already replaced Hyde - Prince George's/ Montgomery Counties), 3rd (Lucas - Prince George's/ Montgomery Counties), 6th (Adams - Queen Anne's/Kent Counties), 7th (Scott - presumably Anne Arundel County) and 9th/Light Infantry (Stricker - Frederick County) Companies were stationed in Annapolis with the HQ. LTC Ware, 2nd MAJ Gist and 2nd Surgeon's Mate Dr. William Augustus Dashiel were stationed in Baltimore Town. With them were the 4th (Ewing - Baltimore/Harford/Cecil Counties), 5th (Ramsey - Cecil County) and 8th (Smith - Baltimore) Companies. Based on a unit muster signed June 10, 1776 by COL Smallwood, there had been officer changes since the initial elections by the Convention in January. In the 1st Company ENS Chambers had resigned with no indicated replacement, This contradicts information from other sources, as discussed above, that Chambers was promoted to 2LT of the 1st Company on July 9th and replaced by newly commissioned Walter Brooke Cox. As noted earlier, Patrick Sims had replaced the resigning William Hyde in 2nd Company. 4th company's 2LT Joseph Baxter had resigned and had not yet been replaced. A month later, on July 9th, ENS Edward Praul was promoted to fill the vacancy. In the 6th Company Alexander Murray is listed as replacing David Plunkett as 2LT. [410]

On January 15, 1776, having "been informed that the counties of Accomack and North Hampton are in need of assistance," the Convention decided to take action. The two Virginia counties were at the southern end of the Delmarva Peninsula. They had heavy populations of loyalists and trouble, i.e. resistance to the "cause," was spilling over into the southern Maryland counties on the Eastern Shore.. The Convention directed minutemen companies from Dorchester, Queen Anne's and Kent Counties to march to Virginia to assist the inhabitants. Those who were unable to go would be replaced by volunteers. The Convention followed with instructions for paying and arming the troops. It appointed a commissary, provided each Captain funds for expenses, and set a time limit for the length of the units' deployment. After eight weeks the companies were to be relieved and, presumably, replaced. [411]

The Council of Safety stayed involved with organizing the regulars throughout the late winter and spring of 1776. On January 19th the Council directed the Treasurer of the Western Shore to pay one hundred and twenty pounds to "subsist and Advance money [possibly bonuses or prepayment of some monthly pay] ..." for the recruits of Ewing's 4th Company, Ramsey's 5th and Scott's 7th. On February 16th the Council promoted Thomas Woolford to Captain and put him in command of the 6th IC, replacing Lemuel Barrett who had resigned. On February 24th CPT Thomas (5th IC) requested that the Council order 1LT John Steward (Stewart) and the men he had enlisted to Leonardtown to join his own men. He further requested a horse for the company. On March 6th the Council ordered "Captain George Stracker's [sic] Company of Light Infantry [9th] immediately march to their station at the City of Annapolis." It also directed the Treasurer of the

Western Shore to pay for monies advanced by CPT Lucas (3rd Co) for "Inlistment and Subsist money."

On March 8th Lucas was ordered to march his company to Annapolis. Also on the 8th, CPT Thomas (5th IC) reported three vessels near the mouth of the Patuxent River. He had captured a vessel ladened with flour, but still needed arms and supplies. He informed them that he was sending 1LT Steward (Stewart) for arms, Steward apparently having joined him by that time. Thomas had stationed troops on both the Patuxent and Patapsco Rivers to repel any British incursions. His 3LT, Henry Neale, and a Benjamin Ford [not one of his officers, but also mentioned in his February 24th letter; possibly 1LT Benjamin Ford of the 2nd Co. from Prince George's County.] were handling the provisions for the troops. Finally, Thomas requested a seine for each division of his company so that the men could catch fish and a frying pan for each mess. On March 14th Thomas' company was ordered return Leonardtown. On the 18th he replied, complaining about having marched his troops to the Patuxent River and then to Point Lookout, the extreme southern tip of St. Mary's County, in response to reported enemy sightings. Further, he wanted confirmation of the order to remain in Leonardtown so that he wasn't held responsible for failing to repel an invasion elsewhere. He complained again on April 22nd. [412]

Thomas was not the only one responding to possible British waterborne raids. To counteract British naval activity on Chesapeake Bay and the Potomac, the Council ordered CPT Beall to station half of his 1st IC at Port Tobacco in Charles County. On March 7th the Council informed Col Smallwood that a "Ship of War and two Tenders [British] have just come in sight." They were sighted in the vicinity of the South River;

just south of the peninsula Annapolis was located on. The town was situated on the north side of the peninsula on the southern bank of the Severn River. Smallwood was requested to immediately come to Annapolis [implying that his HQ was not yet located there, that he hadn't joined it, or that he was elsewhere on business.] and order CPT Stone (2nd Co - PG/ Mont. Cos) to "march with his Company as expeditiously as he can." Stone was to stop at Upper Marlboro enroute to secure such Public Arms" as may be collected there "by the Committee of Observation for Prince George's County.

Several days later the British ship, identified as the <u>Otter</u>, with its tenders, was located in the vicinity of Baltimore. The Council of Safety, located in Annapolis, directed Charles Carroll, Barrister, one of its members, to order CPT Stricker's Company (9th) to Baltimore instead of Annapolis, its original destination, if he thought it necessary. When the ships left the vicinity of Baltimore for Annapolis Stricker could be sent there. MAJ Gist and the regulars in Baltimore marched to Whetstone Point to entrench. The area they proceeded to is near the eastern terminus of the peninsula between the Northwest and Middle Branches of the Patapsco River, roughly in the vicinity of the site of current day Ft. McHenry. The militia was being called in, as well as supplies and ammunition, all to defend against the anticipated British land incursion. About March 10th, with <u>Otter</u> still cruising the Bay, LTC Ware was ordered to take command of the Calvert County militia units. On the 14th, as we have seen, the Council ordered Thomas' 5th IC to Leonardtown. It also ordered CPT Watkin's 3rd IC (Worcester Co.) to Snow Hill and CPT Veazy's 7th IC (Queen Anne's and Kent Cos.) to be split between "Chestertown in Kent County; and ... Blunt's ware-House on Kent Island in Queen Anne's County." [413]

Also during the month of March, CPT Smith (8th Co., Baltimore) and some of his troops served as volunteer marines on the privateer <u>Defense</u> and several accompanying tenders. The <u>Otter</u> had come up the Bay not only to harass and destroy shipping in Maryland ports. It specifically had come to capture or destroy the <u>Defense</u>, which was docked in Baltimore. The <u>Defense,</u> with Smith and his "marines" aboard, was able to drive the <u>Otter</u> off, forcing it to withdraw south down the Chesapeake and return to its Virginia station. Smith's troops became temporary marines because, presumably, the marine company authorized by the Convention hadn't been formed yet, or hadn't recruited and/or trained a sufficient number of men to meet the need.

While all of this was going on, correspondence between Governor Eden and Lord George Germaine of the British ministry was intercepted, showing that the Governor was cooperating with the "enemy," the British. General Charles Lee, then at Williamsburg, VA, forwarded a request to Samuel Purviance, Chairman of the Baltimore Committee of Safety, to arrest the Governor. The Committee not being in session, on his own Purviance requested MAJ Gist's assistance. On April 18th Gist ordered CPT Smith, with ten men, to Annapolis on the tender <u>Resolution</u> to seize Eden and his papers. Upon their arrival they were met by local members of the Annapolis Committee of Safety. They informed Smith that he had no jurisdiction in their community and refused him permission to proceed. They then ordered him back to Baltimore. He obeyed and set sail north. [414]

Aside from reinforcing the fact that localitis was still the prevailing view, the incident raises a number of unanswered questions. Among them: why did Lee deal with a local Committee of Safety in Baltimore instead of the Maryland

Council of Safety in Annapolis; and why did Purviance chose to deal with it personally and, in effect, locally, without involving state officials? There are several possible explanations for why Purviance went to Gist and not Annapolis for troops: he, Purviance, was the senior civil political figure in Baltimore and had influence over the military, even the regulars; he may have had a personal relationship with Gist of long standing; or both may have factored into his decision. What is clear is why Gist sent Smith. He knew Smith and knew his capabilities. Gist had, in fact, commanded him in the Baltimore Independents and may even have recommended him for command. But, why didn't Gist involve Annapolis, and, more specifically, some of the Regimental HQ and six companies that were to be stationed there? We have seen that Stricker and Stone were ordered to Annapolis in March, along with Smallwood. The incident took place almost a month later, in April. However, maybe none of the 6 companies or the Regimental HQ was in Annapolis yet. Gist, Smith and the 8th Company were home in Baltimore and available. The other Regimental companies had to move/march to either Annapolis or Baltimore. Maybe they hadn't had time enough to arrive at their assigned post.

On April 14th the Council ordered Smallwood to send a commissioned officer to apprehend Alexander Ross, suspected of "communicating intelligence to Lord Dunmore [vigorously attempting to campaign up and down Chesapeake Bay from his waterborne headquarters] and other persons inimical to the cause of America ..." They advised him that Russell was probably in the vicinity of Queenstown in Queen Anne's County. The officer was authorized to get assistance from the military units on the Eastern Shore. On April 18th the Council advised LTC Ware that his presence had become necessary. He apparently was in Charles County tending to sick family members. They wanted him to take command of the troops in Baltimore Town. COL Smallwood was deemed "so unwell, that MAJ Price cannot be spared from [Annapolis]." Note that this was the same date that Gist sent Smith to Annapolis. So, at least the HQ, or part of it, was there by then but, possibly, none of the companies. On April 22nd the Council ordered the Commissary of Stores to deliver to CPT Thomas for CPT Beall's 1st IC arms, ammunition and supplies. They further ordered supplies for Thomas. [415]

According to correspondence from the Council of Safety and a local arms manufacturer, MAJ Price was in Frederick Town on May 1st and was also still there on May 25th. This appears to be in conflict with the Council's April correspondence cited above. However, a simple explanation might be that he had returned to Frederick in the interim on Regimental business, pursuing arms and ammunition. In the mean time, LTC Ware had made it to Baltimore. Also on May 1st, he advised the Council that he had been informed of the presence of smallpox in several different locations in Baltimore Town. A doctor advised him to be inoculated (still a dangerous and possibly fatal process) because of his age. It was presumed that an older person would have greater difficulty if he/she contracted smallpox naturally. He, in essence, asked for the Council's instruction on what to do. He also told them that if they disapproved of "Enockulation" they should "contrive some method of getting the troops encamped without the town. Whetstone Point would be the most proper station could we be provided with tents and other camp utensils." He also said that the officers "neither of them (Gist and himself, the field officers?) had a tent nor the ability to find the proper cloth to make one." [416]

While continuing to train and get properly equipped, Smallwood's men experienced some of the more mundane tasks of military life, including guard details. On May 9th he was ordered to provide an officer and thirty men as a prisoner escort for a group of 26 persons being conveyed from North Carolina to Philadelphia. The party was to be detailed from one of the Western Shore companies. They were to pick up the prisoners in Queen Anne on the Patuxent River, on the boundary between Prince George's and Anne Arundel counties. The Queen Anne's bridge over the Patuxent was the main route to Annapolis from Charles, Prince George's and western St. Mary's Counties. From there they were to be taken to Baltimore. The escorts were to be relieved by another 30 man escort and transported through Head of Elk (Elkton) by water or by land, to the "verge of the Province," there to be handed over to the Pennsylvania forces for transmission to Philadelphia. Troops were similarly detached to guard powder shipments throughout the state. Generally, an officer and a small guard of enlisted men were detailed to guard the train of bulk powder shipments. [417]

On May 21st the Council authorized payment to CPT Smith (8th Co.) to cover the cost of boarding and nursing his men. On May 25th Smallwood, in a letter to the Council, outlined problems with obtaining uniforms for all of his troops. Leather breeches and cloth stockings were proving hard to acquire. He suggested that the troops be allowed "breeches and spatterdashes in one piece made of aznobogs [?]." Spatterdashes were knee length leggings worn to protect clothing from mud or water spatters. This would achieve uniformity with the hunting shirts and be a good substitute for the leather breeches. The soldiers were willing to buy a pair if another would be provided. In late May CPT Beall (1st

IC) had informed the council that there were not sufficient quarters to billet the half of his company stationed at Drum Point, on the north bank of the mouth of the Patuxent River, at the southern end of Calvert County. He was authorized to construct barracks and the Calvert County Committee of Observation was instructed to assist him. On May 31st Smallwood was ordered to again provide guards for the "Magazine near CPT James Tootell's" in the neighborhood of Annapolis. [418]

In June 1776, while Maryland was wrestling with the problem of organizing, equipping and training both regular and militia forces, the British Navy became even more active in the lower Chesapeake Bay and lower Potomac River. Military action was required by both Maryland and Virginia forces. The Maryland authorities feared that the lower Bay incidents signaled raids farther north in the Bay and, possibly, an invasion. They were in the process of training and equipping Smallwood's Regiment and the Independent Companies of state troops that would shortly be transferred to the Continental Army. At the same time, they were commencing recruitment, training and gathering equipment for the new soldiers of the Flying Camp. Further build up of those units disrupted the local militia organizations and preempted their very scarce supplies of arms and ammunition.

To release COL Smallwood, the Baltimore Town militia was ordered to place three companies on duty on July 7th; the Anne Arundel County Elkridge Battalion (primarily drawn from areas now in Howard County) was ordered to place two companies in Annapolis. The West River and Severn Battalions of militia (Anne Arundel County) were also ordered to send three companies to Annapolis. Before the militia moves were completed the British were reported to be in the vicinity of Point Look Out at the mouth of the Potomac. Militia units in southern Maryland were quickly mobilized. Two of the regular companies that had started north were turned back and CPT Beall was ordered to send troops to help the militia.

Earlier, on June 23rd, the British ship Fowey had arrived off of Annapolis, under a flag of truce, to take off Governor Eden at his request. On June 24th the Council ordered CPT Thomas (5th IC, St. Mary's Co.) to march to Cedar Point in the southern part of the county to guard from there to the Potomac River to "prevent any servants, negroes [slaves], or others from going on board the Fowey ... as also to repel any violence." Smallwood was also ordered to provide "a Sergeant and six men" to help sail and protect a boat under CPT Pitt, whose orders were to repel any force or violence offered by the Fowey. Also on the 24th, CPT Beall was to be prepared to "repel any violence which he may offer in his passage down the bay, or attempt to procure Provisions." Later in July, partially organized Flying Camp companies moved in to relieve the state troops and the militia. All of the militia had been sent home by early August. The Flying Camp companies were sent north to assist Washington's army when each became armed and fully trained. [419]

On June 28th the Convention, upon receipt of a letter from the Somerset County Committee of Observation, ordered MAJ Price to take command of "so many of the independent companies on the eastern shore ... as he may think proper ..." to march to the lower part of Somerset County, which adjoined Accomack County, Virginia. Price was to "disarm all such persons in that county as shall from good grounds appear ... to be disaffected and to take into custody all such disaffected persons as shall be ordered ..." by a committee appointed by the Convention. The committee was to determine if militia forces were needed and, if so, to call them up. Price would also command the militia.

Accomack County had been vigorously supporting Lord Dunmore and had strong Loyalist sentiments. The Maryland Convention had already ordered Eastern Shore militia into Accomack and Northampton Counties in Virginia during the previous January to assist Virginia authorities in dealing with the Loyalists. George Plater of St. Mary's County and John Hall were appointed as the committee. They were charged to "secure obedience to the resolves of the Convention, and peace and good order" in Somerset County. They were given command of Price, the Independent Companies and the militia. Finally, they were to "report their proceedings to the next Convention," to be held in August. On July 5th Plater and Hall were elected to the 9 member Council of Safety that governed Maryland when the Convention was not sitting.

The Dorchester County Committee of Observation had also expressed concern to the Convention for the safety of their area. They complained that they had been guarding the Bay and the river shores (presumably with their militia) to the detriment of their harvests as well as other "damages to their property ..." They felt exposed and unprotected and asked for help. Pursuant to the Convention's June 28th order, Price took CPT Woolford's 6th IC from Dorchester, splitting it between Somerset County and the mouth of the Nanticoke River in the southeast corner of Dorchester County. The Nanticoke served as the boundary between Dorchester and then Somerset, now Wicomico, Counties. [420]

Troops began to converge on Annapolis, the main point of debarkation and embarkation for all Maryland soldiers. On July 6, 1776, COL Smallwood was ordered "to immediately proceed with your battalion to the city of Philadelphia under the Continental officer commanding there, and be subject to the further orders of the Congress." Several of the Independent Companies were placed under his command and also ordered north. However, as mentioned above, some of the troops had to be recalled to deal with the British threat in southern Maryland. The St. Mary's County men began their march towards Philadelphia, but they were brought back as British threats continued and became more serious. [421]

On July 14th CPT Beall reported the presence of up to 40 sailing vessels off Point Lookout to Alexander Sommerville of the Calvert County militia. Sommerville moved men to Drum Point. He reported hearing firing overnight and subsequently confirmed it to be from the Potomac. Beall, with the men he had available, moved south from Drum Point and requested orders from the Council. On July 15th the Council of Safety ordered Beall to keep his 1st IC in St. Mary's County to foil any British attempts to land, in conjunction with the local militia. Also on the 15th the Council ordered CPT Thomas to stop proceeding up the Bay and return his 5th IC to Annapolis. Finally, on the 15th Beall was seriously wounded in the shoulder during an engagement with the British. Based on a subsequent letter dated July 23rd from the Maryland Deputies in the Continental Congress to the Maryland Convention, CPT James Hindman's 4th IC from Talbot County had also been ordered to St. Mary's County. [422]

On July 18th the Council directed MAJ Price to provide carriages to transport artillery and ammunition to St. Mary's On the same day he was ordered to St. Mary's County (possibly from the Eastern Shore, but it is unclear) to take command of the "regular troops [the Independent Companies] and the militia." On July 19th CPT Thomas was ordered to move his 5th IC to St. Mary's County and put himself under the direction of the commanding officer there. He traveled by water to the mouth of the Patuxent. However, he was not destined to stay in the area long. On July 23rd Thomas was ordered to march his company north to rejoin the other regular troops as soon as the local commander determined that his troops were no longer needed in the area. Also on the 23rd the Council received a letter from Maryland's Congressional delegation highlighting the urgency for releasing the Independent Companies from St. Mary's to move to New York to support Washington.

MAJ Price was actively involved with directing the fighting in southern Maryland. On July 29th he directed the militia and CPT Thomas to engage various ships on the Potomac and be prepared to counteract British raids. He also advised the Council of rotating militia troops, of the sickness among the regulars and the overall fatigue of the troops, indicating that they would have to be replaced if they were there much longer. On July 31st the Council informed him that Peter Mantz, commanding a company of the Frederick Battalion, was marching to relieve CPT Thomas and his company. They, in turn, were ordered north, as we have seen. Mantz's stay was also short. The St. Mary's Committee of Observation informed the Council on August 7th that they were unhappy with the performance of Mantz and his company. Mantz also requested a transfer. He was immediately ordered to Philadelphia via Annapolis. [423]

It is interesting to note that throughout this period of military development in Maryland, there was no functioning executive at any level of government. As the spirit of rebellion grew in the early/mid 1770s, existing governmental authority, under royal auspices, was overthrown or, more usually, superseded by democratically elected extra-legal bodies. Although in modern terms the franchise was limited, this was a radical departure from the existing norms. What provided continuity was the fact that, at least in Maryland, the same people ended up in positions of authority and influence at both the local and state levels. The overwhelming majority of the Deputies to the Convention had been members of the Assembly, elected to represent their fellow citizens. Further, the Council of Safety was chosen from members of the Convention. Significantly smaller, it was still a committee. For several years as this was developing in Maryland, Eden, the Royal Governor, continued to reside in Annapolis. However, his influence completely waned and his power of governing was completely superseded. He was allowed to remain until the late spring of 1775, unlike his Virginia counterpart, Lord Dunmore. The difference was that Dunmore violently resisted the changes and was forced to attempt to govern and maintain control from the deck of a British ship of war on the James River and the Chesapeake Bay. Eden quietly tried to ride out the storm until his position became untenable and he requested to leave.

A single executive authority was also absent at the local level in Maryland where large committees, first of Correspondence and then of Observation, assumed authority and control. The same is true at the Continental level with the Congress. As the war progressed, a military administration and bureaucracy was developed, albeit a very elementary one. At the Continental level a powerful single executive never developed. The states eventually returned to governmental structures that included governors. However, at the time we are considering that was not the case. The affairs of the state were governed and directed by committees and legislative bodies, with all of the problems associated therewith. The individual deputies/delegates/committee members were more susceptible to local pressures which colored their decisions, from who was given leadership positions, to where supplies were procured from, to where troops were recruited from, to where they were stationed. Given the unwieldiness of the political structure, the results in terms of the initial development of a military organization were surprisingly good.

Along with creating a new military organization and structure, the Maryland government also developed its skills in utilizing its military forces, both in terms of what type of force to use where and when, as well as broadening its focus and thinking in terms of larger military units. The "governors" of Maryland at the time were, in the main, experienced political leaders. They were all old enough to have been aware of the British Army units that were deployed through and around their territory during the SY/FI War, the regiments, divisions and armies. Further, a regimental structure had existed in the Maryland militia since the seventeenth century. Although geographically based, with no consistency in the size of and number of companies from county to county, the fundamentals of the organization and structure, as well as the way it worked, were essentially the same as regular army units. However, the militia regiments were never deployed enmass. Rather, they served as administrative organizations to recruit, train and equip local citizens into rudimentary soldiers. The deployments above company level were all ad hoc, made up of volunteers. The deployments the legislators, current and future, would have been familiar with were all company sized or, possibly, smaller. Some of them could have been directly involved as militia officers. These companies may have been aggregated into a larger force, e.g. the garrison at Ft. Frederick, but the directions and actions were all focused exclusively on the company level.

Although the Maryland leaders created one regimental size unit, the Maryland Battalion, they still dealt with it almost exclusively one company at a time. The companies (including the Independent Companies, where it made sense since they had no superior military organization) were dealt with administratively, logistically and tactically as individual entities. There was a decided lack of use of the chain of command. With some minor exceptions, orders or administrative requirements or responses to the companies did not flow through the Regimental Commander, Smallwood, to his subordinates. Rather, they came directly from the Convention or, more normally, from the Council of Safety. There are several possible explanations. The political leaders had not yet achieved a vision of the size and complexity of the military force needed to protect them and provide their share of the troops needed to defeat the British. Calling on their experience, they initially thought that short term small units were the answer. They had been in the past. Hence, they continued business as usual. A more prosaic reason is that early on in 1776 the companies barely existed and there probably was not a superior (Regimental) headquarters in existence capable of controlling all of its subordinate units. As events progressed this changed. Smallwood got better control of his headquarters and subordinate units and his political superiors began to treat through him accordingly. Further, necessity forced the creation of additional forces, regular units (e.g. a portion of the German Battalion), Flying Camps and a large number of militia units. For each of these progressively more complex military structures were created, with Brigadier Generals commanding multiple battalions in the Flying Camps or in regions throughout the state. The very size and complexity of the growing force made a more streamlined command structure and communication system a virtual necessity.

It should also be noted that Smallwood operated under some unique organizational handicaps, especially in the early months of his command. For the first six months of its existence the Regiment was never completely together, gathered in one place, so that he could see them all at one time and they could see him. This may not seem significant, but it is, especially in a unit the size of his. In large military units, divisions or larger, such eyes on leadership is rarely, if ever achieved. Even with brigades it rarely happens. However, with Regiments and below, especially at the time he was fighting, it was critical to the successful engagement of the unit. It developed cohesiveness and gave the commander a chance to determine the capabilities of his soldiers and officers when working together.

The Regimental companies were split 6-3, with the heaviest concentration in Annapolis. However, it was many months before the Regimental HQ was up and running and all of the companies were assembled. As noted above, MAJ Gist and the 8th Company, based in Baltimore, were on home ground. Everyone else was stationed away from their home base. It took a while for their ranks to be filled, to properly equip the new troops, and to train them to a basic level of proficiency. This was done, to a large extent, prior to their moving to Annapolis or Baltimore. So, the Marylanders learned overall unit cohesiveness, essential to their future survival, on the road, literally, during the march to Philadelphia and then Amboy, and, finally, New York.

In modern armies marching together as a unit is one of the first skills taught new soldiers and it continues throughout their training. The initial emphasis is on learning individual skills such as saluting, the various commands and the resultant turns and maneuvers, the manual, or ritual, of arms, i.e. how to move a weapon around in the prescribed manner, how to march with it, and the various positions for it when stationary or on the move. This is followed immediately, by the collective training of just marching. The individual and collective training continues throughout the new troops' introductory period. Modern day new soldiers normally march in a unit wherever they are going. The exception is distant training locations when they will be marched to and from their motor transport. Marching develops both individual and collective skills. The individual soldiers learn to respond to commands automatically, an important lesson to be learned for when they are in combat. They also learn to work together as a unit. The more they do it, the closer together the unit becomes. This cohesiveness is critical if a unit is to perform creditably under the extreme stress of combat.

Aside from the occasional move of units across the ground, from one place to another enmass, after their initial training modern day soldiers' marching is almost exclusively ceremonial. This was not the case for their eighteenth century predecessors. Marching is how the units maneuvered around the battlefield; how units got themselves in the best posture to fight, dependent on the existing circumstances. Learning the various commands and resultant changes in direction and/or position was critical to both their success and survival. In addition to learning the skills of marching and maneuvering, Smallwood's units had to learn how to work together as part of a larger whole. Prior to joining together on their march to Philadelphia, the companies had rarely, if ever, worked together. While the more senior officers may have known some of their fellow officers, most of their men probably did not know anyone outside of their own unit. They needed to learn to work together. Further, based on the sketchy record, William Smallwood had little or no experience in coordinating the actions of military units, especially under the stress of combat. While not exposing them to the immediate dangers of combat, the cross country movement enabled the Regiment to come together and learn how to act together. Based on future results, unlikely as it may seem, it worked.

After forcing the British to withdraw from Boston, Washington assumed that their next assault would be made against New York. It was midway between the New England and Mid-Atlantic states. Commonly accepted wisdom was that British control of New York and the Hudson, or North, River would, in effect, isolate the two regions from each other, making them more readily susceptible to being controlled and defeated. As a consequence, Washington brought most of his army down from Boston in stages in the late spring of 1776. Congress exerted its utmost efforts to reinforce him. It authorized Continental regiments in the surrounding states. It also entered a general call for the militia. Washington was eventually able to muster a paper strength of 28,500 men. However, only 17,000-19,000 were present and fit for duty at any one time. The largest portion of the troops was raw recruits, undisciplined and inexperienced in warfare, and militia, never to be relied on to remain as cohesive units under fire. [424]

Immediately prior to adjournment and the end of a six-teen day session in June/July 1776, the Maryland Convention responded to resolutions and requests of the Continental Congress for troops to support Washington in the middle department. Specifically, on June 25th and 29th and July 4th the Congress had requested troops. Maryland's allocation was 3405. Reinforcing the official Continental directive/request was a letter from John Hancock, President of the Continental Congress. In it he stated that "General Howe having taken possession of Staten Island, and the Jerseys being drained of their militia, for the defense of New York, I am directed by Congress to request you will proceed immediately to embody your militia for the establishment of the flying camp, and march them with all possible expedition, wither by battalion, detachment of battalions, or by companies, to the city of Philadelphia ..." [425]

The Convention response was to order COL Smallwood to immediately proceed, with his Battalion/Regiment of state troops, to Philadelphia "and put himself under the Continental officer commanding there and be subject to the further orders of the Congress." The Independent Companies from Talbot (Hindman's 4th IC), Kent and Queen Anne's (Veazey's 7th IC) and St. Mary's (Thomas' 5th IC) Counties were ordered to immediately proceed to Philadelphia and put themselves under Smallwood's command. Those unfamiliar with the Independent Company structure might conclude that the Convention was ordering four companies north, because they did not identify the companies, but, rather, the counties they came from. However, the 7th IC was split between Kent and Queen Anne's, so only three were included. The "battalion and independent companies [were to] be deducted from the number of the militia

[3405] required by Congress of this colony to compose the flying camp." The Convention assigned them to the Main Continental Army.

Ships were ordered to be procured to transport the troops on the Western Shore to the Head of Elk (Elkton). The Council of Safety was requested to provide the troops with carriages and supplies on their march to Philadelphia. The Convention requested "the good people of the Province ... to give him [Smallwood] every assistance in their power on his march and to furnish him with carts &c which may be proper all necessary expenses will be defrayed by the Council of Safety." The Council of Safety was requested to raise militia companies in the city of Annapolis, Baltimore Town, Talbot, Queen Anne's and St. Mary's Counties to replace the regulars being sent north. Until they were available, the Council was to send two already existing militia companies to Baltimore Town and three to Annapolis, as we have seen. The Continental officer commanding the Flying Camp was requested to separate Maryland regular and militia forces, if possible, to prevent "any ground of discontent about rank." [426]

Upon receiving the request from the Continental Congress for 3405 militia, the Council was confused. They replied that they did not have the authority to order militia to go outside of Maryland and that they had called for a Convention to address the matter. In the mean time, after reviewing their quota, the Convention, on June 25th, decided to form an additional four battalions of soldiers. It assigned responsibility for recruiting and organizing these battalions to the counties. The battalions were to be known collectively as Maryland's Flying Camp. Maryland's Congressional delegates helped clear up the Council's confusion by responding that "[i]t never was intended that any part of the militia was compellable to march out of the Province … It was intended that the flying camp be formed by the voluntary inlistment of the militia." Thus, although the term militia was used to describe Flying Camp troops, they were, in fact, to be short term volunteers in the Continental forces. Once they left Maryland they were to be under the ultimate control of General Washington, and they were to be paid and supported by the Continental Congress, not Maryland. [427]

Upon adjourning on July 6th, the Convention turned its governing powers over to the Council of Safety until it would reconvene. As noted above, the state troops had been assigned to the Main Continental Army at the disposal of Congress, and directed to march north. By another resolution passed in response to the Continental troop requisition, they directed the raising of additional companies, what came to be called, as previously noted, the German Battalion. There were to be two companies of riflemen and four of Germans, each consisting of ninety officers and men, larger than Smallwood's companies, but smaller than the Independent Companies. One of the rifle companies was to be from Harford County, two German companies from Baltimore County, and one rifle and two German companies from Frederick County. The county committees were required to dispatch companies as fast as they were organized to the Flying Camp in Amboy, NJ. The state Council was required to supervise and facilitate the immediate departure of Smallwood's regulars. [428]

On July 7th, the Council of Safety forwarded the resolves of the Convention of July 6th to CPT Veazey and 1LT Harrison ordering the 7th to Philadelphia to join Smallwood "with the utmost dispatch." They were advised to attempt to procure a vessel(s) to transport them. In lieu of that, they were to march to Head of Elk, where wagons awaited them to carry baggage and supplies to Philadelphia. If they could not acquire a vessel(s) they were to get the necessary carriages from Talbot County, along with sufficient provisions for their journey to Head of Elk. They were advised that COL Smallwood's probable departure date was either July 8th or 9th.

Also on July 7th the Council sent a letter to General Archibald Buchanan of the militia, attaching a copy of the Convention's July 6th resolution ordering Smallwood and three Independent Companies into Continental service. The Council indicated to him that the regulars departing from Baltimore should be replaced by local militia units until such time as the Flying Camp was established. Buchanan was requested to select two companies and order them to Baltimore Town when the regulars departed. Colonels Weems and Hammond, also of the militia, received comparable letters and were requested to furnish three militia companies for Annapolis when Smallwood left. [429]

The Council, on July 8th, in a letter to Maryland's Congressional delegation, requested that "as the conveniences may not be provided for Col Smallwood and the Troops by the Time they reach Philadelphia," they "give him all the assistance you can …" The letter also included a recommendation of CPT George Stricker (9th Co/LI) of Frederick as a "Field Officer in the German Battalion" being formed. In a reply on the 12th, Thomas Stone advised the Council that no provisions were made for quartering any troops that passed through Philadelphia. He had checked on the status of the city barracks and found some of the soldiers in them had smallpox. Further, it had spread to almost every part of Philadelphia. He was going to advise Smallwood to put his men on the common. No tents were available "in the Continental

Service," and he recommended that they be made and immediately sent after the troops. He also advised that he thought CPT Stricker would be appointed a field grade in the German Regiment, as recommended. Based on what the militia from Philadelphia was doing, he assumed that Smallwood would march from Philadelphia to "Trent Town [Trenton]," NJ and thence to the Continental Flying Camp at Amboy.

On July 9th the Council ordered COL Smallwood and CPTs Hindman (4th IC) and Veazey (7th IC) to furnish it with a muster roll of the troops in their units present and moving towards Philadelphia. It also asked for "an Account of their Arms, Accoutrements, Camp Utensils and Baggage." On July 10th Smallwood's companies began their journey north. Thomas, Hindman and Veazey also started to move towards Head of Elk, where they would join Smallwood, or, if not there, then in Philadelphia. By July 15th Thomas and Hindman had been ordered to terminate their movement and return to Maryland to help protect southern Maryland from British raids and incursions which had increased in frequency and severity. Thomas, at least, was initially ordered to Annapolis, prior to being directed to St. Mary's County. It is unclear how far either had progressed. Ultimately, neither was retained for very long. Thomas was in St. Mary's County when he was released and ordered to resume his movement north by the end of July. Thomas Stone subsequently reported that Thomas had arrived in Philadelphia on August 13th. Hindman's movements are more uncertain. The records do not clearly indicate that his unit was present in southern Maryland, nor when or how his company moved north. Both he and Thomas reached New York prior to August 27th. However, they may not have been, and probably weren't, with the Regiment during the Battle of Long Island. [430]

COL Smallwood, with his headquarters and six companies, left Annapolis on July 10, 1776. His troops were generally transported up the Bay by barge to Head of Elk (Elkton). From there they were required to march to Philadelphia, a distance of about fifty miles, to report to the Continental Congress. In his October 1776 report to the Maryland Convention, the first since he had departed in July, Smallwood indicated that the unit had marched the entire distance in one body, covering fifteen to twenty miles a day "as the several stages made it necessary." He commented on the "[e]xertions necessary to procure Baggage, Waggons, Provisions and House Room for 750 men." The count included CPY Veazey's large company (7th IC). The three companies and staff that had been located in Baltimore joined the main body at Head of Elk and the consolidated unit proceeded to Philadelphia, arriving on July 17th. Smallwood then reported to John Hancock, as President of the Congress the senior Continental official present. Hancock, in turn, directed Smallwood to report to General Washington with his unit, at the Flying Camp which had been established in the vicinity of Amboy (Perth Amboy) New Jersey. Hancock then wrote to Washington that this "exceeding fine body of men ... will begin their march today."

Hancock wasn't the only one who was impressed with the appearance of Smallwood's men when they arrived in Pennsylvania. One unidentified man, quoted in J. Thomas Scharf's Chronicles of Baltimore, said: "Colonel Smallwood's battalion was one of the finest in the army, in dress, equipment and discipline. Their scarlet and buff uniforms and well burnished arms contrasted strongly with those of New England troops and were distinguished at that time ... by the most fashionable cut coat, the most macaroni cocked hat, and hottest blood in the union." These comments probably referred to the officers. The men were normally in their hunting shirts, although they could have been in their uniforms to march into the city. The "hottest blood in the union" was describing the aristocratic young officers.

Major Joseph Adlum of a Pennsylvania Continental regiment was present the day Smallwood's Regiment arrived in Philadelphia. He subsequently recollected the following, from his diaries and papers of the time: "Smallwood's regiment arrived in Philadelphia about the middle of July, 1776, the day after the York Pennsylvania militia got there. I happened to be on Market Street when the regiment was marching down it ... The regiment was then said to be eleven hundred strong [sic]; and never did a finer, more dignified, and braver body of men face an enemy. They were composed of the flower of Maryland, being young gentlemen, the sons of opulent planters, farmers and mechanics. From the colonel to the private, all were attired in hunting shirts." Contrast the description of their uniforms with that of the previous source. It is unclear which is accurate. The unit did wear hunting shirts by choice. Their dress uniforms were as described above. One or both descriptions contain hyperbole. [431]

On July 15th, as previously noted, the Council ordered CPT Beall (1st IC) to stay in St. Mary's County, where they presumed he was with a portion of his company, to watch the British activity "as long as you apprehend the Enemy may have any design of Landing there ... if they should move from there to any other part of the Potowmack or up the Bay to land on this [Western] Shore you will follow them with all the dispatch you can." They informed him that General Dent was placed in command of the militia and regular forces in his district, and that he, Beall, was under his orders when he received them.

The other part of the 1st IC remained at Port Tobacco. CPTs Thomas (5th IC) and Hindman (4th IC) were ordered to stop their movement north on the Bay, as we have seen, and return south. Thomas was ordered to go to Annapolis until more information was available on what Lord Dunmore's fleet was doing. Hindman probably received the same orders. As subsequently reported to the Council on July 17th by Jeremiah Jordan, CPT Beall was severely wounded in the shoulder on the 15th in an engagement with 300 British troops that had landed on St. George Island and then moved inland. [432]

MAJ Price, on July 18th, was ordered to proceed immediately to St. Mary's County and take command of the regular troops and the militia. On the 19th CPT Thomas was ordered to St. Mary's County and, when there, to put himself under the "[d]irection of the commanding officer there." The Commissary of Stores was ordered to provide his company with ammunition. The Contractor for Provisions was ordered to provide two days rations. The Defense's small tender was ordered to convey the 5th IC to the mouth of the Patuxent. When MAJ Price moved to St. Mary's County to take command, he was accompanied by three field pieces and a nine pounder. In a letter to General Dent informing him of this the Council also asked him to give them CPT Beall's status. In a subsequent report to the Council, Price indicated that he had arrived in the vicinity of St. George's Island on July 21st. On the 23rd the council directed that as soon as "the Enemy which are now in the Potowmack River may leave the Colony of Maryland, or there appears to the Commanding Officer at St. George's … no further occasion for detaining the fifth independent company," CPT Thomas should march his company "to the northward and join the troops already sent there." [433]

458

On July 24th CPT John Gunby (2nd IC) was ordered to march his company to Cambridge, Dorchester County. On the same day CPT Woolford and the 6th IC were ordered south to Princess Anne in Somerset County, adjoining the Virginia Eastern Shore counties with strong Loyalist sentiments. In both instances they were placed under the direction of the local Committees of Observation. Gunby was specifically moved to Cambridge to help protect against any seaborne raids. A month later, on August 16th, the Council ordered the Western Shore Treasurer to pay the 2nd IC an advance. Since there were separate Treasurers for the Eastern and Western Shores, and both were regularly ordered to support the units on their respective shores, this implied that Gunby had moved his company to the Western Shore by this time. Further, it implied that he and his company were still in Maryland to receive the payment. Still further, an advance implies future expenditures away from the payer's location, i.e. a possible movement north. [434]

The Council of Safety informed their Congressional delegation of their July 23rd order to CPT Thomas to move the 5th IC northwards in a letter dated July 26th. They reconfirmed that Thomas' departure was dependent upon his release from his current commanding officer. They further stated that CPT Hindman's 4th IC had also been ordered north to join Smallwood. The Council expressed concern that sending their regulars to join Washington left them in a precarious position. "We feel for the State of New York, but cannot help feeling also for Maryland, and shall endeavor to conduct ourselves in such manner as to give every assistance in our power to them, and to the common cause, without exposing ourselves to destruction. Since the march of our regulars, we are truly in a defenseless [position], and if powerfully invaded know not what may be the consequence, however we hope for the best and are exerting ourselves to the utmost." Note the Marylanders' continuing overriding parochial concerns, as well as their focus on providing assistance to New York, another colony. Although mentioned, the "common cause" is almost an afterthought. [435]

1LT Bennett Bracco of Beall's 1st IC (soon to succeed him in overall command) commanded the portion of the company stationed in the vicinity of Port Tobacco. On July 26th he reported that smallpox had broken out among his troops. He requested instructions on whether to inoculate the troops, a dangerous practice, or "remove them out of the way," i.e. isolate the infected troops. On the 27th Samuel Chase and Charles Carroll of Carrollton reported that they (presumably the Continental Congress, or, at least, the Maryland delegation thereto) had advanced COL Smallwood 1335 dollars to provide necessities for his men "at the Camp [Flying Camp in Amboy, NJ]." They passed on Smallwood's recommendation that Christopher Richmond be appointed his unit's paymaster to fill a position created by the Congress for all of the regiments/battalions in the Flying Camp. They also said that "[a]s the harvest is now over [in late July], we imagine the militia will come in fast to compose the flying camp; and we hope the Maryland Militia will march with all possible expedition." [436]

As previously noted, on July 30th a militia company under CPT Peter Mantz from Frederick County was ordered to Leonardtown, to be deployed as directed by MAJ Price and to replace Thomas' 5th IC. The Council informed Price of the pending deployment of Mantz and the redeployment of Thomas on the 31st. Also on the 30th Thomas Stone informed the Council that the British had not stirred from Staten Island.

General Washington had considerable strength in New York. However, there were only 3,000 in the Jerseys (the Flying Camp), where 10,000 were needed. Further, he informed them that COL Smallwood was in New York. On August 7th the Council asked the Maryland Congressional delegation to give CPT Thomas any assistance he required. Further, in the absence of COL Smallwood, they were asked to give Thomas directions as needed. Mantz arrived in St. Mary's at least by August 7th. However, Dunmore's ships having departed the area, thus eliminating the for troops there, coupled with friction between Mantz and the local authorities, resulted in him being ordered to march to Annapolis, enroute to Philadelphia. He was to leave his baggage at the mouth of the Patuxent, where it would be picked up by ship. [437]

On August 3rd the Council ordered COL Thomas Ewing, commander of the Lower Battalion (southern Maryland) of the Maryland Flying Camp to march his " Battalion in Detachments, or companies, as they shall be armed and accoutered, to the city of Philadelphia, subject to the orders of Congress." Colonel Charles Greenbury Griffith of Frederick County received the same order on August 6th. On August 9th the Council informed the Congressional delegation of the status of the movement to the Flying Camp. CPT Good's company from Frederick was enroute and probably already at Philadelphia. COL Griffith and the rest of the Frederick Battalion should move "in a few days." CPT Mantz's company (from Frederick) was ordered north, and CPT Thomas' 5th IC was enroute. COL Ewing's Battalion from the lower (southern) counties was under marching orders and "two or three companies of the Battalion are near ready, and we are doing all we can to forward the others; they want but ... everything - we have arms for one half of the Battalion ... [T]wo or three

Eastern Shore companies will be ready to march next week, two other companies have borrowed arms, and are to supply the place of CPT Veazey [7th IC], Kent/Queen Anne's] and Captain Hindman [4th IC, Talbot] - the rest will be very slow, we fear, in getting arms." [438]

In the meantime, Smallwood, his regiment and the 7th IC arrived in New York. The exact date varies with the source, July 30th, August 8th or 9th. The discrepancy may have been between their arrival in the New York area (e.g. the Flying Camp in Amboy) and the town itself. However, regardless of the date, the Maryland soldiers were shocked by the reception they received after the warmth given them in Philadelphia. New York was populated overwhelmingly by loyalist Tories. They referred to the Marylanders as "macaronis," a derisive term from the song "Yankee Doodle" and meant to signify a dandified, ineffective fop. Almost one hundred years later John Williamson Palmer, a Baltimore native, wrote a poem entitled "The Maryland Battalion." The first verse speaks of the arrival in New York and the nickname conferred by the Tories:

Spruce Macaronis and pretty to see,
Tidy and dapper and gallant were we;
Blooded, fine gentlemen, proper and tall,
Bold in a fox-hunt and gay at a ball;
Prancing soldados so martial and buff,
Billets for bullets in scarlet and buff -
But our cockades were clasped with a mother's low prayer,
And the sweet hearts that braided the sword knots are fair. [439]

From Philadelphia on August 13th, Thomas Stone informed the Maryland Council that Washington felt that he needed additional troops. With a strong present British force, the anticipated arrival of the Hessians, and continued British preparations for attack, Washington "ordered a reinforcement of 2,000 from Jersey to York, the Maryland Battalion was immediately sent to him, but I believe the camps in Jersey were too weak to spare more." On August 14th, on the opening day of its 9th session, the Maryland Convention ordered "the four independent companies [to] immediately proceed to Elizabethtown [adjacent to or in the vicinity of Amboy] in the Jerseys and put themselves under the command of Colonel Smallwood, subject to the further orders of Congress." Having already ordered the 4th, 5th and 7th ICs to join Smallwood in July (although the 4th and 5th had been diverted for several weeks), the four companies would have been Beall's 1st IC in southern Maryland, Gunby's' 2nd IC from Somerset, Watkin's 3rd IC from Worcester and Woolford's 6th IC from Dorchester. The Council of Safety was requested to expedite their march and provide them with supplies. Further, they were to count towards Maryland's requirement for the Continental Flying Camp. [440]

The Council responded to Stone and his fellow deputies on August 15th, stating "[w]e received yours of the 13th … we have given orders to all the Independent Companies four in number to march[northward]." Note that CPT Beall was promoted to Brigadier General of Maryland's Flying Camp, also on the 16th, and was eventually replaced by his 1LT Bennett Bracco. The Council also informed the deputies that Colonels Hals and Ewing and six or seven companies on the Eastern Shore had also been given marching orders. Those, combined with Griffith's battalion, meant that "we shall have near four thousand men with you in a short time - this exceeds our proportion of the flying camp, but we are sending all that can be armed and equipped, and the people of New York, for whom we have affection, can have no more than our all." They enclosed a list of the Battalions and companies, noting that "[t]hese companies are not all fully armed and equipped, but we hope soon to collect enough … Smallwood's Battalion 9 companies 76 each … 684; CPT Veazey [7th IC] 100, CPT Hindman [4th IC] 100, CPT Thomas [5th IC] [100 … 300; CPT Beall [1st IC] 100, CPT Gunby [2nd IC] 100 … 200; CPT Woolford [6th IC] 100, CPT Watkins [3rd IC] 100 … 200 - 1384. Griffith's Battalion 9 companies 90 men each … 810; Col Carvel Hall ditto, ditto … 810; 3 companies of Col Ewing's … 270; 7 companies of Eastern Shore Battalion … 644. Totaling 3918. The remaining companies of Ewing and the Eastern Shore Battalion must borrow arms from the Militia to do duty here they can get Arms on no other terms." The Council was putting a very favorable light on their efforts. The numbers listed were the authorized strengths of the units and did not reflect their actual on hand numbers, which were probably 2/3 of the authorized strength, at best. Further, while accurately reflecting the units they had committed to Washington, it does not reflect what he would have from Maryland in his early major battles. For a variety of reasons, including the relative slowness of transportation, the lack of arms and equipment to outfit all of the authorized units and the time it took to organize them, most of the units listed did not arrive in the vicinity of Washington's Army until many weeks later, in some cases even much longer. The only exception was Smallwood with Veazey, who was already there. [441]

As an example of the time period involved, on August 24th the Council ordered the Commissary of Stores to deliver to Gunby's 2nd IC "2 ps check linen, 16 camp kettles, 16 tents, 90 knapsacks with Haversacks and ninety wooden Bottles." The Western Treasurer was ordered to pay him over 95 pounds "on Account of his Company." The Paymaster was ordered to advance him "one month's pay, ending the third day of September, 1776." All of this was in preparation for Gunby taking his company northward and implies that he was still in Maryland to receive it all, i.e. he hadn't marched yet. However, since he was from the Eastern Shore it might mean that he had moved to the Western Shore. After Rezin Beall's election as Brigadier General of the Maryland Flying Camp on August 16th, the Convention made some promotions in the 1st IC on August 22nd: 1LT Bennett Bracco to Captain, 2LT John Halkerston to 1LT, 3LT Daniel Jennifer Adams to 2LT and Thomas Beall as 3LT. On August 27th the Convention replaced 2LT Adams, who had been promoted to Beall's Brigade Major, with 3LT Beall and appointed Calmore Williams as 3LT. Newly promoted Brigadier General Beall, now in command of Maryland's four Flying Camp Battalions, arrived in the Continental Flying Camp in the late August time frame. How many of his battalions had arrived for him to command is unclear. When the Council, in accordance with the legislation they had passed in January, informed him, or, at least, suggested to him that he report to Smallwood, he refused; presumably because he thought that he outranked Smallwood. He was not subsequently involved in any of the combat action.

On August 26th the Council ordered the Commissary of Stores of Baltimore Town to deliver to CPT Bracco "fifteen tents and six camp kettles" It also ordered the Paymaster to pay Bracco's company one month's pay, also through September 3rd. Bracco, then, had not departed Maryland. However, he had at least begun to move towards Baltimore Town from Charles and St. Mary's Counties, if he wasn't there already. The Council also ordered the Paymaster to advance CPT Woolford (6th IC) one month's pay through September

3rd. It further ordered the Western Shore Treasurer to pay Woolford half a month's pay in "Continental Currency." As with Gunby and Bracco, Woolford had to still be in Maryland to receive the pay. And, like Gunby, it may mean that he had moved from the Eastern to the Western Shore.

It wasn't until September 19th that the remaining Independent Companies, by then under MAJ Price's command, joined Smallwood's Regiment in the New York area. However, there was one exception. CPT John Watkins' 3rd IC had been stationed at Snow Hill in Worcester County. His unit was the last Independent Company to leave for New York. Why is unclear. It could have been because of the continued possibility of unrest caused by the heavily Loyalist populations of the Virginia Eastern Shore counties abutting southern Worcester County. For whatever reason, on September 20th the Company still remained in Philadelphia. Maryland's Congressional deputies informed the sitting Maryland Convention that of Watkins' established strength of 100 men, he had "only thirty seven effective privates and ... several of that number appeared not really effective." The men were upset about the insufficiency of blankets and also about the beating inflicted on several of them by Watkins (disciplinary floggings?). [442]

The Council wrote COL Richardson on the Eastern Shore on August 17th, informing him that they had "already given orders to many of your Captains in Writing. We have now only to add that you are to march all of the Companies in your Battalion as soon as possible that can be armed and equipped. They are to go to Elizabethtown in the Jerseys [again, in the vicinity of Amboy and on the Hudson] and there receive further directions from the Commander in Chief [Washington]." Richardson's companies, or most of them, appear to have moved north independently. Richardson informed the Council that he was departing on September 1st. [443]

By August 12, 1776, the British Army in the New York area numbered 27,000 troops. As previously indicated, the American paper strength was 28,000. However, due to illness and other reasons especially endemic to poorly organized armies, its on hand strength on any given day was only 17,000-19,000, practically all of whom were ill-equipped and inexperienced. Maryland's previously noted efforts to send as many of their regular and Flying Camp troops northward to New York was their attempt to help balance the scale of military strength. It was still assumed by many, especially government officials at all levels, local, state, and national, but definitely not Washington, that the militia troops were adequate to meet the needs of the American force. One significant reason for their reluctance to more fully embrace the strong regular army concept, aside from a strong philosophical aversion to a standing army, was that the militia was relatively easy for them to get their hands on to get moving. They were generally already existing units that needed merely to get mobilized and get on the march. The politicians didn't have to start from scratch. Further, although when fighting the militia units were under someone else's operational control, they still "belonged" to the state and local governments and would return to their direct control sooner than later. This could not be said for the regular units, especially as time went on. [444]

The American Army was far less homogeneous than the British and Hessian Armies. Each British royal regiment had its distinctive characteristics with the majority of its men

coming from the same region. However, each also drew officers and men from throughout the British Isles, and each was
controlled by one government and one set of regulations and
customs. By contrast, the American forces on Long Island in
August 1776 included regiments from eight states and under
thirteen separate governmental jurisdictions, all under the
operational control of General Washington. Because each
governmental entity established slightly different terms of
service for its troops, used different criteria in selecting officers, and provided different training and regulations, and
because each unit reflected the peculiar characteristics of the
community from which it was drawn, the American Army was
a true conglomeration. Washington already knew what battle would prove; that the quality of his army was as varied as
its origins; and that discipline, morale and effectiveness were
strikingly different from regiment to regiment. [445]

In contrast to the woeful state of training, equipment and
discipline of most of the units under his command at New York,
especially the militia, Washington did have some units which
were fully trained and equipped. He used these as a cadre, or
backbone, to strengthen the masses of untrained and undisciplined troops. Commenting on those "well formed regiments, "which figured prominently in the bloodiest actions in
Brooklyn, Washington would cite his need of them, declaring
that "our liberties" could be lost "if their defense is left to any
but a permanent standing army." He had watched the local
militias "almost by whole regiments" disappear, the field to
be held only by the toughness, loyalty and valor of such units
as Haslett's Delawares or Smallwood's Maryland Regiment.
Unlike the average militia unit, Maryland's soldiers were fully
equipped and were very well drilled. In Maryland the regiment was known as the "Dandy Fifth." When it arrived in New

York, its men were called "macaronis," initially derogatorily by the local citizens, but then in admiration and respect by the rest of the army. [446]

Smallwood arrived in New York possibly in late July, but not later than August 8th or 9th (the sources, as we have seen, vary) and his regiment was assigned to Brigadier General (BG) John Sullivan's Brigade. On August 12th Washington transferred them to the brigade of BG William Alexander. Alexander was in the midst of an extended legal battle to claim a vacant Scottish title of nobility. He referred to himself as Lord Stirling, as did other Americans. The British did so only derogatorily. In July and August the Maryland Convention and Council of Safety had placed the seven Independent Companies of regulars under Smallwood's command and control. However, when he arrived in New York he only had direct control over one, Veazey's 7th IC which had joined him at Head of Elk and marched north with the regiment. The other six were at various stages of their journey to New York, with a number not joining the regiment until mid-September, as previously noted. The Continental Congress assigned Maryland a quota of two "regular" regiments on August 17th. Although it had previously ordered its units to New York to be part of the Army contesting the British, the Convention waited for the formal request to transfer the troops formally to Continental control. To fulfill their quota they transferred Smallwood's regiment and the seven Independent Companies to the Continental army effective August 17th. The number of troops transferred equaled two regiments (16 companies), but they purposely neglected to provide a second regimental staff. The seven Independent Companies were to be controlled and directed by Smallwood. [447]

The number of soldiers under Smallwood's command in New York and, more specifically, the number available for duty on the day of the Battle of Long Island, August 27th, is difficult to determine, as is which specific units were there. As previously noted, not all of the units listed by the Maryland Convention in mid-August as having been committed to Washington's Army in New York had arrived. In fact, some of them hadn't left Maryland yet. Documentary evidence shows that some units were still in Maryland, some enroute and some in New York at the time of the battle. COL Richardson of the Eastern Shore did not leave Maryland until September 1st. Of the soldiers who were with Washington, some remained on Manhattan Island (New York) during the engagement, and some may have been at the Flying Camp at Amboy, NJ, technically under Washington's overall command. Some were sick or engaged in administrative duties. What can be documented is that the 9 regimental companies and Veazey's 7th IC were present. Thomas' 5th IC was in the area, but was not involved with the regiment initially that day. The other Independent Company originally ordered to accompany Smallwood, Hindman's 4th IC, was not present and its exact location is unclear. The other four companies were in various stages of moving north.

The number of troops involved is also difficult to pin down. One source states that Smallwood left for New York with 540 enlisted men. Another says that Smallwood and Veazey combined had an authorized strength of almost 800 men. Still another says that Maryland had 900 men in Washington's Army on August 27th. Thomas' authorized strength of 100, combined with Veazey's and Smallwood's authorized strength would equal almost 900. The actual number that went into the fight is even more difficult to determine. All of the units, Smallwood's included, had men sick and otherwise not available for a variety of reasons. In the last official return of

Washington's Army prior to the battle Smallwood's regiment is listed with an available for duty strength of 600 men. The best available estimate is that the regiment went to battle with a field strength of about 450 men. [448]

A problem for Washington appeared in the "silk stocking" regiments that were joining his Army. The Maryland Regiment was one of them. William Smallwood, a wealthy planter's son, and a wealthy planter himself, commanded a regiment officered and, to some extent, staffed, by the sons of planters, lawyers and merchants, as well as planters, lawyers and merchants themselves. They were primarily from the Western Shore. A Pennsylvania militiaman described them as "city-bred Marylanders (meaning Annapolis and Baltimore) who were distinguished by the most fashionably cut coat, the most macaroni cocked hat, and the hottest blood in the union." Others remarked on their dress uniforms of scarlet and buff, which were thought to be "not fully according with the independence we had assumed."

Unlike most of Washington's Army gathering in New York, the Maryland contingent had been well drilled at home and were so well equipped that they even had bayonets, a rarity for the American Army. Whigs of Maryland were deadly serious about their soldiering. When they joined Washington's army they put away their scarlet coats (the officers) and every man "from the colonel to the private all were attired in hunting shirts." But even privates in what had been the Baltimore Independent Cadets expected to be treated as gentlemen, with the privileges of their social rank, such as immunity from corporal punishment and the right to resign from the Army if the terms of their contract were not honored. [449]

As previously noted, Smallwood and his regiment, including CPT Veazey and the 7th IC, arrived in the New York area by August 8th or 9th. Washington originally placed the regiment in the brigade of BG John Sullivan. On August 12th it was reassigned to a brigade commanded by BG William Alexander, Lord Stirling. It wasn't until five days later, on the 17th, that the Marylanders formally became part of the Continental Army, which at the time was primarily situated in and around New York. Sullivan, in the meantime, had been advanced to Major General (MG) and given command of a Division, which included Stirling's Brigade.

Other troops, regulars, were coming north to New York, including Haslett's Delawares and COL Samuel Atlee's Pennsylvania Rifles. Both of the regiments joined Smallwood's in Stirling's Brigade by the morning of August 27th. Sullivan was under the overall command of MG Israel Putnam, who had replaced a sick MG Nathaniel Greene as Washington's tactical commander on Long Island. On the morning of August 27th Sullivan's Division consisted of the following troops:

Major General John Sullivan (New Hampshire) Commander

Brigadier General William Alexander, Lord Stirling

Maryland Regiment - COL William Smallwood (MAJ Mordecai Gist acting Commander)

Delaware Regiment - COL John Haslett (MAJ Thomas McDonough acting Commander)

Pennsylvania Rifle Regiment - COL Samuel Miles

Pennsylvania Musketeers - COL Samuel John Atlee

Pennsylvania Militia - LTC Peter Kochlein

Lancaster City (PA) Militia - MAJ Hay

Brigadier General Alexander McDougall (Richard Platt Brigade Major)

1st New York Regiment - formerly McDougall's

3rd New York Regiment - COL Rudolph Retzema

19th Continental Regiment (Conn.) - COL Charles Webb

Artificers (e.g. armorers, ammo handlers) (Mass.)

- COL Jonathan Brewer [450]

On August 14th Sergeant William Sands of the 7th IC wrote his parents. "Our Maryland Battalion is Encamped on a hill about one mile out of Newyork [sic] where we lay in a very secure place... We are advised to hold our-Selves in readiness we expect an attack hourly we have lost a great many of our Troops Thay have deserted from us at Philadelphia and Elizabeth Town and a Great Many Sick in the ospitals [sic] There is Rations Given out at New York for 600 men dailey ... We Expect Please God to Winter in Annapolis those that Live of us." Sgt. Sands was killed on August 27th. [451]

It is difficult to determine how far Washington's Army had been savaged by camp fever in late August, or to what extent the newly arrived units, including the Marylanders, were infected. A 30% disability rate seems likely. The fever was taking out an alarming number of field grade officers. COL Fish Gay of Connecticut was already dead; others were too sick to accompany their units to Long Island. There were barely enough healthy ranking officers to hold a court-martial for LTC Herman Zedwitz. Washington insisted that Zedwitz be tried. His case had been pending a long time due to the inability to gather enough senior officers together to try it. Hence Smallwood and Haslett, with their Lieutenant Colonels, had to sit on the trial commencing August 25th while their units deployed to Long Island and took the field.

Sickness had a significant, albeit sometimes temporary, impact on the ranks of the Marylanders. It was recorded that "[t]he flower of these [American] troops was Smallwood's Battalion of about 680 men. They were composed of young men from all of the best Maryland families. These brave soldiers were later reduced by camp disease to about 450 men." The desertions noted by Sgt. Sands would also have contributed to the reduction in strength. Many of the men were emaciated by what was called camp distemper caused by drinking foul water from New York's public pumps. Those who had money learned to buy water from vendors. Despite these difficulties, they would have been active. Smallwood was known to be a strict disciplinarian. The men, unless confined by illness, would have spent their days keeping their camp sites and equipment clean, marching and drilling. [452]

In a letter dated August 24th, Daniel of St. Thomas Jennifer informed COL Smallwood that CPT Beall had been appointed by the Maryland Convention as Brigadier General of the Maryland Flying Camp (i.e., the senior Maryland officer) on August 23rd. The commission had been offered to Smallwood's First Major, Thomas Price, who declined it because the Convention would not allow him to also retain his rank of Major in the "regular service." Jennifer also informed Smallwood that if he and Beall were to "act together, you are to command." Beall had also been informed of this potential command structure. It was in accordance with the Convention's resolution passed early in 1776 dealing with the seniority of officers. It was an attempt to avoid the conflicts among the officers that proved so divisive during the SY/FI War. As mentioned earlier, Beall refused to agree to honor the command structure dictated by the Convention and, in effect, faded from the military scene. [453]

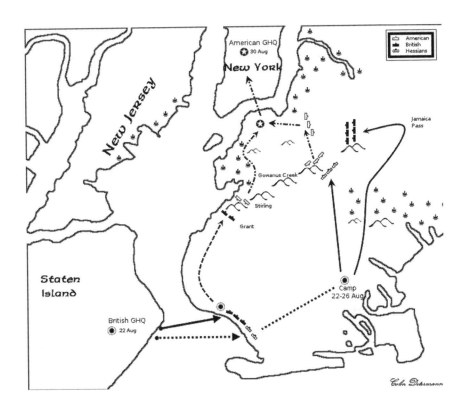

From August 21st to August 17th the British ferried troops from their base on Staten Island to the south-eastern corner of Long Island through Sheepshead Bay. There were American troops already on Long Island. Both sides exchanged shots daily, with little damage. Between the British landing sites and the growing American fortifications in Brooklyn, essentially in the vicinity of the East River across from New York and Manhattan Island, was a range of hills, the Heights of Gowan. The hills extended generally east north east from the Narrows on the Hudson River to Jamaica. There were known to be four passes through the hills that were large enough to accommodate the movement of troops with artillery. The most direct road was along the Bay, cutting through the hills just behind Red Lion (the Red Lion Inn) where Mortense Lane joined the Gowanus Road. A second was directly in front of Flatbush. The road through it led directly to the American entrenchments. It was the Flatbush Pass, subsequently referred to by some as the Battle Pass. The third was by the road from Flatbush to Bedford, the Bedford Pass. The fourth, the Jamaica Pass, which extended as far as Flushing, crossed the Bedford and Jamaica Road nearly three miles east of Bedford.

On August 26th the Maryland and Delaware troops under Stirling were ordered to Long Island. They, along with the other units that were moving, joined the American formations already in place, some of whom had been steadily skirmishing with the British and Hessian troops. COL Haslett of Delaware and his LTC Bedford joined COL Smallwood and LTC Ware on LTC Zedwitz's court-martial, as specifically ordered by GEN Washington. Their troops were under the command of MAJ Thomas McDonough and MAJ Mordecai Gist, respectively. General Howe, after months of delay and preparation was ready to use his army. [454]

John McCasland of Cumberland County, PA, joined CPT Thomas Campbell's company of volunteers in COL Brown's Seventh Regiment, Pennsylvania militia in August 1776. After the company was "madeup," officer elections were held and he was elected as Ensign at the age of twenty-six. The company "marched to Philadelphia and then went by water to Trenton [NJ, up the Delaware River], and from Trenton … marched to Perth-Amboy, while at Amboy the British lay on Staten Island there was occasional cannonading, but the distance was so far that no damage was done … [F]rom Perth Amboy, went to Long Island under the command of General Putnam. We found troops on Long Island (American troops), and soon after our arrival an engagement took place with the British, who I think were commanded by General Howe. We were defeated with a considerable number killed and a number taken prisoner, and among the number taken prisoners by the British was Captain Campbell." [455]

On August 17th, the day the Maryland Regiment and Independent Companies formally became part of the Continental Army. Smallwood's Regiment, augmented by the 7th IC, was assigned to General Stirling's Brigade, as we have seen. Major General Putnam had been given overall command of the American troops on Long Island. Major General John Sullivan, commanding the Division that Stirling's Brigade was part of, was on the American right (i.e. western) flank, generally facing south/southeast. Sullivan, in turn, assigned Stirling to the right flank of the American Army, with responsibility for covering the Gowanus Road. His Brigade, as previously noted, consisted of: Smallwood's Maryland Regiment, Haslett's Delaware Regiment, COL Samuel Miles' Pennsylvania Rifle Regiment, COL Samuel Atlee's Pennsylvania Musketeers, LTC Peter Kochlein's Pennsylvania militia and MAJ Hay's Lancaster City (PA) militia. Stirling had positioned pickets from Atlee's Musketeers on his extreme right, in the vicinity of the Red Lion Inn, at the intersection of the Gowanus Road and Martense Lane in the Martense Pass through the Heights of Gowan.

General Howe, and his subordinates, conceived an attack plan to take advantage of a perceived American weakness. British scouts had found that the Jamaica Pass through the Heights of Gowan was virtually unguarded and open for significant troop movement. The pass was beyond the flanks of both Armies (the American left and the British right) and well to the east of the main American forces. General Henry Clinton developed and wrote an operations plan to capitalize on the American mistake. If the British could advance through the pass relatively unscathed, they would be in position to advance west southwest against the American left flank and roll them up (i.e. attack the Americans from the side when they were focused to the front, completely disrupting units, forcing them to retreat and, if the British were lucky, to fall apart under the unexpected, overwhelming pressure.). Troops under Clinton and General Cornwallis made up the main attack through the Jamaica Pass. British troops to their west (left), after suitable delay to allow Clinton and Cornwallis to march to and get control of the pass, were to attack the Americans through the passes to their front and attempt to fix the Americans; i.e., through vigorous attacks, cause the Americans to focus on them and not pay attention to their left flank. The Hessians were to go through the Flatbush Pass. A force under Major General Grant was to move through the Martense Pass on the British extreme left flank.

Grant's Division consisted of his own 4th Brigade (17th, 40th, 46th and 55th Regiments), BG James Agnew's 6th Brigade (23rd, 44th, 57th and 64th Regiments), the 42nd Royal Highlanders (from the reserves), two New York provincial companies (Loyalists), and a detachment of Royal Artillery with ten guns. Later in the day he was joined by about 2,000 Marines, culled from the fleet. They brought his total force to about 5,000 troops. Grant allowed Howe's column, with Clinton and Cornwallis, destined for the Jamaica Pass, a three hour head start. Shortly before midnight on August 26th he began to move his column up the Shore or Narrows or Gowanus Road

(The name varies with the source, probably because local usage varied over time. Gowanus will be used subsequently.) He was marching towards Martense Lane and the Red Lion Inn. Prior to 1 AM on the 27th his scouts were attracted by watermelons growing in a patch near the Red Lion Inn. The American pickets, including COL Edward Hand's riflemen and COL Atlee's Pennsylvania Musketeers, saw the scouts and fired on them, driving them away. Grant brought his main force up but stopped them short of the intersection, from where he proceeded to observe the American positions at the inn for several hours. He then began to move his units forward towards the pass and a spirited fight broke out along the line of American outposts. As the British forces moved steadily forward, some of the American troops broke and ran, terrified, up the Gowanus Road.

Messengers quickly informed General Putnam of the skirmishing at the watermelon patch. He rapidly began alerting his troops. For several hours he and his subordinates assumed that the main British attack was being made on the American right and moved to counteract it. Stirling subsequently wrote that "I fully expected, as did most of my officers, that the strength of the British army was advancing to our lines." Putnam rode down to insure that Stirling had been informed and, more importantly, to get him moving. Stirling's headquarters encampment was at the Vechte-Cortelyou (Old Stone) house, located at the intersection of Gowanus and Porte Roads, the latter a short, direct route to the Flatbush Pass. Putnam arrived at Stirling's HQ at about 3 AM. Stirling had not heard the firing and had not been informed of the skirmishing. Putnam roused him and ordered him to collect as many troops as he could and to move immediately to stop Grant.

Shortly after Putnam's arrival, Stirling had troops marching towards the British. There is disagreement among authors concerning exactly which units he took with him and, more specifically, which portions of which units. There is no disagreement, however, on two salient points. First, Smallwood and Haslett, along with their LTCs, were still in New York sitting on a court-martial on Washington's orders. The Marylanders and the Delawares, then, were led, as we have seen, by their Majors, Mordecai Gist and Thomas McDonough. Gist was the 2nd Major, the fourth in command of the regiment. Second, the core of the fighting force was the Maryland and Delaware Regiments, which Stirling quickly led to battle. He was soon followed by BG Parsons of Spencer's Division, with another two hundred men and more from Atlee's Battalion. After being notified of the contact by Putnam, Sullivan dispatched another 400 men to aid Stirling. Wright said that the 400 joined with Stirling during his movement. Carrington indicated that they didn't arrive until about 9 AM. Although the timing of the arrival of the various detachments isn't known with exactitude, Stirling ultimately led about 2,000 troops to reinforce Atlee. [456]

Smallwood and Ware weren't the only senior Maryland leaders not present of the 27th. CPTs Barton Lucas (3rd Co.) and Peter Adams (6th Co.) were both ill the day of the battle. In their absence, command fell to their inexperienced 1LTs. Both CPTs Benjamin Ford (9th Co.) and Patrick Sim s (2nd Co.) were young and inexperienced. Ford, only recently promoted, was from Charles County and probably knew Smallwood. Sims was from neighboring Prince George's County. There is some evidence that CPT John Hoskins Stone probably served as Gist's second in command. As 1st Company Commander Stone was the most senior of the Captains and appeared to have at least some militia experience. While a successful business man and, apparently, a persuasive leader, Gist had little military experience. What he had was limited to what he had gained organizing, training and leading the Baltimore Independent Cadets and the Maryland Regiment. He had no combat experience. He had never been under fire. The situation called for additional leadership. [457]

Grant, the British left wing as we have seen, began advancing against the Americans, aiming toward the Red Lion Inn at the intersection of the Gowanus Road and Martense Lane. The position was defended by a variety of American troops, including the 2nd New York, the 1st Continentals (Penn.) under Edward Hand of a Brigade of Greene's Division, the Penn Musketeers under COL Atlee (as we have already seen) and, possibly, a portion of Huntington's Connecticut Regiment, a total of about 600 men. Grant's scouts ran into the Americans in a watermelon patch in the middle of the night, as we noted. The American pickets were from a unit commanded by MAJ Buford of the Pennsylvania Flying Camp, Pennsylvania's portion of the Continental 10,000 man Flying Camp, which was to be placed under instructions as the ultimate reserves. As with Maryland, the emergency caused many Pennsylvania units to be sent to New York before they had, in fact, been fully organized. Buford's pickets initially held. However, they were ultimately forced back and some fled. The rest were captured by Grant's advanced guard. Carrington states that the pickets were aided by the presence of General Parsons of Spencer's Division who had just been promoted to Brigadier General. Others, including John Gallagher, put Parsons' arrival, with 200 troops he had gathered along the way, after Stirling's. The 400 troops that Sullivan ultimately sent had been detached from the forces defending the Flatbush (Battle) Pass. It was not yet under attack when they departed.

COL Atlee had pushed forward to the crest of the hill by which the British had to approach the American position. A portion of his three companies united with the advance guard and maintained such vigorous skirmishing just back of Red Lion that the British advance was halted until daylight. Midway between Red Lion and the American lines a well developed ridge extended from the general line of hills (the Heights of Gowan) across the Gowanus Road, nearly to the shore of New York Bay. The ground in front, to the southwest, was low and marshy at places, while an orchard occupied the slight upland immediately in front of this ridge. Stirling was to select it as his primary position. Atlee concentrated his regiment and the retiring picket guard upon the side of the main hills, east of the road on the British right and what was to be the American left. He did so to have a superior position from which to open fire on the British. They were then preparing to descend from the summit near the pass to the low ground and orchard which they had to pass to eventually attack Stirling. Atlee made his move to the wooded higher ground under grape shot with the loss of only one man.

Facing the gathering Americans was the ad hoc Division sized force under MG Grant. It consisted, as we have seen, of Grant's 4th Brigade and Agnew's 6th Brigade of Lord Percy's Second Line and First Line, respectively, the 42nd (Black Watch) Regiment from the reserve, two companies of New York Loyalists and an artillery detachment with ten guns. After the initial encounter Grant began applying pressure before dawn, primarily with heavy cannon fire. The guns began to run low on gunpowder and shot and were resupplied from the fleet. In addition, the previously noted 2,000 marines were landed to reinforce Grant, bringing his force total to between 5,000 and 9,000 troops (depending on the source, the marines increased his force to 5, 7, or 9 thousand). The marines increased the size of Grant's force, but did not necessarily increase its effectiveness for several reasons. The marines served on the fleet's war ships in detachments of varying size depending on the size of the ship and its particular mission. For example, if coastal raids were anticipated the size of a ship's detachment might be increased over its normal strength. These detachments rarely acted together as part of a larger force, nor were they organized along traditional land force lines, so coordination and cohesiveness were difficult to achieve. Further, their shipboard life, while often uncomfortable, dangerous and physically demanding, did not prepare them well to serve for extended periods ashore as army infantry units. In simple terms, the only way to prepare soldiers to march relatively long distances carrying heavy loads of cumbersome equipment in all kinds of weather, quickly and effectively, arriving at their destination ready to fight, and to do so day after day after day, is to do it a lot. Serving aboard shops, the marines did not receive that type of conditioning.

Taking advantage of the lull in firing, Atlee withdrew several hundred yards, through Stirling who, in turn, withdrew to Atlee's position. Stirling formed his line with Atlee's troops on the right, nearest the coast, under cover of trees. His main formation was positioned on Blockje"s Hill, east of the Gowanus Road. He placed two companies forward to break an English charge. A detachment of Marylanders was also in front and to the left. The units formed an inverted "V", developed by Frederick the Great of Prussia (a kettle or "kessel"), with the legs of the "V" ready to envelope any British force attacking the main force at the juncture of the two arms. In addition to occupying the higher ground, the Americans had the further advantage of a small stream in front of them crossed only by a narrow bridge on the Gowanus Road. [458]

Stirling had moved his forces to within a half mile of the Red Lion to confront and halt Grant. He formed his troops across Gowanus Road, including two guns of an artillery company which had joined him. The British had also drawn themselves up in several lines to attack the Americans. Stirling had deployed the Delawares, the Marylanders and part of Kochlein's rifle battalion from right to left on the field. The Maryland Regiment, with Veazey's 7th IC, probably deployed in two wings of five companies each, which combined to form a continuous line from the Gowanus Road. It appears that the 1st, 2nd, 5th, 7th and 8th Companies formed the left wing; while the 3rd, 4th, 6th, 9th (Light) and 7th IC formed the right. Since the Regiment had presumably conducted little, if any training as a complete unit, except during its march north and possibly in New Jersey and/or New York after they arrived, this disposition made sound military sense given the circumstances. The case for two separate wings of the above composition is reinforced by later returns which showed that the companies in the left wing (1st, 2nd, 5th, 7th, and 8th) suffered very few losses in the battle. However, the other companies on the right wing (3rd, 4th, 6th 9th, 7th IC) had casualties of 60% to 80%.

A member of Ramsey's 5th Company later recalled that following the subsequent retreat the English advanced towards the Americans and General Stirling "immediately drew us up in a line and offered them battle ..." As the British advanced to within three hundred yards the American line came under fire from both cannons and mortars. The Americans were under fire from sunrise to midday. MAJ Gist probably fought somewhere near the juncture of the two wings. An anonymous source, presumably Gist, subsequently reported that the Maryland line was under artillery fire and observed that the right wing was also under fire from Light Infantry deployed from the British left. Gist commented that "the men ... maintained their ground until ten o'clock" At this point the British retreated. [459]

About 7AM the Scottish Highlanders and Hessians under Philip von Heister and Carl von Donap, engaged the Americans in a wooded area to Stirling's left in the vicinity of the Flatbush Pass. This too was a holding action, not an all out drive. On the 26th COL Samuel Miles of Stirling's Brigade had been ordered to protect the east, Stirling's and Sullivan's left flank. He stationed his troops, including 600 in his Pennsylvania Rifle Regiment and some New York troops, in the American front line near Bedford Pass, east of Flatbush (Battle) Pass. Sullivan had already sent 400 men from Flatbush Pass to Stirling on the far right, making the job of the Highlanders and Hessians easier. [460]

Grant, who disdained the Americans and their fighting capabilities initially sent a body of men forward against Stirling's right, advancing to within 200-300 yards of their lines, and recommenced his artillery fire. The American troops were under orders not to fire until the enemy was within 50 yards, on the premise that the first opponent to discharge his weapons was immediately at a disadvantage, forced to continue on with only bayonets. The Americans apparently had not yet mastered the technique of rolling, continuous fire from two or three lines of infantry, with one line reloading while the other fired. This technique, initially unique to the British, enabled them to defeat the French and their allies 30-40 years later. One participant claimed to have been under fire from "sunrise to 12 o'clock, the enemy firing on us the chief portion of the time." When they not only held, but opened fire with their two cannon, Grant pulled his troops back, switching to a steady artillery barrage that still failed to dislodge the Americans. They, still unaware what was happening on the rest of the battlefield, continued to believe that they were holding back the enemy's main thrust.

Grant and Stirling faced each other at Red Lion for at least two hours and probably closer to four. The artillery of both sides had been in action all along, but it was now felt more keenly because of the lack of any other visible activity on the main front. The troops had little else to distract them from the results of the cannonades on their fellow soldiers, if not themselves. The troops of both sides stood, literally, in position, the Americans spaced in more extended order than the British simply because there were fewer of them to cover their front. None of the Americans, and few of the British, especially the Privates, had ever been in a formal, European style combat situation before. In keeping with the traditional procedure, neither commander sought cover for his men (In the late eighteenth and early nineteenth centuries Wellington was considered an innovative combat leader for many reasons. Main among them is that he always sought to have his troops positioned behind a hill or ridge and laying down before conducting an attack or receiving one from the enemy. This rested the troops until they were needed. It concealed them from the enemy, making it more difficult to know exactly where and how many of them there were. Finally, it protected them from the enemy's artillery, which was still a direct fire weapon. They couldn't see the English troops to shoot at them.). The danger to each army, however, lay not in the number of actual casualties - which were not heavy at all - but in the ghastly effect cannon balls had on living flesh and the impact it had on their messmates, let alone themselves. Inexperienced troops normally would be expected to give into their fears, break ranks and flee. Yet the Americans all stood the ordeal like veteran campaigners for hours. The British were especially surprised by their steadfastness. [461]

Grant then sent a detachment of two regiments and part of a third to Stirling's right, overlapping Atlee with the intention of flanking him and, ultimately, Stirling's whole line. Stirling responded, sending two companies of Delawares and General Parsons with a portion of Huntington's Regiment (Parsons' 200?) that was on the ground to extend and cover Atlee's left flank. Two strong attacks were made on Atlee with limited success. However, it was not necessary for Grant to overcome the Americans, just hold them in place.

When Grant sent a detachment to link up with the Hessians he was expecting from von Heister in the British center, to his right, Stirling detected the attempt to encircle him and ordered units to seize the high ground on his left flank. They held off three British charges and inflicted the highest losses on them that were incurred at any point during the whole day of fighting. As the morning developed, the Americans under Stirling had lost only a handful of men and appeared to be holding back the British left wing successfully. However, by 10 AM there was nothing remaining of the American lines east of Stirling. All cohesion there had been broken; the men remaining on the field were either dead, captives of the British, or fugitives hiding in the brush and woods in the hills. The Hessians and Highlanders had smashed through the American center at Flatbush (Battle)

Pass. Cornwallis, with the bulk of the British forces, had continued from Jamaica Pass, dispersing the American left to come up upon their remaining right wing from behind. [462]

By 8AM on the 27th, as a result of hard night marching and poor American reconnaissance, the majority of Howe's forces were in position behind the American advanced lines. At the other attack points: de Heister had his Hessian Division and Highlanders in position in front of Flatbush (Battle) Pass; and Grant had advanced along the Shore (Gowanus or Narrows) Road and was already in a heavy firefight at Martense Lane. However, he had not yet fully committed his field force. Both waited for a signal from Clinton to the northeast. Sullivan, at Flatbush Pass, having detached 400 men to help Stirling on the Gowanus Road where the main British thrust was expected, now faced de Heister's imminent assault with 800 men.

Atlee's Pennsylvanians had borne the brunt of the skirmishing with Grant's troops so far. Around 8 AM Stirling ordered him to drop back so the British would have to face the fresh units he had brought with him and additional ones that he had just received. These new contingents were placed in open order across the road. Stirling's strongest unit, the Maryland Regiment, was on his left, anchored in a hilltop copse of trees to take advantage of the only height available. They had waited there since first light, about four hours, and had also been the target of Brant's artillery. [463]

Around 8 AM Howe fired a cannon to indicate that he was safely through the Jamaica Pass. Hearing the signal, Cornwallis and his grenadiers continued to move strongly across the American rear, moving down the Old Jamaica Road, north of the Heights of Gowan (Long Island Heights), beginning to put pressure on Sullivan. Clinton's light troops and dragoons peeled off south down the Flatbush Road, the light infantry fanning out into the woods on either side of the road to descend on Sullivan's men who were preoccupied with the Hessians and Highlanders to their front. The Hessian Jaegers - expert riflemen - deployed as skirmishers/light infantry and uniform ranks of Scots and German infantry broke through Flatbush Pass and began to move up through the woods, flushing out the Americans at the points of their bayonets. As they fled out of the woods in a desperate attempt to reach their interior lines and the fortifications to their rear, the Americans had to cross an intervening plain. It was there that the British dragoons, from their left and rear, swept down, while the jaegers, combining with the Hessians and the Scots, systematically corralled and destroyed groups of Americans in the woods. The Hessians and Highlanders gave no quarter, killing many of the surrounded and surrendering Americans. The Hessians, in particular, were egged on by reports that the Americans themselves were going to give no quarter. While their actions were subsequently praised by some British officers, others praised the Americans' bravery and were shocked by the massacres made by the Hessians and Highlanders after victory was decided. [464]

As previously noted, COL Miles of Stirling's Brigade had been ordered to protect the area east of Sullivan's left flank. He had positioned the 600 members of his Pennsylvania Rifle Regiment near Bedford Pass, east of Flatbush Pass. Hearing firing coming from his left, the British breakthrough, he ordered COL Samuel Wylly's 22nd Continental (Conn.) Regiment and other units, some 800 strong, to hold the pass. With the remainder of his units he went in search of Clinton. Bypassing the main force, he came upon the British baggage train at the rear of the column. Miles attacked with his forward elements and directed the rearmost battalion to return and alert Sullivan of his danger. Clinton, in turn, overwhelmed Miles' detachment, capturing some, including Miles, and killing or scattering the rest. The survivors withdrew in small groups to the American entrenchments.

Sullivan had heard the firing coming from his rear, heard the signal cannon, and was joined by Broadhead's returning battalion just as remnants of Miles' unit came straggling in. He now realized that the main British thrust had come up on the left and was now behind him. Sullivan turned the greater part of his force to face the new threat, leaving the pass to be defended by his skirmishers and the artillery in a redoubt built earlier. The combined pressure of Howe's (Clinton's and Cornwallis') troops from the left and de Heister's Hessians and Highlanders, as well as his artillery, from the front overwhelmed the American left and center. Those troops on the left were rolled up from their left; units disintegrated and the survivors fled. In the center, pressure from the left and front combined to produce the same result, forcing General Sullivan to retreat from Flatbush Pass. The battle for the center was over by 11 AM. All that remained was to finish off Stirling's forces on the Gowanus Road. [465]

Only on their right were the Americans able to provide sustained, organized opposition. Although that opposition was the result as much of British restraint as of American discipline, it did allow hundreds of American troops time to escape to Brooklyn. MG Grant, who was ordered to create a diversion on the American right while Howe turned their left, was slow to press the Americans on the Gowanus Road. Throughout the morning he was content to skirmish and exchange cannon fire. The forces opposing him under Lord Stirling were some of the best in the Continental service, including the Marylanders and the Delawares. Those regiments were not to be broken by a mere show of force. They stood firm against Grant, gaining confidence in themselves and allowing the stragglers from the left and center of the American line to pass behind them to Brooklyn. When, at around 12 PM, Cornwallis, leading Howe's force, came down on the flank and rear of Stirling's men and Grant attacked from their flank, the Americans continued to fight, even though Stirling was unable to coordinate their efforts. His main body, including Haslett's regiment, faced about, broke through the British and retreated "up to the middle of this a Marsh of Mud and brought off with them 23 prisoners." However, his left flank, failing to receive orders to retire, was soon cut off and broken into small groups, many of which continued to fight stubbornly until forced to retire. Stirling, with a substantial portion of Smallwood's Regiment, stayed behind to cover the retreat and was captured. The American right had at last collapsed under the combined weight of Clinton's Cornwallis', de Heister's and Grant's men. However, it had fought well enough to save hundreds, if not thousands, of men to help prevent the British from completing their victory. [466]

Stephen Kimble, with Clinton's column, in summarizing the action, stated that "the Grenadiers continued on the road to Brooklyn with the general [Clinton] at their head to cut off the Enemy's Retreat from Brookland Heights [the Heights of Gowan] which was happily executed. Lieut.-Gen. de Heister attacked from Flatbush at the same time [in the center] and [on the British left] Major-Gen. Grant, with the Fourth and Sixth Brigades from the Heights of the Narrows by which measure the Rebels were cut off from all Retreat and cooped up in the woods to the right of the road in the morning, but the Enemy being strongly posted in the woods could not proceed. The action between them and part of the Main body continued until late afternoon." With Grant and de Heister pressing from the south and Clinton sealing off retreat on the north and east, the American outer defenses were surrounded. [467]

Michael Graham, an eighteen year old volunteer in the Pennsylvania Flying Camp, later wrote that he had been part of an eight man picket posted near the Flatbush Pass on August 26th. On the 27th "the battle commenced about the break of day or perhaps a little more. At the Narrows [i.e., on the American right], where Lord Stirling commanded, there was a pretty heavy cannonading kept up and occasionally the firing of small arms fire, and from the sound appeared to be moving slowly towards Brooklyn. This continued for hours. At length the firing commenced above us and kept spreading until it became general in almost every direction. We continued at our post until ... about twelve o'clock, when an officer ... told us we were surrounded. We immediately retreated ... [and] had went but a small distance before we saw the enemy paraded in front of us."

Despite his efforts, and those of his fellow soldiers, Graham was continually surrounded and forced to flee. "Our Troops were routed in every direction. It's impossible for me to describe the confusion and horror of the scene that ensued: the artillery flying with chains over the horses' backs, our men running in almost every direction, and run which way they could, they were almost sure to meet the British or the Hessians. And the enemy huzzahing when they took prisoners made it truly a day of distress to the Americans. I escaped by going behind the British that had engaged hard with Stirling and entered a swamp or marsh through which a great many of our men were retreating Some of them were mired and crying to their fellows ... to the side of the marsh was a pond which I took to be a mill pond. Numbers, as they come to the pond jumped in, and some were drowned. Soon after I entered the marsh, a cannonading commenced from our batteries on the British, and they retreated, and I was safely in camp. Out of the eight men that were on guard the day before ... only I escaped. The others were either killed or taken prisoner." [468]

As the morning wore on, Stirling's command, while not suffering heavy casualties, diminished in number through the casualties they were taking. After the initial infusion of troops under Parsons and the 400 from Sullivan, he hadn't received any further reinforcements. Grant, on the other hand, had been constantly, and significantly, reinforced. As previously noted, he had Highlanders with him, members of the 42nd Regiment, the Black Watch, which de Heister had sent him. Later, as we have also seen, Admiral Howe directed that he be sent 2,000 of the fleet's marines, a numerical increase if not a increase in the quality of the land troops available. The Hessians poured through Flatbush Pass, coming down Porte Road to join the Cornwallis column coming down the Jamaica Road from Jamaica Pass, closing towards Stirling's rear unimpeded. Cornwallis, with part of the 71st Regiment - Frasier's Highlanders - and the Second Grenadiers, plus his growing contingent of Hessians, seized the thick-walled field stone and brick Vechte-Cortelyou (Old Stone) House, on the Gowanus Road, just southwest of the intersection with Porte Road. Constructed in 1699 to withstand Indian raids, it was a natural fortification and had served as Sullivan's headquarters. [469]

From dawn until about 11AM Stirling's troops remained strongly positioned in the woods on or near the Gowanus

Road, primarily trading artillery fire with Grant. However, Grant had begun to apply pressure. Firing had already been heard in the direction of Flatbush, generally east of Stirling's position. It increased between 1100 and 1130. Shortly thereafter Stirling discovered that he had enemy troops coming from his rear. In short order, he had British and Hessian troops pressing him from his front (Grant), left (the Hessians), and rear (Cornwallis with a mixture of units). As they converged on his position, Stirling quickly realized that he had to cover the retreat of the disorganized and fleeing American Army, a major portion of which was throwing his lines into confusion. Further, he had to withdraw his own units to avoid annihilation. He decided to withdraw back up the Gowanus Road. His goal was to move his troops to the safety of the American fortifications and entrenchments on Brooklyn Heights.

He didn't realize that in addition to the troops bearing down on him, there were two significant impediments to his successful movement to Brooklyn Heights. The first was the force under Cornwallis at the Vechte-Cortelyou House which served as a virtual road block at or near the intersection where the American troops would swing west to cross Gowanus Creek at the Yellow Mill. The second was the bridge over the Gowanus Creek at the Yellow Mill. It had been destroyed by a New England regiment under COL Ward in the process of its hasty retreat. After the battle Smallwood, in effect, accused the New Englanders of cowardice and panic in destroying the bridge resulting in his men's isolation in front of the enemy. The New Englanders responded that the bridge had been destroyed and the mill burnt only when it was under direct threat from the British, to prevent them from gaining easy access to the American battlements. The only escape route left, then, was directly across the creek near Freeke's

Mill. However, the land bordering the creek was swampy and marshy, a muddy morass with deep and tangling thickets. The creek at that point was 80 yards wide, possibly wider at Denton's millpond near the Yellow Mill, deep and swiftly running with an incoming tide. It was a crossing fraught with danger, but if the Americans could get across, they might be able to reform under the guns of Forts Box and Greene, two of the fortifications they had constructed. Further, Stirling, or someone who informed him, had observed wounded men being carried away on a trail through the marsh, apparently successfully. It was passable.

Stirling managed to disengage from Grant and got his units moving back up the Gowanus Road, where they ran into Lord Cornwallis' advance elements with Haslett's Delaware's in the lead. The original American intention had been to go around the pond and cross dry-shod at the dam, where part of Sullivan's column had already crossed. General Parsons had apparently been left with forces to hold off Grant while the brigade was withdrawing. However, the pressure finally became too great. Even Atlee's Pennsylvanians finally broke. The bridge they wanted to use was the one Smallwood complained had been burned. However, that would have made no difference because the British were already blocking the approaches. A platoon of the Delawares was already crossing the salt marshes with their prisoners, intending to swim the creek and gain the safety of the American entrenchments. However, if the brigade followed suit - and there was no real alternative - then the entire column would be vulnerable to attack on its exposed right flank and rear. Stirling deemed it absolutely necessary to keep Cornwallis occupied at the Upper Mills. He detached MAJ Gist with five companies, ordering all other troops to make their best way through the creek. They kept formation down to the edge of the marsh, and then dispersed in the wet ground.

There is a general consensus among historians on the events up to this point and on Stirling's actions. There is no question that he selected Maryland troops under MAJ Gist as a covering force for the rest of the brigade trying to get through the marshes and across the water. However, there is significant disagreement on which of the Maryland companies were involved in the covering force and how big the force was. Five companies are generally agreed on. A total of 400 men is normally used and has become part of the myth, enshrined on the monument in the vicinity of the Vechte-Cortelyou House. Linda Reno's research led her to state that the companies were the 1st, 2nd, 3rd, 6th and 9th. She states that she only researched the regiment. There may have been other units from Maryland involved, but since they were not in the regiment, she didn't deal with them. Howard Henry, in a work on Cecil County in the Revolution, stated that Gist had the 1st, 2nd, 3rd, 6th and 7th IC. He points out that CPTs Adams (6th) and Lucas (3rd) were sick with camp fever and not present for duty. Further, CPT Veazey (7th IC) had already been killed. Mark Tacyn has an alternative theory, following his identification of the makeup of the wings of the regiment when facing Grant.

Between 1100 and 1200 Stirling discovered he had pressure on three sides and quickly determined that he needed to withdraw. He ordered Gist to retreat with a portion of the Brigade "and force our way through to our camp." The troops in the Maryland right wing (3rd, 4th, 6th, 9th and 7th IC) were in the most advantageous position to cover the retreat since they affectively straddled the most open terrain in front of the British and were the closest to the Gowanus Road. If the British were to pursue an advance in this sector, the path of least resistance would, therefore, pass directly through the position. Occupying more heavily wooded terrain, the left wing was in a better position to disengage and withdraw, with the right's protection, up the Gowanus Road.

At this point the left wing of the Maryland line, accompanied by Haslett's Delawares (possibly in the lead) and some prisoners, retreated. The 5th and 7th Companies were in the van, followed by the 1st, 2nd and 8th companies (and, possibly, the Delawares). They withdrew along the Gowanus Road. Either when they encountered enemy troops, or under the threat of doing so, they veered left and entered the marshy area bordering Gowanus Creek. During the movement Gist ran into a group of British soldiers who appeared to want to surrender, but subsequently opened fire on him. They missed and the Marylanders drove them away. The five Maryland companies crossed both the marsh and Gowanus Creek, losing only four men (one battle death and three drowning). With a portion of his men across Gowanus Creek, Gist apparently rejoined Stirling and the other half of the regiment. He probably only accompanied the first group to the edge of the marsh, but surely no further than the edge of the stream. [470]

In his after battle report Stirling stated that to buy the bulk of his retreating brigade time to withdraw through the marshes "I found it Absolutely Necessary to attack a Body of Troops commanded by Lord Cornwallis … this I instantly did, with about half of Smallwood's" He led them to "[a]ttack a considerable time the Men having been rallied and the Attack renewed five of Six times." According to Stirling, the attackers were making headway until Cornwallis was reinforced. He, Stirling, soon "found a Considerable body of troops in my front, and Several in pursuit of me on the Right and left and a Constant fire on me." Facing overwhelming numbers, the Marylanders finally broke and ran. [471]

MAJ Gist, in his report on the battle, stated that after forcing the British attackers to withdraw around 10AM (Grant) there was a lull in the action.

> "We soon heard the fire continue round our left, and in a short time discovered the enemy in our rear, going on to our lines in short order to cut communication between us. Being thus surrounded and no probability of reinforcement, his Lordship [Stirling] ordered me to retreat with the remaining part of our men, and force our way to our camp." They ran into a larger enemy party, but forced them to retire "to a larger body that was lying in ambuscade." "During this interval the main part of our force [Stirling's Brigade] retreated from the left through the marsh, We were left with only five companies of our battalion, when the army returned, and after a warm and close engagement for near ten minutes, our little line became so disordered we were under the necessity of retreating to a piece of woods to our right, where we formed and made a second attack, but being overpowered with numbers, and surrounded on all sides by at least 20,000 men, we were drove with much precipitation and confusion ... The impracticality of forcing through such a formidable body of troops, rendered it the height of rashness and imprudence to risk the lives of our remaining party in a third attempt, and it became necessary

for us to endeavor to effect our escape in the best manner we could. A party immediately retreated to the right through the woods and CPT Ford [2nd Co/9th Co?] and myself and 20 others, to the left through the marsh; nine only of whom got safe in. The killed, missing and wounded amounted to 259." [472]

The CPT Ford that MAJ Gist referred to was, presumably, CPT Benjamin Ford, originally 1LT of the 2nd company and subsequently promoted to Captain and given command of the 9th Company. If he was with Gist, his company should have been also. This, in turn, weakens Howard Henry's contention on which five companies were with Gist because he doesn't include the 9th Company among them. It does not resolve the disagreement between Reno and Tacyn over which five companies were with Gist. Both list the 3rd, 6th and 9th. The disagreement comes over the other two. Reno said it was the 1st and 2nd, Tacyn the 4th and 7th IC. Tacyn's justification, based on an assessment of the respective companies' casualties, among other things, is more plausible. It is interesting to note that the company commanders of two of the three companies they agree on were not present. CPTs Lucas (3rd) and Adams (6th) were sick with camp fever. If Henry is correct on the time sequence, CPT Veazey of the 7th IC, who was killed during the fighting on the 27th, was already dead before his company became part of Gist's covering force.

Michael Smith, a sixteen year old member of a New York Continental regiment, and a native New Yorker, accompanied his regiment to Long Island in May 1776 and continued on duty there until August 29th, when the Army retreated. He said that "[a]t the Battle of Flatbush I was one of the picket guard. We were drove in and retreated according to orders to [sic] General Washington's headquarters at Brooklyn. General Greene, Lord Stirling, and General Sullivan are the regular officers ... at that battle [Greene was ill and did not participate. That is why Putnam was in overall command.]. Smallwood's regiment of regulars, part of Paulding's regiment, Drake's regiment of militia, and also Lasher's regiment were present. Sullivan and Stirling were taken prisoner." [473]

A letter from "an unknown Patriot Soldier," dated September 1, 1776, gives a general description of the portion of the Battle of Long Island involving the Marylanders. Based on the in-depth detail he provided, the "Patriot" was either a member of the Maryland Battalion or a unit attached to it. The troops ordered to defend that right flank against Grant's attack numbered "near 3,000 men," including the Delaware and Maryland regiments and COL Atlee's Pennsylvania regiment. Upon seeing the British approach and deploying Atlee to his left, Stirling drew the rest of his force in a line. The British advanced within 300 yards and began engaging the American lines with artillery, "now and then taking off a head." The Americans withstood the barrage. Their orders were to not fire until the British were within 50 yards. They never got that close.

At around 12 PM, upon learning that the main body of British had surrounded the Americans and virtually scattered all of the American units except those of Delaware and Maryland under Stirling, the Delaware and Maryland units were ordered to withdraw, fighting their way through the British forces "who had posted themselves and nearly filled every road and field between us and our lines." Within a quarter of a mile the enemy's advance guard engaged the retreating Americans while those now in their rear continued the artillery bombardment. They came to a marsh which some

crossed, and a small river. They were led by Ramsey's (5th)
and Scott's (7th) Companies. The right wing of the "Patriots"
battalion, thinking it was impossible to march through the
marsh, attempted to force their way through the woods, where
they "almost to a man were killed or captured." Major Guess
(Gist) commanded the Maryland Battalion. Captains Adams
(6th) and Lucas (3rd) were sick. Gist, Ramsay (Ramsey) and
Lieutenant Plunket (6th) led the attack against the British. [474]

With the exception of having Ramsey join MAJ Gist in
leading the right wing's attack in the British, this account
generally agrees with the other accounts. Ramsey led the
5th Company and, in all probability, took it across the marsh
and Gowanus Creek while the attacks against the Cortelieu
House were taking place. He may have participated as one of
the leaders, but without his company.

In a report to General Washington on August 29, 1776,
two days after the battle, detailing his activities on August 27th,
Lord Stirling stated that around 11 AM he found out that
General Howe, with the main body of the British Army, was
between his (Stirling's) forces, on the American right flank
at the direction of General Putnam, and the American lines.
Stirling felt that the only way his troops could escape being
killed or captured was to cross the Gowanus Creek, near the
"Yellow Mill." In order to make this possible, he would have
to attack the troops under Lord Cornwallis - by that time
located in the vicinity of the "Upper Mills (the Cortelieyu/
Vechte/Old Stone House)." The rest of the troops, including, presumably, the other half of Smallwood's, were ordered
to "make the best of their way through the creek." The attack
continued for a considerable time, "the men having been rallied and the attack revived five or six times and were on the
point of driving Lord Cornwallis from his station, but large

succors [additional troops, presumably Hessians] arriving rendered it impossible to do more than provide for safety." Stirling, eventually cut off, purposely surrendered himself to the Hessian commander, General de Heister, rather than to the British. [475]

Withdrawing his units to preclude being surrounded, Stirling proceeded up the Gowanus Road. Running into greater and greater British opposition, he chose to split his forces. The majority he sent to their left with directions to withdraw through the swamps and fast flowing tidal creek, with the tide on the ebb, to the American forces. Stirling was left with a smaller force by choice, 5 companies of Smallwood's regiment under MAJ Gist. Although having sustained fire throughout the morning, Gist's troops were relatively fresh. The Marylanders were considered one of the elite American units on the field, the best Stirling had available for a serious fight. With their training, discipline, muskets and bayonets they were the best troops available to take on a superior British force. It was probably never Stirling's intention to sacrifice a portion of his command to cover the retreat of his units. With the left wing out of the way he faced two bad choices. Following the majority of the brigade into the swamp would invite disaster since his men would be unable to defend themselves while in the water. The only alternative, then, was to skirt along the marshy area and proceed by the Gowanus Road to Porte Road. Once on Porte Road Stirling could maneuver around Denton's Millpond, cross Gowanus Creek at Yellow Mills and enter the American lines. Stirling reported that "in order to render this more practicable [I] found it absolutely necessary to attack a body of troops commanded by Lord Cornwallis, posted at the house near Upper Mill." [476]

Stirling's attempt to cross at Yellow Mills was too late. As we have seen, the bridge had been destroyed to prevent the quickly advancing British from crossing it and having a straight and easy route to the American fortifications. They would have been able to cut off many of the scattered and disintegrated units, as well as individual troops, who trying to reach the safety of the American lines. The passage to Ft. Box, the redoubt at the nearest point on the American lines, was cut off, blocked by British troops. Cornwallis' troops had reached the Vechte-Cortelyou House, roughly at the intersection of Gowanus and Porte Roads, and had immediately begun to fortify the position. Cornwallis also brought up a light cannon. The British tried to draw the Marylanders into a trap. They sent forward a party with arms reversed and hats removed in a gesture of capitulation. However, the bait apparently lost its nerve. At 60 yards they presented their pieces and fired, inflicting minimal damage. They quickly retired under American fire to the British lines that were laying in wait for the Americans. The Marylanders continued on.

Stirling placed himself at the head of the Maryland column as it prepared for an assault upon at least five times their number, with the enemy forces constantly being reinforced and increasing in size. Forming hurriedly in the vicinity of present day Fifth Avenue and Tenth Street, the column advanced along the Gowanus Road towards the Vechte-Cortelyou House, into heavy volumes of fire. There is some evidence to suggest that Stirling attacked with the 4th and 6th Companies and the 7th IC, while the 3rd and 9th Companies followed in a supporting role. A return of the regimental troops on September 27, 1776 indicates that the 4th suffered 80% casualties, the 6th 77% and the 7th IC 73%; while the 3rd sustained losses of 60% and the 9th 57%. While these companies had been involved in additional fighting in the intervening month, none of that equaled the intensity of the combat the covering force had been involved in on August 27th.

As noted above, the Marylanders drove the British advance party (the faux capitulators) back and continued their attack on the Vechte-Cortelyou House with musket and bayonet until they were ultimately halted and then driven back, with heavy casualties. In fact, the Americans' bayonet attack appeared on the verge of success, the first use of the bayonets by the Americans in the day's battle. They were driving the British back, preventing their advance. However, the British deployed two cannon and used them to halt the Americans with canister and grape shot that eventually forced them back. Stirling could see that the bulk of his troops had not yet crossed Gowanus Creek, so he ordered anther attack. The second charge penetrated to the Vechte-Cortelyou House, drove the gunners from the battery at the corner of the building and nearly seized the objective. Then withering fire from within the house and from adjoining high ground, as well as the overwhelming numbers of approaching enemy, compelled another slow retreat.

The Americans attacked three more times, in the face of ever growing opposition and with ever greater casualties. Each attack was smaller due to ever mounting casualties, but two of the assaults drove the British from the house. Each attack, however, was ultimately halted and repulsed, forcing the Americans to withdraw. They regrouped and mounted a sixth attack. The British column reeling from repeated shocks, gave way in confusion. Cornwallis was ready to retire when more reinforcements arrived. Hessians, relatively fresh troops, had come through Flatbush Pass and came to Cornwallis' aid. He immediately attacked. At almost the same time, Grant's force finally caught up with the Marylanders and assaulted them in the rear. Outnumbered ten to one, with their ranks thinned down by long fighting, the Marylanders could no longer make any headway against their opponents, or withstand their growing pressure. They withdrew again.

Faced with overwhelming forces, the surviving Marylanders "were drove with much presipitation and confusion." They disintegrated, breaking into smaller groups to fight their way to safety. About this point they discovered that Stirling wasn't present. Seeing Grant's advance into his rear, Stirling attempted to continue the fight. Finding his avenues of escape closed and Grant's troops coming from his rear, he moved rapidly into the woods to the right. He went up the slope of a hill, only to be confronted by a Hessian column which had crossed over from Prospect Hill, to the left (west) of the Flatbush Road. He finally surrendered. However, he searched until he found LTG de Heister, the Hessian commander, to whom he gave his sword. He refused to surrender to Cornwallis, the senior British commander present. Cornwallis later said that "General Lord Stirling fought like a wolf."

In the absence of Stirling, Gist had to make some quick decisions, He thought that the situation "rendered it the height of rashness and imprudence to risk the lives of our remaining party in ... [another] attempt." The decision was made to attempt escape. A portion of the Marylanders had been with Lord Stirling and surrendered to the Hessians when he did. Three companies cut their way through the British and maintained their order until they reached the marsh, where they were compelled to break ranks and escape as quickly as possible to the banks of the creek. The remaining men split up into at least two groups, one to the woods on the right and the other to the marsh on the left. Some melted into the woods and made their way back to the American lines. According to his later report, MAJ Gist and CPT Ford led a party of over twenty through the marsh and creek; with more making it successfully back to the American lines. [477]

General Washington came over from New York to observe the battle. He and his generals were able to see the action from the Cobble Hill Fort which was perched on a small hill inside the American fortified lines. COL Smallwood, upon his "Dismisison" (as he characterized it) from the court-martial he had been involved in in New York, crossed over to Long Island with the intent of joining his regiment in battle. He arrived about noon, but he was too late. The regiment was fully engaged. During one of the Marylanders charges Washington, according to an observer, had cried "My God, what brave men I must lose today." Smallwood joined Washington and the others observers on the hill.

Faced with the prospect of losing his entire regiment, Smallwood asked Washington for troops "to march out to sup-port their retreat" across the creek. Washington initially denied his request, being reluctant to risk losing more troops to what he felt were overwhelming forces. However, he eventually relented. He ordered Smallwood to Gowanus Creek and gave him a covering force: COL William Douglas" 5th Connecticut levies, CPT John Allen Thomas' heavy company, the 5th IC, which had just reported to Long Island from New York, and two field pieces. Henry P. Johnston claims that Washington did not reverse his original decision to give Smallwood com-mand of a covering force. However, the units listed were sent to the mouth of the creek to cover the retreating troops. [478]

Smallwood described what he saw from the inner fortifi-cations near Freeke's tidal-mill dam: "Between the place of action and our lines there lay a large marsh and deep creek, not above 86 yards across at the mouth, (the place of action upon a direct line did not much exceed a mile from a part of our lines) towards the head of the creek was a mill and a bridge, across which a certain Col. Ward from New England [21st Massachusetts Continentals], who is charged with having acted a bashful part that day, passed over with his regiment, and then burnt them down, though under cover of our cannon, which would have checked the enemy's pursuit at any time, otherwise this bridge might have afforded a secure retreat. There then remained no other prospect but to surrender or attempt to retreat over this marsh and creek at the mouth, where no person had ever been known to cross. In the interim I applied to Gen.Washington for some regiments to march out to support and cover their retreat, which he urged would be attended with too great risk to the party and its lines." [479] As noted above, Washington subsequently changed his mind and gave Smallwood some troops. Smallwood is accusing Ward and his troops of cowardice. It serves to illustrate both his tendency to quarrel with subordinates, peers and superiors, which only got worse over time, and his provincialism. The colonies may be supplying troops to the common cause, but at their most rock bottom core of beliefs, everyone not from their home colony, or even locale, is a foreigner and not quite trustworthy. Further, COL Smallwood was probably wrong. COL Ward, in his subsequent defense, stated that he burned the bridge only in the direct face of the enemy and when it (the bridge) was under imminent danger of being captured, opening a clear, unobstructed route to the American fortifications. If the British had been able to utilize the bridge about the time Ward had it burned they would have been able to cut off even more fleeing American troops.

The British may not have been seriously trying to capture the bridge but, rather, feinted towards it with a sizable force to force its destruction, helping to cut off fleeing Americans. However, in the end it made no difference if the bridge was destroyed or standing. By the time Stirling and the Marylanders were heading towards it their route was blocked by British units and some artillery located between them and the bridge. The Americans couldn't get to it without a major fight. That is one of the reasons Stirling decided to change direction and attack Cornwallis at the Vechte-Cortelyou House.

Joseph P. Martin was a fifteen year old Private in a Connecticut unit. It, along with a twelve pound cannon, had been ordered to join the covering force for Stirling's with-drawal. He later wrote: "We were soon called upon to fall in and proceed ... Our officers ... pressed forward toward a creek, where a large party of American[s] and British were engaged. By the time we arrived, the enemy had driven our men into the creek, or rather mill pond (the tide being up), where such as could swim got across; those that could not swim, and could not procure anything to buoy them up, sunk. The British having several field pieces stationed by a brick house [the Vechte-Cortelyou House] were pouring canister and grape upon the Americans like a shower of hail; they would doubtless have done them much more damage than they did for the twelve pounder. ... The men having got it within sufficient distance to reach them, and opening fire on them, soon obliged them to shift their quarters! There was in this action a regiment of Maryland troops (volunteers), all young gentlemen. When they came out of the water and mud to us, looking like water rats, it was truly a pitiful sight, many of them were killed in the pond and more drowned. Some of us went into the water after the fall of the tide and took a number of corpses and a great many arms that were sunk in the pond and creek." [480]

Smallwood quickly moved the troops Washington had assigned him, including the two artillery pieces, to Gowanus Creek's western shore, opposite Stirling's retreating force. He found the trenches by the creek already occupied by Broadhead's 2nd Pennsylvania Battalion of riflemen, posted there immediately after their run from the American lines. Douglas' Connecticut Levies were sent to the extreme right of the American position, at the mouth of the creek. The retreating troops were under constant carronade from four to six British field pieces (sources differ on the number). A strong column of Hessians were advancing to attack the fleeing Americans, the Delaware, Pennsylvania and Maryland troops of Stirling's Brigade, and then the remnants of the Maryland covering force. The Pennsylvania, Connecticut and Maryland troops opened fire on the oncoming British and Hessians, shooting over the heads of the retreating Americans. The two American cannon opened fire on the British field pieces. The concentrated fire drove the British back, out of the marsh, almost 600 yards. The American artillery silenced the British cannon and forced them to withdraw. The American fire then held the British at bay while the Americans continued to flee through the marsh, the creek and the mud.

CPT Thomas' troops were instrumental in pulling many of Stirling's exhausted Marylanders through the mud to safety. Some members of Stirling's Brigade drowned, but the efforts of Smallwood's ad hoc covering force greatly reduced the number of fatalities. Some sources claim that only 12 men were lost in the crossing. While this seems too low a count, it may be fairly accurate. The retreat was a trying one, but without considerable loss except that of the battle field and of prisoners. Exaggerated reports were current during that period as to the number of men drowned or suffocated while crossing the creek and the marsh. Many of the men abandoned their equipment and weapons and swam the narrow belt of deep water. However, Henry Carrington, among others, contends that the number of drowned men did not exceed seven. COL Haslett, whose Delawares withdrew along with the Marylanders, only mentions one drowning. [481]

There is great difficulty in accurately determining the casualties in Smallwood's Regiment on August 27th, or, more specifically, those during the covering force action attacking the Vechte-Cortelyou House. There also is difficulty in determining how many men participated in the Battle as a whole and then the covering force attacks. There are numerous reasons for these difficulties in arriving at accurate figures. Chief among them is the absence of any direct and timely reports for that day. The reports and letters detailing casualties were generally written some time after the battle and, in some cases, include on hand strengths and casualty figures for a much longer period than just August 27th. The issue breaks down into two broad areas, on hand strength and losses. What was the strength of the Regiment and then the five companies in the covering force, on the day of the battle? How many casualties and what kind were sustained during the battle?

The original organized strength of Smallwood's regiment in January 1776 was 671 men. Eight Infantry companies with 4 officers, 8 NCOs, 1 Drummer, and 60 Privates (73x8=584). 1 Light Infantry Company with 4 officers, 8 NCOs, a Drummer, and 64 Privates (77). Regimental Headquarters was 10 men, including the Field Officers (10). 584+77+10=671. The Independent Company was authorized 4 officers, 8 NCOs, 1 Drummer, and 92 Privates (105). On its departure Smallwood's command had an authorized strength of 776 (Regiment - 671; Veazey's 7th - 105). Prior to the unit's departure it had incurred losses due to resignations (at least among the officers), transfers, illness and disease, and, probably, desertion. The unit left with no more than 700 men, and probably less. Tacyn said that when Smallwood's Regiment left for New York it numbered approximately 540 enlisted men. If it included NCOs, the authorized strength was 716, if only Privates, it was 636. Either way, it started off considerably under strength. This was not unusual in the 18th Century. The replacement process was primitive, if it even existed. Often, when a regiment's strength got too low for it to be an effective fighting force it was combined with another. It is a problem for modern day combat leaders as well. In the heaviest fighting we saw in Cambodia in the spring of 1970, my mechanized infantry company's on hand fighting strength, i.e. present for duty on the battlefield, was just over 100 officers and men, out of an authorized strength of about 150. Further, we had just received replacements late the previous afternoon and it was the most men we had ever had in the field at one time, or ever would.

By the end of August, as the battle approached, the Regiment's strength was greatly reduced. Ross Kimmel estimates that desertions during the march to New York and after arrival, combined with illness and disease (primarily acquired in New York, so called "camp fever" was prevalent, affecting many units), had reduced the Regiment's on hand strength to 400 on the eve of the battle. This seems somewhat low. But it may be accurate. How many of these men were placed into Stirling's and Gist's covering force? What is agreed on by virtually every source is that it consisted of five companies. How many men are open to question. The traditional, mythic number is 400 who, through valorous conduct, became immortal. Many authors use that number as a starting point. Linda Reno is among them. However, the five companies she claims were with Gist and Stirling (the 1st, 2nd, 3rd, 6th and 9th Companies) had an authorized strength of 369 officers and men, well below 400 if they were at full strength. Mark Tacyn's covering force units (3rd, 4th, 6th, and 9th Companies and the 7th IC) had an authorized strength of 401. Everything indicates that they were probably under strength. It is more probable that the Regiment under Gist started the day with an on hand, present on the battlefield strength of over 400 soldiers, probably 450+. Since only half of the Regiment's companies were in Gist's covering force, it didn't have 400 troops. There could have been about 250, since two of the five companies, (the 9th and 7th IC) had higher authorized strengths than the other 8 Infantry companies and, hence, probably had higher on hand strengths. Ross Kimmel stated that Stirling detached MAJ Gist and 265 men as the covering force. This appears to be about right. [482]

How severe were the casualties of the covering force? How many Marylanders gave their lives to protect the fleeing American troops, allowing them to regroup and, ultimately, continue fighting? How many survived to fight again? One myth, perpetuated by several authors, was that only MAJ Gist and 9 of his men were able to successfully escape through the marsh and creek. The rest became casualties (killed, wounded or captured). This is based on a misinterpretation of MAJ Gist's subsequent report. He said that he and CPT Ford gathered a group of 20 men and attempted to make the American lines. Of his group of 20 - 22 men, only 9 made it through. However, they weren't the only members of the covering force that were trying to escape injury or capture and weren't the only ones that made it. [483]

In response to a request from the Maryland Convention, on October 12th COL Smallwood forwarded them a report on the Regiment's activities since its departure from Maryland in July. In it he stated that 256 men had been killed or were missing, including officers. He said this right after describing the Regiment's involvement in the Battle of Long Island. The implication is that these were casualties from that battle. However, they could have been from all of the engagements the Regiment had been involved in. [484] Numerous authors have used this figure over the years with several variations: 256 men lost; 256 men captured, killed or dying; 256 killed or captured; 256 killed, wounded or captured; 256 lay dead in front of the Vechte-Cortelyou House with more than 100 wounded and/or captured; and some claimed a 90% casualty rate. Further, exasperated by the Marylanders' resistance, Hessian and Highland soldiers bayoneted to death most of those wounded and captured that fell into their hands. [485]

There are, however, different opinions, some minor variations on the amount of 256 casualties and some significantly different. In a letter written September 1, 1776, four days after the battle, the writer said: "The Maryland Battalion lost two hundred and fifty-nine men, amongst whom were twelve officers: CPTs Vezey [Veazey] and Bowie, Lieuts Butler, Sterrett, Dent, Coursey, Morse, Praul, Ensigns Corts [Courts] and Fernandes. Who are killed and who are prisoners is yet uncertain." On September 10th Washington reported the same number of losses for the Maryland Regiment, 259. [486] John Gallagher gives the August 27th casualties as 267, including 11 men killed prior to Stirling's covering force, hence

256. The history of the 175th Regiment, modern day successor to Smallwood's Maryland Regiment, claims that after repeated charges against the British, all conducted within the space of an hour, the Marylanders were reduced to 93 effectives, i.e. 93 not killed, captured, or wounded so badly that they were unable to fight. Of course, some of those 93 could subsequently have become casualties during the withdrawal. Morris Radoff uses still another set of figures: 250 Marylanders killed in action, 19 died of wounds, 100 were wounded, and only a handful escaped unscathed. [487]

Linda Reno, working on the premise that 400 Marylanders were in the covering force and conducted the attacks, chose to focus her attention only on the units of Smallwood's Regiment, consciously ignoring anyone else that may have participated. She accepted that 256 men were killed attacking Cornwallis. However, she had a dilemma. She claimed to have found records that 225 members of the Regiment survived. In attempting to correlate this to the 256 figure traditionally used for the eventual mass grave in the vicinity of the Vechte-Cortelyou house, she stated that the remainder buried were probably from Maryland units that fought with the Regimental Companies (e.g. CPT Veazey's 7th IC). David Daugherty, in a review of The Maryland 400, questions where Reno got her figure of "400" for the Regiment. He also questions why 256 men are said to have been killed and then, later in the book, 256 were given as the number of killed, captured or wounded. He contends that out of Gist's command of 357 men, 213 survived (Close to the 225 Reno claims survived.). He then asks, rhetorically, if 256 men were killed, captured or wounded, where did they come from? And, finally, there is Mark Tacyn. His figure of losses during the entire Battle of Long Island is 147 men, approximately 27% of its strength. Regardless of the exact number, the number of casualties among the Marylanders was significant. The rate of casualties as a part of the available strength on August 27th was extremely high for the Companies involved. The casualties of Stirling's Brigade were one-half, and those of the Maryland Regiment one-fourth, of the aggregate American losses on August 27th. [488]

Linda Reno's research into the post August 27th status of the companies she concluded were involved in Stirling's covering force (Note that the original authorized strengths for the 1st - 8th Companies, including officers, NCOs, musicians and Privates was 73 and for the 9th Company was 77.):

First Company
Seventy five soldiers were originally enrolled. Of those, seventy one were still assigned on August 27th (four transferred). Forty nine men are known to have survived and twenty one are unaccounted for, excluding LT Bowie who died in captivity. LT Courts and ENS Fernandes were also captured.

Second Company
Seventy five soldiers were originally enrolled. Of those, seventy were still assigned on August 27th. Forty six were known to survive and twenty four were unaccounted for.

Third Company
Eighty soldiers were originally enrolled. Seventy were still assigned on August 27th, not including CPT Lucas, who was sick. Forty two survived and twenty eight were unaccounted for. Thirteen were taken prisoner.

Sixth Company

Seventy two soldiers were originally enrolled. Of these, sixty nine were still assigned on August 27th. Thirty five are known to have survived and thirty four were unaccounted for. Ten men were taken prisoner.

Ninth Company

Eighty one soldiers were originally enrolled. Of these seventy six were still assigned on August 27th. Forty one are known to have survived and thirty five are unaccounted for. Fourteen men were taken prisoner.

Henry Peden, Jr., in Revolutionary Patriots of Frederick County, 1775-1783, contends that the fate of the 9th company was disastrous: "… so great was the havoc in its ranks, in the conflict and during the retreat, that scarcely none of its members escaped death or a wound." Reno contends, then, that of the five companies involved (383 soldiers were enrolled in early 1776, versus authorized strengths of 379), 213 were known to have survived the battle, with 142 unaccounted for and 40 taken prisoner. The numbers of the original enrollees appear high. However, they may include the total number enlisted to achieve the lower authorized strengths. The number still assigned on the day of the battle is an indicator, but not the significant figure. That is the number of troops present for duty. The unaccounted for figures appear to be the result of a simple calculation and not necessarily indicative of what happened on August 27th. While still carried on the Companies' official strengths that day, some could have deserted, transferred, gotten sick and/or died, as well as become lost during and/or after the battle. [489]

On September 5, 1776 the "Maryland Gazette" printed an extract of a soldier's letter of August 28th, the day after the battle: "... Major Gist, with about 100 men, kept the ground while the rest of the brigade crossed a creek, which we were obliged to do. The major and his party were drove, and I expected never to see them again, but the greatest part got off with the major. We lost some men in the creek that got stuck in the mud and were drowned. ... Captain Veazey is dead. Lieutenant's Butler, Steret [Sterrett], Wright, Fernandes and de Coursey [de Courcy] with 250 of our battalion [the rest, presumably, NCOs and Privates] are missing. Steret (sic) is a prisoner, I believe ...." [490]

Different reports of casualties present sometimes conflicting information. From the American Archives, Northern Illinois Community Libraries: "A list of the killed and missing in the Maryland Battalion: CPT Veazey, killed; LT Butler, said to be killed; Ensign Fernandes, LT Dent, CPT Bowie, missing; LTS Sterrett, Coursey (sic) and Wright, Ensign Ridge, 13 Sergeants and 259 privates. From the "Maryland Historical Magazine" Volume 14: "At Long Island, early in the war, CPT Daniel Bowie, LTS William Steret (sic), William Ridgley (sic), Hatch Dent, Walter Muse, Samuel Wright and Joseph Butler were captured by the British. LTs Edward Praul and Edward Courcy [sic], Ensigns James Fernandez [sic] and William Courts were wounded." MAJ John Adlum of Pennsylvania later recollected that "Edward de Courcy, CPT Herbert [?] ... and a Doctor Stuart [?] of Smallwood's were among the prisoners taken at Long Island, with whom I became acquainted, while I was a prisoner in New York." [491]

James H. Fitzgerald Brewer, in his History of the 175th Infantry (Fifth Maryland), and Ella Dorsey, in her Smallwood' Immortals, A Historical Abstract, both contend that during the Battle of Long Island the principal losses occurred in the companies of CPTs Bowie (1st), Ford (2nd), Lucas (3rd), Adams (6th) and Veazey (7th IC). This implies that these were the companies of Stirling's covering force because they suffered the highest casualty rate and, hence, were involved in the heaviest fighting. Reno probably generally followed them, since she published in 2008 and Brewer and Dorsey published in 1955 and some unspecified earlier date, respectively. Reno said that the fifth company was Smallwood's 9th. Tacyn points out that CPT Lucas' 3rd Company lost nearly all of its men on the 27th. Brewer stated that of the original 404 officers and men, the probably original present for duty strength on August 27th, 96 men were subsequently listed as returned and 35 fit for duty. The discrepancy between the original muster of 404 and 352 (256 casualties and 96 returned) is unexplained. He lists most of the same officer casualties, includes General Stirling among the officer casualties, and concludes by stating that 248 enlisted men were casualties (killed/wounded/captured). Dorsey also includes many of the oft mentioned officer casualties, pointing out that Bowie (1st), Ford (2nd), Lucas (3rd) and Adams (6th) fell at the head of their companies. Bowie was wounded, captured and died in captivity. No other author mentions Ford as a casualty. Multiple other sources state that both Lucas and Adams were ill, probably with camp fever, and did not lead their troops during the fighting on the 27th. [492]

While the estimates of the number of enlisted casualties vary, there is some consensus on the officer casualties. These are the ones that the majority of sources agree on: 1st Co. - CPT Daniel Bowie, wounded/captured, died on Long Island in 1776; 2nd Co. - ENS James Fernandes - wounded/probably captured; 3rd Co. - LT William Ridgely - wounded,

LT William Sterrett - wounded (He was probably in command; the Company Commander, Lucas, was sick.); 4th Co. - LT Joseph Butler - wounded/captured and died on Long Island in 1776, LT Edward Praul - wounded/captured; 5th Co. - LT Walker Muse - wounded/possibly captured, ENS William Courts - wounded; 9th Co. - LT Hatch Dent, Jr. - captured; 7th IC - CPT Edward Veazey - killed; CPT/LT William Harrison - mortally wounded, LTs Samuel Turbutt Wright and Edward de Courcy - captured (Note that all four officers of the 7th IC were either killed or captured.). Several of the sources note that LT John Stockton of the 4th Battalion of the Flying Camp and LT Daniel Cresap, late of a Maryland Rifle Company, then assigned to Stephenson's Rifle Regiment, were also captured. [493] Not including the last two officers, out of a maximum of 41 - 43 officers of the Maryland Regiment and attached unit engaged with the enemy on the 27th, and the actual figure was probably 35 - 38, 13 were casualties, for a possible officer casualty rate of over 30%. As noted above, there is significantly less agreement on the overall casualties for the Regiment for the 27th in general, and the attacks on Cornwallis in particular. The Regiment started the day with between 400 - 450 officers and men, probably closer to 400. They had upwards of 250 casualties for the day, but possibly fewer, and, maybe, significantly fewer than that, especially if you follow Tacyn's 147 enlisted casualties. The actual figure was probably around 200 +/-. Whatever the exact number, it was a large, horrific casualty rate for one day's action, no matter which war it took place in

Washington spent the latter part of the battle on a hill in the American sector, where he was able to watch Stirling's repeated assaults on Cornwallis' overwhelming force. During the attacks, as they were repeatedly being driven back, but also were covering the retreat of much of the rest of the American force, he said "My God, what brave men I must lose today." He subsequently stated that "they [the Marylanders] have bought in blood that hour more precious to American liberty than any other hour in its history." As noted above, the Marylanders were the first American troops to use bayonets in their attacks. A late eighteenth century unit's ability to attack massed troops firing muskets at them without firing their own and only utilizing "cold steel," their bayonets, was considered the ultimate mark of its discipline and professionalism. The Regiment's successor, the Maryland Line, was to become famed for its willing and forceful use of this weapon. [494]

The action on August 27th was the largest battle of the American Revolution in terms of both participation and casualties. In Brooklyn both sides had hopes of ending the conflict with one great victory, and massed their forces accordingly. As it turned out, however, the British were able to bring to bear nearly all of their 32,000 men. The Americans, meanwhile, employed 11,000 troops, only part of their strength and just a fraction of their force as it looked on paper. By comparison, at Yorktown, the British, French and Americans together totaled only 19,000 men. The only redeeming feature from the American point of view was the astonishing bravery, fortitude and discipline showed by the Continental regiments from Delaware and Maryland, especially the latter. By their courage and ability these troops may have saved the American Army on Long Island from complete annihilation. [495]

The behavior of the Marylanders on the battlefield can be attributed to training and leadership. Without it, the discipline of fire and movement they exhibited would have been impossible on such a battlefield. In withstanding a British artillery barrage which "now and then took a head," they showed a discipline uncharacteristic of green, inexperienced troops. There is no indication that any Marylander retired from the field without orders. The troops which attacked Cornwallis displayed a great deal of courage and resolution under fire. This is further underscored by their multiple attempts to force a passage through to the American lines. Their heroism in this, the first major encounter of the war, showed the British that the Americans were a force to be reckoned with. [496]

Shortly after the fighting around the Vechte-Cortelyou House the Marylanders were at Ft. Putnam in Brooklyn Heights, within 250 yards of the enemy lines. They were one of the units Washington called on to cover his withdrawal from Long Island. After the heavy fighting on August 27th and the subsequent withdrawals (an accurate description in some cases, but in most instances unit disintegrations and fleeings) to the previously prepared positions and the advance of the British towards those fortifications, Washington and his subordinates met. General Howe's land forces, combined with his brother's fleet which could move up the East River to the Americans' rear and block their access to Manhattan Island, had them almost completely cut off. They needed to withdraw from Long Island over the East River immediately, and to do so surreptitiously to avoid British attacks on their weakened units that could very well result in their annihilation. The Council of War decided to withdraw as soon as possible.

Soon after daylight on the morning of August 28th, in a heavy rain, the remnants of Smallwood's regiment, the Pennsylvania regiments of Shee and Magaw and Glover's Marblehead (Massachusetts) Regiment were hurried to the extreme left of the American entrenchments, on the ground between Wallabout Bay and Ft. Putnam. Glover's regiment was made up primarily of fishermen from the Marblehead, Massachusetts area, well versed in handling boats. They manned the boats that were used in the withdrawal. On several other occasions they handled Washington's waterborne transportation needs, to include rowing boats during the crossing of the Delaware River during the attack on Trenton, NJ in late December, 1776.

On August 29th, in a heavy fog, the Americans began to withdraw from Long Island to New York and Manhattan. General Mifflin, commanding Smallwood's, Shee's, and Magaw's units, covered the retreat. Under pretense of attacking the enemy, they marched and countermarched all night, providing a covering force for the retreat. The British did not discover the withdrawal until the last detachment of Marylanders and Pennsylvanians was half way across the East River and out of reach. [497]

Meanwhile, back in Maryland, two weeks later, on September 13th, the Council ordered Thomas Price to take custody of three men who had "gone over to the Enemy and deserted from them ..." He was to deliver them to the Committee of Observation of Somerset County at the southern end of the Eastern Shore. This implies that Price was present in Maryland, available to carry out the order. As will be seen below, this was not true. At the time of the order Price was in northern New Jersey, or on Manhattan Island in the vicinity of New York. He, and the companies under his command, participated in an engagement with the British on September 16th, three days after the order. He may have carried out the order, but if he did so he did it at a distance, and merely directed that it be done. [498]

COL Richardson, from the Eastern Shore, received his first orders from the Convention, to march to the Flying Camp in the vicinity of Amboy/Elizabethtown, NJ. There he was to join other Maryland troops under the command of COL Smallwood, who, as the senior regular Maryland officer was the Commander of all Maryland forces in Washington's army. Richardson's troops arrived in the area o/a September 9th. On September 15th, having landed on Manhattan at Kip's Bay, GEN Howe's main force headed up the Post Road on the eastern side of the Island. Washington ordered what was left of Smallwood's Regiment to march down towards New York to cover the Army's retreat and protect the baggage.

The Marylanders were positioned a mile south of McGowan's Pass, through which the Americans were withdrawing. This would give the Americans at Ham's Hook and further north along the Harlem River more time to retreat. At McGowan's Pass the Post Road ran between two hills before descending steeply to Harlem Plains. This was the most advantageous spot for a small detachment to impede the progress of a much larger force. Smallwood posted his men behind rocks on the hilly terrain and planned to attack the British column as it approached along the road. If necessary, he planned to give ground slowly and retreat to the pass to make a stand.

When the British encountered Smallwood's men a brief exchange of musket fire convinced them that the Americans were ready to stand their ground. So, they headed west to Bloomingdale road, being used by GEN Putnam's men to withdraw northward. However, by the time Howe's troops reached Bloomingdale Road the Americans had essentially passed and they encountered only skirmishers. Smallwood's men pulled back and left McGowan's Pass to the British as planned. [499]

On September 16th Marylanders again participated in attacks against the British forces which were advancing across Manhattan in the Battle of Harlem Heights. MAJ Thomas Price led three Independent Companies. Which three is unclear; presumably not Veazey's 7th or Thomas' 5th, who were by that time probably considered integral parts of Smallwood's Regiment, in fact if nor formally. The Convention directed the Western Treasurer to pay Gunby's 2nd IC, Bracco's 1st IC, and Woolford's 6th IC a month's pay through September 3rd, on August 26th. Further, on August 26th the Convention ordered supplies and equipment for the 1st IC. All of this implies that the companies were in Maryland to receive the pay and equipment, although the 2nd and 6th ICs may have moved to the Western Shore. So, the 3 ICs under Price may have been Watkin's 3rd, Hindman's 4th, and either Gunby's 2nd or Woolford's 6th. It could also have been the 7th, 5th and 4th ICs, the original three companies ordered north.

Price's companies were joined by other units from the Flying Camp, COL Richardson's (Eastern Shore) and COL Griffith's (Frederick County) Battalions (Regiments). The Marylanders were part of a force which also consisted of Connecticut and Virginia troops. They repelled a British attack with low casualties. In a letter on September 20th the Maryland Continental Deputies (Thomas Johnson, Jr., William Paca, Samuel Chase and Thomas Stone) informed the Council of Safety that COL Richardson's and COL Griffith's Battalions/Regiments had been involved with the British "on Monday last [16th] … and behaved well."

On September 19th, after some had already been involved in combat operations, the actions of the Maryland Convention were completely formalized, while being completely obviated. In August the Convention had assigned the Independent Companies to the Continental Army to fulfill both a man-power requirement (3405 troops) and a specific unit require-ment, an additional regiment. They just, purposely, failed to designate another regimental commander and staff. On the 19th MAJ Price and six Independent Companies were incorporated in Smallwood's Regiment. The six companies were, presumably, the 1st, 2nd, 3rd, 4th, 5th and 6th. I think that after more than two months and several significant combat actions, including August 27th, the 7th was already part of the Regiment.

The new companies brought the Regiment's assigned strength up to 840 men. However, only 427 men were fit for duty. The strength of the Flying Camp at this time was 2189 men, with 1717 fit for duty. Smallwood utilized his new troops later in September. At Washington's request, after oth-ers of his units had deserted him, the Regiment covered the withdrawal into lines below Ft. Washington. They attacked the enemy, drove them from their positions and were in full pursuit when recalled. [500]

On October 2nd , as previously noted, the Maryland Council of Safety wrote COL Smallwood, asking for "a particu-lar account of the Troops at present under your command, as well as regulars [the Regiment and Independent Companies] as militia [the Flying Camp Battalions/Regiments. A com-pletely different type of unit from the regular militia] ...." They wanted a list of effectives as well as sick, wounded, cap-tured and those who had been killed. They repeated their request for an inventory of arms as well as other stores. They indicated that they were "surprised you have never wrote us a Line since you left Annapolis and more especially since the battle of Long Island ... " Smallwood responded on the 12th with a letter forwarded through the Council to the Convention describing the march to New York and the fighting to date in some detail. It was in this letter that he used the figure of 259 casualties. His details on the Battle of Long Island were relatively sparse, presumably because he hadn't been present for virtually any of it except the end. Apparently he was unaware of any report of MAJ Gist, chose not to use it, and/or chose not to obtain details of the battle from him. [501]

The request of the Council, and Smallwood's subsequent report, point out the dual environment in which Smallwood had to operate. His unit was part of the Continental Army and he reported to GEN Washington through his Brigade Commander. Washington had at least a primitive staff that worked on keeping track and maintaining unit strengths, as well as providing them with food, arms, ammunition and supplies. However, there was also a very real connection with Maryland and the political leadership there. They considered Smallwood's troops theirs and wanted to be kept informed on their status and what was going on. Since Congress did not have the wherewithal to supply the Continental Army, the states were tasked to do so, with a promise of Congressional reimbursement of funds eventually. This obviously created confusion on occasion that detracted from the unit's effectiveness. The situation with the Flying Camp units and the militia units which periodically deployed for short periods of time with the Continentals was even more complex and confusing. Lines of authority were often tangled. As will be seen, late in 1776, when the Continental units were being expanded and reorganized, representatives of the Council and Convention were active participants in the process.

Smallwood's Regiment, along with other Maryland units, continued to serve with Washington throughout the remainder of 1776 and into 1777. They suffered through defeats in an around New York and the victories at Trenton and Princeton. However, severe casualties greatly reduced the Marylander's strength, especially the Regiment's. Often it had been parceled out in various administrative reorganizations. In January 1777 it stood no bigger than as a solitary company under the command of CPT John Hoskins Stone (nee 1st Co.). [502]

In late October 1776 COL Smallwood led the Regiment in the fighting at White Plains. They met Hessians commanded by Rowle under the fire of fifteen British cannon. With over 100 casualties, Smallwood was forced to withdraw, but did so in good order. He was also among the casualties, being wounded in the hip and through the arm. With MAJ Gist in command, about 400 Marylanders, including members of the Rifle Regiment, were taken prisoner at Ft. Washington. By December 26th the Maryland Regiment, due to casualties, sickness and the expiration, or immediately pending expiration, of enlistments, had an effective strength of 190 men under the command of MAJ Gist. Earlier in December COL Smallwood had been ordered to return to Maryland to recuperate from his wounds and to raise and organize Continental units in Maryland and Delaware.

The surviving members of the Maryland Regiment, with part of the German Regiment and what remained of Stephenson's Rifle Regiment, participated in Washington's daring and successful attack on Trenton, NJ in late December. On January 3, 1777, the remaining Marylanders, under, as we have seen, CPT John Hoskins Stone, in less than seven weeks the commander of the 1st Regiment of the Maryland Brigade, participated in the fighting at Princeton, NJ. After the victory Washington took his remaining troops into winter quarters in Morristown, NJ. At this time, according to then LTC James Wilkinson (subsequently an acolyte of Horatio Gates and on the fringes of the Conway Cabal and those who were trying to supplant Washington; and much later of Aaron Burr and on the fringes of his possible/probable treasonable involvement with the Spanish in the then West) there was "... a detachment consisting of fragments of Smallwood's Regiment commanded by Captain Stone ... [with] other elements ... in the whole certainly not exceeding 300 men." Washington's record of the Marylanders was: "Smallwood's troop had been reduced to a mere handful of men, but they took part in the engagement with their usual gallantry and won great renown." [503]

As the early winter fighting was continuing, the Flying Camp had outlived its usefulness. The scene of the fighting was shifting. The camp was dissolved on December 1, 1776, with many of the officers and men from the various states joining the newly organizing Continental Army regiments. As the fall wore on the fighting, with mostly negative results for the Americans, brought home to the leaders, specifically the members of the Continental Congress, that their organizational and personnel models were not effective. They needed more troops in more units serving for longer periods of time. The relatively short terms of enlistment, even for the regulars, continued to prove devastating for unit cohesiveness, morale, and even the very existence of the American Army. Congress' and the states' leaders had thought that they could solve the problem by extending the enlistments to one year, in most instances a major leap from the periods of time traditionally used in mobilizing troops to defend the then colonies. However, as the Americans began to engage the British in late August around New York and continued through the fall and early winter into the New Year, the problems created by the relatively short enlistment periods came more and more to the fore, especially as their expiration dates got nearer. Soldiers in combat with known departure dates become increasingly less interested in participating in the fighting and the rigors associated with existing in an army at war and more and more interested in leaving and going home. In Viet Nam, for example, with a fixed, limited tour length of 12 or 13 months, the soldiers kept "short-timer" calendars, marking off the days left until they could leave. Most of them, including me, could give the exact number of days they had left off of the top of their heads. The impact on their units was obvious.

As a consequence, in the fall of 1776 Congress passed the "Eighty-eight Battalion Resolve" which directed that a significantly larger Continental Army be organized. It provided that the population numbers of the respective states would govern the number of regiments to be raised. It also mandated longer enlistment terms. Maryland's quota was eight regiments, including responsibility for half the German Regiment. The regiments' strengths would total 4,000 men who would serve for three years or the duration of the war, whichever was longer. Despite the fact that the number was disproportionate to the state's population, the Maryland convention agreed to their allocation. From September 1776 to February 1777 the recruiting went on, spurred by an enlistment bounty of $10.00. Newly promoted Brigadier General Smallwood and Colonel Gist were leading the recruiting efforts on Maryland to organize the new units, both having been returned to Maryland in December 1776.

The Convention decided to use the remnants of Smallwood's Regiment as the core of the first five regiments/battalions. It was only as this recruitment and expansion process was going on that the terms gradually came to have different meanings and regiment became the primary designation of the multi-company (up to 9 or 10] units. Four commissioners, with authority to reorganize the command, went to Morristown to Washington's 1776-1777 winter quarters. Note the intimate involvement of the local (Maryland) political polity in the Continental Army reorganization. The commissioners carried broad powers to commission promising officer candidates and to promote veteran officers, all subject to the approval of the Commander -in-Chief. In CPT Stone's contingent the commissioners found sufficient cadre material to constitute two regiments. By March 27, 1777 the officers were all certified. BG Smallwood commanded the Brigade (The Line). Stone, initially promoted to LTC in the 1st Regiment, was promoted to COL and command of the Regiment when COL Ware was forced to resign due to illness and infirmity. Now COL Gist commanded the 3rd Regiment. He was subsequently promoted to Brigadier General and succeeded Smallwood in command of the Brigade.

By April 1777 the Maryland regiments had achieved operational strength. The Continental Army reports show the following strengths:

1st Maryland COL John Hoskins Stone (nee 1st Co. Cdr and 1st Rgmt LTC) from COL Ware - 235 men

2nd Maryland COL Thomas Price (nee 1st MAJ) - 147 men

3rd Maryland COL Mordecai Gist (nee 2nd MAJ) - 136 men

4th Maryland COL Josias Carvel Hall - 262 men

6th Maryland COL Otho Holland Williams (nee Rifle Company) - 142 men

7th Maryland COL John Gunby (nee 2nd IC) - 109 men

The 5th Maryland, organized in Queen Anne's, Kent, Caroline and Dorchester Counties, was retained in Maryland as the major defensive force for the Eastern Shore. The First, Third, and Sixth Maryland Regiments and the Delaware Regiment comprised the First Maryland Brigade under BG Smallwood. The Second, Fourth and Seventh Maryland Regiments and the German Regiment were part of the Second Maryland Brigade under Philippe-Hubert, Chevalier de Preudhomme de Barre. [504]

On Long Island, trusting in their discipline and courage, Washington used the Maryland troops in positions that were vital to the success of the American Army. They displayed soldierly conduct that rivaled or exceeded the best in the Continental Army. The performance and conduct of the troops was the product of their time spent drilling before joining the ranks of the Continental Army - training that differentiated them from the other states' troops. While other states responded to Congress' call for recruits with untrained militia, the Maryland Convention, working under the assumption that paid soldiers furnished with rations and suits of clothes would be better soldiers, established, in essence, two regiments worth of uniform regulars. The Convention's assumption proved correct as the Maryland troops exemplified a cohesive, disciplined military unit, especially in comparison to the throngs of untrained militia that formed the bulk of the Continental Army of that time. [505]

From 1776, throughout the entire Revolutionary War, the state of Maryland was represented on nearly every battlefield.

Although its troops were relatively few in numbers, they were distinguished for valor, so that their failure in an emergency was a sign of great peril, or of some over-mastering enemy superiority, not panic. The Marylanders sacrifice, especially at Long Island, was remembered throughout the war. In the words of someone not in any history book, "[t]he Declaration of Independence that was signed in Philadelphia was signed in blood in south Brooklyn." [506]

The Maryland Brigade served throughout the war in various configurations, with many of its most significant battles taking place in the South. On January 5, 1949, the Army Historical Division authorized the following Revolutionary War battle streamers for the regimental colors of the modern successor unit to Gist's Independent Cadets and Smallwood's Regiment, the 175th Infantry Regiment: Long Island, New York 1776, Trenton, Princeton, Brandywine, Germantown, Monmouth, South Carolina 1780-1781, North Carolina 1781. They missed the end at Yorktown, like they had missed the beginning at Lexington/Concord/Boston. However, without them much, if not all, of what happened after August 27, 1776, would have been vastly different. They saved the American Army. [507]

Conclusion

Fighting has been an innate part of man's existence since before "he" was deemed a "man;" witness conflicts among groups of primates. As man became more organized and sophisticated, so too did his fighting, moving to the level of organized warfare. The types of warfare and the levels of organization and sophistication of the groups conducting it, the "armies," have ebbed and flowed over the course of recorded history, sometimes very simplistic, sometimes very complex. The Egyptians, the Assyrians, Alexander's Greeks/ Macedonians, the Persians, and the Romans, among others, all developed and maintained regular standing armies which dominated large portions of their "worlds" and their eras.

Between and after their eras warfare became very decentralized and localized. This was especially true in Europe after the Roman Empire in the west disintegrated. The Eastern Empire carried on with primarily mercenary armies. The Western Empire fell apart and then slowly coalesced into feudal land groupings supported by levies. These grew into militia formations that, in turn, were replaced, or at least supplemented, by standing regular forces. England, for a host of reasons, was late in developing a regular army, not doing so until well after the initializations of many of its American colonies in the early seventeenth century.

The organizers of the new English colonies realized that they needed some defense against the local inhabitants

(Indians) as well as their European competitors/enemies (the French, Dutch and Spanish). They used what they were familiar with and all that was available to them, a universal militia. The militia worked moderately well as long as the danger came from marauding Indians. While early on there had been danger of complete destruction of the first settlements, the actual danger lessened over time to a level the colonists could handle locally. While being on an outlying farm or in a frontier outpost under threat of attack, or being attacked and terrorized by Indians did not seem a small thing to the victims, it actually was in the overall scheme of settlement and development. It wasn't until the mid-eighteenth century and the growing involvement of outside, or European, adversaries that the colonists needed military help, in the form of regular soldiers. By this time England had developed regular forces it could send. They were somewhat at loose ends, needing someone to help pay for their upkeep, and the home government had come to view the problems in America as part of the world-wide military conflicts with France and Spain. They wanted to win and if the colonists would help pay their soldiers to defeat their European enemies in the American wilderness, even involuntarily, so much the better. The irony is that the introduction of British regiments into America during the SY/FI War ultimately, and fairly quickly, led to the loss of the American colonies.

Maryland's colonial military experiences were not untypical, but nowhere near as extensive as those of Virginia or the northern New England colonies. While there was some fighting with Indians throughout the seventeenth century, most of the military conflicts were between internal groups within Maryland or with neighboring colonies over land disputes. Even during the SY/FI War, Maryland's troops' actual involvement in military campaigns and fighting was relatively limited in comparison to other colonies. However, this lack of an extensive military tradition did not seem to have negatively impacted on the Marylanders ability to organize and train a very effective fighting force in a short period of time. By all rights, there is no way that Smallwood's Regiment should have been able to do what it did during the Battle of Long Island. That it was speaks volumes for the courage and determination of both the troops and their leaders. Most impressively, they fought under the command of only the third or fourth ranking officer, with no real planning or training to do so. Their actions saved the American Army from destruction, so that it could survive to fight again. They saved the American Revolution. While missing the surrender at Yorktown, they enabled the rest of the Army to get there.

Author's Note

I first heard of William Smallwood's Maryland Regiment in 1974 while a student in the Infantry Officer Advanced Course at Ft. Benning, GA. In lieu of taking another graduate course, I prepared a briefing on a defensive maneuver. I choose Washington's withdrawal from Long Island to Manhattan in the late summer of 1776. As part of my research I learned about the relatively small unit of Marylanders who attacked and delayed thousands of British and Hessian soldiers, allowing a significant portion of the overwhelmed and disintegrating American Army to withdraw to fortifications on Brooklyn Heights. In essence, they saved Washington's Army, allowing it time to reorganize, withdraw further shortly thereafter, and eventually, through much travail, survive long enough to win. How they were able to do that caught my interest. I wanted to learn more about them, who they were, where they came from, how they became such a cohesive military unit so relatively quickly, able and willing to repeatedly engage a vastly superior force. I began to think about writing a thesis about them. Over time this coalesced into wanting to write a book about them. However, I really didn't have the time. Life intervened.

Finding out about this unit became one of my retirement dreams, one of the things I planned to do after I finally stopped working. While I never really pursued it, I kept thinking about it, not quite to the point of obsession, but close sometimes. After retiring from the Army in Maryland I went into the retail industry. As I could see the end of my career approaching, I began to think even more about beginning the research. I started making topic outlines and identifying possible research sources. When you retire you are supposed to find something, or several somethings, to do that you enjoy, maybe always wanted to do or see, to keep you somewhat busy and mentally engaged. The research was going to be mine, and I talked about it, definitely too much, both at home and at work.

After I retired, I made a list of projects and things I wanted/needed to do, primarily around the house, in addition to spending more time going places with my wife Nancy. The research was on the list, but buried deep. I got busy elsewhere, did more volunteering, etc., and the idea of the research began to recede further. Some months later I saw a friend of 30 years from the Army and several jobs we had worked on together. He asked me, "Have you started writing your book yet?" I said no, but I was going to. The next day, in January 2008, I pulled out the outlines and other things I had prepared, reviewed and revised them, found some relevant books on my own shelves, and began work.

After eighteen months I had written and typed the first draft. As I was proof reading and correcting the last page of footnotes, I realized that I didn't have enough information, especially on Smallwood's unit. So, I started again. Just under two years later (I'm old school. I can only think at the speed of a pen and I am a slow typist.) I finished again and began the process of finding out how to get it published and how to get permission to use maps and sketches prepared by someone else. The latter has been quite interesting. Given that they are in the business of providing something to the public, I found it amazing how unresponsive many mega-corporate publishing institutions were, even if only to indicate that I was at the wrong place and where the right one may be found. There were exceptions. One publishing house, no longer controlling the rights, referred me to an agent that did, they thought. In response to a letter, a representative of the agent called me from New York to give me the contact information for the next person in the chain.

The library staffs I dealt with have all been great and extremely helpful. Howard County's Central Library staff gave me suggestions on where and how to find things. They also introduced the wonders, to me, of their computer system, especially MARINA, the interactive system that links all of the public libraries in Maryland. This allowed me to find and receive books from throughout the state. The librarians at Ft. Meade's library used a comparable system which helped me to get books from their federal/military network. Also providing assistance were the staffs of the Baltimore County Catonsville Library, the Enoch Pratt Central Library in Baltimore, the Southern Maryland Studies Center at the College of Southern Maryland, and the University of Maryland College Park library system. Dr. Balkoski, historian with the Maryland National Guard, gave me good advice and source suggestions, as well as a good source in his book. The staff of the Howard County Historical Society as well as the staff and archivists of the Maryland Historical Society and its Imaging and Permissions office, all provided key support and suggestions, especially how to wander around in Maryland's State Archives on the internet. My friend of many years, Dave Doy, gave me the final push to get it started.

My children, Geoff, Adam and his wife Courtney, Matt, and Jessica and her husband Colin, have given me help and support and assistance, some near and some far. They put up with my excitement over obscure and, to them, uninteresting information. They have helped me learn the intricacies of the computer and word processing. Colin, especially, has used his computer skills and worked his computer magic in many ways. Most of all, they have loved me and tolerated me and worried about me and taken care of me, especially for the last three years.

The person who helped me most is no longer here. My wife Nancy left us and went home to God in November 2010. Given the time that has passed since then, an initial reaction might be that she is missing the conclusion and product of our hard work. However, that's not accurate. She doesn't need to be here to see this part, because she was involved in the hard part and lived through it all. Nancy went to school on Staten Island and spent four years in the New York area. However, she really wasn't interested in the Heights of Gowan. She was a scientist, not a historian. She could have cared less about Revolutionary War battles, or the many battlefields I dragged her and then the kids to, except in a general sense that she was glad the Americans won. But she loved and cared about me. She typed the original paper that started all of this in 1974. She put up with my meanderings and research trips, sometimes accompanying me and sometimes packing my lunch and sending me on my way. She suffered through many lectures at dinner, detailing my excitement about finding or figuring out some obscure fact. Only rarely did she wish out loud that it would end. It finally has, dear. She was the love of my life and this is for her.

January 1, 2014
Columbia, Maryland

540

Bibliography

Manuscripts/Documents

Balch, Thomas, edit., Papers relating Chiefly to the Maryland Line During the Revolution, Seventy Six Society, Philadelphia: 1857, Courtesy of the Southern Maryland Studies Center,
    College of Southern Maryland.

Force, Peter, American Archives, published from 1837-1853; digitized by Northern Illinois University @www.lib.niu.edu/amarch.

Proceedings of the General Assembly, January 1637/
    38-September 1664, Archives of Maryland, Volume 1 @ www.mdsa.net.

Proceedings of the Council of Maryland, 1636-1667, Archives of Maryland, Volume 3 @www.mdsa.net.

Journal of the Maryland Convention, July 26 to August 14,
    1775, Archives of Maryland, Volume 11 @www.mdsa.net.

Journal and Correspondence of the Maryland Council of Safety, August 29, 1775 - July 6, 1776, Archives of Maryland
    Volume 11 @www.mdsa.net.

Journal and Correspondence of the Maryland Council of Safety, July 7 - December 31, 1776, Archives of Maryland, Volume 12
    @www.mdsa.net.

Muster Rolls and Other Records of Service of Maryland
    Troops in the American Revolution, 1175 - 1783, Genealogical Publishing Co., Inc., Baltimore: 1972; originally Archives of Maryland, Volume 18, Maryland Historical Society, 1900.

Proceedings of the Conventions of the Province of Maryland, 1774 - 1776, Archives of Maryland, Volume 78 @www.mdsa.net.

Tacyn, Mark Andrew, "To the End": The First Maryland Regiment and the American Revolution, Doctoral Dissertation, University of Maryland: 1999, Courtesy of the Enoch Pratt Library, Baltimore, MD.

Books

Ahern, Mariel, The Rhetoric of War: Training Day, the Militia and the Military Sermon, Greenwood Press, Inc., Westport Connecticut, 1989.

Andrews, Charles M., The Colonial Period of American History, Vol. 2, New Haven: Yale University Press, 1936.

Andrews, Matthew P., The Founding of Maryland, Baltimore: The Williams and Wilkens Company, 1933.
  - History of Maryland: Province and State, Garden City, NY: Doubleday, Doran and Co., Inc., 1929.

Ansel, William H., Frontier Forts Along the Potomac and Its Tributaries, Parsons, WV: McClain Printing Co., 1984.

Axelrod, Alan, America's Wars, New York: John Wiley and Sons, 2002.

Balkoski, Joseph M., The Maryland National Guard: A History of Maryland's Military Forces, 1634 - 1991, Baltimore: The Maryland National Guard, 1991.

Barker, Charles A., The Background of the Revolution in Maryland, Yale University Press, 1940.

Barnett, Corelli, Britain and Her Army, 1509-1970: A Military, Political and Social Survey, New York, William Morrow, 1970.

Berg, Fred Anderson, Encyclopedia of Continental Army Units: Battalions, Regiments, and Independent Corps, Harrisburg, PA: Stackpole Books, 1972.

Bertzell, Edwin W., St. Mary's County, Maryland in the American Revolution, Calendar of Events, St. Mary's County, MD Bicentennial Commission, 1975, courtesy of the Howard County, MD Historical Society.

Brewer, James H. Fitzgerald, History of the 175th Inf. (Fifth Maryland), Baltimore: Mary-land Historical Society, 1955.

Brewer, John, Sinews of Power: War, Money and the English State, 1688-1783, New York: Alfred A. Knopf, 1989.

Browne, William H., Maryland: The History of a Palatinate, Boston: Houghton, Mifflin and Company, 1897.

Buchanan, John, The Road to Valley Forge, Hoboken, NJ: John Wiley and Sons, Inc., 2004.

Carr, Lois G., Menard, Russell R., and Peddicord, Louis, Maryland - at the Beginning, Hall of Records Convention: Maryland, 1984.

Carrington, Henry B., Battles of the American Revolution, New York: A. S. Barnes and Co., 1888.

Chandler, David, edit., The Oxford Illustrated History of the British Army, Oxford: Oxford University Press, 1994.

Chartrand, Rene, Colonial Troops - 1610 - 1774, Chicago: Raintree/Osprey, 2002.

Clark, Murtie June, Colonial Soldiers of the South, 1732-1774, Genealogical Publishing Co., Inc., Baltimore, MD: 1986, courtesy of the Howard County MD Historical Society.

Clements, S. Eugene and Wright, F. Edward, The Maryland Militia in the Revolutionary War, Family Line Publications, Silver Spring, MD: 1987.

Cochrane, Laura, et. al., History of Caroline County Maryland, From Its Beginning, 1920, courtesy of the Howard County, MD Historical Society.

Commanger, Henry Steele, and Morris, Richard B., edits., The Spirit of 'Seventy-Six, Harper and Row, 1958.

Craven, Wesley Frank, The Southern Colonies in the Seventeenth Century, 1607 - 1689, LSU Press, 1949.

Dale, Esther M., Maryland During the American Revolution, 1941.

Dann, John C., The Revolution Remembered, Eyewitness Accounts of the War for Independence, London, 1980.

Dederer, John Morgan, War in America to 1775: Before Yankee Doodle, New York University Press, New York 1990.

Dorsey, Ella Loraine, Smallwood's Immortals; a historical abstract, courtesy of the Maryland Historical Society.

Doubler, Michael D., Civilian in Peace, Soldier in War: The Army National Guard, 1636 - 2000, University of Kansa Press, Lawrence, Kansas: 2003.

Draper, Theodore, A Struggle for Power, the American Revolution, New York: Random House, 1996.

Dupuy, R. Ernest, The National Guard, A Compact History, New York: Hawthorne Books, 1971.

Dupuy, R. Ernest and Dupuy, Trevor N., The Compact History of the Revolutionary War, New York: Hawthorne Books, 1963.

- The Harper Encyclopedia of Military History: from 3500 BC to Present, Harper Collins, New York, Fourth Edition, 1993.

Eliot, Charles W., The Harvard Classics, Vol. 43, American Historical Documents, 1000 - 1904, New York: P. F. Collier and Son Corp., 1938.

Ellis, John, Armies in Revolution, Oxford University Press, New York: 1974.

Everstine, Carl N., The General Assembly of Maryland, 1634 - 1776, Charlottesville, VA: The Mitchie Co., 1980.

Fisher, David Hackett, Washington's Crossing, Oxford University Press @www.books.google.com.

Gallagher, John J., The Battle of Brooklyn, 1776, SARPEDON, New York: 1995.

Gallay, Alan, Colonial Wars of North America, 1512 - 1763, An Encyclopedia, Garland Publish-ing, Inc., New York: 1986.

Gilbert, Adrion, The Encyclopedia of Warfare, Guilford, CT: The Lyons Press, 2003.

Gray, Edward G., Colonial America, A History in Documents, New York: Oxford University Press, 2003.

Hallowak, Thomas, Maryland Genealogies, A Consolidation of Articles from the Maryland His-torical Magazine, Vol. II, Genealogical Publishing Co., Inc., Baltimore: 1980.

Hartzog, William W., American Military Heritage, Center of Military History, U. S. Army, Washington, DC: 2001.

Hawke, Daniel Freeman, Everyday Life in Early America, New York: Harper and Row, 1988.

Heller, Charles E. and Stafft, William A., edits. America's First Battles: 1776 - 1965, University of Kansas Press, Lawrence, KS: 1986.

Henry, Howard G., et. al., (Cecil County Bicentennial Book Committee), Cecil County in the Revolutionary War, no date, courtesy of the Howard County, MD Historical Society.

Hienton, Louise J., Reminders of Revolutionary Days in Prince George's County, 1975, courtesy of the Howard County, MD Historical Society.

Higginbotham, Don, <u>The War of American Independence</u>, New York: The Macmillan Co., 1971.

<u>The History of the 175th Infantry, (Fifth Maryland)</u>, Baltimore, MD: 1974, courtesy of the Howard County, MD Historical Society.

Homes, Richard C., edit., <u>The World Atlas of Warfare</u>, New York: Penguin, 1988

James, Lawrence, <u>Warrior Race, A History of the British at War</u>, New York: St. Martin's Press, 2001.

Jennings, Francis, <u>Empire of Fortune</u>, New York: W. W. Norton and Co., 1988.

Johnston, Henry P., <u>The Campaign of 1776 Around New York and Brooklyn</u>, Long Island Historical Society, Brooklyn, NY, 1878.

Jones, Archer, <u>The Art of War in the Western World</u>, Chicago: University of Illinois Press, 1989.

Karsten, Peter, edit., <u>The Military in America: From the Colonial Era to the Present</u>, New York: The Free Press, 1980.

Katcher, Philip R. N., <u>Armies of the American Wars, 1753-1815</u>, Hastings House, Publishers, N.Y.: 1975.

Keegan, John, <u>A History of Warfare</u>, New York: Alfred A. Knopf, 1993.

- <u>Fields of Battle: The Wars for North America</u>, New York: Alfred A. Knopf, 2002.

Keegan, John and Holmes, Richard, <u>Soldiers, A History of Men in Battle</u>, New York: Viking, 1985.

Keith, Arthur L., "Smallwood Family of Charles County Maryland" in <u>Maryland Genealogies, Vol. II</u>, Genealogical Publishing, Baltimore, MD: 1980.

Kilbourne, John Dwight, <u>A Short History of the Maryland Line in the Continental Army</u>, The Society of the Cincinnati of Maryland, Baltimore, MD, 1992.

Kimmel, Ross M., <u>In Perspective: William Smallwood</u>, Smallwood Foundation, Inc.: 2000,courtesy of the Southern Maryland Studies Center, College of Southern Maryland.

Kimmell, Ross M. and Harp, David W., <u>The Maryland Soldier/ A Revolutionary War Portrait</u>, Annapolis: Maryland Magazine, 1975.

Klapthor, Margaret and Brown, Peter Dennis, <u>The History of Charles County, Maryland</u>, Charles County Tercentenary, Inc., La Plata, MD: 1958.

Lancaster, Bruce, <u>From Lexington to Liberty</u>, Garden City, NY: Doubleday and Co., Inc., 1955.

Land, Aubrey, <u>Colonial Maryland, A History</u>, KTO Press: 1981.

Leckie, Robert, <u>A Few Acres of Snow: The Saga of the French and Indian Wars</u>, New York: John Wiley and Sons, 1999.

- <u>The Wars of America, Vol. 1: Quebec to Appomattox</u>, New York: Harper and Row, 1968.

Mackenzie, George Norburg, edit., <u>"The List of " 'The Ark' and 'The Dove' Passengers,"</u> <u>Colonial Families of the United States of America</u>, 1912; reprinted by Genealogical Publishing Co., Inc., Baltimore, 1965, 1995, pp 593 - 606, courtesy of the St. Mary's City Foundation.

McSherry, James, <u>History of Maryland</u>, Baltimore: The Baltimore Book Company, 1904.

Mahon, John K., <u>History of the Militia and the National Guard</u>, New York: Macmillan Publishing Co., 1983.

Manders, Eric I., <u>The Battle of Long Island</u>, Philip Freneau Press, Monmouth Beach, NJ: 1978.

Martin, James Kirby and Linden, Mark Edward, <u>A Respectable Army: The Military, Origins of the Republic, 1768 - 1789</u>, Arlington Heights, IL: Harlan Davidson, Inc., 1982.

Matloof, Maurice, edit., American Military History, Washington, DC: Office of the Chief of Military History, 1969.

Mereness, Newton Dennison, Maryland as a Proprietary Province, Cos Cob, CT: John E. Edwards, 1968 (1906).

Millis, Walter, Arms and Men: A Study in American Military History, G. P. Putnam's Sons, New York: 1956.

Mitchell, Joseph B., Decisive Battles of the American Revolution, New York: G. P. Putnam's Sons, 1968.

- Military Leaders in the American Revolution, EPM Publications, Inc., McLean, Virginia, 1967.

Newman, Harry Wright, The Flowering of the Maryland Palatinate, self published, Washington, DC: 1968.

Offutt, Thieman Scott, et. al., Patriotic Maryland and the Maryland Society Sons of the American Revolution, Baltimore: 1930, courtesy of the Howard County, MD Historical Society.

Papenfuse, Edward, et. al., A Biographical Dictionary of the Maryland Legislature, 1635 -1789, Vols. I and II, The Johns Hopkins University Press, Baltimore: 1985, courtesy of the Howard County MD Historical Society.

Peden, Henry C., Revolutionary Patriots of Charles County , Willow Bend Books, Westminster, MD, 2001.

Powell, Alan, Forgotten Heroes of the Maryland Frontier: Christopher Gist, Evan Shelby, Jr., Thomas Cresap, Baltimore: Gateway Press, Inc., 2001.

- Fort Cumberland, Parsons, WV: McClain Publishing Co., 1989.

- Fort Frederick: Potomac Outpost, Parsons, WV: McClain Printing Co., 1988.

- Maryland and the French and Indian War, Baltimore: Gateway Press, Inc., 1998.

Radoff, Morris L., The Old Line State, A History of Maryland, Annapolis: Pub 16, Hall of Records Commission, State of Maryland, 1971.

A Relation of Maryland, London, 1635, University Microfilms, Inc., Ann Arbor, 1966.

Reno, Linda Davis, The Maryland 400 in the Battle of Long Island, 1776, McFarland and Company, Inc., Jefferson, NC: 2008.

Richardson, Mrs. Hester Dorsey, Side-Lights on Maryland History, Cambridge, MD: Tidewater Publishers, 1967.

Ross, John F., War on the Rim, The Epic Story of Robert Rogers and the Conquest of America's First Frontier, Bantam Books, 2009.

Ross, Steven T., From Flintlock to Rifle: Infantry Tactics, 1740-1860, Associated University Presses, Inc., Canbury, NJ: 1979.

Russell, George Ely and Russell, Donna Valley, edits., The Ark and The Dove Adventurers, Genealogical Publishing Co., Inc., Baltimore, MD 2005.

Scharf, John Thomas, The Chronicles of Baltimore, Turnbull Brothers, Baltimore, 1874.

- History of Baltimore City and County, Part I, Regional Publishing Company, Baltimore: 1971 (1881).

- History of Maryland from the earliest Period to the Present Day, Volume 1, Hatboro, PA: Tradition Press, 1879.

Schecter, Barnett, The Battle for New York: The city at the Heart of the American Revolution, New York: Wilkes and Company, 2002.

Shepherd, Ruth, edit., Empires Collide, Oxford: Osprey Publishing, 2002.

Simmons, R. C., The American Colonies, From Settlement to Independence, New York: W. W. Norton and Co., Inc., 1976.

Skagg, David Curtis, Roots of Maryland Democracy, 1753 - 1776, Greenwood Press, Inc., Westport, Connecticut: 1973.

Sparks, Francis Edgar, Causes of the Maryland Revolution of 1689, Johns Hopkins University Studies, 1973.

Stephenson, Michael, Patriot Battles, How the War of Independence Was Fought, New York:Harper Collins, 2007.

Steuart, Rieman, A History of the Maryland Line in the Revolutionary War, Society of the Cincinnati of Maryland, 1969.
- Maryland in the Revolutionary War, The Society of the Cincinnati of Maryland, 1969.

Stockbridge, Henry, The Archives of Maryland, Baltimore: Maryland Historical Society, 1886.

Strachan, Hew, European Armies and the Conduct of the War, London: George Allen and Unwen, 1983.

Streissguth, Thomas, Maryland, San Diego: Lucient Books, Inc., 2002.

Taylor, Allen, American Colonies, New York: Penguin, 2001.

Vexler, Robert and Swindler, William F., edits., Chronology and Documentary Handbook of the State of Maryland, Oceana Publications, Inc., 1978.

Ward, Matthew C., Breaking the Backcountry: The Seven Years War in Virginia and Pennsylvania, 1754 - 1765, Pittsburgh: The University of Pittsburgh Press, 2003.

Warfield, J. D., A. M., The Founders of Anne Arundel and Howard Counties Maryland, Baltimore: 1962 (1905).

Weigley, Russell F., History of the United States Army, New York: Macmillan Co., Inc., 1967.

Whisker, James B., The American Colonial Militia (MD, NJ, NY, Del), Edwin Mellen Press, Lewistown, NY: 1997.
- The Citizen Soldier and U. S. Military Policy, North River Press, 1979.

White, Frank F., Jr., The Governors of Maryland, 1777-19709, Hall of Records Commission, State of Maryland, Annapolis: 1970, courtesy of the Howard County, MD Historical Society.

Wilcox, John, Masters of Battle, London: Arms and Armour Press, 1996.

Williams, T. Harry, The History of American Wars from 1745 to 1918, New York: Alfred A. Knopf, 1981.

Wilson, Rufus Rockwell, Rambles in Colonial Byways, Vol. 2, @ books.google.com.

Wright, Robert K., Jr., The Continental Army, Center of Military History, U. S. Army, Washington, DC: 1983 @www.history.army.mil/books.

Wright Robert K., Jr., and MacGregor, Morris J., Jr., Soldier - Statesmen of the Constitution, Center of Military History, U. S. Army, Washington, DC: 1987 @www.history.army.mil/books.

Periodicals/Magazines/Encyclopedias

Elting, John R., Encyclopedia Americana 2008, Grolier Online, 2 April 2008.<http:es.Grolier.com/cgi-bin/article?a sseted+0270840-00>

"Encyclopedia Britannica," http://www.britannica.com/EBchecked/topic.

"Encyclopedia Wikipedia," http://www.en.wikipedia.org/wiki.

Gruber, Ira D., "Of Arms and Men: Arming America and Military History, The William and Mary Quarterly, January 2002, <http:www.historycooperative.org/cgi-bin/justtop. cgi?act=juststopandurl==http:www.historycooperative. org/journals/wm/59.gruber.html> 25 April 2008.

Keith, Arthur L., "General William Smallwood," Maryland Historical Magazine, Volume 19,1924, courtesy of the Maryland Historical Society.

Mereness, Newton D., "William Smallwood," Dictionary of American Biography, Volume 17, Charles Scribner's Sons, New York: 1933, courtesy of the Maryland Historical Society.

Mordecai Gist @http://www.en.wikipedia.org/wiki/Mordecai_Gist.

Internet

Bell, David, Passenger List of the Ark and the Dove, originally compiled on 3/30/03, revised 11/01/05 @calvertgene-alogy.net/Baltimore/passenger_list_of_the_ark_and_th.html. Bell compiled the list from various sources: Robert E. T. Pogue, Yesterday in Old St. Mary's County, self pub-lished at Bushwood, MD, 1985; Harry Wright Newman, The Flowering of the Maryland Palatinate, Baltimore Genealogical Publishing Co., Inc., 1985 [Newman's List]; The US GEN Web project, compiled by Rhoda Fine and Carole ?, 2001; Gentlemen and Gentlewomen of the Voyage; John T. Marck, The Founding of Maryland, Maryland Historical site; and Passenger List of the Ark and the Dove, The Society of the Ark and the Dove @www. thearkandthedove.com from Gus Skordas, edit.; The Early Settlers of Maryland, An Index to Names of Immigrants Compiled from Records of Land Patents, 1633 - 1680,

Genealogical Publishing Company, Baltimore, MD, 1968 and a companion volume by Carson Gibb, <u>A Supplement to Early Colonial Settlers of Maryland</u>, 1997.

Carr, Dr. Lois Green, <u>Biographical Files of 17th and 18th Century Marylanders</u> @www.msa.md.gov/msa/speccol.html/carr.html.

"The Continental Army" @www.historycarper.com/resources/tra/chap4.htm.

"Descriptions of General William Smallwood's family and education" @www.gilderhrman.org/search/collectionpdfa/01/20/51.

Daugherty, David M., "Review of <u>The Maryland 400</u>" @www.amazon.review.com.

"The First Maryland Regiment in the Revolutionary War" @ www.myrevolutionarywar.com/states/md-01.html.

Hill, Scott, "Leading the Old Line: General William Smallwood" @www.thebaynet.com/news/index.cfm/fa/viewtory/story_id/7784.

Miller, John, "The Flying Camp Battalion," <u>Emmitsburg Area Historical Society</u>, @www.emmitsburg.net/archive_list/articles.

- "The Forgotten Patriots of the Tom's Creek Hundred," <u>Emmitsburg Area Historicald Society</u>, @www.emmitburg.net/archive_lists/articles.

Peale, Charles Wilson, <u>Portrait of William Smallwood in the Old Senate Chamber</u> @http://www.msa.gov/msa/mdstatehouse/html/wsmallwood.html.

Peden, Henry C., <u>Revolutionary Patriots of Charles County, 1775-1783</u>@www.book.google.com/books?id=rCSNb74p-fusC&pg=PA 273&lpg=PA273&dq+William...

Polk, Ryan, <u>The Origin of "The Old Line State,"</u> Maryland State Archives:2005@www.oldline vanners.com/history.htm.

Re: <u>Brigadier General William Smallwood</u> @www.genforum. genealogy.com/smallwood/messages/1815.html.

"Richardson's Company-Looking for a Few Good Men" @www.rivewrheritage.org/Riverguide/Stories/html/Richardson_-_enlistments.html.

"Richardson's Regiment at the Battle of Harlem Heights" @ www.riverheritage.org/Riverguide/Stories.

"The Second Maryland Regiment in the Revolutionary War" @ www.myrevolutionarywar.com/statesmd-02.htm.

"Smallwood State Park History" @www.dnr.state.us/publiclands/smallwoodhistory.html.

Stewart, Richard W., edit., <u>American Military History, Volume 1: The United States Army and the Forging of a Nation, 1775 - 1917</u>, Center of Military History, U. S. Army, Washington, DC: 2004@www.history.army.mil/books/amk-vol1/index.htm

"William Richardson - American Revolutionary" @www.riverheritage.org/Riverguide/Stories/html/Richardson_-_revolutionary.html.

"William Smallwood" @www.answers.com/topic/William-smallwood-1.

Zimmerstutzen, "When Maryland Invaded Pennsylvania" ##636719@www.huntingpa.com/forums/webthreads.

Notes

Introduction

[1] Ira D. Gruber in Haller, Charles E. and Stafft, William A., edits., <u>America's First Battles</u>, 1776 - 1965, University of Kansas Press, Lawrence, KS: 1986, pp 1-2.

[2] Gruber in Haller, <u>Ibid.</u> p 13.

1. Amateur to Professional, The Old Country

[3] Matloof, Maurice, edit., <u>American Military History</u>, Washington, DC: Office of the Chief of Military History, 1969, pp 18-19.

[4] Keegan, John, <u>A History of Warfare</u>, New York: Alfred A. Knopf, 1993, p 228.

[5] Etling, John R., <u>Encyclopedia Americana</u>, 2008, Grolier online.<http:ea.Grolier.com/cge-bin/article?asseted=0270840-00>

[6] Jones, Archer, <u>The Art of War in the Western World</u>, Chicago: University of Illinois Press, 1987, p 245.

[7] Keegan, <u>A History of Warfare</u>, p 232; Doubler, Michael D., <u>Civilian in Peace, Soldier in War: The Army National Guard, 1636 - 2000</u>, University of Kansa Press, Lawrence, KS: 2003, p 7.

[8] Jones, <u>Op. cit.</u>, pp 245-246.

[9] Keegan, <u>A History of Warfare</u>, pp 231-232.

[10] Whisker, James B., <u>The Citizen Soldier and United States Military Policy</u>, North River Press, pp 4-5.

[11] Keegan, <u>A History of Warfare</u>, p 233.

12 Jones, <u>Op. cit.</u>, pp 645-646.

13 Whisker, <u>The Citizen Soldier ...</u>, p 3.

14 Dederer, John Morgan, <u>War in America to 1775, Before Yankee Doodle</u>, New York University Press, New York: 1990, pp 80-92.

15 Keegan, John and Holmes, Richard, <u>A History of Men in Battle</u>, New York: Viking, 1985, pp 113-14.

16 <u>Colonel</u>, "Encyclopedia Wikipedia," http//en.wikipe-dia.org.wiki; Millis, Walter, <u>Arms</u> <u>and Men: A Study in American Military History</u>, G. P. Putnam's Sons, New York: 1956, p 18.

17 <u>Regiment</u>,"Encyclopedia Britannica," http://www.britan-nica.com/EBchecked/topic.

18 <u>Colonel, Op. cit.</u>

19 Keegan and Holmes, <u>Op. cit.</u>, p 211.

20 Gilbert, Adrian, <u>The Encyclopedia of Warfare</u>, Guilford, CT: The Lyons Press, 2003, p 72.

21 Holmes, Richard, edit., <u>The World Atlas of Warfare</u>, New York: Penguin, 1988, p 77-78.

22 Wright, Robert K., Jr., <u>The Continental Army</u>, Center of Military History, Washington, DC: U. S. Army, 1983 @his-tory.army.mil/books, p 4.

23 Dupuy, R. Ernest and Dupuy, Trevor, N., <u>The Harper Encyclopedia of Military History: from 3500 BC to Present</u>, Harper Collins, New York: Fourth Edition 1995, pp 576-577.

24 Wright, <u>The Continental ...</u>, pp 4-5.

25 Chandler, David, edit., <u>The Oxford Illustrated History of the British Army</u>, Oxford: Oxford University Press, 1994, p 41.

26 Brewer, John, <u>The Sinews of Power: War, Money and the English State</u>, New York: Alfred A. Knopf, 1989, pp 7-8.

27 Strachan, Hew, <u>European Armies and the Conduct of War</u>, London: George Allen and Unwen, 1983, pp 8-9.

28 Williams, T. Harry, <u>The History of American Wars from 1745 to 1918</u>, New York: Alfred A. Knopf, 1981, pp 4-5.

29 Matloof, <u>Op. cit.</u>, pp 20-22.

30 Ross, Steven, <u>From Flintlock to Rifle: Infantry Tactics, 1740 - 1866</u>, Associated University Presses, Inc., Cranbury, NJ: 1979, pp 17-19.

31 Matloof, <u>Op. cit.</u>, p 22.

32 Ross, <u>Op. cit.</u>, pp 21-22.

33 Mahon, John K., <u>History of the Militia and National Guard</u>, New York: Macmillan Publishing Co., 1983, pp 6-7; Prestwich, Michael in Chandler, <u>Op. cit.</u>, p 17; Etling, <u>Op. cit.</u>, p 1; Doubler, <u>Op. cit.</u>, p 7.

34 Karsten, Peter, edit., <u>The Military in America: From the Colonial Era to the Present</u>, New York: The Free Press, 1980, p 19; Doubler, <u>Op. cit.</u>, p 8; Weigley, Russell F. , <u>History of the United States Army</u>, New York: Macmillan Publishing Co., Inc., 1967 p 3. Etling, <u>Op. cit</u>, p 1; Mahon, <u>Op. cit.</u>, pp 7-8.

35 Williams, <u>Op. cit.</u> , p 8.

36 Barnet Correlli, <u>Britain and Her Army, 1509 - 1970</u>, New York: William Morrow and Co., 1970, pp 10-11.

37 Mahon, <u>Op. cit.</u>, pp 8-9; Barnett, <u>Op. cit.</u>, pp 23-24; Doubler, <u>Op. cit.</u>, pp 8-9.

38 Keegan, John, <u>Fields of Battle: The Wars for North America</u>, New York: Alfred A. Knopf, 1995, pp 150-151; Mahon, <u>Op. cit.</u>, pp 9-10.

39 James, Lawrence, <u>Warrior Race, A History of the British at War</u>, New York: St. Martin's Press, 2001, pp 142-144; Doubler, <u>Op. cit.</u>, p 9.

[40] Roy, Ian, in Chandler, Op. cit., pp 35-36.

[41] James, Op. cit., pp 133-134.

[42] Barnett, Op. cit., pp 32-37.

[43] Roy, Ian, in Chandler, Op. cit., pp 37-42.

[44] James, Op. cit., pp 140-142.

[45] Hawke, Daniel Freeman, Everyday Life in Early America, New York: Harper and Row, 1988, p 135.

[46] Stephenson, Michael, Patriot Battles: How the War of Independence Was Fought, New York: Harper Collins, 2007, pp 13-14.

[47] Strachan, Op. cit., p 57.

[48] Brewer, John, The Sinews ..., pp 32-33.

[49] Dederer, Op. cit., pp 115-116; Wright, Op. cit., p 5; Ross, Op. cit., p 23.

[50] Mahon, Op. cit., p 7.

[51] Prestwich, Michael in Chandler, Op. cit., p 17.

[52] Brewer, John, The Sinews ..., pp 7-12.

[53] James, Op. cit., p 145.

[54] Whisker, The Citizen Soldier ..., pp 3-4.

[55] Barnett, Op. cit., pp 3-4.

[56] Brewer, John, The Sinews ..., p 8.

[57] Weigley, Op. cit., pp 3-4; Gilbert, Op. cit., p 90.

[58] Barnett, Op. cit., pp 112-115; Childs, John in Chandler, Op. cit, pp 47-52.

[59] Higginbotham, Don, The War of American Independence, New York: Macmillan Co., Inc., 1971, p 15; Weigley, Op. cit., pp 5-7.

[60] Brewer, John, The Sinews ..., pp 28-32.

[61] Williams, Op. cit., p. 4.

[62] Holmes, Op. cit., p 90; Ross, Op. cit., p 17.

[63] Keegan, Fields of Battle ..., pp 45-46.

64 Martin, James Kirby and Lender, Mark Edwards, <u>A Respectable Army: The Military Origins of the Republic, 1763 - 1789</u>, Arlington Heights, IL: Harlon, Davidson, Inc., 1982, pp 6-11.

2. New World Militia

65 Eliot, Charles W., edit., <u>The Harvard Classics, Vol. 43, American Historical Documents, 1000 - 1904</u>, New York: P. F. Collier and Son, Corp., 1938, pp 52-55.

66 Whisker, <u>The Citizen Soldier ...</u>, p 7; Weigley, <u>Op. cit.</u>, pp 3-4.

67 Higginbotham, <u>Op. cit.</u>, p 1; Simmons, R. C., <u>The American Colonies, From Settlement to Independence</u>, New York: W. W. Norton and Company, 1976, pp 151-152; Dederer, <u>Op. cit.</u>, p 112; Clements, S. Eugene and Wright, F. Edward, <u>The Maryland Militia in the Revolutionary War</u>, Family Line Publishing, Silver Spring, MD: 1987, p 1; Whisker, James, <u>The American Colonial Militia (MD, NY, NJ, Del), Vol. 4</u>, Edwin Mellen Press, Lewiston, NY: 1976, pp 97-98.

68 Andrews, Matthew Page, <u>History of Maryland: Province and State</u>, Garden City, NY: Doubleday, Doran and Company, Inc., 1929, pp 30-32; Andrews, Matthew Page, <u>The Founding of Maryland</u>, Baltimore: The Williams and Wilkins Company, 1933, pp 63-64.

69 Vexler, Robert I. and Swindler, William F., edits., <u>Chronology and Documentary Handbook of the State of Maryland</u>, Oceana Publishing, Inc., 1978, p 93; Scharf, John Thomas, <u>History of Maryland From the Earliest Period to the Present Day, Volume 1</u>, Hatboro, PA: Tradition Press, 1879, p 79.

70 Gray, Edward G., <u>Colonial America, A History in Documents</u>, New York: Oxford University Press, 2003, pp

52-53; Richardson, Mrs. Heather Dorsey, <u>Sidelights on Maryland History, 1634 - 1776</u>, Charlottesville, VA: The Mitchie Co., 1980, p 39.

[71] Mahan, <u>Op. cit.</u>, pp 14-16; Ahern, Marie, <u>The Rhetoric of War, Training Day, the Militia and the Military Sermon</u>, Greenwood Press, Inc., Westport CT: 1989, pp 11 and 143.

[72] Mahan, <u>Op. cit.</u>, pp 14-16; Whisker, <u>The Citizen Soldier ...</u>, p 6; Ahern, <u>Op. cit.</u>, p 14; Scharf, <u>History of Maryland ...</u>, p 66.

[73] Dupuy, R. Ernest, <u>The National Guard, A Compact History</u>, New York:, Hawthorne Books, 1971, pp 2-3; Simmons, <u>Op. cit.</u>, p 152; Mahan, <u>Op. cit.</u>, p 15; Hawke, <u>Op. cit.</u>, p 131;Wright, <u>The Continental ...</u>, p 6; Doubler, <u>Op. cit.</u>, p 12.

[74] Weigley, <u>Op. cit.</u>, pp 4-5.

[75] Doubler, <u>Op. cit.</u>, pp 14-16; Ahern, <u>Op. cit.</u>, p 1; Wright, <u>The Continental ...</u>, p 6.

[76] Balkoski, <u>The Maryland National Guard: A History of Maryland's Military Forces, 1634 - 1991</u>, Baltimore: The Maryland National Guard, 1991, p 3; Bell, David, <u>Passenger List of the Ark and the Dove</u>, originally compiled 3/30/03, revised 11/01/05 @calvertgenealogy.net/ Baltimore/passenger_list_of_the   _ark_and_th_html; Newman, Harry Wright, <u>The Flowering of the Maryland Palatinate</u>, self published, Washington, DC: 1968, pp 155-156, 189, 220-223, 229, 233-234, 266-267, 339-349; <u>A Relation of Maryland</u>, London, 1635, University Microfilms, Inc., Ann Arbor, 1966, Chapter 1; Russell, George Ely and Russell, Donna Valley, edits., <u>The Ark and The Dove Adventurers</u>, Genealogical Publishing Co., Inc., Baltimore, MD, 2005, pp 1-14, 58-59, 104-105; Mackenzie, George Norbury, edit., "List of 'The Ark' and 'The Dove' Passengers," <u>Colonial Families of the United States of</u>

America, 1912, reprinted by Genealogical Publishing Co., Inc., Baltimore, 1966, 1995, pp 593-606, courtesy of the Historic St. Mary's City Foundation; Proceedings of the Council of Maryland, 1636-1637, Archives of Maryland, Volume 3, @mdsa.net, pp 5, 59-60,64,74,85,98,106,108, 127-132; Proceedings of the General Assembly, January 1637/38 - September 1664, Archives of Maryland, Volume 1, @mdsa.net, pp 2-3; Carr, Dr. Lois Green, Biographical Files of 17th and 18th Century Marylanders@www.msa. md.gov/msa/speccol/carr.html.

[77] Ahern, Op. cit., p 11.

[78] Williams, Op. cit., pp 7-8; Dederer, Op. cit., pp 112-113.

[79] Hawke, Op. cit, p 131; Ahern, Op. cit., p 1.

[80] Keegan, A History of Warfare ..., p 347; Weigley, Op. cit., p 4.

[81] Axelrod, Alan, America's Wars, New York: John Wiley and Sons, 2002, p 16.

[82] Wright, Robert K., Jr., and MacGregor, Morris, Jr., Soldier Statesmen of the Constitution, Center of Military History, U. S. Army, Washington, DC: 1987 @http://www.history. Army.mil/books, p 4.

[83] Weigley, Op. cit., pp 6-7.

[84] Higginbotham, Op. cit., p 4.

[85] Doubler, Op.cit., pp 6-7.

[86] Hartzog, William W., American Military Heritage, Center of Military History, U. S. Army, Washington, DC: 2001, p 8.

[87] Shepherd, Ruth, edit., Empires Collide: The French and Indian War, 1754 - 1763, Oxford: Osprey Publishing, 2006, pp 26-27.

[88] Jennings, Francis, Empire of Fortune, New York: W. W. Norton and Company, 1988, p 221.

89 Hawke, Op. cit., p 134

90 Simmons, Op. cit., p 152

91 Stephenson, Op. cit., pp 6-7.

92 Williams, Op. cit., pp 8-9.

93 Weigley, Op. cit., p 6.

94 Ibid. p 5; Dupuy, The National Guard ..., p 3.

95 Dupuy, The National Guard ..., pp 3-7.

96 Ibid., pp 3-4.

97 Karsten, Op. cit., p 13.

98 Jennings, Op. cit., p 86.

99 Weigley, Op. cit., pp 7-8.

100 Mereness, Newton P., Maryland as a Proprietary Province, Cos Cob, CT: John E. Edwards, 1968 (1901), pp 280-281; Brewer, James H. Fitzgerald in Radoff, Morris, The Old Line State, A History of Maryland, Annapolis: Pub. No. 16, Hall of Records Commission, State of Maryland, 1971, p 247; Scharf, History of Maryland..., pp 132-133.

101 Stockbridge, Henry, The Archives of Maryland, Baltimore: MD Historical Society, 1886, pp 44-45.

102 Ibid., p 47.

103 Powell, Allen, Maryland and the French and Indian War, Baltimore: Gateway Press, Inc., 1998, p 133; Warfield, J. D., A. M., The Founders of Anne Arundel and Howard Counties Maryland, Baltimore: 1905 (1967), pp 34-36; Klapthor, Margaret Brown and Brown, Peter Dennis, The History of Charles County, Charles County Tercentenary, Inc., La Plata, MD: 1958, pp 9-10.

104 Mereness, Op. cit., p 282.

105 Chartrand, Renee, Colonial Troops, 1610 - 1774, Chicago: Roundtree-Osprey, 2002, p 33; Mereness, Op.cit., pp 282-284; Whisker, The American Colonial ..., pp 100-101.

[106] Sparks, Francis Edgar, <u>Causes of the Maryland Revolution of 1689</u>, Johns Hopkins University Studies, 1973, pp 77-78; Simmons, <u>Op. cit</u>, p 173; Mereness, <u>Op. cit.</u>, pp 284-288; Whisker, <u>The American Colonial ...</u>, pp 102-103.

[107] Whisker, <u>Op. cit.</u>, pp 114-115.

[108] <u>Ibid.</u>, pp 122-123.

[109] Higginbotham, <u>Op. cit.</u>, pp 17-18.

[110] <u>Ibid</u>, p 17.

[111] Weigley, <u>Op. cit.</u>, pp 5-6.

[112] Craven, Wesley Frank, <u>The Southern Colonies in the Seventeenth Century, 1607 - 1689</u>, LSU Press, 1949, pp 276-277; Simmons, <u>Op. cit.</u>, p 44.

[113] Weigley, <u>Op. cit.</u>, p 7; Whisker, <u>The Citizen Soldier ...</u>, pp 9-10.

[114] Mereness, <u>Op. cit.</u>, p 184; Sparks, <u>Op. cit</u>, p 25.

[115] Craven, <u>Op. cit.</u>, pp 203 and 206.

[116] Sheppard, <u>Op. cit.</u>, p 29; Dupuy, <u>The National Guard ...</u>, p 6.

[117] Williams, <u>Op. cit.</u>, pp 8-9; Mahon, <u>Op. cit.</u>, pp 15-16.

[118] Simmons, <u>Op. cit.</u>, p 101; Weigley, <u>Op. cit.</u>, Dupuy, <u>The National Guard ...</u>, p 4; Ahern, <u>Op. cit.</u>, p 14; Wright, <u>The Continental ...</u> p 67.

[119] Mereness, <u>Op. cit.</u>, p 406; Sparks, <u>Op. cit.</u>, pp 23-24.

[120] Mereness, <u>Op. cit.</u>, p 406; Sparks, <u>Op. cit.</u>, pp 23-24.

[121] Richardson, <u>Op. cit.</u>, pp 267-268.

[122] Leckie, Robert, <u>A Few Acres of Snow: The Saga of the French and Indian Wars</u>, New York: John Wiley and Sons, Inc., 199, pp 58-59.

[123] Sheppard, <u>Op. cit.</u>, p 27; Higginbotham, <u>Op. cit.</u>, p 12; Weigley, <u>Op. cit.</u>, pp 6-7.

[124] Mahon, <u>Op. cit.</u>, pp 15-16; Ahern, <u>Op. cit.</u>, pp 14-16.

[125] Karsten, Op. cit, p 14.

[126] Stephenson, Op. cit., p 12.

[127] Sheppard, Op. cit, p 29; Hawke, Op. cit., pp 138-139.

[128] Weigley, Op. cit., p 6; Mahon, Op. cit., pp 16-17; Stewart, Richard W., edit., American Military History, Volume 1: The United States Army and the Forging of a Nation, 1775 1917, Center of Military History, U. S. Army, Washington, DC: 2004 @www.history.army.mil/books/amh-vol1/ index.htm, p 30.

[129] Chartrand, Op. cit., p 33; Mereness, Op. cit., pp 16-17.

[130] Chartrand, Op. cit., pp 43-45; Sheppard, Op. cit., p 111.

[131] Leckie, A Few Acres of Snow ..., p 61; Karsten, Op. cit., p 13.

[132] Leckie, A Few Acres of Snow ..., pp 59-60.

[133] Williams, Op. cit., pp 9-10.

[134] Weigley, Op. cit., p 6; Sheppard, Op. cit, p 26; Williams, Op. cit., p 9; Mahon, Op. cit., p 18.

[135] Sheppard, Op. cit., p 27; Mahon, Op. cit., pp 9-10.

[136] Ahern, Op. cit., pp 21-23.

[137] Weigley, Op. cit., p 6; Hawke, Op. cit., p 136.

[138] Kimmel, Ross M. and Harp, David W., The Maryland Soldier: A Revolutionary War Portrait, Annapolis: "Maryland Magazine," 1975, pp 9-10.

[139] Weigley, Op. cit., p 9.

[140] Ibid., pp 10-11; Leckie, A Few Acres of Snow ..., p 53.

[141] Whisker, The American Colonial..., p 121.

[142] Hawke, Op. cit., pp 135-136.

[143] Dederer, Op. cit., p 117; Ahern, Op. cit., p 16.

[144] Wright and MacGregor, Soldier Statesmen ..., pp 5-6.

[145] Scharf, John Thomas, History of Baltimore City and County, Part I, Regional Publishing Company, Baltimore: 1971 (1881), p 47.

3. Militia Employment

[146] Higginbotham, Op. cit., p 3.

[147] Hawke, Op. cit., pp 137-138; Higginbotham, Op. cit., p 3.

[148] Stephenson, Op. cit., pp 7-11; Hawke, Op. cit., p 139.

[149] Ahern, Op. cit., p 6.

[150] Hawke, Op. cit., p 140.

[151] Dederer, Op. cit., pp 120-121.

[152] Mahon, Op. cit., p 19; Whisker, The Citizen Soldier ..., p 10.

[153] Dupuy, The National Guard ..., pp 1-2.

[154] Keegan, Fields of Battle ..., pp 150-151.

[155] Jennings, Op. cit., pp 209-210.

[156] Mahon, Op. cit., pp 20-22; Wright and MacGregor, Soldier Statesmen ..., p 5; Dederer, Op.cit., Steward, American History ..., p 35.

[157] Whisker, The American Colonial ..., pp 101-102.

[158] Martin and Lender, Op. cit., pp 16-17.

[159] Gruber, Ira D., Gruber, "Of Arms and Men, Arming America and Military History," The William and Mary Quarterly, January 2002, from www.historycooperative. org, April 25, 2008, p2.

[160] Weigley, Op. cit, p 8.

[161] Mahon, Op. cit., pp 19-20; Matloof, Op. cit., pp 32-33.

[162] Mahon, Op. cit., pp 21-27.

[163] Higginbotham, Op. cit., p 9.

[164] Dupuy, The National Guard ..., pp 5-6.

[165] Weigley, Op. cit., p 8.

[166] Sheppard, Op. cit., pp 29-30.

[167] Ward Matthew C., Breaking the Backcountry: The Seven Years' War in Virginia and Pennsylvania, 1754 -1765, Pittsburgh: University of Pittsburgh Press, 2003, pp 95-98.

[168] Shy, John W., "A New Look at Colonial Militia" in Karsten, Op. cit., p 7.

[169] Martin and Lender, Op. cit., pp 17-18.

[170] Simmons, Op. cit., p 151.

[171] Gallay, Alan, Colonial Wars of North America, 1512 - 1763, An Encyclopedia, Garland Publishing, Inc. NY: 1996, p 136.

[172] Higginbotham, Op. cit., p 3; Keegan, Fields of Battle ..., p 151.

[173] Ward, Op. cit., p 92.

[174] Weigley, Op. cit., p 13; Powell, Maryland and the French ..., pp 24-25; Mahan, Op. cit., p 28.

[175] Andrews, Op. cit., p 250; Powell, Maryland and the French ..., pp 33-36.

[176] Mahan, Op. cit., p 30.

[177] Williams, Op. cit., 19; Keegan, Fields of Battle ..., p151.

[178] Mahon, Op. cit., p 33.

[179] Keegan, Fields of Battle ..., p 152.

[180] Browne, William H., Maryland: The History of a Palatinate, Boston: Houghton, Mifflin and Company, 1897, p 18; Land, Aubrey C., Colonial Maryland, A History, KTO Press: 1981: p 6; Whisker, The American Colonial ..., p 106.

[181] Brewer, James, in Radoff, Op. cit., p 247; Clark, Murtie June, Colonial Soldiers of the South, 1732 - 1774, Genealogical Publishing Co., Inc., Baltimore, MD: 1986, p xiii, courtesy of the Howard County, MD Historical Society.

[182] Chartrand, Op. cit., pp 24-33; Axelrod, Op. cit., p 32; Balkoski, Op. cit., p 3.

[183] Browne, Op. cit., pp 27-34; Land, Op. cit., p 12.

[184] Brewer, James, in Radoff, Op. cit., p 247; Scharf, History of Maryland ..., p 129.

185 Brewer, James in Radoff, Op. cit, pp 247-248; Scharf, History of Maryland ..., p 129; Browne, Op. cit, p 41.

186 Stockbridge, Op. cit., p 44; Brewer, James in Radoff, Op. cit., p 247.

187 McSherry, James, History of Maryland, The Baltimore Book Co., 1904, pp 39-40; Andrews, History of Maryland ..., pp 75-77; Scharf, History of Maryland ..., pp 133-134.

188 Andrews, History of Maryland ..., pp 75-77; Scharf, History of Maryland ..., pp 133-134; Stockbridge, Op. cit., p 45. Stockbridge dated Calvert's commission to Harvey in January 1639. Andrews and Scharf placed it in 1640. This illustrates graphically the problems with interpreting the sketchy records that remain. I placed it in 1640 because that seemed the most logical chronological fit.

189 Andrews, History of Maryland ..., pp 75-77.

190 Ibid., pp 73-75.

191 Browne, Op. cit., p 54; Whisker, Op. cit., p 99.

192 Scharf, History of Maryland ..., pp 141-142.

193 Axelrod, Op. cit., pp 31-31; Scharf, History of Maryland ..., pp 144-145; Stockbridge, Op. cit. pp 49-51; McSherry, Op. cit., pp 44-46.

194 Carr, Lois G., Menard, Russell R., Peddicord. Louis, Maryland... at the beginning, Hall of Records Commission, Maryland, 1984, p 35; Brewer, James in Radoff, Op. cit., pp 247-248; Andrews, History of Maryland ..., pp 82-85; McSherry, Op. cit., pp 44-46; Whisker, The American Colonial ..., p 99.

195 Brewer, James in Radoff, Op. cit., p 248; Stockbridge, Op. cit., p 51.

196 Richardson, Op. cit., pp 182-184; Browne, Op. cit., pp 81-81; Brewer, James in Radoff, Op. cit., pp 248-249;

Axelrod, <u>Op. cit.</u>, p 33; Whisker, <u>The American Colonial ...</u>, pp 99-100; Warfield, <u>Op. cit.</u>, pp 16-26.

[197] Browne, <u>Op. cit.</u>, pp 91-92.

[198] Whisker, <u>Op. cit.</u>, p 102.

[199] Streissguth, Thomas, <u>Maryland</u>, San Diego: Lucient Books, Inc., 2002, pp 21-33; McSherry, <u>Op. cit.</u>, pp 95-97.

[200] Streissguth, <u>Op. cit.</u>, pp 34-35; Browne, <u>Op. cit.</u>, pp 130-131; Klapthor, <u>Op. cit.</u>, p 30.

[201] Mereness, <u>Op. cit.</u>, pp 306-307.

[202] Whisker, <u>The American Colonial ...</u>, pp 106-107.

[203] Taylor, Alan, <u>American Colonies</u>, New York: Penguin, 2001, pp 282-283.

[204] Whisker, <u>The American Colonial ...</u>, p 113.

[205] Chartrand, <u>Op. cit.</u>, p 33.

[206] Mereness, <u>Op. cit.</u>, p 307; Powell, Alan, <u>Forgotten Heroes of the Maryland Frontier: Christopher Gist, Evan Shelby, Jr., Thomas Cresap</u>, Baltimore: Gateway Press, Inc., 2001, pp 119-125; Zimmerstutzen, "When Maryland Invaded Pennsylvania," #636719, www.huntingpa.com/forum, p 2; Scharf, <u>History of Baltimore ...</u>, pp 64-66.

[207] Barker, Charles, <u>The Background of the Revolution in Maryland</u>, Yale University Press, 1940, p 203.

[208] <u>Ibid.</u>, pp 204-205; Richardson, <u>Op. cit.</u>, pp 267-272; Scharf, <u>History of Maryland...</u>, p 429; Chartrand, <u>Op. cit.</u>, p 34. Klapthor, <u>Op. cit.</u>, p 47.

[209] Powell, <u>Forgotten Heroes ...</u>, pp 131-132.

[210] <u>Ibid.</u>, pp 166-167; Barker, <u>Op. cit.</u>, p 202.

[211] Browne, <u>Op. cit.</u>, pp 220-222; Vexler, <u>Op. cit.</u>, p 103.

[212] Powell, <u>Maryland and the French ...</u>, pp 40-41; Brewer, James, in Radoff, <u>Op. cit.</u>, p 249; Andrews, <u>History of Maryland ...</u>, p 250.

[213] Scharf, <u>History of Maryland ...</u>, p 447.

214 Chartrand, Op. cit., p 34; Brewer, James in Radoff, Op. cit., pp 249-250; Andrews, History of Maryland ..., p 250; Scharf, History of Maryland ....

215 Andrews, History of Maryland ..., pp 250-252.

216 Scharf, History of Maryland ..., pp 450-451; McSherry, Op. cit., p 104.

217 Chartrand, Op. cit., p 34.

218 Sheppard, Op. cit., p 89; Scharf, History of Maryland ..., p 460; Powell, Maryland and the French ..., pp 77-83; Powell, Allen, Fort Frederick: Potomac Outpost, McClain Printing Company, Parsons, WV: 1989, pp 9-10; Scharf, History of Baltimore ..., pp 37-38.

219 Andrews, History of Maryland ..., pp 256-257; McSherry, Op., cit., Scharf, History of Maryland ..., p 471.

220 Ansel, William H., Frontier Forts along the Potomac and its Tributaries, McClain_Publishing Co., Parsons, WV: 1984, pp 12-14, 28.

221 Ibid., pp 40-42, 135.

222 Ibid., pp 51-57.

223 Ibid., pp 62-64, 68, 83, 148; Powell, Allen, Fort Cumberland, McClain Printing Company, Parsons WV: 1989: pp 9-16. Ansel, writing in 1984, gives the date of 1750 for the construction of the "New Store" on the south side of the Potomac. Powell, in 1989, gives the date of 1752 and states that it was called the "New Storehouse."

224 Ansel, Op. cit., pp 183-185.

225 Ansel, Op. cit., pp 102-105; Powell, Maryland and the French ..., pp 95-98; Powel, Fort Frederick ..., pp 10-19; Clark, Op. cit., pp 75-91.

226 McSherry, Op. cit., pp 109-110; Powell, Maryland and the French ..., pp 37-39.

227 Scharf, History of Maryland ..., p 481.

228 McSherry, Op. cit., p 112.

229 Powell, Maryland and the French..., p 225; Ansel, Op. cit., pp 28-29.

230 Chartrand, Op. cit., pp 34-35; McSherry, Op. cit., pp 110-111.

231 Powell, Maryland and the French ..., pp 92-92; McSherry, Op. cit., pp 110-111.

232 Powell, Maryland, and the French ..., p 229.

233 Chartrand, Op. cit, p 34.

234 Ansel, Op. cit., pp 27-28.

235 McSherry, Op. cit., pp 112-113.

236 Chartrand, Op. cit., pp 34-45; Powell, Forgotten Heroes ..., p 88; McSherry, Op. cit., p 114.

237 McSherry, Op. cit., p 115.

238 Barker, Op. cit., pp 209-210.

239 Draper, Theodore, A Struggle for Power, The American Revolution, New York: Random House, 1996, p 173; Barker, Op. cit., pp 210-211; Whisker, The American Colonial ..., pp 133-134.

240 McSherry, Op. cit., p 116; Mereness, Op. cit., pp 308-309.

241 Everstine, Carl N., The General Assembly of Maryland, 1634 - 1776, Charlottesville, VA: The Mitchie Co., 1980, pp 373-382.

242 Balkoski, Op. cit., p 4; Powell, Maryland and the French ..., pp 105-117; McSherry, Op. cit., p 117; Jennings, Op. cit., p 407.

243 Powell, Forgotten Heroes ..., pp 94-95.

244 Radoff, Op. cit., p 250; McSherry, Op. cit., pp 118-120; Klapthor, Op. cit., p 48.

245 McSherry, Op. cit., pp 120-121.

246 Powell. Maryland and the French ..., pp 176-181.

247 Everstine, Op. cit., p 383.

[248] Andrews, History of Maryland ..., p 253.

[249] Everstine, Op. cit., pp 375-376.

[250] McSherry, Op. cit., p 135.

[251] Hawke, Op. cit., p 140.

[252] Weigley, Op. cit., pp 11-12.

[253] Hawke, Op. cit., pp 136-140.

[254] Leckie, A Few Acres of Snow ..., pp 235-236.

[255] Higginbotham, Op. cit., pp 9-10.

[256] Dederer, Op. cit., p 119; Stewart, Op. cit., p 31.

[257] Wilcox, John, Masters of Battle, London: Arms and Armour Press, 1996, p 95; Leckie Few Acres of Snow ..., pp 55-59; Higginbotham, Op. cit., p 17.

[258] Dupuy, The National Guard ..., p 46; Hawke, Op. cit., p 140; Weigley, Op. cit., p 14; Martin and Lender, Op. cit., pp 18-19.

[259] Weigley, Op. cit., p 16.

[260] Higginbotham, Op. cit., p 7.

[261] Jennings, Op. cit., p 207.

[262] Ward, Op. cit., pp 93-94.

[263] Stephenson, Op. cit., pp 13-14.

[264] Mahon, Op. cit., p 131; Matloof, Op. cit., Simmons, Op. cit., p 283.

[265] Ward, Op. cit., p 93.

[266] Weigley, Op. cit., p 15.

[267] Matloof, Op. cit., pp 32-33.

[268] Sheppard, Op. cit., p 30; Shy, John W., "A New Look at Colonial Militia" in Karsten, Op. cit., p 8.

[269] Mahon, Op. cit., pp 33-34.

[270] Dupuy, The National Guard ..., p 6; Mahan, Op. cit., p 25.

[271] Whisker, The American Colonial ..., pp 125-130; Clark, Op. cit. p XIV.

[272] Weigley, Op. cit., p 15; Ward, Op. cit., pp 119, 147.

[273] Clements, <u>Op. cit.</u>, p 1.

[274] Doubler, <u>Op. cit.</u>, pp 35-36.

4. The Regulars

[275] Weigley, <u>Op. cit.</u>, pp 12-16.

[276] Leckie, Robert, <u>The Wars of America, Vol. 1: Quebec to Appomattox</u>, New York: Harper Row, 1968, pp 39-43.

[277] Leckie, <u>A Few Acres of Snow ...</u>, p 280.

[278] Sheppard, <u>Op. cit.</u>, pp 24-25.

[279] Taylor, <u>Op. cit.</u>, pp 289-290; Mahon, <u>Op. cit.</u>, p 24; Barnett, <u>Op. cit.</u>, p 196; Higginbotham, <u>Op. cit.</u>, p 17.

[280] Sheppard, <u>Op. cit.</u>, pp 21-22.

[281] Katcher, Philip R. N., <u>Armies of the American Wars, 1753 - 1815</u>, Hastings House, Publishers, New York: 1975, pp 22-23.

[282] Powell, <u>Maryland and the French ...</u>, p 43.

[283] Weigley, <u>Op. cit.</u>, pp 14-17; Keegan, <u>Fields of Battle ...</u>, p 109.

[284] Scharf, <u>History of Maryland ...</u>, p 452.

[285] <u>Ibid.</u>, p 480; Shy in Simmons, <u>Op. cit.</u>, p 8.

[286] Matloof, <u>Op. cit.</u>, pp 36-37.

[287] Sheppard, <u>Op. cit.</u>, p 33.

[288] Higginbotham, <u>Op. cit.</u>, p 19.

[289] Gilbert, <u>Op. cit.</u>, p 119; Chandler, <u>Op. cit.</u>, p 105.

[290] Ross, John F., <u>War on the Run: The Epic Story of Robert Rogers and the Conquest of America's First Frontier</u>, Bantam Books: 2009, p XXV.

[291] Jennings, <u>Op. cit.</u>, pp 206, 207.

[292] Barnett, <u>Op. cit.</u>, p 196; Guy, Alan J. in Chandler, <u>Op. cit.</u>, p 97; Ansel, <u>Op. cit.</u>, p 5; Sheppard, <u>Op. cit.</u>, p 23; Katcher, <u>Op. cit.</u>, pp 41-41.

[293] Sheppard, <u>Op. cit.</u>, pp 22-23.

294 Ibid., p 25; Scharf, History of Maryland ..., p 451; Chandler, Op. cit., p 116; Ansel, Op. cit, p 7-9; Weigley, Op. cit., pp 17-18; Katcher, Op. cit., pp 35-39; Powell, Fort Frederick ..., p 5.

295 Powell, Fort Frederick ..., p 9.

296 Keegan, Fields of Battle ..., pp 112-113; Holmes, Op. cit., p 90; Chandler, Op. cit., p116; Strachan, Op. cit., p 28; Sheppard, Op. cit., p 23; Barnett, Op. cit., pp 199-200.

297 Matloof, Op. cit., p 37; Chandler, Op. cit., pp 116-117.

298 Matloof, Op. cit., pp 36-37.

299 Scharf, History of Maryland ..., pp 453, 457-458.

300 Draper, Op. cit., p 177; Mahan, Op. cit, pp 30-32.

301 Jennings, Op. cit., pp 207-208; Dupuy, The National Guard ..., p 13.

302 Leckie, The Wars of America ..., p 45; Higginbotham, Op. cit., pp 21-22; Dederer, Op. cit., p 120.

303 Gilbert, Op. cit., p 49.

304 Ward, Op. cit., pp 119-120; Jennings, Op. cit., p 220.

305 Martin and Lender, Op. cit., pp 15-16.

306 Simmons, Op. cit., p 29.

307 Wilcox, Op. cit., p 82.

308 Chandler, Op. cit., pp 119-123.

309 Keegan, Fields of Battle ..., p 136; Barnett, Op. cit., pp 213-215.

310 Keegan, Fields of Battle ..., pp 152-153.

311 Powell, Maryland and the French ..., p 207.

312 Gruber, Ira in Heller, Op. cit., p 101.

313 Draper, Op. cit., p 178; Martin and Lender, Op. cit., p 19.

5. The Regulars

314 Martin, Op. cit., p 37; Mereness, Op. cit., pp 287-288.

[315] Land, <u>Op. cit.</u>, pp 296-304; <u>Proceedings of the Convention of the Province of Maryland, 1774 - 1776, Archives of Maryland, Volume 78</u> @mdsa.net, p 1.

[316] Skagg, David Curtis, <u>Roots of Maryland Democracy, 1753 - 1776</u>, Greenwood Press, Inc., Westport, CT: 1973, pp 156-157.

[317] Radoff, <u>Op. cit.</u>, pp 37-38; Mereness, <u>Op. cit.</u>, pp 287-288; Andrews, <u>History of Maryland ...</u>, pp 305-306; McSherry, <u>Op. cit.</u>, pp 147-148; Clements, <u>Op. cit.</u>, p 3; <u>Archives of Maryland, Vol. 78</u>, pp 8-9.

[318] "Richardson's Company - Looking for a Few Good Men," @riverheritage.org/Riverguide/Stories/html/ Richardson _-_enlistments.html, p 1; Tacyn, Mark Andrew, <u>To the End: The First Maryland Regiment and the American Revolution</u>, Doctoral Dissertation, University of Maryland, 1999, Courtesy, Enoch Pratt Library, Baltimore, MD, p 20.

[319] Balkoski, <u>Op. cit.</u>, p 5.

[320] McSherry, <u>Op. cit.</u>, pp 152-153.

[321] Draper, <u>Op. cit.</u>, p 491.

[322] Skagg, <u>Op. cit.</u>, pp 158-159.

[323] Clements, <u>Op. cit.</u>, p 4; Skagg, <u>Op. cit.</u>, pp 158-159.

[324] Weigley, <u>Op. cit.</u>, p 29; Martin, <u>Op. cit.</u>, p 40; Matloof, <u>Op. cit.</u>, pp 46-47.

[325] Clements, <u>Op. cit.</u>, pp 4-5.

[326] Ibid., pp 5-6; Skagg, <u>Op. cit</u>, pp 158-259; Land, <u>Op. cit.</u>, pp 306-307; Radoff, <u>Op. cit.</u>, pp 37-38; <u>Muster Rolls and Other Records of Service of Maryland Troops in the American Revolution, 1775 - 1783</u>, Genealogical Publishing, Inc., Baltimore: 1972, originally <u>Archives of Maryland, Volume 18</u>, Maryland Historical Society, 1972, pp 14-23; Whisker,

The American Colonial ..., pp 137-138; Bertzell, Edwin W., St. Mary's County, Maryland in the American Revolution, Calendar of Events, St. Mary's County, MD Bicentennial Commission: 1975, Courtesy, Howard County, Maryland Historical Society, p 2.

[327] Leckie, The Wars of America ..., pp 46-47; Martin, Op. cit., pp 45-46.

[328] Ellis, John, Armies in Revolution, Oxford University Press, New York: 1964, pp 47-48.

[329] Matloof, Op. cit., p 49; Mahan, Op. cit., p 37; Heller, Op. cit., pp 12-13.

[330] Maryland, Vol, 78, p 39; Clements, Op. cit., p 9; Land, Op. cit., p 308; Archives of Radoff, Op. cit., p 251; Wright, The Continental ..., p 81; Skagg, Op. cit., p 60.

[331] Archives of Maryland, Vol. 78, p 47.

[332] Steuart, Rieman, A History of the Maryland Line in the Revolutionary War, 1775 - 1783, Society of the Cincinnati of Maryland, 1962, p 2; Steuart, Rieman, Maryland in the Revolutionary War, 1775 - 1783, Society of the Cincinnati of Maryland, 1969, p 2; Tacyn, Op. cit., p 9; Archives of MD, Vol. 78, pp 65 - 66; Committee to Report Resolutions for Raising and supporting the Forces to be raised, in Force, Peter, American Archives, published from 1837 - 1853, digitized by the Northern Illinois University @ www. lib.nui.edu/amarch/pn4:728

[333] "The First Maryland Regiment in the Revolutionary War" @www.myrevolutionarywar.com/states/md-01.htm, p 1; Archives of MD, Vol. 78 , pp 92 - 96; Clements, Op. cit. , p 9; Steuart, A History of ..., p 2; Skagg, Op. cit., pp 160-161; Wright, The Continental Army, p 81; Steuart, Maryland ..., p 2.

[334] <u>Archives of MD, Vol. 78</u>, pp 108, 116-117.

[335] "Record of Maryland Troops in Continental Service during the War of the American_Revolution, 1775 - 1783" @oakline.org/OgGatewers/faster/fast51.htm, p 3; Miller, John "The Flying Camp Battalion," <u>Emmitsburg Area Historical Society</u> @emmitsburg.net/archive__list/articles, p 1; Steuart, <u>Maryland ...</u>, p 5.

[336] <u>Journal and Correspondence of the Maryland Council of Safety, July 7 - December 31, 1776, Archives of Maryland, Volume 12</u> @mdsa.net, pp 3, 28, 46, 53.

[337] Steuart, <u>A History of ...</u>, p xi.

[338] Cochrane, Laura C., et. al., <u>History of Caroline County, Maryland From Its Beginning</u>, 1920, Courtesy, Howard County MD, Historical Society, pp 54-70; Johnston, Henry P., <u>The Campaign of 1776 around New York and Brooklyn</u>, Long Island Historical Society, Brooklyn, N. Y.: 1878, p 15; Scharf, John Thomas, <u>The Chronicles of Baltimore</u>, Turnbill Brothers, Baltimore: 1874, pp 138-140.

[339] Berg, Fred Anderson, <u>Encyclopedia of Continental Army Units: Battalions, Regiments and Independent Corps</u>, Harrisburg, PA: Stackpole Books, 1972, pp 51-53; Matloof, <u>Op. cit.</u>, p 55.

[340] Mereness, <u>Op. cit.</u>, p 289.

[341] Clements, <u>Op. cit.</u>, p 3.

[342] Reno, Linda Davis, <u>The Maryland 400 in the Battle of Long Island, 1776</u>, McFarland and Company, Inc., Jefferson, NC: 2008, p 8; Scharf, <u>History of Baltimore City and ...</u>, p 70; Chartrand, <u>Op. cit.</u>, p 34; Brewer, James H. Fitzgerald, <u>History of the 175th Infantry (Fifth Maryland)</u>, Baltimore, Maryland Historical Society, 1955, p 3; Radoff, <u>Op. cit.</u>, pp 250-251.

343 Brewer, James, History of the ..., pp 3-5; The History of the 175th Infantry (Fifth Maryland), Baltimore, MD: 1974, Courtesy, Howard County, MD, Historical Society, p 1; Scharf, The Chronicles ..., p 139.

344 Miller, "The Flying ...", Op. cit., pp 1-3; Miller, John, "The Forgotten Patriots of The Tom's Creek Hundred," Emmitsburg Area Historical Society, @emmitsburg.net/archive_list?atricles, pp 1-4; Steuart, A History ..., p 5; Muster Rolls ..., Archives of MD, Vol. 18, p 504; Clements, Op. cit., pp 53, 108, 180.

345 "William Richardson - American Revolutionary," @rivewrheritage.org/Riverguide/stories/html/Richardson_-_revolutionary.html, p 1; Miller, "The Flying ...," Op. cit., p 2.

346 Berg, Op. cit., pp 47, 67-68; Balkoski, Op. cit., p 5; Radoff, Op. cit., pp 38, 250; Brewer, James, History of the ..., p 4; Steuart, Maryland ..., p 3; McSherry, Op. cit., p 152; Committee of Observation for Frederick County, Maryland in Force, Op. cit., p n2: 104-10 5; Clements, Op. cit., p 5; Dale, Esther Moher, Maryland During the American Revolution, 1941, pp 119-120; Steuart, A History ..., p 1; Kilbourne, John Dwight, A Short History of the Maryland Line in the Continental Army, The Society of Cincinnati of Maryland, Baltimore, MD: 1972, p 1. In one place Brewer states that on June 27, 1776 Congress authorized the German Battalion to have four Pennsylvania companies and four from Maryland. Elsewhere he stated that the Battalion was to include four Virginia companies and three from Maryland. The latter, which I used, generally agrees with other sources.

347 Brewer, Op. cit., p 4; Land, Op. cit., pp 310-311.

348 Weigley, <u>Op. cit.</u>, p 33; Berg, <u>Op. cit.</u>, p 108; Radoff, <u>Op. cit.</u>, p 251; Reno, <u>Op. cit.</u>, p 10; "The Continental Army ' @www.historicalcarper.com/resources/tra/chap4.hgtm, p 81.

349 <u>Archives of MD, Vol. 78</u>, pp 66-67; Steuart, <u>Maryland ...</u>, p 3; <u>Persons Commissioned in</u> the Regular Forces cannot serve in the Convention, nor hold any civil office, in Force, <u>Op. cit.</u>, pp n4: 728-729.

350 <u>Archives of MD, Vol. 78, pp 67-68;</u> Brewer, James, <u>History of ...,</u> pp 5-6.

351 Steuart, <u>A History ...</u>, p 3; Scharf, <u>The Chronicles ...</u>, p 138.

352 "1st Maryland Regiment" in "Encyclopedia Wikipedia" @ http//en.wikipedia.org/wiki; Reno, <u>Op. cit.</u>, pp 51, 75, 95, 115, 130; Tacyn, <u>Op. cit.</u>, p 21; "The First Maryland ..." @...myrevolutionary..., p 1.

353 Klapthor, <u>Op. cit.</u>, pp 56-57.

354 <u>Archives of MD, Vol. 78</u>, p 96; Balkoski, <u>Op. cit.</u>, p 5; Scharf, <u>History of Baltimore...</u>, p 72.

355 <u>Archives of MD, Vol. 78</u>, pp 92-93; <u>Archives of MD, Vol. 12</u>, p 16. The Council did not give any Company designations in its order. However, based on the original assignments and the rank of 3Lt only being used in the 9th Co/ LI, it was possible to determine all of the 1LTs and 2LTs. Since they were listed in chronological company order, it is safe to assume that the Ensign assignments were listed the same way.

356 "The Continental Army," p 81.

357 <u>Archives of MD, Vol. 78</u>, p 96; Steuart, <u>Maryland ...</u>, p 4; Steuart, <u>A History ...</u>, p 4; <u>The History of Charles ...</u>, p 56; Beitzel, <u>Op. cit.</u>, p 3.

358 "The Second Maryland Regiment in the Revolutionary War" @www.myrevolutionarywar.com/states/md-02.htm, p 1.

[359] Archives of MD, Vol. 78, pp 73-79.

[360] Kilbourne, Op. cit., p v; Berg, Op. cit., pp 47, 120.

[361] Archives of MD, Vol. 78, p 204.

[362] Archives of MD, Vol. 18, p 29; Steuart, A History ..., pp 6-9; Archives of MD, Vol. 78, pp 170-175, 189-190, 218-220; Archives of MD, Vol. 12, pp 94, 104-105, 147.

[363] Stephenson, Op. cit., pp 66-67; "The Continental ...," p 81; Force, Op. cit., pp 711, 728, 759.

[364] Keith, Arthur L., "Smallwood Family of Charles County," Maryland Genealogies From the Maryland Historical Magazine, Genealogical Publishing, Baltimore, MD: 1980, Courtesy, Maryland Historical Society, p 326; RE: Brigadier General William Smallwood @genforum.gene-alogy.com/smallwood/messages/1815.html, p 1; Kimmel, Ross M., In Perspective: William Smallwood, Smallwood Foundation, Inc.: 2000, Courtesy, Southern Maryland Studies center, College of Southern Maryland, pp 3-4; Mereness, Newton A., "William Smallwood," Dictionary of American Biography, Vol. 17, Charles Scribner's Sons, New York: 1933, Courtesy of the Maryland Historical Society, p 225; Hallowak, Thomas, Maryland Genealogies, A Consolidation of Articles from the Maryland Historical Magazine, Vol. II, Genealogical Publishing Co., Inc., Baltimore: 1980, pp 325-332.

[365] Hallowak, Op. cit., p 337; Re: Brigadier General ..., p 1; Keith, Arthur L., "General William Smallwood," Maryland Historical Magazine, Volume 19 (1924), Courtesy of the Maryland Historical Society, pp 304-306; Keith, "Smallwood Family ..." Op. cit., p 354; Kimmel, Op. cit., pp 3-4; "Description of General Smallwood's family and education" @www.thebayonet.com/news/index.cfm/fa/viewstory/collection.pdfs/01/20/51, p 1; White, Frank

F., Jr., <u>The Governors of Maryland, 1770 -1970</u>, Hall of
Records Commission, State of Maryland, Annapolis,
MD: 1920, Courtesy, Howard County, MD Historical
Society, pp 21-22; Mereness, "William Smallwood," p 225;
"Smallwood State Park History" @www.dnr.state.md.us/
publiclands/smallwoodhistory.html, p 1.

[366] "Smallwood State ...," p 1; Steuart, <u>A History ...</u>, p 130;
Warfield, <u>Op. cit.</u>, pp 237-238; Reno, <u>Op. cit.</u>, p 36;
Klapthor, <u>Op. cit.</u>, pp 87-88; Papenfuse, Edward C., edit.,
<u>A Biographical Dictionary of the Maryland Legislature,
1635 - 1789, Vol. I and II</u>, The Johns Hopkins University
Press, Baltimore,: 1985, Courtesy, Howard County, MD
Historical Society, p 741.

[367] <u>Re: Brigadier ...</u>, p 1; "Description of General ...," p 1;
Warfield, <u>Op. cit.</u>, pp 237-238; Kimmel, <u>Op. cit.</u>, pp 3-4;
Peden, Henry C., <u>Revolutionary Patriots of Charles County,
1775 - 1783</u> @www.book.google.com/books?id=rcsn-
674pjusc&pg=PA273&lpg=PA273&dq=William..., p 1;
"William Smallwood" @www.answers.com/topic/William-
smallwood-1, p 1; Steuart, <u>A History ...</u>, p 130.

[368] <u>Officers recommended for appointment by the Committee
for Charles County</u>, in Force, <u>Op. cit.</u>, p 4N: 1494.

[369] <u>Peden, Revolutionary ... (Internet)</u>, p 1; Reno, <u>Op. cit.</u>,
Mereness, "William Smallwood," pp 225-226; Peale,
Charles Wilson, <u>Portrait of William Smallwood in the
Old Senate Chambers</u> @http://www.msa.md.gov/msa/
mdstatehouse/html/ws-smallwood.html; Hill Scott,
"Leading the Old Line: General William Smallwood"
@www.the bayonet.com/news/index.cfm/fa/viewsto-
ry/D/7784, p 2; Tacyn, <u>Op. cit.</u>, p 12; Papenfuse, <u>Op. cit.</u>,
p 741; White, <u>Op. cit.</u>, pp 21-22; Kimmel, <u>In Perspective
...</u>, pp 4-5, 7.

370 "Smallwood State Park ...," p 1; Hill, <u>Op. cit.</u>, p 2; "William Smallwood," p 1; Papenfuse, <u>Op. cit.</u>, p 741.

371 <u>Meeting of the Inhabitants of Charles County, MD</u>, in Force, <u>Op. cit.</u>, p N2: 668; Kimmel, <u>In Perspective ...</u>, pp 5-7; Klapthor, <u>Op. cit.</u>, p 51; <u>Charles County (Maryland) Resolutions June 14, 1774</u>, in Force, <u>Op. cit.</u>, pN1: 438. Two of the cited reports in Peter Force's <u>American Archives</u> have contradictions. <u>Meetings ...</u> stated that Charles County appointed nine Deputies to the June Convention. <u>Charles ...</u> said that sixteen were appointed, any five of whom had the power and authority to bind the County. This may actually refer to the Committee of Correspondence with eighteen members.

372 Klapthor, <u>Op. cit.</u>, pp 52-53; <u>Charles County (MD) Committee</u> in Force, <u>Op. cit.</u>, p vi: 985-986.

373 Klapthor, <u>Op. cit.</u>, pp 53-54; <u>Charles County (MD) Committee</u> in Force, <u>Op. cit.</u> pp vi: 1080-1082; White, <u>Op. cit.</u>, pp 21-21; <u>Archives of MD, Vol. 11</u>, p 67; Mereness, "William Smallwood," pp 225-226.

374 <u>Archives of MD, Vol. 11</u>, Force, <u>Op. cit.</u>: <u>Meeting of Inhabitants...</u>, pp N3: 694-695, <u>Committee for Charles ...</u>, p N3: 695, <u>Maryland ...</u>, pN4: 711.

375 Papenfuse, <u>Op. cit.</u>, p 741; Klapthor, <u>Op. cit.</u>, pp 87-88.

376 Papenfuse, <u>Op. cit.</u>, p 741; Klapthor, <u>Op. cit.</u>, p 67; Peale, "Portrait of ...".

377 White, <u>Op. cit.</u>, pp 21-22.

378 Clark, <u>Op. cit.</u>, p 87; Papenfuse, <u>Op. cit.</u>, p 861; Peden, Henry C., Jr., <u>Revolutionary Patriots of Charles County Maryland, 1775 - 1783</u>, Willow Bend Books, Westminster, MD: 2001, p 313; <u>Officers recommended for appointment</u> ... in Force, <u>Op. cit.</u>, p N4: 1494.

379 Papenfuse, <u>Op. cit.</u>, p 861.

[380] Ibid., p 861;Skagg, Op. cit., p 24; Klapthor, Op. cit., p 50.

[381] Force, Op. cit.: Meeting of the Inhabitants ..., p N2: 668, Charles County ..., pp v1: 985-986, Maryland ..., p N1: 438, Charles County ... Resolutions, p N1: 409, The History of Charles ..., pp 45-54. Parenthetically, the original number of men elected to the Committee of Correspondence varied with the source, from thirteen to eighteen. I used eighteen because it conveniently is twice the number of Deputies selected. However, it could have been sixteen, because it appears that only eight attended, half of sixteen.

[382] Klapthor, Op. cit., b p 54; Force, Op. cit.: Charles County ..., pp vi: 1081-1082, Meeting of ..., pp V3: 694-695, Committee for ..., p N3: 695, Maryland ..., p N4: 711.

[383] Klapthor, Op. cit., Archives of MD, Vol. 78, p 1131; Papenfuse, Op. cit., p 861; Steuart, A History ..., p 10; Peden, Revolutionary ... (Book), p 313.

[384] Force, Op. cit.: Frederick County (Maryland) Resolutions, p N1: 433, Maryland Convention, p N1: 438, Frederick County (Maryland) Committee, pp N1: 174-175, Committee of Observation for Frederick County, Maryland, p N2: 1045; Papenfuse, Op. cit., Steuart, A History..., p 121.

[385] Steuart, A History ..., p 85 (Steuart stated that Mordecai Gist was born on February 22, 1742. However, every other source used 1743.); Carrington, Henry B., Battles of the American Revolution, 1775 - 1781, Promontory Press, New York: 1888, p 682; Skagg, Op. cit., p 144; Scharf, History of Baltimore ..., pp 70-71; Scharf, The Chronicles ..., p 130; Archives of MD, Vol. 11, p 33; Force, Op. cit.: Committee of Observation for Baltimore County, in Maryland, appointed, p vi: 795, Committee of Observation

appointed for Baltimore County, p 3N: 776; Reno, Op. cit, p 48; Polk, Ryan, The Origin of "The Old Line State", Maryland State Archives: 2005 @oldlinevannes.com/history.htm, p 1.

[386] Klapthor, Op. cit., p 89; Kimmel, In Perspective ..., p 7.

[387] Klapthor, Op. cit., p 81; Reno, Op. cit, p 51; Archives of MD, Vol. 11. pp 3 & 67; Officers Recommended for appointment by the Committee for Charles County, in Force, Op. cit., p N4: 1494; Clements, Op. cit., p 126; Tacyn, Op. cit., pp 14-15; Steuart, A History ..., p 137; Papenfuse, Op. cit., pp 784-785; Peden, Revolutionary ... (Book), pp 286-287.

[388] Steuart, A History ..., p 59; Reno, Op. cit., p 56.

[389] Reno, Op. cit., pp 57-70.

[390] Ibid., p 75; Ross, Op. cit., p 14; Tacyn, Op. cit., pp 14-15; Hieton, Louise J., Reminders of Revolutionary Days in Prince George's County, 1975, Courtesy of the Howard County, MD Historical Society, p 30.

[391] Reno, Op. cit., pp 81-82, 94, 132.

[392] Ibid., p 95; Tacyn, Op. cit., pp 14-15; Clements, Op. cit., p 98.

[393] Reno, Op. cit., pp 107-109.

[394] Clements, Op. cit., p 114; Archives of MD, Vol. 11, pp 5 & 67; Henry, Howard G., et. al. (Cecil County Bicentennial Book Committee), Cecil County in the Revolutionary War, no date, Courtesy of the Howard County, MD, Historical Society, p 39. Tacyn, Op. cit, pp 14-15; Papenfuse, Op. cit., pp 671-672.

[395] Reno, Op. cit., pp 126-127.

[396] Ibid., pp 115-121.

[397] Clements, Op. cit., p 123; Offutt, Thieman Scott, et. al., Patriotic Maryland and the Maryland Society Sons of the

American Revolution, Baltimore: 1930, Courtesy of the Howard County, MD, Historical Society, pp 45-46; Tacyn, Op. cit., pp 14-15.

398 Clements, Op. cit., p 120; Reno, Op. cit, p 140; Miller, "The Forgotten Patriots ...'" p 3; Papenfuse, Op. cit., p 791; Tacyn, Op. cit., pp 14-15.

399 Clements, Op. cit., p 123; Reno, Op. cit., pp 140 & 156.

400 Hienton, Op. cit., p 1; Clark, Op. cit., p 87.

401 Bertzell, Op. cit., pp 1-3; Papenfuse, Op. cit., pp 808-809.

402 Bertzell, Op. cit., p 20.

403 Stephenson, Op. cit., p 29; Tacyn, Op. cit., pp 24-29.

404 Bertzell, Op. cit., pp 3-6, 25-28.

405 Steuart, A History ..., pp 53, 63, 77, 83-84, 90-91, 114.

406 Miller, "The Flying Camp ...," p 2; Reno, Op. cit., p 10.

407 Tacyn, Op. cit., pp 11-12.

408 Journal and Correspondence of the Council of Safety of Maryland, August 29, 1775 - July 6, 1776, Archives of Maryland, Volume 11 @mdsa.net; Reno, Op., pp 16, 45-46.

409 Journal and Correspondence of the Council of Safety of Maryland, August 29, 1775 - July 6, 1776, Archives of Maryland, Volume 11 @mdsa.net; Reno, Op., pp 16, 45-46.

410 Archives of MD, Vol. 18, pp 5-20. The information on Alexander Murray is suspect. It is based on the Muster Report cited. Linda Reno in The Maryland 400 also puts Murray in the 6th Company. However, there is significant data to the contrary. The 5th Company's Commander, Ramsey, was from Cecil County and, presumably, did much, if not most, of his recruiting there. Murray apparently was from Cecil County. While it borders on the southeast with Kent County, it was still., in those days of poor roads and limited transportation, a significant distance

from the 6th Company's general home base of Kent, Queen Anne's and Caroline Counties. The <u>Proceedings of the Convention</u> show Murray and Plunkett tied for fifth in the election of 2LTs at nine votes each, with Murray listed first. In every other instance of a tie in the officer elections the officers were assigned to companies in the order they were listed, with the first one named going to the lowest numbered company that did not already have an officer of the rank in question assigned. Several other sources also show Murray originally in the 5th Company. Therefore, although he may have replaced Plunkett in the 6th Company, the preponderance of available evidence indicates that Murray started in the 5th Company, with a good chance that he stayed there.

[411] <u>Archives of MD, Vol. 78</u>, pp 106-107.

[412] <u>Archives of Maryland, Vol. 11</u>, pp 97-98, 163, 202-203, 214; Bertzell, <u>Op. cit.</u>, pp 5-6.

[413] <u>Archives of MD, Vol. 11</u>, pp 207-219, 236, 245.

[414] <u>Archives of MD, Vol. 78</u>, pp 5-7; Scharf, <u>History of Baltimore ...</u>, p 73.

[415] <u>Archives of MD, Vol. 11</u>, pp 332 & 356; Bertzell, <u>Op. cit.</u>, p 6.

[416] <u>Archives of MD, Vol. 11</u>, pp 399-403, 444-445.

[417] <u>Ibid.</u>, pp 421-422; Tacyn, <u>Op. cit.</u>, pp 40-44.

[418] <u>Archives of MD, Vol. 11</u>, pp 435,445-446, 463-464.

[419] Clements, <u>Op. cit.</u>, pp 19-20; <u>Archives of MD, Vol 11</u>, pp 511-513; Bertzell, <u>Op. cit.</u>, pp 7-8.

[420] <u>Archives of MD, Vol. 78</u>, pp 175 & 197; <u>Archives of MD, Vol. 12</u>, p 38.

[421] Reno, <u>Op. cit.</u>, p 11.

[422] <u>Archives of MD, Vol 12</u>, pp 44-45; <u>Archives of MD, Vol 12</u>, pp 44-45; Bertzell, <u>Op. cit</u>, pp 12-16.

[423] Bertzell, <u>Op. cit.</u>, pp 15-21; <u>Archives of MD, Vol. 12</u>, pp 138-139.

[424] Matloof, <u>Op. cit</u>, p 63.

[425] <u>Archives of MD, Vol. 12</u>, pp 203-204; Brewer, James, <u>History of the 175th</u> ..., pp 8-9.

[426] Manders, Eric I., <u>The Battle of Long Island</u> , Philip Freneau Press, Monmouth Beach, NJ: 1978, p 26; Bertzell, <u>Op. cit.</u>, p 9; "The First Maryland Regiment ...," p 1; "... Wikipedia," <u>1st Maryland Regiment</u>; <u>Archives of MD, Vol. 78</u>, pp 203-204; Tacyn, <u>Op. cit.</u>, p 44; Brewer, James H., <u>History of ...</u>, pp 8-9.

[427] Clements, <u>Op. cit.</u>, pp 18-19.

[428] McSherry, <u>Op. cit</u>, pp 160-161.

[429] <u>Archives of MD, Vol. 12</u>, pp 4-5.

[430] Ibid., pp 12,16,35,194, 199; Tacyn, <u>Op. cit.</u>, p 44; Bertzell, <u>Op. cit.</u>, 21.

[431] <u>Archives of MD, Vol. 12</u>, p 339; Johnson, <u>Op. cit.</u>, p 115; Brewer, James, <u>History of</u> ..., pp 8-9; Reno, <u>Op. cit.</u>, pp 36-37.

[432] <u>Archives of MD, Vol. 12</u>, pp 49-50, 65-66, 80.

[433] Ibid., pp 72-78, 90, 97-98.

[434] Ibid., pp 113-114, 208.

[435] Ibid., pp 119-120.

[436] Ibid., pp 125, 129-130.

[437] Ibid., pp 140-142, 146-147, 181, 189.

[438] Ibid., pp 166,179,181.

[439] Wright, <u>Op. cit.</u>, p 81; Steuart, <u>Maryland</u> ..., p 154; "The Continental Army," p 81; Reno, <u>Op. cit.</u>, pp 13-14.

[440] Reno, <u>Op. cit.</u>, p 14; <u>Archives of MD, Vol. 78</u>, p 215.

[441] Reno, <u>Op. cit.</u>, p 14; <u>Archives of MD, Vol. 12</u>, pp 211-213; Bertzell, <u>Op. cit.</u>, p 22.

[442] Archives of MD, Vol. 12, pp 235, 240-242; "The Continental Army," p 81; Tacyn, Op. cit., p 32; Archives of MD, Vol. 78, p 226; Steuart, Maryland ..., p 154.

[443] Archives of MD, Vol. 12, pp 216-217, 251.

[444] Brewer, James, History of ..., pp 9-10.

[445] Gruber, Ira D. in Heller, Op. cit., p 11.

[446] Gallagher, John J., The Battle of Brooklyn, 1776, SARPEDON, New York: 1995, p 54.

[447] Steuart, A History ..., p 154; "The Continental Army," p 81; Johnston, Op. cit., p 115.

[448] Tacyn, Op. cit., p 144; Brewer, James, History of ..., p 10; Johnston, Op. cit., pp 125-129.

[449] Fisher, Daniel Hackett, Washington Crossing, Oxford University Press @book.google.com, p 29; "1st Maryland Regiment".

[450] Steuart, Maryland ..., p 154; "The First Maryland Regiment ... '" p 1; "1st Maryland Regiment"; Carrington, Op. cit., p 197; Gallagher, Op. cit., p 179.

[451] Gallagher, Op. cit., pp 14-15.

[452] Manders, Op. cit., p 37; Reno, Op. cit., p 15.

[453] Balch, Thomas, edit., Papers Relating Chiefly to the Maryland Line During the Revolution, Seventy-Six Society, Philadelphia: 1857, Courtesy of the Southern Maryland Studies Center, College of Southern Maryland, p 64.

[454] Steuart, Maryland ..., p 154; Carrington, Op. cit., p 201; Reno, Op. cit., p 37.

[455] Dann, John C., edit., The Revolution Remembered: Eyewitness Accounts of the War for Independence, The University of Chicago Press, Chicago: 1980, pp 155-156.

[456] Henry, Op. cit, p 37; Schecter, Barnett, The Battle for New York, New York: Walker and Company, 2002, pp 141-142;

Carrington, <u>Op. cit.</u>, p 110; Andrews, Charles M., <u>The Colonial Period of American History, Volume 2</u>, Yale University Press, New Haven: 1936, pp 130-134; Wright, <u>Op. cit.</u>, pp 237-238; Brewer, James, <u>History of ...</u>, pp 10-11. Exactly which units Stirling led towards Grant and what their makeup was is open to question. James H. Fitzgerald Brewer states that Stirling had Atlee's and Haslet's battalions and Smallwood's regiment with him, although part of Atlee's unit was already deployed in the vicinity of the Inn. Robert Wright said that he moved Smallwood's and Haslet's units. Henry Carrington said that Stirling took 400 men (6 companies) from Smallwood's unit in their hunting shirts and almost all of Haslet's troops in full regimental dress. The figure of 400 men has taken on a life of its own and is embedded deeply in the mythology of the Marylanders' actions on the 27th during the battle. Wright contends that Stirling took six companies from each regiment, Other authors are of the opinion that Smallwood's entire regiment, all nine companies and the 7th IC, was initially, engaged against Grant. This appears to be the most probable action. Stirling assumed that he was going against the main British attack. It is logical that he would seek to deploy everyone he had available to him. If he only took six of Smallwood's companies, where were the other four?

[457] Reno, <u>Op. cit.</u>, pp 44-45.

[458] Carrington, <u>Op. cit.</u>, pp 207-208; Gallagher, <u>Op. cit.</u>, pp 124-125.

[459] Schecter, <u>Op. cit</u>, p 143; Carrington, <u>Op. cit.</u>, pp 208-209; Tacyn, <u>Op. cit.</u>, pp 56-57.

[460] Wright, <u>Op. cit.</u>, p 230; Gallagher, <u>Op. cit</u>, 136.

[461] Carrington, Op. cit., pp 208-209; Schecter, Op. cit., Gallagher, Op. cit., pp 125-127; Henry, Op. cit., p 43.

[462] Carrington, Op. cit., pp 208-209; Schecter, Op. cit., p 146; Gallagher, Op. cit., pp 125-127.

[463] Gallagher, Op. cit., p 113.

[464] Wright, Op. cit. , pp 238-239.

[465] Gallagher, Op. cit., p 136; Schecter, Op. cit., p 148.

[466] Heller, Op. cit., pp 27-28.

[467] Gallagher, Op. cit., p 117.

[468] Scharf, History of Baltimore ..., pp 48-50.

[469] Gallagher, Op. cit., p 127.

[470] McSherry, Op. cit., p 164; Gallagher, Op. cit., pp 10-11; Wright, Op. cit., p 239; Carrington, Op. cit., pp 209-210; Andrews, Charles, Op. cit., pp 130-134; Schecter, Op. cit, pp 149-150; Henry, Op. cit., pp 44-45; Tacyn, Op. cit., pp 58-59; Johnson, Op. cit., pp 187-188.

[471] Buchanan, John, The Road to Valley Forge, John Wiley and Sons, Inc., Hoboken, NJ: 2004, p 59.

[472] Reno, Op. cit., pp 48-49.

[473] Dann, Op. cit., p 113.

[474] Onderdonk, Henry, Revolutionary Incidents of Suffolk and Kings Counties: With an Account of the Battle of Long Island ... , in Commanger, Henry Steele and Morris, Richard B., edits., The Spirit of 'Seventy-Six, De Capo Press, Inc., 1995 (1975), pp 439-440.

[475] Dawson, Henry B., Battles of the United States by Sea and Land, in Commanger, Op. cit., p 436.

[476] Tacyn, Op. cit., pp 59-60; Andrews, Charles, Op. cit., pp 130-134; Brewer, James, History of ..., pp 11-12; Henry, Op. cit., pp 44-45; Gallagher, Op. cit., p 129; Lancaster, Bruce, From Lexington to Liberty, Garden City, NY, Doubleday

and Company Inc., 1955, pp 208-209; Carrington, Op. cit., pp 2209-210.

[477] Weigley, Op. cit., p 36; Lancaster, Op. cit., pp 208-209; Gallagher, Op. cit., p 129; Henry, Op. cit., pp 44-45; Andrews, Op. cit., pp 130-134; The History of the 175th ..., p 1; Carrington, Op.cit., pp 209-210; Reno, Op. cit., pp 22-25; Brewer, James, History of ..., pp 11-12; McSherry, Op. cit., p 165; Tacyn, Op. cit., pp 62-62; Warfield, Op. cit., p 238. How many attacks the Marylanders under Stirling made against the British and the Cortelyou House is still being debated. Gist, and Tacyn following him, said two. Stirling, and most others following him, said five or six. One source said seven, but that is clearly too many. Stirling may have included forays that Gist thought inconsequential, as well as his final movement that ended up being blunted by the Hessians, as attacks. Smallwood, in his belated fall report to the Maryland Convention, does not provide much detail on the events of August 27th, presumably because he missed the main action. I followed the overwhelming majority of sources and worked with six attacks.

[478] Schecter, Op. cit., p 152; Andrews, Charles, Op. cit., pp 130-134; Henry, Op. cit., p 46; Johnston, Op. cit. p 189; Reno, Op. cit., pp 24-25; Brewer, James, History of ..., pp 12-13; Steuart, Maryland ..., pp 154-155; Steuart, A History of ..., pp 154-155.

[479] Gallagher, Op. cit. , pp 131-132.

[480] Ibid., pp 132-133; Joseph P. Martin, A Narrative of Some of the Adventures, Dangers and Sufferings of a Revolutionary Soldier in Commanger, Op. cit., pp 442-443.

[481] McSherry, Op. cit., pp 165-166; Steuart, Maryland , pp 154-155; Brewer, James, History of ..., pp 12-13; Reno,

Op. cit., pp 24-25; Henry, Op. cit., p 46; Steuart, A History ..., pp 154-155; Carrington, Op. cit., p 210.

[482] Mitchell, Joseph B., Decisive Battles of the American Revolution, New York: G. P. Putnam Sons, 1962, p 56; Gallagher, Op. cit., p 130; Tacyn, Op. cit., p 114; Kimmel In Perspective ..., p 8.

[483] Reno, Op. cit., o 25; Kimmel, In Perspective ..., p 8; Gallagher, Op. cit., p 130.

[484] Archives of MD, Vol. 12, p 341; Reno, Op. cit., p 39.

[485] Brewer, James, History of ..., pp 11-12; Reno, Op. cit., pp 22-25; Kimmel, In Perspective ..., p 8; Steuart, A History ..., pp 154-155; Steuart, The Maryland ..., p 155; 1st Maryland Regiment; Wright, Op. cit., p 239; Gallagher, Op. cit., p 130.

[486] Scharf, The Chronicles ..., p 215.

[487] Gallagher, Op. cit., p 137; The History of the 175th ..., p 51; Radoff, Op. cit., p 251.

[488] Reno, Op. cit., p 45; Dougherty, David M., "Review of The Maryland 400" @amazon.review-com, p 1; Tacyn, Op. cit., p 114; Carrington, Op. cit., p 212.

[489] Reno, Op. cit., pp 74-156.

[490] Ibid., p 27.

[491] Ibid., pp 12-13, 107.

[492] Tacyn, Op. cit., p 14; Brewer, James, History of ..., pp 13-14; Dorsey, Ella Loraine, Smallwood's Immortals, A Historical Abstract, Courtesy of the Maryland Historical Society, p 10.

[493] Steuart, A History ..., pp 154-155; Steuart, Maryland ..., p 155; Tacyn, Op. cit., pp 17-19; Reno, Op. cit, pp 12-13, 27, 107.

[494] Brewer, James, History of ..., pp 12-13; The History of the 175th ..., p 1.

[495] Gallagher, Op. cit., p 2; Mitchell, Joseph B., Military Leaders in the American Revolution, EPM Publications, Inc., McLean, VA, 1967, pp 28-30.

[496] Tacyn, Op. cit., p 71; Gallagher, Op. cit., p 168.

[497] Warfield, Op. cit., pp 238-239; Scharf, John Thomas, History of Maryland, in Reno, Op. cit. , pp 27-29; Steuart, Maryland ..., p 155; Steuart, A History ..., p 155.

[498] Archives of MD, Vol. 12, pp 270-271.

[499] Richardson's Regiment at the Battle of Harlem Heights," reverheritage.org/Riverguide/Stories, p 1; Steuart, Maryland ..., p 155; Steuart, A History ..., p 155; Schecter, Op. cit., pp 190-191.

[500] Wright, Op. cit., p 81; "Richardson's Regiment ...," p 1; Archives of MD, Vol. 12, pp 291-292;Steuart, Maryland ..., p 155; Steuart, A History ..., p 155.

[501] Archives of MD, Vol. 12, pp 316, 338-343.

[502] Brewer, James, History of ..., pp 20-21.

[503] Steuart, Maryland ..., p 156; Warfield, Op. cit., pp 238-239; Kilbourne, Op. cit., pp 4-6.

[504] Steuart, Maryland ..., p 5; Brewer, James, History of ..., pp 20-21; Kilbourne, Op. cit., pp 4-6.

[505] Polk, Ryan, The Origin of "The Old Line State", Maryland State Archives: 2005@oldlinevanners.com/history.htm, p 1.

[506] Carrington, Op. cit., p 491; Gallagher, Op. cit., p 130.

[507] Brewer, James, History of ..., p 251.

Index

Jamaica, West Indies, 157
Jamaica, Long Island, NY, 470
Jamaica Pass, 471-73, 482, 488
Jamaica (Old Jamaica) Road, 471, 483, 488
James I, 67
James II, 51, 55, 194, 197
James River, VA, 92, 441
Jamestown, VA, 67, 71, 74, 89, 92, 114, 155, 182, 221
Jennifer, Daniel of St. Thomas, 350, 413, 469
Jennifer, Elizabeth, 413
Jerseys, The (New Jersey), 210, 228, 234, 258, 349-50, 359-62, 386-87, 389, 417, 446, 451, 456, 458, 462, 479, 515
Johnson, Thomas, Jr., 345, 386-87, 399, 427, 518
Johnson, William, 312
Johnston, John, 165
Jordan, LTC, 122
Jordan, Jeremiah, 453
Jordan, ENS/LT John, 371, 371, 419
Joseph, Gov. William, MD, 197-98
Justice of the peace, 125, 395
Justice/Judge, County Commission, 117, 393, 398, 409

Keeports, LT George, 376
Kendal (Quaker) school, 396
Kent County, England, 40
Kent County, MD, 84-5, 189, 200, 212, 247, 290, 326, 334-35, 346, 374, 379-80, 386, 388, 395-396, 424, 427-31, 447, 457, 525, 578n410
Kent Island, MD, 82, 84-86, 102, 104, 116, 121, 174-77, 181, 185-87, 192, 276, 427, 431
Kent COL James, 388
Key, Francis Scott, 417

Made in the USA
Charleston, SC
18 April 2014